IMAGES OF ASIA

New Chinese Cinema

D0209780

New Chinese Cinema

Kwok-kan Tam & Wimal Dissanayake

OXFORD

UNIVERSITY PRESS

OXFORD
UNIVERSITY PRESS

Oxford University Press is a department of the University of Oxford.
It furthers the University's objective of excellence in research, scholarship,
and education by publishing worldwide in

Oxford New York

Auckland Bangkok Buenos Aires Cape Town Chennai
Dar es Salaam Delhi Hong Kong Istanbul Karachi Kolkata
Kuala Lumpur Madrid Melbourne Mexico City Mumbai Nairobi
São Paulo Shanghai Singapore Taipei Tokyo Toronto

and an associated company in Berlin

Oxford is a registered trade mark of Oxford University Press

Published in the United States
by Oxford University Press Inc., New York

© Oxford University Press 1998

First published 1998
This impression (lowest digit)
3 5 7 9 10 8 6 4 2

British Library Cataloguing in Publication Data
available

Library of Congress Cataloging-in-Publication Data

Tam, Kwok-kan, date.
New Chinese Cinema / Kwok-kan Tam and Wimal Dissanayake.
p. cm. — (Images of Asia)
Includes bibliographical references and index.
ISBN 0-19-590607-1 (alk. paper)
1. Motion pictures—China—History. 2. Motion picture producers
and directors—China. I. Dissanayake, Wimal. II. Title. III. Series.
PN1993.5.C4T34 1998
791.43'0951—dc21

97-51578

CIP

Printed in Hong Kong
Published by Oxford University Press (China) Ltd
18th Floor, Warwick House East, Taikoo Place, 979 King's Road, Quarry Bay
Hong Kong

Contents

Preface

FIRST OF ALL, we would like to make it clear what this book is not. This is not a work intended for the specialist. This is not a book on the history of Chinese cinema; nor is it a comprehensive discussion of each of the films made by each of the directors we have selected for analysis. This is meant for the non-specialist, the interested layperson. Within the brief compass of the book, we have sought to select six of the most important Chinese film directors (there are, of course, other equally distinguished and talented Chinese directors), and to focus on some of their works as a means of generating greater interest in the new Chinese cinema. To this end, we have used many illustrative photographs. In the ensuing pages, we use the generic term 'New Chinese Cinema' to designate films made in China, Taiwan, and Hong Kong during the past twenty years.

Such evaluations and judgements as we make in this book are tentative and provisional; the best subtitle for the book would be 'An Interim Report'. Many of the film-makers we discuss are in their forties. Their careers are ahead of them. They are bound to find new paths, broach new areas, and evolve, perhaps, in unanticipated ways. All are serious film-makers, who use the apparatus of cinema to reflect on how we live and how we think about how we live in rapidly changing Chinese cultures. Clearly, the diverse ways in which they construct the contemporary Chinese imagination compel our admiration and invite sustained study.

We are deeply grateful to Zhang Yimou, Tian Zhuangzhuang, Hou Hsiao-hsien, Edward Yang, and Stanley Kwan for granting us extended interviews and supplying us with photographs. Dai Jinhua of Peking University, Bey Logan of Media Asia Group, Jade Hsu of Tomson (H.K.) Films Co. Ltd., Liu Desheng of Southern Film Corporation and Andrew Leung of Era International (H.K.) Ltd. also kindly provided us with photographs from their own collections. We would like to express our gratitude to William S. Tay of the University of California, San Diego, for his advice on the project. Katherine Li helped us in the preparation of the manuscript, and we are thankful to her. We would also like to acknowledge the Ho Sin Hang Education Endowment Fund for a grant in support of the research for this book.

Kwok-kan Tam
Wimal Dissanayake
Hong Kong, 1997

1

Chinese Cinema:
Lines of Development

WHEN WE SEEK to understand the historical evolution of any cinema, whether it is Chinese or Indian or German, it is always useful to bear in mind that cinema is a cultural practice. Thus, the different dimensions of cinema—artistic, commercial, industrial, technological, political, and ideological—are vitally interconnected. The complex ways in which film-makers, the audience, officialdom, critics, and custodians of taste and industrialists interact merit very close study. As all cinemas are distinct products of cultural geographies and historical moments, these aspects of cinema invite careful analysis as we chart the growth of film cultures.

From 1896 onwards, China was exposed to the art of cinematography, which quietly opened the door of the Middle Kingdom to the West through the tea-house variety film shows in Shanghai. However, until very recent times, cinema in China was considered an imported art form by the general public. Indeed, it is not without significance that at the early phase, cinema in China was popularly referred to as 'Western peep shows'. This perceived sense of alienness operated at a number of different levels. Until 1949—the year of the victory on the Mainland of the Chinese Communist Party (CCP)—much of the cinematic fare offered to the Chinese was of foreign origin. Many of the films that were actually shot in China were produced by foreign companies. Moreover, a substantial number of films were based on Western works of literature, ranging from Shakespeare's plays to Hardy's novels, as well as Russian and Japanese works. All of these phenomena, understandably enough, nurtured the notion that cinema and alienness were closely related.

To put it differently, for most of this century the attitude was widespread that the art of cinema was not a native form of entertainment and communication. However, with the passage of time, this notion began to fade away. The emergence of the Fifth Generation of film-makers (some of whose works we will discuss here), including Chen Kaige, Zhang Yimou, Tian Zhuangzhuang, Zhang Junzhao, Wu Ziniu, and Zhou Xiaowen, changed the situation significantly. Ideas of cultural identity, the distinctiveness of Chinese film aesthetics, and cinema as a vital part of the public sphere began to gain greater attention.

A connection persisted in the minds of both film directors and audiences, from the earliest times, that cinema and didacticism were inseparably linked. Later, this belief gave way to the idea of cinema as a politically educative medium of communication. Perceiving cinema's vast possibilities for inculcating a political consciousness in the mass of people, the Communist Party in 1932 established the Mingxing (Star) Film Company, located in Shanghai. It is evident, as we look back, that the CCP and intellectuals with a leftist orientation exercised a profound influence on film-making in China. This is, of course, not to suggest that foreign influences emanating from capitalist societies, and motives of profit-making and commercial success, were totally absent. By the end of the First World War, local industrialists had clearly realized the value of cinema as a profit-making venture. In 1917, the Commercial Press established a Department of Motion Pictures, which four years later produced the first Chinese feature-length film. In 1923, this department built the first film studio in China.

By about the 1940s, there was discernible in China an

interesting connection between the art of cinematography and the literary and dramatic arts. Many of the film directors were conversant with the arts of literature and the theatre; some of them were closely involved with these arts. This close linkage between literature and film had two significant consequences. First, in view of the fact that literature was highly regarded by the educated classes in China, it served to legitimize the newer art of cinematography and to invest it with a greater degree of respectability as a medium of entertainment. Second, until comparatively recent times, in Chinese cinema the writer of the screenplay was held in greater regard than even the director of the film.

Policy-makers in China came to realize increasingly the value of cinema as a form of mass communication and education after the victory of the Communist revolution in 1949. Despite the fact that by that time the value of cinema as a mode of public consciousness-raising had been clearly established, it was apparent to officialdom that one could move still further down this road. Cinema continued to cater to specialized audiences drawn mainly from the élite segments of society. One of the primary goals was to secure a larger national audience that would patronize the art of cinema, and through this means expand the process of political education.

As a result of this deeply felt need to make cinema a medium of political education, as well as to widen the audiences for cinema, films that subscribed to the idea of 'socialist realism' began to be produced in increasing numbers. The models for this approach to film-making were provided by the Soviet Union. The display of revolutionary zeal and fervour, the actions of positive heroes primarily interested in the betterment of the masses, class struggle, the eventual triumph of the progressive forces over reactionary forces: all were given enthusiastic emphasis. During this period, films imported from countries other than the Soviet bloc were banned. This restriction resulted in locally produced films winning a much wider market in China than was the case before 1949.

The Cultural Revolution was launched in 1966, unleashing great revolutionary fervour, and for nearly a decade the followers of Jiang Qing, the wife of Mao Zedong, exercised unchallenged authority in nearly all aspects of Chinese life. These tendencies resulted in the further strengthening of the concept of a nationalist-socialist cinema. On the basis of the available body of evidence, one can say that the Cultural Revolution sought to call attention to two interconnected themes: the political function of art and the importance of indigenous art. As a result, one observed a resolute effort to utilize traditional art forms, with a distinctive indigenous cultural imprint, to communicate contemporary experiences and a vision of society that was consistent with the accepted political blueprint. Revolutionary operas, such as *Taking Tiger Mountain by Strategy* (Zhi qu Weihushan), were offered as models worthy of emulation. However, in terms of the exploration of complex and multifaceted human experiences and the creative exploitation of the possibilities of the art of cinema, these films fell far short of the mark.

As most commentators would agree, the Cultural Revolution turned out to be a disaster for the country, setting it back by a number of years. In October 1976, the so-called Gang of Four, who had spearheaded the movement, were arrested and publicly disgraced. People began to raise doubts about the wisdom of some of the policies of Mao, something that had been unthinkable a decade before. When Deng Xiaoping succeeded Mao as the leader of China, he sought to liberalize the economy and put in place a more open-door policy. In this newer atmosphere of liberalism, the film industry began to show signs of health and vitality. The traumatic experiences associated with the Cultural Revolution and the increasing exposure to good Western cinema, and the constructive role played by the Beijing Film Academy, no doubt, contributed to this newer vibrancy. A film like Chen Kaige's 1984 release, *Yellow Earth*, which will be discussed later, is emblematic of this new vitality in the Chinese cinema.

A new group of talented craftspeople, generally referred to as the Fifth Generation of film-makers from the timing of their graduation from the Beijing Film Academy (Beijing dianying xueyuan), ushered in the 'new wave' in Chinese cinema. These film-makers were interested in moving away from traditional ways of making films, and in relating Chinese cinema to modernism and internationalism. Members of the Fifth Generation succeeded in generating great international interest in modern Chinese cinema, and in winning for it a high global profile. Their films were eagerly sought by organizers of international film festivals. This is, of course, not to suggest that everything was going smoothly. Many of these film-makers, at one time or another, had to contend with a hostile officialdom, who disapproved of their representations of Chinese society and the kind of vision they projected, and a less than enthusiastic audience that at times found their work lacking in narrative energy.

The film-makers of the Fifth Generation were followed by those of the Sixth Generation, who are seeking to negotiate the forces of localism and globalism and to create works of cinematic art that are true to the deeper currents of Chinese culture. In this regard, the work of Sixth Generation directors, such as He Jianjun, Hu Xueyang, Lu Xuezhang, Wang Xiaoshuai, and Zhang Yuan, merits closer study.

As an international city situated between China and Taiwan and with relatively fewer political restrictions, Hong Kong presents a compelling example of a small place with a vibrant film industry and film culture. Hong Kong, with its successful economy and its position as a centre of international finance, displays a number of interesting features and trends in film production. It is generally believed that the first Hong Kong feature film, *To Steal a Roasted Duck*, was produced by the American theatre owner Benjamin Polanski in 1909 and directed by Liang Shaobo. Since that time the film industry has grown steadily, facing challenges of different sorts. Hong Kong people love their movies, and it is said that there have been years in which more than three hundred movies were made in this small enclave alone.

Before and during the Second World War, a substantial number of people associated with the film industry moved to Hong Kong from the Mainland. Some saw the making of films as a way of resisting Japanese aggression. Others sought to escape the decree of the Guomindang government that all films should be made in Mandarin Chinese. Cantonese-language film-makers came to Hong Kong for a variety of reasons and took advantage of available financial resources there. Consequently, the 1940s saw a dramatic increase in the number of Cantonese films made. As one surveys the growth of Hong Kong commercial cinema, one realizes the vital role played by the Shaw Brothers and Golden Harvest studios in its development. These two organizations succeeded in placing cinema on a firm industrial footing and made it a significant part of Hong Kong's popular culture and popular consciousness.

When most people think of Hong Kong cinema, they picture scenes from the martial arts (kung fu) films that have become so closely identified with Hong Kong culture.

6

Although examples of many other film forms, with diverse styles and subject-matter, are made in the Territory, the general tendency is to associate martial arts actors, plots, and settings with the Hong Kong cinema. The martial arts films grow out of deep roots in Chinese culture, while making diverse connections with the voices of cultural modernity. Among the names that are most often cited with regard to the growth of this genre, those of Cheng Cheh, Wang Yu, King Hu, Bruce Lee, Ng See-yuen, Liu Chia-liang, Yuen Woo Ping, Samo Hung, Jackie Chan, Tsui Hark, and Wong Kar-wai deserve special mention. It is indeed true that the majority of these martial arts films seek to provide cheap escapist fantasies to the vast mass of moviegoers. There are among them, however, a substantial number of films that attempt to grapple with vexed issues of nationalism, cultural modernism, technologization of society, and Westernization. The work of a film director like Wong Kar-wai, particularly his *Chungking Express*, is most significant in this regard.

During the last ten or fifteen years a distinctly Hong Kong mode of cinema has emerged which combines elements of the popular and the artistic. Film-makers such as Ann Hui, Tsui Hark, Allen Fong, John Woo, Stanley Kwan, and Wong Kar-wai represent this trend. As Ackbar Abbas (1997: 26) has commented, 'The new Hong Kong cinema is interesting... not essentially because it has caught up in terms of technical competence and sophistication with the rest of the world; what is really interesting about it is the way film is being used to explore and negotiate a problematic and paradoxical cultural space, without abandoning its role as popular entertainment.' Tsui Hark's *Zu: Warriors from the Magic Mountain*, Ann Hui's *Boat People*, Allen Fong's *Father and Son*, and Stanley Kwan's *Rouge* bear testimony to the strengths of this new Hong Kong cinema. The Hong Kong film industry, of course, has its own share of problems. The number of films produced has decreased sharply in recent years, and producers and directors are challenged to think of ways of winning back audiences from competing modes of entertainment. In recent years, Taiwanese cinema and Taiwanese film directors have been gaining wide international acclaim. Directors such as Hou Hsiao-hsien, Edward Yang, and Ang Lee have generated a great deal of interest among international audiences. When compared to most other Asian countries, for understandable historical reasons, the film industry took root in Taiwan in comparatively recent times. During the Second World War, the Japanese established the Taiwan Motion Picture Association. In 1945, this amalgamated with the Taipei News Picture Association to form Taiwan Film Studio, which is important to an understanding of the evolution of Taiwanese cinema for its role in putting the island's film industry on a firm footing. In 1949, several film organizations and film directors came to Taiwan from the Mainland, influencing appreciably the growth of the art of cinematography in Taiwan.

In the 1950s, four studios owned by the government played a central role in Taiwan's movie production, and during the late 1960s and 1970s more than two hundred films were produced annually. This number fell in the 1980s. Various reasons, ranging from restrictive government regulations to the costs of production, have been advanced as having brought about this situation. However, amidst the ups and downs of the Taiwanese film industry, a number of immensely gifted directors, Hou Hsiao-hsien and Edward Yang among them, have continued to produce films of a high order that can compare with the best in the world.

Although generalizations are always perilous, it is tempting to make some broad comparative statements about

Hong Kong and Taiwanese cinema. The Hong Kong cinema, from its very inception, had a commercial character, and it was nourished by Chinese film-makers who arrived in the Territory from the Mainland after 1949. The Taiwanese cinema, on the other hand, had its origins in the documentaries and newsreels produced by the Guomindang government. These different origins continue to shape the two cinematic traditions. Moreover, while Hong Kong cinema has focused on martial arts films and the agility of male actors in physical combat and swordplay, Taiwanese films largely have dealt with women's privations in a sentimental way. There is also, in many Taiwanese films, a glorification of rural culture, in contradistinction to urban culture, a juxtaposition which is rarely seen in Hong Kong films.

The film industries and film cultures of China, Hong Kong, and Taiwan present us with an interesting set of contrasting developments. Each place has its own distinctive problems and issues. China's film-makers are grappling with issues of state interference, as well as attempting to develop the most productive ways of negotiating the competing demands of localism and globalism. Since the 1980s, they have also had to contend with the imperatives of the box office and the lure of television. Hong Kong's film directors are faced with the problem of maintaining a vibrant film industry in the face of diminishing output, as well as confronting new social and political challenges prompted by the Territory's July 1997 return to Chinese sovereignty.

For their part, Taiwanese film directors are seeking to produce quality films while not forfeiting the strength of their economic base. The challenges here, too, are formidable. The relationship with China always looms in the background of Taiwanese film discourse, affecting art, entertainment, and industry alike. Amidst the challenges and problems with which each tradition has to contend, there are also co-productions taking place under the initiative of artists and financiers from all three societies. This cooperative spirit could have a positive impact on the growth of Chinese cinema.

Since the 1980s, the film industries of China, Taiwan, and Hong Kong have similarly entered a new phase in their different historical developments, producing the 'new Chinese cinema', in which there are conscious attempts to probe a new subjectivity in the face of contemporary challenges. These works deal squarely with issues of cultural change, such as the role of tradition in modernity, quests for identity, and explorations of the self, gender, and sexuality. The films made by Chen Kaige, Zhang Yimou, Tian Zhuangzhuang, Hou Hsiao-hsien, Edward Yang, and Stanley Kwan are representative of this newly emerging aesthetics and new sensibility in the depiction of contemporary Chinese subjectivity, which places emphasis on the inner psychological over the outer social representation.

2
Chen Kaige: Steps Toward a
Personal Cinema

THE NAME of Chen Kaige is perhaps more closely associated with the new Chinese cinema than that of any other director. His *Yellow Earth* (Huang tudi), made in 1984, served to inaugurate a new phase of Chinese film. Many of the most discerning commentators on Chinese cinema are united in their opinion that this film constitutes the first major work of the Fifth Generation and that it had the effect of reformulating Chinese film language and aesthetics for the newer generations. It is hardly surprising that Chen's *Yellow Earth* has become a reference point in the discussion of contemporary Chinese cinema.

Chen Kaige (Fig. 2.1) was born Chen Aige in Beijing on 12 August 1952. His father, Chen Huai'ai, was a film director himself. At the age of fifteen, when the Cultural

2.1 Chen Kaige, 1986. Photo courtesy of Southern Film Corporation.

Revolution was in its initial stages, Chen was sent down to Yunnan province, where he was engaged in clearing the jungle for expansion of a rubber plantation. Three years later, he joined the People's Liberation Army and was stationed on the Yunnan border. In 1975, he resigned from the army and returned to Beijing, where he landed a job in the Beijing Film Processing Laboratory, the country's main film processing laboratory. In 1978, he gained admission to the Beijing Film Academy, from which he graduated four years later.

Chen made *Farewell to Yesterday* (Xiang zuotian gaobie) for Fujian Television in 1980, and he later worked as an assistant director for the children's film *Brother Echo* (Yingsheng a'ge) and for two other films, *The Fragile Skiff* (Yiye xiaozhou) and *26 Young Ladies* (26 ge guniang). When Chen released *Yellow Earth* in 1984, he won for himself and for modern Chinese cinema great international acclaim. He has since completed five other films, *The Big Parade* (Da yuebing), *King of the Children* (Haizi wang), *Life on a String* (Bian zou bian chang), *Farewell to My Concubine* (Ba wang bie ji), and *Temptress Moon* (Feng yue). With these films Chen established himself as one of the most important modern film-makers in China and the world.

Yellow Earth (Fig. 2.2) recounts a fairly simple story. A soldier comes to a mountain village with the intention of collecting folk-songs. While in the village he lives in a house where a young woman is married to an older man to whom she was betrothed in infancy. The soldier explains to her how women are treated under the Communist regime in the capital, Yan'an. The young woman's mind is filled with hopes and expectations. She sets out in search of the city and is accidentally drowned. Chen presents this simple story movingly and persuasively on the screen, paying close attention to composition, exquisite visual images, and

2.2 *Yellow Earth*, 1984. Photo courtesy of Southern Film Corporation.

a careful use of sound and music. As a result, the film yields a complex sense of personal and social destiny. The cinematographer, Zhang Yimou, who later emerged as an outstanding film director in his own right, assisted greatly in this effort, presenting the landscape, as well as the relationship between people and nature, in a manner deeply reminiscent of classical Chinese paintings. This is a film full of symbolic and allegorical meaning, and the interplay between humans and nature, past and present, culture and politics, propaganda and reality is at the heart of the experience communicated by this work (Fig. 2.3).

On 12 April 1985, *Yellow Earth* was shown at the Hong Kong International Film Festival, and many who saw it realized that day that the new Chinese cinema had arrived. Quickly the word got around, and the film went on to win numerous awards at international festivals. Eschewing the dictates of socialist realism that had dominated Chinese

2.3 *Yellow Earth*, 1984. Photo courtesy of Southern Film Corporation.

cinema up until that time, Chen had made a film that focused on narration through images and communal self-reflexivity. Although *Yellow Earth* won great international acclaim, it did not do well at the box office domestically. What is more, the film-maker had to contend with the hostilities of the officialdom in Beijing, who saw it as an unfriendly film depicting Chinese backwardness.

Chen's next production, *The Big Parade* (Fig. 2.4), was completed in 1986. In a sense this film, although perhaps artistically not as successful as *Yellow Earth*, extends the concerns of the earlier work while at the same time moving in a different direction from it. *The Big Parade* presents a psychological probing into the lives of soldiers in the People's Liberation Army. As in the plotting of *Yellow Earth*, here the director has chosen a specific situation in order to comment on the contours and life of the larger society. His focus on images and composition, clearly in

2.4 *The Big Parade*, 1986. Photo courtesy of Southern Film Corporation.

evidence in the earlier film, finds ample artistic expression in this film as well, with sound playing an even more significant role. In some respects, *The Big Parade* is different from *Yellow Earth*. The former focuses on a contemporary subject and on male values, while the latter is set in the past and is more concerned with the situation of women. *The Big Parade* deals with a group of army volunteers preparing themselves to take part in the National Day parade. Although the director focuses on six characters, ranging from a callow youth to a despairing intellectual, no one character emerges into a position of dominance. The accent is on the group mentality and the webs of interconnections that make up the whole. At the centre of the film rests a strong impulse to question and challenge accepted beliefs and sanctioned discourses. Throughout the film, powerful and appealing visual images are contrasted with voices heard from off screen. As Tony Rayns (1989a: 31) points out, 'Visual certainties are undermined by aural uncertainties, and this disjunction helps to push the film into a symbolic register.'

As with *Yellow Earth*, *The Big Parade* addresses issues that are of great concern to Chinese society and culture. In this case, the focus is on notions of Chinese patriotism, nationhood, citizenship, and a selfless devotion to the betterment of the country. A certain tentativeness characterizes this film, as the director experiments with both theme and visual grammar in a search to find his cinematic signature. The ostensible subject of *The Big Parade* is the army, but the real subject is the Chinese nation state itself.

Chen's *King of the Children* was completed in 1987. This anguished work demonstrates how contemporary history can be explored allegorically with great artistic power. The 'king of the children', Lao Gan, is sent to a school in Yunnan province, where many of the students are poor and lead unhappy lives. He is a dedicated teacher who has come to realize the futility of learning by rote, and he is keen to stimulate the creative and critical faculties of his students. His teaching methods are unorthodox by approved standards, and since the local élite disapproves of his teaching style and philosophy, he is dismissed.

Chen successfully expands this story visually into a powerful and allegorical indictment of the Cultural Revolution that caused irreparable damage to Chinese society. The self-destructive education system portrayed in the film becomes a symbol for the Cultural Revolution in general. As Chen has remarked, he did not directly depict the violent social confrontation that took place during the Cultural Revolution. Instead, he chose the language and syntax of film to create the atmosphere of the era. The forest, the fog, and the sound of trees being chopped are all, according to him, 'reflections of China during that period of time'.

King of the Children is based on a novel of the same title by Ah Cheng, but the director has modified the story to enhance its visual power. The mute cowherd, for example, who helps in defining Lao Gan's character and interests, is not found in the original story. Chen's experiments with the visual language of film can be seen very clearly in this work. He invests the film with a certain mystic aura, through his deft use of sight and sound, to create a multifaceted experience which has a pointed relevance to the audience's perspective on the Cultural Revolution.

King of the Children was followed by *Life on a String*, Chen's most philosophical film to date. This work inhabits the region of the sublime and aesthetic wonder, in which the play of images and sound trembles on the verge of new insights. Made in 1991, *Life on a String* is a mesmerizing parable full of memorably vivid images. A blind boy is told that he will surely gain his sight if he devotes his life to

17

the pursuit of music. Years pass, and the boy is now a blind old man, who regards music as the pathway to superior knowledge and wisdom. His disciple, however, regards music as a pleasurable sensual experience that serves to celebrate and define the present. Both are caught between the contradictory pulls of the desire for wisdom and the desire to see the world. The older musician has a deep faith in the ancient belief that his blindness could be cured by a prescription carefully kept in the Chinese harp. He will be allowed to try this prescription only if he wears out a thousand harp strings. After the thousandth string is broken, the musician removes from the harp a sheet of paper. Unfortunately, the paper turns out to be blank.

In *Life on a String*, Chen addresses questions of the redemptive power of art and the human need for spiritual values. Commenting on this work, Chen has remarked:

This film deals with human ideals and hopes. The old master lives with spiritual strength because of his objective in obtaining the secret cure to his blindness. Although he is briefly disappointed to find the prescription is nothing more than a blank sheet of paper, the old man realizes he has been able to grow spiritually strong simply because of that hope. Pursuit of an object enables the old man to live a better and higher life.

Despite the visual power of the film, it was both a critical and commercial failure, and in its wake Chen wanted to make a different kind of film. His next work, *Farewell to My Concubine* (Plate 1), represents the cinematic shape of this desire.

Farewell to My Concubine was both a critical and commercial success. It was the co-winner of the Palme d'Or, the top prize at the Cannes International Film Festival and received the International Film Critics' Prize for 'its incisive analysis of the political and cultural history of China and for its brilliant combination of the spectacular and the intimate'. It was a box-office hit in Hong Kong and did well internationally as well. *Farewell to My Concubine*, in many ways, represents a new departure for Chen in its attempt to combine the popular and the artistic. The success in this regard achieved by his friend and colleague Zhang Yimou may have impelled Chen to take this new path.

Farewell to My Concubine is based on a widely read novel that recounts the relationship between two Peking opera stars. The period of their friendship covers their boyhoods, the turbulence of the Cultural Revolution, and their old age. A three-hour epic, *Farewell to My Concubine* is visually stunning and dazzling in its exoticism. The relationship between the two opera stars is complex, taking place within the larger contexts of a boyhood friendship based on mutual suffering, as they learn the art of opera from cruel masters, unreciprocated love, opium addiction, the traumatic experiences of the Cultural Revolution, and encounters with bullying Red Guards. Chen's focus is on the complicated emotional relationship between the two actors, but some critics have maintained that he does not adequately probe this phenomenon. Chris Berry (1993: 22), for example, has maintained that the original story allowed Chen the opportunity to explore deeply his evident fascination with male–male relationships, but the director's homophobia undermined his ability to achieve that goal.

Despite the fact that *Farewell to My Concubine* was both an indubitable critical and commercial success, there are many commentators on Chinese cinema who feel that this movie indicates that Chen is heading down the wrong path artistically. They argue that this is a highly conventional film, with an obvious eye to commercial acceptability and displaying little of the stylistic innovation that characterized his earlier films. At the time of the film's release, Chris Berry (1993: 22) wrote:

Although *Farewell to My Concubine* may resuscitate Chen's career and make him a bankable director, it indicates dangerous thematic and stylistic self-limitation. Since leaving China for New York some years ago, his work has tended toward increasingly abstract reworking of well-known themes. The perils of blind faith, historical repetition from one Chinese generation to another, and bad faith among men as symbols of China's cultural condition with the Cultural Revolution as dominant trope have been reworked in one Chen Kaige film after another. Distant from contemporary China and showing absolutely no sign of making any connection with the culture of his adopted home, he is in danger of being as condemned to repetition and historical abstraction as he believes China to be. Is this price worth paying?

This is indeed a sentiment shared by many of Chen's admirers.

Chen's latest film, *Temptress Moon* (Plate 2), is in many ways closer to *Farewell to My Concubine* than to his earlier films. It is an elegantly shot work but the story is clumsily told, with many unnecessary convolutions. The film centres on the character of Zhongliang, played by Leslie Cheung, who as a child grew up at the country estate of the decadent Pang family. His playmate at the estate was Ruyi, played as an adult by Gong Li (Plate 3). Around these two characters are many others caught up in the decadence, the temptations of opium and lust for power, and the progressive erosion of human values. *Temptress Moon*, while drawing on some of Chen's established strengths as a filmmaker, such as his persuasive visual rhetoric, does not in any way represent an advance over his earlier work.

At the time of this writing, Chen is at an interesting crossroads in his career. Will he continue with the line of innovative work established in his earlier films? Or will he delve more deeply into the kinds of themes and treatments exemplified by *Farewell to My Concubine*? Only time will tell. There is no doubt, however, that Chen has already contributed significantly to the growth of the new Chinese cinema.

Multifaceted and driven by a strong moral vision, Chen's films established a new standard for film-making in China. The setting of the film *Yellow Earth* clearly demonstrates the director's subtlety and skill. The heartland of both the Communist revolution and Chinese civilization itself, the yellow earth and the Yellow River basin that contains it nurtured the ancient Chinese people. Chen's selection of a setting rooted in that earth and close to Yan'an, the headquarters of the CCP during the Chinese civil war and the war of resistance to Japan, allows him to explore the role of the Communist Party while making significant connections to China's distant past.

Chen, along with the other film-makers associated with the Fifth Generation, ushered in the new wave in Chinese cinema. A clear emphasis on the visual image in constructing a narrative, use of unconventional camera movements, an absence of melodrama, minimalist acting, a careful contrast of light and dark, and a move away from theatricality all contributed to the emergence of a new form of film-making in China and a new language for Chinese cinema. Not all critics of the cinema were equally enthusiastic about these innovations. Certainly, the officialdom in Beijing has viewed Chen's work with a great degree of cynicism and anxiety. Some of his films have been repeatedly banned and unbanned. Others have been subject to severe criticism in the official media. Clearly, his relationship with the czars of cinema in China has been full of tension, even antagonism.

Chen's work, understandably enough, has generated much discussion among film commentators. His attempt to create a cinema that departs radically from the theatrical and socialist realist works that continue to dominate the film scene in China has been justly commented on. His focus on vivid images and composition, a clever use of sound, an imaginative intertwining of personal biography and social history, and his attempt to make cinema a vital part of the public sphere have also been discussed at length. Similarly, his attempts to draw on Chinese aesthetics, his direct and indirect critiques of the Cultural Revolution, his interest in a variety of metaphysical outlooks, as well as the presentation in his films of a subversive 'other', as represented by the use of an unfamiliar landscape, mute children, social failures and outcasts, and simple peasants, have received extensive scholarly attention.

Chen Kaige is an absorbing, resolute, and innovative filmmaker with a fine visual sense supported by a speculative mind. Reflexivity is the ruling virtue in his work: for him films are a way to think about the world and its unpredictabilities. Abstract speculation and human specificity meet in his memorable images. He may present a certain pessimism, a personal testament of a society divided against itself and moving away from its deepest and most nurturing strengths. Yet, beneath it all, there is a sense of wonder and a celebration of freedom in the flow of his images, an undercurrent of hope for social renewal and human solidarity. The society he admires most is the society we have as yet failed to create, but one which he feels is within the human grasp.

3

Zhang Yimou: Dramas of Desire and the Power of the Image

ZHANG YIMOU is now the Chinese film-maker whose work is most widely known in the West, and he has done more than any other director to give modern Chinese cinema an international profile. His films have won many of the most prestigious awards at the international film festivals, while achieving wide popularity domestically as well. The first film Zhang directed, *Red Sorghum* (Hong gaoliang)(Plate 4), not only won for its director the Golden Bear award at the 1988 Berlin Film Festival, the highest international honour a Chinese film had earned up to that point, but it also found a wide audience in China. It became a kind of cult film, and songs and sequences from it became prominent elements of new folk performances.

Zhang is a multitalented artist, who first displayed his gifts as a cameraman for such films as Zhang Junzhao's *One and Eight* (Yige he bage, 1984) and Chen Kaige's *Yellow Earth*. Later, Zhang showed his talents as an actor by playing the lead role in Wu Tianming's *Old Well* (Lao jing), made in 1987, for which he won the best actor award at the Tokyo Film Festival. The film itself won the top award at the same festival. Since making his directorial debut with *Red Sorghum*, Zhang has made a number of films that have been both critical and commercial successes. His 1997 work, *Keep Cool* (You hua haohao shuo)(Plate 5), is a comic exploration of contemporary urban life in Beijing, which the director promises will make the audience laugh, while pressing them to entertain deep thoughts about the meaning of life. This latest film from Zhang signifies his

23

shift in interest from historical and ethnic themes to a depiction of urban life in contemporary China.

Zhang (Fig. 3.1) was born in Xi'an, Shaanxi province, in 1950. When the Cultural Revolution broke out, he was sent to the countryside for three years to work on a production team. Subsequently, he was employed for seven

3.1   Zhang Yimou, filming *Shanghai Triad*, 1995. Photo courtesy of Zhang Yimou.

years as a textile worker in the town of Xianyang. From his younger days he was interested in drawing, photography, and the art of the cinema, and so he decided to apply for a place in the department of photography at the Beijing Film Academy. His request was turned down initially, but later he was admitted to the program. After graduation he was affiliated with the Guangxi Film Studio, where he was the cinematographer for three films, *One and Eight*, *Yellow Earth*, and *The Big Parade*. In 1987, he made his appearance as a highly gifted director with *Red Sorghum*, the first film by a Fifth Generation film-maker to win a broad-based appeal in China.

1. *Farewell to My Concubine,* 1992. Photo courtesy of Tomson (H.K.) Films Co., Ltd.

2. *Temptress Moon*, 1996. Photo courtesy of Tomson (H.K.) Films Co., Ltd.

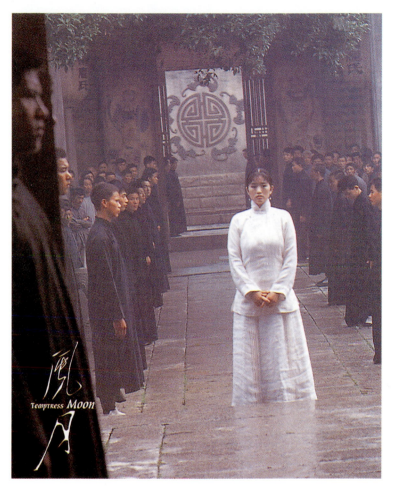

3. Gong Li in *Temptress Moon*, 1996. Photo courtesy of Tomson (H.K.) Films Co., Ltd.

4. *Red Sorghum*, 1987. Photo courtesy of Southern Film Corporation.

5. *Keep Cool*, 1997. Photo courtesy of Zhang Yimou.

6. *Raise the Red Lantern*, 1991. Photo courtesy of Era International (H.K.) Ltd.

7. *The Story of Qiu Ju*, 1992. Photo courtesy of Zhang Yimou.

8. Tian Zhuangzhuang filming *The Blue Kite*, 1992. Photo courtesy of Tian Zhuangzhuang.

9. On the set of *The Blue Kite*, 1992. Photo courtesy of Tian Zhuangzhuang.

10. *The Puppetmaster*, 1993. Photo courtesy of Hou Hsiao-hsien.

11. *The Puppetmaster*, 1993. Photo courtesy of Hou Hsiao-hsien.

12. *Goodbye South, Goodbye,* 1996

13. *A Confucian Confusion*, 1994. Photo courtesy of Edward Yang.

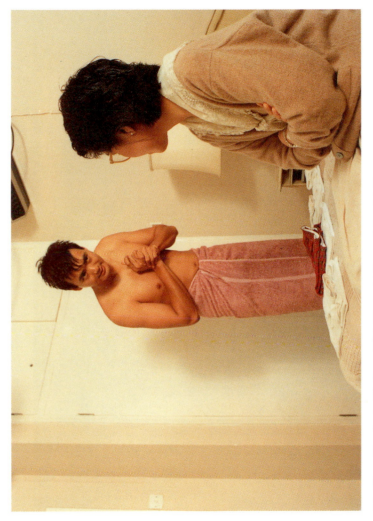

14. Chow Yun-fat in *Women*, 1985. Photo courtesy of Stanley Kwan.

15. *Love Unto Waste*, 1986. Photo courtesy of Media Asia Group.

16. *Rouge*, 1988. Photo courtesy of Media Asia Group.

17. *Centre Stage*, 1991. Photo courtesy of Media Asia Group.

18. Maggie Cheung in *Centre Stage*, 1991. Photo courtesy of Media Asia Group.

In addition to its other successes, *Red Sorghum* is the film that gained international recognition for the actress Gong Li, who has since played central roles in a number of Zhang's films. *Red Sorghum* (Fig. 3.2), set in the 1920s and 1930s, tells the story of a young woman, played by

3.2 *Red Sorghum*, 1987. Photo courtesy of Southern Film Corporation.

Gong, who is sold into marriage to a leper. Based on two short stories by the well-known writer Mo Yan, the film portrays the marriage of the man and woman who will later become the grandparents of the narrator. The film begins with an arranged marriage, follows with a rape, and concludes with the Japanese invasion of China in the 1930s. *Red Sorghum* has many memorable events: a bride being carried to her wedding, the same woman raped in a field of sorghum, a rite of cleansing, punishment in the form of a beating, orgies of drunkenness, a worker in an expression of rebellion urinating into a vat of newly brewed wine, and the concluding scenes of torture associated with the war.

3.3 *Judou*, 1990. Photo courtesy of Zhang Yimou.

26

In this film, as indeed in all his films to follow, Zhang makes effective use of colour symbolism. The colour red occurs throughout the film—in images of the bridal sedan, in the liquor distilled in the winery from red sorghum, in the blood shed during the war, in bright fires throughout— creating a dominant leitmotif. After seeing the film, one is left with the sensation of having partaken of an aesthetic ritual that celebrates life, love, and rebellion. There is a raw energy, a physical absorption in the world, and a yearning for a primal consciousness that have the effect of enlarging the circumference of our emotional topography.

Zhang made his second film, *Judou* (Fig. 3.3), in 1990; it received an American academy award nomination in 1991. The film is set in a small village in the 1920s and recounts the story of a tragic love relationship between Judou and Tianqing. Yang Jinshan is an old and wealthy dye-mill owner. He is also very miserly, and in order to run his business productively he exploits the labours of his forty-year-old nephew, Tianqing. Jinshan buys himself a beautiful and young bride, Judou, so as to make sure that his patriarchal lineage continues. His sexual impotence and sadistic practices, however, result in Judou starting a relationship with Tianqing. The desired male heir is produced from this union.

From the beginning of the film, the viewer senses a certain tragic inevitability about the story. Ultimately, Jinshan and Tianqing come to a tragic ending at the hands of the boy, Tianbai. Judou becomes insane, and she destroys the dye factory as well as herself. The film clearly highlights the nature of feudal exploitation, the dynamics of a patriarchal society, and the tragedy of the victimization of women. The film is based on a story, 'Fuxi, Fuxi', by Liu Heng, but Zhang effects changes in the original story so as to make the film more interesting and visually appealing. In the film, for example, the story unfolds against the backdrop of the dye mill, while this setting is not so apparent in the original story. The change allows the director to make use of colour symbolism to great effect.

Raise the Red Lantern (Da hong denglong gaogao gua) (Plate 6), made in 1991, was Zhang's third full-length film. Once again the victimization of women and the injustices and indignities to which they are subject form the core of the work. *Raise the Red Lantern* is based on *Wives and Concubines*, a novel by Su Tong. Set in the 1920s, the film recounts the passions, intrigues, and injustices associated with a polygamous household. A nineteen-year-old university student named Songlian arrives in a feudal manor house presided over by a wealthy and powerful patriarch. She is to become his fourth wife. The title of the movie refers to the practice of lighting a red lantern in the courtyard outside the apartment of the wife who is selected for the night.

Within the enclosed world of the manor house, each wife has her own ways of making the master happy. Very quickly, Songlian catches on to how the game is played. She pretends to be pregnant, and her lanterns are lit all night and all day. The intrigues among the wives, the feudal and patriarchal practices exemplified by the polygamous relations, are captured in a series of memorable images. The story of the film takes place in the feudal manor house, where the four wives plot against each other to obtain the favours of the master each night. The women internalize this oppressive system completely, ultimately leading to madness and death. The master is never shown clearly, but his weighty presence is felt from the beginning to the end of the film.

In 1992, Zhang completed *The Story of Qiu Ju* (Qiu Ju daguansi)(Plate 7), which went on to win the Golden Lion award at the Venice Film Festival. A film that depicts a quest for social justice, *The Story of Qiu Ju*, unlike Zhang's earlier films, is set in modern times, where economic liberalism and political repression are interwoven. In terms of style, as well as setting, this film differs from Zhang's earlier works. Within it there is a pronounced element of the documentary and the aesthetics of neo-realism. Much of the film was shot with a hidden camera in the streets of towns in northern Shaanxi. There are only four professional actors in the film; the remainder of the cast comes from the community itself. Some of these play minor roles, while others, unaware of the fact that they are being filmed, simply play themselves. Unlike Zhang's earlier films, here there are no visually striking landscapes or sets—one sees only the milling crowds. *The Story of Qiu Ju* is, in short, a very different kind of film from the director's earlier ones, avoiding the exuberant and distended visual rhetoric that characterized those works.

The Story of Qiu Ju is based on a novel by Chen Yuanbin. The title character, Qiu Ju, is an illiterate farmer's wife who simply wants to see justice done; she is seeking official help to obtain an apology from the local government official, Wang Shantang, for kicking her husband in the groin. She first takes the matter up with a local policeman, Li Shunlin, who regards the matter as settled after Wang has agreed to pay the Qius' medical bills. What Qiu Ju wants, however, is an apology. The court upholds the settlement, but Qiu Ju does not give up her struggle to obtain justice, and she appeals to a higher court.

Contrary to expectations, as Qiu Ju meets people on the higher rungs of the bureaucratic ladder, they are unfailingly courteous and helpful to her. By the time Qiu Ju has followed her appeals to the higher court, her husband has recovered from the injury, and as far as he is concerned the matter of the insult is behind him. His more pressing concern is that Qiu Ju is spending the farm's product—chillies—for court expenses. An interesting point to this story, as Zhang seems to be implying, is that it takes a strong-willed woman's efforts to maintain a man's honour. It is evident from the film's reception that Chinese officialdom liked the way the bureaucracy was portrayed within it, and this good reception resulted in a more favourable response to his earlier films as well. Discussing this film, Zhang has said, 'In terms of film language or film style, it's totally different from my previous work. Of course, there are inner connections among all my films; the mentality remains consistent. But if you look at *The Story of Qiu Ju* by its "look", you might not recognize it as my work.'

In 1994, Zhang released *To Live* (Huozhe), that year's winner of the jury award at the Cannes festival. *To Live* is an epic love story that charts the fortunes of a number of generations in a Chinese family. Fugui, the eldest son of a prominent household, makes a living by performing shadow puppetry. He has been performing from early in his life with his wife, Jiazhen, in a small village, and he has been doing so through the years he spent as a soldier in the Nationalist (Guomindang) army, upon his return to his village after it was put under Communist administration, during the Great Leap Forward of the late 1950s, and in the turbulence of the Cultural Revolution. At the time the film is set, Fugui and Jiazhen find joy in the raising of their grandson. In making *To Live*, Zhang sought to capture in human terms the joys and sorrows, triumphs and defeats, seen as a society moves forward, making right and wrong turns. As Zhang has remarked, there are tears and there is laughter, one following the other in gentle rhythm like the breath of a bellows. How the forces of the wider society influence and shape the lives of individuals, however remote they may be from the well-springs of those forces, is vividly brought out in this film.

Zhang completed *Shanghai Triad* (Yao a yao, yao dao waipo qiao)(Fig. 3.4) in 1995, winning the jury award at the Cannes International Film Festival for a second time. The

3.4   Zhang Yimou on the set of *Shanghai Triad*, 1995. Photo courtesy of Zhang Yimou.

visual style, the use of colour, and the striking pictorial compositions that characterized his earlier films, such as *Red Sorghum*, *Judou*, and *Raise the Red Lantern*, are in evidence in this film as well. *Shanghai Triad* takes us to the gangster world of the 1930s. The film deals with the life of a popular cabaret singer, Xiao Jingbao, who is the mistress of Tang, reputed to be the 'godfather' of Shanghai's underworld. Jingbao, played by Gong Li, desires autonomy for herself. With the intention of obtaining it, she allies herself with Tang's second in command, a move that produces tragic results. The story is told from the point of view of a young boy entrusted to watch Jingbao. How

31

compassion and understanding are embroiled with a hunger for power and cruelty is portrayed memorably in this work. Zhang is a different kind of film-maker from his friend and colleague Chen Kaige. If the latter is more philosophically minded and comfortable with abstract concepts, the former likes to convey his thoughts and experiences as directly as possible. Zhang has always desired to combine popular and artistic elements in his work, while Chen's films, with the exception of *Farewell to My Concubine*, display a certain austerity and have little interest in the melodramatic imagination that characterizes Zhang's work.

Women are central to the work of Zhang in a way that they are not in Chen's films, but despite their strong wills and strength of character, women in Zhang's films are victimized and subject to numerous indignities. They are chained to a highly repressive system from which they desire release. As Rey Chow (1995: 47) points out, in Zhang's films the woman's body becomes the 'living ethnographic museum that, while putting "Chinese culture" on display, is at the same time the witness to a different kind of origin. This is the origin of human sexuality, which should be free but is imprisoned in China.' Chow continues, pointing out that the woman becomes a 'way to localise China's "barbaric" cultural institutions, from which she seeks to be set free'.

Ritual figures prominently in many of Zhang's films, often as a way of presenting shared experiences symbolically and with power and beauty. Zhang's vision is itself connected to the idea of ritual in interesting ways. In *Red Sorghum, Judou*, and *Raise the Red Lantern*, in particular, this connection becomes clearly evident. It is well to remind ourselves that ritual is at the centre of Chinese culture, and that the idea of *li* is closely connected to social norms and morality in the Confucian tradition. Similarly, in

Communist societies ritual plays a central role in many varieties of symbolic communication.

There is a certain contradiction at the heart of Zhang's films. On the one hand, he is deeply interested in illuminating the plight of women, to show how they are victimized by a patriarchal social order. On the other hand, women are presented as objects of male desire and voyeurism. His concern for the predicaments of women is crossed by a penchant for exuberant specularity. As Rey Chow (1995: 47) again accurately points out, women in Zhang's films 'draw attention to themselves precisely as spectacular, dramatic bodies.' It is this latter aspect of his films that may ensure their mass appeal. The body, both male and female, is central to the meaning of Zhang's films, and the female body is singled out as an object of male desire, a site of display, and the bearer of inscriptions of social power. The masculine body, on the other hand, displays a raw and brutal energy, 'flames of fierce desire', to use William Blake's phrase, a primeval sensuality which seeks to capture the mythic depth of our collective imagination.

Zhang's films might be described as dramas of desire and sensation. The intense visual energy, the pulsing surfaces of erotic desire, the joyous celebrations of life, the luminous images, and the portrayal of cultural worlds dense and rich in texture hold a special appeal to local as well as international audiences. In many of his films, Gong Li, through her sheer force of presence and her remarkable face, with its mobility and subtlety, add to this broad-based appeal. The ways in which Zhang visualizes the flow of sensations through representational strategies of melodrama displays the special shape of his sensibility and merits deeper investigation. For Zhang, it seems, reality is a theatrical spectacle that has to be captured in all its vividness and raw power.

Not all observers, of course, are equally enthusiastic about Zhang Yimou's films. There are those who lament that he is textualizing a kind of ethnic primitivism, constructing a mythified China, is a willing prey to orientalism, displaying characteristics of misogyny and pandering to the whims of Western audiences, and that he has deviated from the deepest impulses of the Fifth Generation. How he responds to these charges and how he makes use of his immense gifts for the enrichment of Chinese cinema is something that all lovers of cinema will be watching with great eagerness. In an interview conducted in 1996 by the authors of this book, Zhang denied any Western influences on his film-making, and he raised thought-provoking questions about the future direction of the Fifth Generation, now facing the rapid social, economic, and philosophical changes seen in the China of the 1990s. The Fifth Generation directors, he says, are at a crossroads, negotiating how best to transcend the historical and ethnic themes that have distinguished them from Chinese film-makers of earlier periods.

4

Tian Zhuangzhuang: Reconfiguring the Familiar and the Unfamiliar

CHEN KAIGE and Zhang Yimou, whose works we have already discussed, and Tian Zhuangzhuang are the three most widely discussed of the Fifth Generation film-makers. These film-makers sought to usher in a new wave of Chinese cinema by relating it to modernism and internationalism, while drawing, as well, on facets of a particularly Chinese aesthetics. To understand the significance and the trajectories of development of these Fifth Generation film-makers, one has to pay attention to the cultural politics of China, and to the political environment of the international film scene. The Fifth Generation, like artists associated with other artistic movements, are products of a specific historical moment, a specific cultural geography.

When we talk of the Fifth Generation, it is important that we recognize that this term is only a convenient short-hand to identify a group of like-minded and innovative film-makers. This is of course not to suggest that all of them, Chen, Zhang, Tian, Zhang Junzhao, Wu Ziniu, and Zhou Xiaowen, among them, follow and have followed the same artistic path. This is clearly not the case. In addition, in the work of some of these directors, one begins to see a movement away from cultural élitism to a kind of cultural populism. The work of Tian, while interesting in its own right, testifies to a set of newer ambitions in his search to see the familiar in the unfamiliar, the unfamiliar in the familiar.

Tian Zhuangzhuang (Fig. 4.1) was born in 1952. His parents were closely associated with the cinema; both his father and mother were widely known actors. During the Cultural Revolution, Tian spent time in Jilin province, and later he joined the army. He was successful in obtaining

4.1 Tian Zhuangzhuang, filming *The Blue Kite*, 1992. Photo courtesy of Tian Zhuangzhuang.

an apprenticeship in the photographic department of the government's Agricultural Film Unit. In 1978, he entered the Beijing Film Academy, two years later co-directing a video film called *Our Corner* (Women de jiaoluo). After graduating from the Beijing Film Academy, he co-directed a children's film, *Red Elephant* (Hong xiang), which was completed in 1982. One year later, he made a film for television, *A Summer Experience* (Xiatian de jingli). In 1984, he made *September* (Jiuyue), a somewhat sentimental film dealing with a children's choir.

The following year, Tian made *On the Hunting Ground* (Liechang zhasa), which gained wide international recognition. He directed *The Horse Thief* (Daoma zei) in 1986, and this film went on to win for him even greater international recognition. In 1992, Tian made *The Blue Kite* (Nan fengzheng), which won awards at Cannes and other international film festivals. In this short essay, we will focus our attention on just these three films, each of which displays Tian's characteristic preoccupations and lines of growth.

On the Hunting Ground (Fig. 4.2), filmed in Inner Mongolia, addresses the lives and experiences of a Chinese minority and is without a plot in the conventional sense of the term. Instead, it deals with a hunter's violation of established codes of behaviour and the ways in which he has to face the consequences of his actions. This setting allows the film-maker to portray local rituals, the embodiments of the codes of behaviour of these exotic people, who seem to fascinate him. There are numerous shots of animals being brutally killed, reflecting the film-maker's sense of shock and puzzlement in this alien world. The whole is presented with an ethnographic quality that is consciously imposed on the film by its director.

In this film, as in Tian's next work, narrative austerity and ethnographic meditativeness meet creatively. *On the Hunting Ground* did poorly at the box office, Chinese cinema-goers showing little interest in ethnographic presentation of the rituals and codes of behavior of an alien minority, despite the deep fascination they held for Tian. Like most other film-makers associated with the new wave, Tian was not overtly addressing contemporary social problems. In an oblique way, however, his film had much to do with the Cultural Revolution. It was his way of commenting on the ritualism, the highly codified behaviour, and the cruelty associated with a mass mobilization of the people.

On the Hunting Ground presents, in the style of a documentary, the hunting rules subscribed to by China's

4.2 *On the Hunting Ground*, 1985. Photo courtesy of Southern Film Corporation.

Mongolian minority. Many of the actors were non-profes-
sionals and native Mongolian speakers, a language which
was not understood by the majority of the Chinese audience. The film relies on a monotonous voice-over to trans-
late the utterances of people belonging to different age
groups and genders. This intercession has the effect of distancing the audience from the experience of the film.
Similarly, the uses of natural lighting, a camera that is constantly surveying the landscape, and documentary-style
shots present the audience with an experience into which
they could not readily enter. It is hardly surprising that
this film did so poorly at the box-office. At the same time,
one has to applaud Tian's courage in going against the
prevalent tastes of the time and creating a film that was
in keeping with his deepest artistic impulses.

Discussing *On the Hunting Ground*, Tian (1989: 14) has
remarked, 'In the early days of the Cultural Revolution
people were extremely cruel to each other; I feel they'd
lost a certain basic humanity. In *On the Hunting Ground*,
it seems the way that animals are hunted is very cruel,
very wild, and that the other scenes on the grasslands are
very peaceful, but in fact that relationship between the
human beings is even more terrifying.' Clearly, the excesses
and cruelties of the Cultural Revolution were not far from
Tian's mind as he was making this film.

The Horse Thief (Fig. 4.3) also deals with the experiences
of members of a Chinese minority, in this case Tibetans.
The story, if one can call it that, centres around the character of Norubu. It was Tian's intention to let the narrative unfold in an unspecified time. However, officialdom
felt otherwise, and so at the opening of the film it is indicated that it takes place in 1923. In that year, Norubu is
thrown out of his community for violating accepted codes
of behaviour. He is a horse thief and a defiler of sacred

4.3 *The Horse Thief,* 1986. Photo courtesy of Southern Film Corporation.

grounds. The film covers the period from a settled if impoverished life, to the family's banishment and existence as nomads, the death of Norubu's son, the birth of a second child, and Norubu's determination to sacrifice himself for the betterment of his family.

The Horse Thief deals extensively, and often poetically, with the customs and rituals associated with the Tibetan people. The film opens and ends with scenes of the famous 'sky burial' rites associated with the Tibetans, in which corpses are placed in the open so as to be eaten by vultures. This practice, it is believed, hastens one's rebirth. There are many other rituals ethnographically presented in the film. Once again, the memorably vivid images of the Tibetan plateau, its inhabitants, their rites and customs, all somewhat exoticized, have the effect of distancing the audience from the narrative (Fig. 4.4). At the same time, as Dru Gladney (1995: 172) points out, 'the themes of individual persecution and group survival, individual guilt and social exoneration, private attachment and private betrayal, thematically relate to the turbulent and catastrophic events intimately known by every viewer of the film in China: the Great Proletarian Cultural Revolution.'

4.4 'Sky burial' scene in *The Horse Thief*, 1986. Photo courtesy of Southern Film Corporation.

A complex simplicity is radiated by both *The Horse Thief* and *On the Hunting Ground*. They aspire to attain new perceptions and strain toward new social insights. Tian's ambitions and desires declare themselves allegorically. His camera, which is that of an ethnographer, displays a detached fascination with what it surveys. In these two films, the director mounts a rebellion not only against social oppression but also against the demands of mainstream narration.

Commenting on *The Horse Thief*, Tian has made the observation that during the Cultural Revolution, the

41

spiritual worship of politics and political leaders was rampant in China. Mao was a virtual god. The attitude of the people towards their leader, and politics in general, was nothing short of religious. According to Tian, real religion has the effect of prompting human beings to probe deeper into themselves, to be more introspective, while political religion inculcates a mentality of blind and unquestioning belief. As he was making *The Horse Thief*, these ideas, he says, were uppermost in his mind.

A general criticism has been levelled against both *On the Hunting Ground* and *The Horse Thief* that their author, rather than exploring the lives and privations of these minorities, Mongolians and Tibetans, is making use of their experiences—exploiting them, in a way—so as to comment on greater Chinese social experiences and crises. In responding to this type of criticism, Tian (1989: 15) has remarked,

I did think about the problem of using Mongolian and Tibetan customs to represent China at the outset, and because I wasn't really sure how to deal with it, I decided that in making the films my primary concern had to be to respect these people's religions; I wouldn't fool them into doing anything false to serve the ends of my film. I think that's a matter of politeness and quality. Second, the problems these nationalities have been through are ones they share with the Han Chinese majority. The Cultural Revolution was very traumatic for them, too. Therefore, I don't feel the films constitute exploitation of the national minorities for my own ends.

In 1992, Tian made *The Blue Kite* (Plate 8), a film that represents a stylistic change on the part of the film-maker. There is a much stronger narrative in the work, and as with Zhang Yimou's films, a certain penchant for melodrama and a focus on specularity are apparent. In 1989, Tian made the remark that Zhang's *Red Sorghum* marked the end of Fifth Generation film-making. Zhang's film relied on a strong narrative, specularity, and melodrama as means of reaching a mass audience, a goal which had never up to that time been the intention of the Fifth Generation artists. Chen Kaige's *Farewell to My Concubine*, released the same year as *The Blue Kite*, also indicated a departure from the style of film-making previously associated with the Fifth Generation.

In this context, it is particularly interesting that Tian should follow suit with *The Blue Kite*. The film focuses on Tietou, a child born in 1954, and his mother. It explores the events of more than a decade in modern Chinese history, and the story is told from two perspectives: that of the boy and that of the mother. In this work, Tian is concerned to point out the complex and powerful ways in which politics impinges on the daily lives of ordinary people, how their lives are shaped and broken by the dictates of politics. Tian calls attention to a number of important stages in the evolution of modern China: Mao's Hundred Flowers Campaign of 1957, the Great Leap Forward, begun in 1958, and the Cultural Revolution. Tian dramatizes these events, and traces their impacts on the lives of ordinary people, with the eye of a critical humanist (Plate 9).

Although the excesses of the Cultural Revolution, its persecution of intellectuals and the general inhumanity that was unleashed by the movement, had been dealt with directly or indirectly in earlier films, what is interesting about *The Blue Kite* is that the film brings within a single narrative the Hundred Flowers Campaign, the Great Leap Forward, and the Cultural Revolution, pointing out the vacillations, uncertainties, and muddle-headedness that have often characterized official policy-making. This point is illustrated through the failure of three marriages, as the partners succumb to the dictates of the larger political discourses. In making this film, Tian ran into numerous difficulties with officials, who were clearly unhappy with his treatment of contemporary Chinese history. Not only was post-production delayed, but he had to do a kind of 'long-distance editing' of the film. Tian, who had been vocal in his opposition to the government in its attitude to the student protests, the release of political prisoners, and so on, had to face severe hostility from the officialdom.

Between the years 1987 and 1991, Tian made four easily forgettable commercial films. *Rock 'n Roll Kids* (Yaogun qingnian), for example, made in 1988, deals with music and dance, and it was very popular in China. Over 160 prints of this film were sold domestically, as opposed to *On the Hunting Ground*, of which only two copies were sold. The official bureaucracy was also very pleased with this film. Tian, however, was not satisfied, and understandably so. As he remarked later, 'I was miserable making the film.... I never really liked the film.'

A study of Tian's works enables us to understand better the contours of the film landscape and film culture in China. His earlier works, such as *On the Hunting Ground* and *The Horse Thief*, reflect his boldness of mind in going against the accepted styles of Chinese film-making, as well as displaying many of the central concerns of the Fifth Generation. The structure of cinematic thought displayed in *The Horse Thief* and *On the Hunting Ground*, with the economy of the director's art, its narrative parsimony and expansive reflexivity, made a deep impression on discerning film critics both locally and internationally. The commercial films Tian made between 1987 and 1991 testify to the relentless pressures exerted by the film industry for adequate returns from the box-office. A film like *The Blue Kite*, which manifests a different order of sensibility from his earlier work, is indicative of the strong pulls of the international film culture. All these are vital forces with which not only Tian, but the other innovative film-makers in China as well, have to contend. Tian's more accomplished films bear witness to the necessity of capturing facets of compelling reality, while registering at the same time the impossibility of capturing it.

Similar to many Chinese film-makers, Tian finds it puzzling to try to predict the direction contemporary Chinese film will go in the 1990s and beyond. He admits that film is a product of industry, technology, commerce, and mass entertainment, but as a director he is determined to uphold his principle that there should be a vision of society and culture in every film he makes. In an interview conducted by the authors of this book in 1997, Tian admitted that he has been deeply fascinated by the philosophical vision embedded in the filmic techniques of Ingmar Bergman (as seen in, for example, *Wild Strawberries*), Michelangelo Antonioni (as in *Blow-Up*), and Martin Scorsese (as exemplified by *Taxi Driver*).

Tian Zhuangzhuang's latest production is a 1997 experimental film titled *Steel is Made this Way* (Gang tie shi zheyang liancheng de), a collaboration with the young Sixth Generation film-maker Lu Xuezhang. In this film, Tian worked as a co-producer and actor, but his primary work was to help guide members of the younger generation of Chinese film-makers to search for a new mode of representation that blends personal desires with social changes, inner psychology with outer human relationships, and the initiation of the individual to life with dilemmas between reality and the ideal. This effort is not only a search for a new mode of representation beyond that of the Fifth Generation; it is also a quest for the meaning of art and life for both Tian and the Sixth Generation.

45

5

Hou Hsiao-hsien: Critical Encounters with Memory and History

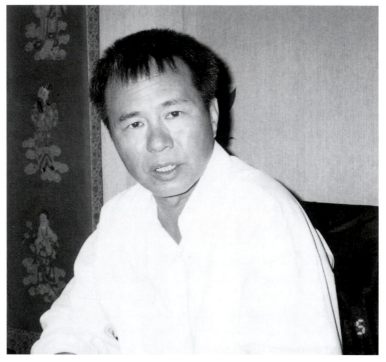

5.1 Hou Hsiao-hsien at an interview, 1997. Photo by Kwok-kan Tam.

Hou Hsiao-hsien (Fig. 5.1) is a thoughtful film-maker, who has carved out a distinct cinematic style admirably suited to the themes he persistently seeks to explore. He has brought international recognition and acclaim to Taiwanese cinema as have few other directors. Going against the tradition of slick comedies and films that achieve their impact

through the latest dazzling special effects, as many popular Taiwanese film directors are wont do, Hou has sought
to create a reflective and humanistic cinema that critically
foregrounds the trajectory of Taiwanese history and social
evolution. With Ozu-like patience and meditativeness,
particularly such as the elder Japanese director demonstrated in his *Tokyo Story* (Tokyo monogatari), Hou draws
us into the lives and relationships of his chosen characters, thereby enlarging our understanding of human motives
and behaviour, as well as deepening our perception of the
transformations taking place in Taiwanese culture. The
manner in which Hou holds characters and history in tension gives his films a special resonance.

Hou's earlier works, including *That's the Way She Strolls
Around* (1981), *The Naughty Wind* (1982), *Green, Green
Grass of Home* (1982), and *The Sandwich Man* (1983), can
best be described as works of apprenticeship in which he
was seeking to discover his true cinematic signature. *The
Boys from Fengkuei* (Fenggui lai de ren), made in 1983, is
the first feature film that indicates his mature style and
vision. The film explores the nature of urban life. The protagonist, Ah-ching, along with two of his friends, leaves his
small town to look for work as well as social adventure.
In the city they are drawn more and more towards the
moral decadence it has to offer: pornographic movies, petty
thefts, superficial amusement, purposeless living.

With the patience and reflectiveness that we have since
come to expect from Hou, against a background of the perils of urbanism, he explores the lack of meaning in the
lives of these youths. Some of the most memorable images
in the film present the protagonist being overwhelmed by
the dense traffic in the city of Kaohsiung. How the protagonist begins to understand more about himself and the
world in which he lives is central to the meaning of the

film. In this work, as in a number of Hou's other films, we see the presence of a passive and inactive father and an active mother, one who takes charge of the household and the life of the growing protagonist.

A Summer at Grandpa's (Dongdong de jiaqi), completed in 1984, also presents the growing social awareness of a young boy. As Tung-tung, the young protagonist of this film, confronts the social world around him, he is increasingly convinced of its oppressive nature and the punishments that inevitably follow when one seeks, for whatever reason, to violate or challenge accepted codes and norms. Hou's stories are deeply embedded in a discourse of the social evolution of Taiwan. In viewing *A Summer at Grandpa's*, an appreciation of the temporal setting of the story—at a time when the agriculture-based economy of the island was gradually being transformed into an export-led one, with the new presence of free-trade zones and multinational corporations and a migration of the labour force from the rural areas to the cities—is important in helping to make greater sense of the film's resonances. That the director has certain misgivings about these transformations is evident from the way in which Tung-tung looks back at his childhood experiences with a nostalgia tinged with a certain romanticism.

Tung-tung's mother is sick, and so he and his sister are sent to the home of their grandfather, a physician with a prominent reputation and a quiet disposition. Here, Tung-tung makes friends with other boys and is involved in various adventures. Through the exploration of such episodes as the family's disapproval of an uncle's marriage, the behaviour of local thugs, and the attachment to tradition displayed by the grandfather, the director confronts the world of adults with that of the young boy in interesting and illuminating ways.

A Time to Live and a Time to Die (Tongnian wangshi), made in 1985, won for Hou wide international acclaim. The director's most autobiographical work, this film covers a period of about twenty years, chronicling the growth of the protagonist, Ah-hsiao, from childhood to young adulthood. The film deals with the experiences of a family from Guangdong province but living at the time of the film on Taiwan. The grandmother of the family is still very much attached to the Mainland, and she hopes that very soon she will be able to return to her native land. The father of the family is a pious educator, who is some-what sickly and dies. His mother, as in most of Hou's films, is strong and takes control of family matters. She exercises a great influence over Ah-hsiao throughout his growing up. It is she, and not the father, who constantly warns the boy against gambling and deceitful practices. During the course of the film she dies of throat cancer and Ah-hsiao, who has become a recognized 'tough', cries unashamedly at her funeral.

As the film progresses, against the backdrop of a rapidly changing Taiwan we see the growth of Ah-hsiao, from a child betting with the money stolen from his mother, to a teenager, given to body-building, ever ready to fight, and obsessed with gambling. Even more than in the earlier two films discussed here, in *A Time to Live and a Time to Die* Hou forges a cinematic style perfectly fitted to the theme. Like Ozu Yasujiro before him, Hou allows his camera to meditate on a location before and after the action has taken place in a way that provokes deeper reflection. He makes use of lighting unostentatiously but sensitively and effectively to register the exact mood. A tree whose branches are lit by the sun, a room lit by a single bulb, a road that runs toward a village in the afternoon sun: each is captured with great delicacy and sensitivity through his lighting.

Talking about his films, Hou openly admits the stylistic influence of Ozu on his work. In *A Time to Live and a Time to Die*, the director also makes use of linguistic diversity to great effect. The voice-over by the eldest son is in a southern-accented Mandarin, indicating that it is a second language for the narrator. His younger brothers, who have grown up on Taiwan, speak a purer Mandarin. The grandmother and mother speak a Cantonese dialect which the children understand but do not themselves speak. As Chris Berry (1994: 57) observes, 'With this linguistic diversity, Hou marks out Taiwan as a space criss-crossed by a specific and intricate network of nuanced and subtle differences.'

Dust in the Wind (Lianlian fengchen), released in 1987, is once again a film that intertwines the stories of personal lives with the larger historical and cultural discourses of Taiwan. The theme of urban migration is central to the intent of the film. Young Wan, although not exactly a picture of health, detests high school; he leaves his family and goes to Taipei in search of work. He is accompanied by his girlfriend, Wuen. Once there, they are caught between the contradictory pulls of home and city, and their relationship is troubled. The young protagonist displays a greater interest in the opposite sex than do those in Hou's earlier films.

In *Dust in the Wind*, with its dream sequences and fantasies, Hou adopts an elliptical style that gives greater emphasis to juxtaposition and montage. As Godfrey Cheshire (1993: 61) points out, this shift of emphasis from *mise en scène* to montage 'signals more than just an interest in expanded stylistic possibilities. For this was the time when Hou was becoming prominent on the international festival circuit, which surely brought with it an implicit dilemma: whether to broaden his subject matter and approach to attract still larger audiences, or remain idiosyncratically indigenous.' If his later films are any indication, Hou seems to have chosen the latter path.

Hou's next film, *Daughter of the Nile* (Niluohe nu'er), made in 1987, seeks to capture the qualities of a newly emerging city life in developing countries and the associated plight of their wayward youth. The spread of mass culture and consumerism and the relentless focus on wealth and capital that are widespread in contemporary cities form the backdrop to the human drama of the film. Unlike in Hou's earlier works, the protagonist in *Daughter of the Nile* is a young woman. She works for a fast-food chain owned by a company in the United States and, from the margins, observes the rapid social and economic transformation taking place around her. There are two main characters in the film. One is a young man, desirous of making it in the newly emerging capitalist society but seemingly unable to achieve his goal. The central protagonist is his sister, who transfers her anxieties and desires onto the adventures of a heroine living in ancient Egypt. Despite its powerful visual imagery, the film does not quite succeed in achieving its ambitions. It is said that Hou regards *Daughter of the Nile* as one of his least successful films.

In 1989, Hou made *A City of Sadness* (Beiqing chengshi), which won the prestigious Golden Lion award for the best film at the Venice festival. An expansive panorama of Taiwan family life during the turbulent years from 1945 to 1949, *A City of Sadness* proved to be a box-office success. This is surprising in view of the style of the film, which is very different from the flashy, slick films that are generally the more popular. This work also won for Hou the best director honours at the Golden Horse Film Festival in Taipei.

The first installment in Hou's 'sadness trilogy', *A City of Sadness* deals with four vitally important years in the growth of the nation state of Taiwan: from the end of Japanese colonization in 1945, to the ascent of Communist power on the Mainland and the establishment in 1949 by Chiang Kai-shek of the Guomindang government-in-exile in Taipei. This was a fateful moment in Taiwan's history. It was, of course, a period of tumultuous change on the island, and Hou explores aspects of these transformations through the fortunes of one family, consisting of an elderly widower, Ah-lu, and his four sons.

Lin Wen-heung, the eldest son, is a black marketeer, a nightclub owner, and a gangster, who dies as a consequence of violence. He is the one most attuned to the social realities of the emergent nation state of Taiwan. Lin Wen-ching, the youngest son, is deaf and mute and stays somewhat aloof from the crisis that has beset the family. Lin Wen-sun, the second son, was recruited into the Japanese army to serve as a doctor in the Philippines and has not returned. Lin Wen-leung, the third son, was also recruited by the Japanese army as a translator, and his unhappy experiences have left him mentally deranged.

Through the interplay of these diverse characters, *A City of Sadness* focuses on an episode that has largely been swept under the carpet by official historians, namely, the massacre on 28 February 1947 of supporters of the Taiwan independence movement by supporters of the Guomindang troops. This is a very sensitive topic in Taiwan, and as a director Hou was fully aware of the controversies and clashes of opinion that his film was likely to generate. He is on record as saying that he made this film,

not for the sake of opening up old wounds, but because it's vital that we face up to this incident if we are to understand where we come from and who we are as Taiwanese. The Chinese way has always been to cover over domestic scandals, to pretend they never happened, but I am not at all persuaded that that's a good thing. My own feeling is that problems must be acknowledged and discussed if we are ever to resolve them in our minds (Hou, 1989: 41).

A City of Sadness is an attempt to interrogate the official stories that each nation tells itself. It is not so much the terror of history as the official manipulations and erasures of history that engage Hou's cinematic interests.

The style of the film invites closer analysis. With a meditative camera, the film-maker draws the viewer into this family saga through carefully constructed and beautifully composed episodes: weddings, family banquets, scenes of life within prison houses and in the countryside. Through a series of deeply moving sequences he portrays the anguish, powerlessness, and inner uncertainties of the family. In this film, we see clearly the gift of the director for interweaving interpersonal relationships with the larger tides of Taiwanese history. *A City of Sadness* represents very powerfully the cinematic style, the maturity of judgement, and the thematic interests that we have come to associate with Hou's work. The film, of course, was not without its critics. Some felt that Hou was venturing into unwanted areas. Others felt that he did not venture far enough. There were yet others who felt that a greater attention to feminist issues would have strengthened the film.

In 1993, Hou released *The Puppetmaster* (Xi meng ren-sheng)(Fig. 5.2), the second piece of his sadness trilogy. *The Puppetmaster* won the 1993 jury prize of the Cannes International Film Festival and the 1993 best sound effects award of the International Festival of Flanders-Ghent (Belgium), and it was exhibited the same year in the non-competition section of the Hawaii International Film Festival. Through exquisite cinematography (Plate 10), it explores

5.2 Hou Hsiao-hsien, filming *The Puppetmaster*, 1993. Photo courtesy of Hou Hsiao-hsien.

five decades of Taiwanese history and the nature and significance of the evolving Taiwanese identity. With a tranquillity born of maturity of judgement and a confidence in his cinematic style, Hou confronts the historical evolution of Taiwan with great self-assurance.

The film recounts the life of an actor who spent many years as a puppetmaster (Plate 11). He returns to the puppet stage and observes performances, which are presented in continuous long takes. The aged actor who recreates his life in this film is Li Tien-lu (Li Tian-lu). Li has lived a long life, but the film focuses on events from the turn of the century to 1945. These were the years when Taiwan was under Japanese rule, and so it is hardly surprising that his memories deal primarily with his experiences of the Japanese. Hou portrays the complex emotions generated during the occupation. Some Japanese subjected Li to various forms of suffering, while others treated him kindly and

5.3 *Good Men, Good Women*, 1995. Photo courtesy of Hou Hsiao-hsien.

with dignity. In this, as in his other films, Hou displays a remarkable ability to portray the complex movement of history through vividly realized individual lives.

Good Men, Good Women (Hao nan hao nu)(Fig. 5.3), made in 1995, is Hou's last film in his sadness trilogy. In making this film he experimented with a new mode of presentation, in which different levels of time and space are intermingled to show the interconnectedness of history and geography. Through the memory of the female character, Liang Jing, who plays the lead role in a film-within-a-film, the past is shown to be related to the present, and the Mainland to Taiwan. Liang lives in Taiwan in the 1990s; the portrayal of her real life presents vividly the confusion of identity in present-day Taiwan. In her role in the film-within-a-film, however, she first lives on the Mainland in pursuit of a national identity and then later back in Taiwan suffering persecution during the Guomindang reign. Through vivid cinematic images of political changes in Taiwan and on the Mainland, Hou shows the hardships and sufferings of both the Mainlanders and the Taiwanese in their search for a new life and a new identity at both the personal and national levels. In the context of his other works, one observes that with this film Hou turned more and more inward in the psychological depiction of his characters.

Goodbye South, Goodbye (Nanguo zaijian, nanguo) (Fig. 5.4), made in 1996, is Hou's latest production, and was nominated for the Golden Palm award at the Cannes film festival. This film can be considered a sequel to *Good Men, Good Women* in its exploration of contemporary social changes in Taiwan. The split between the historical and the contemporary in *Good Men, Good Women* is also a sign of a split in Hou's career. With *Goodbye South, Goodbye* (Plate 12), Hou moves away from a process of rethinking Taiwan's history to one of interrogating its

5.4 *Goodbye South, Goodbye*, 1996. Photo courtesy of Hou Hsiao-hsien.

5.5 *Goodbye South, Goodbye,* 1996. Photo courtesy of Hou Hsiao-hsien.

present. The contemporary element represented by the neon-lit karaoke bar frequented by the hollow youth in *Good Men, Good Women* is fully expanded in *Goodbye South, Goodbye* into a world of gangsterish businessmen (Fig. 5.5), a world in which commerce and corruption are indistinguishable and quick money is the only objective. The use of long, expressive tracking shots in the film highlights the aimlessness of life and the ceaseless movement toward future uncertainties.

Hou Hsiao-hsien is a self-conscious craftsman who places his craft at the service of a creative exploration of the oscillations of personal memory and national history. In his films, idea and image, character and rumination, act in cinematic synergy to create unforgettable sequences. The conviction that underlies his work is interrogative and humanistic, always seeking to challenge received wisdom.

In many of his films, the visual rhetoric perfectly matches his reflective desires, and his images quiver with manifold cultural associations. In his later films, as he finds his personal voice, one discerns a great assurance and purposefulness in the use of the camera. Hou is a film-maker unafraid to cut to the nerve of society, to register its inner oscillations. His preoccupation with the deeper vibrations of culture-in-the-making gives his films a special poignancy.

6

Edward Yang: Visions of Taipei and Cultural Modernity

EDWARD YANG, with Hou Hsiao-hsien, is one of the two best known and most internationally acclaimed of contemporary Taiwanese film directors. Each has a substantial body of work to his credit, yet they may be seen to represent two distinct impulses of Taiwanese cinema. Hou is interested in repossessing childhood memories and cinematizing the countryside. In some of his work, nostalgia for the past is elevated to a condition of redemption. Yang, on the other hand, is concerned with the convulsions of urban life and its dark underside. How the complex imperatives of urbanism press on groups of human beings engages his deepest interest. To say that Hou is interested in the countryside and Yang in the city is, of course, to simplify their art and reduce their intentions. Both of them do much else. There is a healthy competition and cooperation between these two gifted film-makers, and it is interesting to note that each has acted in the other's films.

Edward Yang (Yang Dechang, or Yang Te-ch'ang) (Fig. 6.1) was born in Shanghai in 1947. Two years later, his family migrated to Taiwan. Until around the age of six, he was not interested in films. Talking about his career as a film-maker in an interview conducted by the authors of this book in 1997, Yang revealed that his initial artistic inspiration came from local and Japanese comics, and he started writing his own from a young age. In 1970 he went to the United States to study computer science. While there, Yang studied film production for one semester at the University of Southern California. Dissatisfied with what

6.1 Edward Yang at an interview, 1997. Photo by Kwok-kan Tam.

he perceived as an overemphasis on technological training, he decided to give up film studies and worked as a computer expert in Seattle for eleven years.

At one time Yang was deeply impressed by the new wave in German cinema, and he tried to experiment with it in some of his short productions. Many critics have compared Yang's work with that of Antonioni, but he openly disclaims any direct influence from Western directors. Instead, he thinks that the philosophical inspiration and satiric vision he learned from Japanese comics in his early childhood is larger than any influence he might have received from Western film-makers.

In 1981, Yang travelled to Hong Kong and participated in the production of *The Winter of 1905* (1905 nian de dongtian), working both as a scriptwriter and actor. He also directed a television movie. In 1982, he made his first feature film, *Desires* (Zhi wang), which formed a part of the series titled *In Our Time* (Guangyin de gushi). Yang not only directs but also writes the scripts for his films, sometimes with the help of a co-writer. The following year, he made *That Day, On the Beach* (Haitan de yitian). In 1985, he directed *Taipei Story* (Qingmei zhuma), which gained him international acclaim. One year later, he made *The Terrorizer* (Kongbu fenzi), a film that, once again, generated a great measure of international interest. In 1991, Yang's *A Brighter Summer Day* (Guling jie shaonian sharen shijian)(Fig. 6.2) was released. Three years later still, he made a satiric film, *A Confucian Confusion* (Duli shidai), which may be said to have a post-modern visage. His latest film, *Mahjong*, was completed in 1996. As of this writing, Yang has made seven major films, and all bear his distinct cinematic signature. Exploration of the meaning of being in a society in a hurry, and the implications of living and not living in rapidly transforming social spaces, is central to his intentions.

A brief discussion of a few representative films allows us to point out some of the distinctive traits of Yang as a film-maker. As a beginning, a look at *That Day, On the Beach* allows us to enter the characteristic thought-world of Yang, to explore his thematic and formal preoccupations. This film, with its complex narrative structure, intricate web of flashbacks, non-theatrical acting style, non-linear story, deployment of long takes, avoidance of emotional distensions, use of off-screen space and voice-over

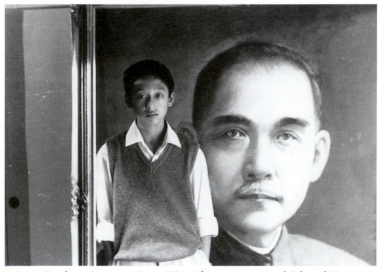

6.2 *A Brighter Summer Day*, 1991. Photo courtesy of Edward Yang.

narration, and a pervading sense of critical detachment, departs significantly from the normal run of Taiwanese films. Indeed, Yang shows himself here to be a film-maker with a modernist and transformative mission.

That Day, On the Beach deals with the complex relationship between Jia-li, the main character and narrator of the film, and De-wei, her husband. There is a secondary, and in many ways complementary, love story in this film, the relationship between Ching-ching and Jia-sen, Jia-li's brother. The lives and entanglements of Jia-li and De-wei serve to focus attention on the rapid economic development of Taiwan and its harsh impact on human relationships. The secondary love story has the effect of focusing the audience's gaze on the interplay between traditional values and Westernization, and the increasing penetration of American cultural values into the lives of the rising generation. The story of the film is told by Jia-li to

Ching-ching, through the use of flashbacks within flash-backs. The disjointed and fragmented nature of the film mirrors the disconnected and fissured being of a society living on contradictions, and it suggests as well the ensu-ing laceration of bonds between human beings. In this film, the complexity of form echoes the complexity of the social vision.

Taipei Story also manifests a complex awareness of the tensions that shadow and inform contemporary urban living. This film explores the troubled dislocations of the contemporary moment, focusing on the life of a couple engaged since adolescence but never married. Also present is a gallery of other characters, who represent a diversity of backgrounds and attitudes and who impinge on the life of the couple. Chin, the film's protagonist, works as a per-sonal assistant to an unmarried woman executive. When a large conglomerate decides to take over the company, Chin, along with her boss, resolves to leave. She sudden-ly has much time on her hands, and she moves away from her parents and obtains her own apartment, displaying a certain rebelliousness of spirit. Lon, Chin's fiancé, repeat-edly fails in his business endeavours. While Chin displays an antipathy to her father, who she is convinced has mis-treated her mother, Lon feels a measure of sympathy for him.

The film textualizes the anguished relationship between Chin and Lon over a period of a few important weeks. Both actions and non-actions during this period have a deeply freighted meaning for each of these characters. *Taipei Story*, like others of Yang's films, consists of multiple strands of narratives that intersect in a complex and, at times, self-subverting manner. The result is a film that captures the flow of urban life, reflecting the director's characteristic energy of perception and gift for precise imagery, producing a kind of poetry of urban banality. *Taipei Story*, with its de-theatricalization, accuracy of placement, sensitivity to logics of spatiality, and the reticent power of its images, is redolent of the work of Antonioni, such as *L'Eclisse*. It needs to be said, however, that Yang's images and their visualities have an unmistakably Chinese flourish. They grow out of a distinctly indigenous sensibility.

The Terrorizer, released in 1986, won for Yang the Grand Prix Special du Jury at the 1987 Locarno Film Festival. That the structure, controlling mood, and paraphrasable meaning of the film always seem to exceed our grasp is a feature we have now come to associate with the work of Yang. These opacities are memorably present in this film as well, as the dislocating power of urbanism pulses through the narrative. The film focuses on the intersecting lives of a girl trapped in her loneliness, a young couple, and a triangular relationship between two men and a woman. The girl finds herself on the wrong side of the law. The young couple are a photographer and his girlfriend; they are on the brink of separation. The triangular relationship is between a woman novelist, her husband, who is a doctor, and a magazine editor. At the beginning of the film, the camera's perspective cross-cuts between these various characters as they go about their business of living. As the film moves forward, we begin to perceive, dimly at first, the interconnections among their lives.

The girl is locked up at home by her irate mother. The girl, for her part, spends her time making prankish telephone calls that are not without venom. One of these catalyses the break up of the marriage of the woman writer. It is a world in which sinister shadows openly embrace everyday realities. Commenting on this film, Tony Rayns (1989b: 7) observes, 'As the links become closer and more complex, the film recognizes the weight of fiction it is con-

structing and turns it into an ironic reflection of the way
that fiction neatly tidies up life's loose ends: the woman's
novel not only draws the events that led to the ending of
the marriage but also seems to prefigure the events that
form its aftermath.' The word 'terrorizer' in the title of
this film carries its special connotative associations, call-
ing attention to the explosively dark underside of urban
living. There is a post-modern logic to the narrativization
of this work.

The eminent American cultural critic and theorist Fredric
Jameson has written at length on *The Terrorizer*. Jameson
(1992: 151) remarks:

> What we must admire... is the way in which the filmmaker
> has arranged for these two powerful interpretive temptations—
> the modern and the postmodern, subjectivity and textuality—to
> neutralize each other, to hold each other in one long suspension
> in such a way that the film can exploit and draw on the bene-
> fits of both, without having to commit itself to either as some
> definitive reading or formal and stylistic category.

A Brighter Summer Day (Fig. 6.3) is a typical Yang film,
with its complex narrative structure embodying the complexity of the foregrounded themes. This is a long film, with
a large cast of characters. It deals with an uncertain Taiwan
seen through the window of post-modern preferences. The
film deals with the Zhang family, the father and mother
of which came with their five children from Shanghai to
Taiwan in 1949. The narrative focuses largely on the fourth
child, a boy nicknamed Xiao Si'er. The family occupies a
position of centrality in the narrative; however, as with
others of Yang's films, there are multiple plot strands, giving it his characteristic density of texture. *A Brighter
Summer Day* is in many ways the least 'Westernized' (to
repeat a term meant disparagingly when used by some of

6.3 *A Brighter Summer Day*, 1991. Photo courtesy of Edward Yang.

Yang's detractors) of his films. In this film the director reconfigures, within a multifaceted cinematic form, the tensions and troubled awarenesses in familial relationships, the way history reconceives differently understood phenomena, the meaning of Taiwaneseness, the island's complicated relations with the Mainland, and the ambiguities of hope and despair all these dynamics engender (Fig. 6.4).

A Confucian Confusion (Fig. 6.5) is a comedy that connects in an interesting way to the current debates on human rights and their applicability to the life of Asian societies. It was shortlisted in the competitive section of the 1994 Cannes festival. The story takes place in Taipei, and among the characters are a group of young people with a primarily modernist outlook, who are caught in the cross-fire of traditional and contemporary values. The conflict between group loyalty and individual fulfillment that assumes ever greater importance in the film is portrayed with a sardonic wit. Indeed, satire guides the film as it shifts from one

6.4 *A Brighter Summer Day*, 1991. Photo courtesy of Edward Yang.

6.5 *A Confucian Confusion*, 1994. Photo courtesy of Edward Yang.

narrative lane to another. The meaning of individuality is a question repeatedly raised in the film, and it is not without significance that the Chinese title of the film means 'Age of Autonomy'. The various characters, such as K. K, Siu Fung, Siu Ming, Lap Yen, Yum, Larry, Molly, and Birdy, who continuously come and go from the narrative, carry the burden of the self-alienation and confused atomism that seem to be the natural extension of super-modernism (Plate 13). Eschewing traditional sentimental pieties, Yang seeks in this film to explore new configurations of values relevant to modern society. The confused world that takes shape through his chosen images is not a world drained of values, but it is one that is struggling with them.

Yang's latest film, *Mahjong* (Fig. 6.6), in many ways of a piece with his earlier works, summons into cinematic existence a world swollen with power and corrupted self-importance. A greater narrative presence asserts itself in it than appears in the earlier films. The director seems to be saying that the apparent glossy surface of life, seductive

6.6 *Mahjong*, 1996. Photo courtesy of Edward Yang.

and glitzy, covers up deep fissures and dark motivations that can have unforeseen consequences. At its release, there was almost a prophetic ring to this film, in that some of the events and trends textualized within it came to achieve an embarrassing visibility in contemporary Taiwanese society. The vision of a society that octopus-like is seeking to move in different directions all at once commands our terrified assent regarding the accuracy of the diagnosis.

Edward Yang and Hou Hsiao-hsien, in their different ways, are two of the most significant makers of the new Taiwanese cinema. Yang, with his inclination toward modernism and post-modernism, the capturing of the flow of urbanism, and the interplay of localism and globalism, compels our sustained attention. Yang has said that we need to face up to the complex and inevitable imperatives of globalization with hope and assurance. Recognizing the ineluctability of the ever-accelerating velocity of change, we must develop what he terms a 'cultural confidence' to participate usefully and productively in this newly emerging world.

Yang is, of course, not without his detractors. They argue that he is too Westernized, that his films are not adequately entertaining, that they lack a coherent structure and his characters inhabit a cartoonist's world. We would dissent from such judgements. Yang, in our opinion, is a highly innovative film-maker, one who is grappling with the possibilities of the medium of cinema. With a teasing charm, he takes us into the heart of some of the most troubling issues of our time. His films capture the ways in which facts and fantasies of the contemporary mind operate in a world somewhat out of joint. He has sought to evolve, not always with the desired measure of success, a cinematic style equal to the perplexities of our time. In his work, a certain justified and incoherent fragmentation informs time and space. The abrupt juxtapositions, presented without obvious narrative connectives, are a result of this disposition. Yang is a film-maker who merits and rewards the closest attention.

7
Stanley Kwan: Narratives of Feminine Anguish

7.1 Stanley Kwan at an interview, 1997. Photo by Kwok-kan Tam.

THERE ARE A NUMBER of distinguished film directors in Hong Kong who have imparted a new vitality and seriousness of purpose to the Hong Kong cinema. Among them, Ann Hui, Allen Fong, Tsui Hark, John Woo, Stanley Kwan, and Wong Kar-wai deserve special mention. Each of these directors, from her or his distinctive vantage point and guided by her or his deepest instincts, has significantly enriched the Territory's cinema. All invite close and sustained study. In this essay we focus on the work of one, Stanley Kwan (Guan Jinpeng).

Stanley Kwan (Fig. 7.1) was born in 1957 in Hong Kong. After attending Pui Ching Middle School, he entered Hong Kong Baptist College (now Hong Kong Baptist University), where he studied communication. After graduation, he joined the Hong Kong Television Broadcast Company Limited (TVB) as a production assistant. In 1979, he left the station and began working as an assistant director to Dennis Yu. Subsequently, he worked as assistant director to such well-known film-makers as Peter Young, Ronnie Yu, Ann Hui, Patrick Tam, Yim Ho, Leung Po-chi, and Tony Au.

In 1984, Kwan made his first feature film, *Women* (Nuren xin)(Plate 14), a work that probes into the lives and loves of a number of career women. The film focuses on the women's psychological complexity, which is shown to grow out of dimly graspable emotionalities and a weight of despair. The film was criticized by some commentators as being too male-centred in its orientation. Two years later, Kwan made *Love Unto Waste* (Dixia qing)(Plate 15), a much more accomplished work of cinematic art. Kwan counts it among the best of his films.

As a general practice, the director selects materials for his films from the worlds he knows best, and he creates works of cinema by transforming his felt experiences, as well as those of his acquaintances, into stories conceived in warmth and sympathy (Fig. 7.2). In recreating these intimate worlds, he relies heavily on the evidence of his senses. *Love Unto Waste* is no exception. Once again the predicaments of women figure prominently in the narrative. In this work, reminiscent of Federico Fellini's *La Strada*, the idea of decadence and its ways of inflecting human behaviour is central to the film-maker's cinematic intentions.

In 1988, Kwan made *Rouge* (Yanzhi kou), a film that has delighted international audiences with its unusual story and memorably visual scenes. Kwan himself seems to have certain reservations about some parts of this film. In the following year he released *Full Moon in New York* (Ren

7.2 *Love Unto Waste*, 1986. Photo courtesy of Media Asia Group.

zai Niuyue), a film set in New York that deals with the lives of three Chinese women, one each from China, Taiwan, and Hong Kong. In 1991, he directed *Centre Stage* (Ruan Lingyu), a film based on the life and privations of a charismatic actress of Chinese silent films. He made a short film titled *Too Happy for Words* in 1992, and in 1994, *Red Rose White Rose* (Hong meigui bai meigui), based on a popular Chinese short story by Eileen Chang and dealing with similar themes as those explored in *Love Unto Waste*. In 1996, he directed *Yang and Yin: Gender in Chinese Cinema* (Nan sheng nu xiang).

In this essay, we wish to focus our attention on four of Kwan's films, in order to higlight his directorial preoccupations, strengths, and stylistic innovations. Each of his films is different from the previous one, manifesting his innovative energies and experimental desires. Through these diverse films, however, winds an identifiable pattern that is connected to the imaginative and sympathetic exploration of the suffering of women. This consistency serves to generate a moral admiration for his work. In one sense, Kwan's films are moral chronicles, in which private anguishes have their public reverberations. Indeed, it is on women characters that he bestows his most memorable cinematic touches. And it is those episodes and sequences that highlight the predicament of women that command the greatest authority, displaying his complex representational richness to the greatest effect.

The troubling truths of life need cinematic witnesses, and Kwan steps forward as one who can fulfill this desideratum most effectively. What he has consistently sought to do, even in those films that do not quite reach the mark, is to provide complex re-articulations of human problems whose full force we sometimes fail to recognize. Through this means, Kwan sponsors a cultural diagnostics allied to a deep human sympathy that eschews moral simplifications.

Rouge (Fig. 7.3) is an imaginative and stylish film that has generated much interest both locally and internationally. What is most remarkable about this remarkable film is the play of imagination that coordinates with a light touch the apparent irreconcilables of realism and fantasy, past and present, natural and supernatural, melodrama and gravitas. *Rouge* shuttles back and forth between two distinctly different worlds, the Hong Kongs of the 1930s and the 1980s, yet the two places are connected by a single-minded quest. Kwan's gift for establishing the feel of place and atmosphere through the controlled flow of images adds significantly to the power of the film.

Rouge is based on a novel of the same name by Li Bihua, the author of a dozen or so popular novels that have drawn inspiration from the Chinese literary tradition. This film

7.3 *Rouge*, 1988. Photo courtesy of Media Asia Group.

contains two topoi that characterize traditional Chinese literature: the ghost story and the encounter between a literary scholar and a courtesan (*caizi jiaren*). The film, through a series of flashbacks, recounts the fate of a couple—the rich and flamboyant Chan Chen-bong (Chen Zhenbang), who is also known as Twelfth Master, and the beautiful courtesan Fleur—whose lives end in disaster. They cannot marry as a consequence of family disapproval. Hence, they resolve to commit suicide by swallowing opium. She dies and he survives.

The film recreates the opulence and decadence of the Hong Kong of the 1930s with remarkable visual energy and compelling power. This backdrop provides an admirable setting in which the rituals and practices, the romance and suicide, can be presented exotically but credibly. The collocation of images Kwan constructs recreates for us in all its vividness and immediacy the visage of Hong Kong sixty years ago. The more important part of the story, however, takes place in contemporary Hong Kong, where the ghost of the dead woman decides to return to Hong Kong from the other world in search of her lover. She appears suddenly in a newspaper office to place a notice, and this arrival leads to an unanticipated intervention in the lives of the journalist Yuen (Yuan) and his girlfriend Ah Chor (A'chu), with unanticipated consequences.

The interplay of realism and fantasy, the imperatives of the past and present, the commingling of the natural and supernatural, give the film its unique texture and imaginative power (Plate 16). What gives the film a special resonance is the realized conviction that the past inhabits the present just as much as the supernatural inhabits the natural. Kwan nicely introduces the idea of a film-within-a-film, with all the artifice of popular cinema deployed carefully to underscore its constructedness. Another interesting point about the film is that unlike the original book, the focus of the film's interest is not on the supernatural but on the contested and fissured cultural space of contemporary Hong Kong. As Ackbar Abbas (1997: 41) acutely observes, 'The paradox is that one of the most popular and fantastic of genres is used as a rigorous method of representing the complexities of Hong Kong's cultural space.'

One year after making *Rouge*, Kwan released another new film, *Full Moon in New York* (Ren zai Niuyue) (Fig. 7.4). Kwan has a predilection for selecting new areas for cinematic exploration with each new film. He says that

7.4 Stanley Kwan filming *Full Moon in New York*, 1988. Photo courtesy of Stanley Kwan.

he has learned from the admonition of Ann Hui that 'a director should treat each of the films he makes as the last chance given in experimenting with film-making.' *Full Moon in New York* is not an accomplished work of cinema in the way that *Rouge* is. Commenting on his film, Kwan (1993: 13) has remarked:

My fourth film was a project assigned to me by an independent producer who had lined up three famous actresses from Hong Kong, Taiwan, and mainland China for a Chinatown story. I feel deeply for the Chinese who have migrated. They will always feel anguished about being Chinese. Despite the fact that they will never return, leading a better life overseas, they cannot forget the past and nothing is forgiven. Though I am sensitive to their plight, the theme was alien to me. I could only feel for the character played by Maggie Cheung, because we are both from Hong Kong. The film turned out to be an embarrassment.

Full Moon in New York explores the terrain of cross-cultural understanding, cultural readjustment, cultural identity, and the ideas of freedom and memory. Three Chinese women from China, Taiwan, and Hong Kong meet in New York; there they enter into a friendship. The three women share very little in common except their Chineseness. Even this attribute, as the film progresses, turns out to be more problematic than one would have anticipated. The three women interact more with the new cultural environment in which they find themselves than with each other. Although they seem to exult in a new found freedom, both emotional and sexual, the idea of Chineseness and the different ways in which it has been inflected in their respective homelands gives the film its tension and urgency. Although the experience itself contains many possibilities, they have not been adequately explored, and the director has not quite followed the deepest insights of the chosen problematic. As a film that chooses to investigate a novel area of experience, however, it merits closer consideration.

In 1991, Kwan made *Centre Stage* (Plate 17), a film that testifies to his maturity of outlook and his careful use of the cinematic medium. *Centre Stage* won the 1992 Golden Horse award in Taipei as the best film from Hong Kong. Constituted by an admixture of the documentary and the fictional, this is a very different kind of film from the ones Kwan had made previous to it. At a deeper level of artistic apprehension, however, one finds in it a number of discursive threads that run throughout this director's work: a sensitivity to the nuances of interpersonal relations, the despair and suffering that is ingrained in feminine experiences, the reaching for newer perceptions of human living, and a search to provide society with compelling reflections of itself.

Centre Stage (Fig. 7.5) deals with the short and famous life of Ruan Lingyu, possibly the best known star of the

7.5 *Centre Stage*, 1991. Photo courtesy of Stanley Kwan.

Chinese silent cinema. The director blends fact and fiction, documentary and narrative, to convey a more complex awareness of this actress and the demands of her time. Black-and-white footage of the director and his cast discussing their roles and perceptions of Ruan are interpolated

80

with the basic narrative of her life. However, as Ackbar Abbas (1997: 46) has pointed out, there is a kind of role-reversal in the use of documentary and narrative: 'It is the fictional or narrative part of the work that recounts the known facts of Ruan Lingyu's life, while it is the documentary part that provides the elements of speculation and exploration.'

Ruan, whom some have described as Greta Garbo of China, brought a special aura of sensitivity and sensuality to her portrayals of tragic characters (Plate 18). Her own personal life, in many ways, reflected the tragedies of the characters she played on the screen. In 1935, at the young age of 25, she committed suicide, yielding to a dark despair and insurmountable pain in her life. It is hardly surprising that she is an inviting subject for filmic representation. In *Centre Stage*, however, Kwan has given the story a new inflection. *Centre Stage* constitutes a daring attempt in its incorporation of documentary footage into the flow of narration. The self-reflexivity and imaginative blending of forms give the experience a depth of perception and critical detachment, as it confronts certain dominant ambivalences of society. The sensitive and inspired performance by Maggie Cheung, as Ruan, adds significantly to the impact of the film.

Although *Centre Stage* textualizes the biography of Ruan, the aim is not merely that; in fact, there is a larger ambition in the film. Kwan intends to explore the complex ways in which legends, especially those connected to public performers, are produced and circulated in society, throwing certain common patterns of desire into relief. *Centre Stage* is an intelligent, mature, and innovative film that testifies to a director in full possession of his powers.

In making *Red Rose White Rose*, Kwan experimented with a new interpretation of feminine psychology. This adaptation of an Eileen Chang story bears the imprint of Kwan's personal vision of feminine sensibility. The film won five awards, including that for best screenplay, best film music, and the best artistic design, in the 1995 Golden Horse Film Festival, and it was nominated for the Golden Bear award at the 1995 Berlin Film Festival. Through the narration of a male voice, instead of exploring the sexual fantasies of the male protagonist, Dong Zhenbao, the film probes the psychoanalytic dimension of femininity as defined in a way closer to the Freudian interpretation than to the traditional Chinese view of the female as a gender-moral role. As Kwan admits, the film seeks to provide a new vision of femininity, one which has often been distorted in traditional Chinese culture. While Red Rose stands for the male sexual fantasy and White Rose for the outer social-familial role expected of a wife in traditional Chinese culture, they are now turned into two psychoanalytic aspects of femininity through which Kwan attempts to reinstitute a new human relationship.

Stanley Kwan has recently stated the view that all the films he has made so far are concerned with the re-envisioning of human relationships in their most naked and undistorted ways. He openly admits his indebtedness to Japan's Ozu. In Kwan's films there is a rare intelligence and human empathy that are wholly admirable and that go to form his cinematic signature. The deep congruence between form and content (which is, at times, not apparent superficially), the reinvigorating stylistic hybridity, the calculated counterposition of feeling, and the moral imagination surveying the predicaments of women serve to release the creative energies of the films.

8

Conclusion: In Search of an Inner Space

The six film directors whom we have discussed in the preceding pages, along with a number of other highly gifted
film-makers, represent the contours of the new cinema on
the Chinese mainland, in Taiwan, and in Hong Kong. These
directors, with all their imperfections, excesses, and vulner-
abilities, have succeeded in charting new and exciting paths
for the Chinese cinema. Their deficiencies, in a significant
sense, are interwoven with their larger strengths and transformative imaginations. All of them are serious artists, who
are vibrantly attuned to social experience, the anxieties of
social mobility, and the historical dynamics of their societies. They seek to register the dislocations of society and
are uncannily alive to the grotesque shapes of social oppression, injustice, and cruelty. Despite their different stylistic and formal inflections, they are united in a conviction
that cinema should become a site for the negotiation of
meaning and the interrogation of received wisdom. Hence,
it is hardly surprising that enforced degradation (Chen and
Tian), mindless victimization (Zhang), confusions of
values (Yang and Kwan), and the deceptions of sanctioned
histories (Hou) figure so prominently in the thematics of
their films.

Chen, Zhang, Tian, Hou, Yang, and Kwan are thoughtful film-makers, keen to mobilize the resources of cinema
to reach new awareness and new insights related to men,
women, culture, politics, and society. There is a salutary
moral imagination at work in all their films. A moral
anguish, which at times rises to indignation, infuses their
cinematic images. One has only to examine such films as
King of the Children, *Judou*, *The Horse Thief*, and *A City*

83

of Sadness to realize the force of this statement. Their anxious concern with individual fulfillment and moral issues is allied to a desire to introduce a new vision of society. The major source of their imaginative energy has its origins in this moral space. Yet, their moral imaginations do not yield to didactic simplifications or easy certitudes, as in the work of many of their predecessors, but display a capacity for self-doubt and the narration of the controlling mind struggling with itself. In their quest for a new dimension of the moral space, they have not forgotten the inner psychological space of their characters. A strong sense of humanism is thus found in the films of the new Chinese cinema, which vividly captures the fate of the Chinese in the three communities. Political ambiguities, cultural reevaluation, a revisioning of history, and personal anguish are all blended in capturing and recapturing the dilemmas of the individual and the nation as they face the forced choice between tradition and modernity, the East and the West.

The six film-makers whom we have discussed in this book are, in their different registers, experimenters and innovators in form and style. Departing from established and mainstream styles of film-making, these directors have sought to combine fact, memory, reflection, and narrativization in new blendings and rhythms of revelation. There are, of course, similarities among them, notably, among the earlier work of Chen and Tian and the later films of Hou. The use of the camera, the art of the editing, the involvement of the soundtrack, the styles of acting, and the de-theatricalizing impulses of these film-makers register significant differences from the work of their predecessors. These are all artists who are deeply committed to thinking through images. These six film-makers, along with others, such as Ann Hui and Wong Kar-wai, are seeking to formulate a new visual rhetoric, a new aesthetic for Chinese cinema. The new aesthetic that they are bent on formulating has clear political and moral resonances. Some, such as Chen, are desirous of drawing on traditional Chinese views of art and philosophy for this purpose.

Cinema as an art form was introduced to China, as indeed to other Asian countries, from the West. However, in most Asian countries—and in this regard mainland China, Taiwan, and Hong Kong are no exceptions—this newly imported art form quickly became indigenized, beginning to develop from local roots and native sensibilities. The West, however, most notably Hollywood, continues to exercise a profound influence on Asian cinemas. Consequently, how these Chinese film-makers respond to, absorb, challenge, and subvert these Western influences is a fascinating question. The six film-makers discussed here approach this question from their distinctive vantage points and domains of imagination. Yang, for example, draws on post-modernist Western cinematic sensibilities with remarkable results, while the early Chen and Tian were more cautious in their assimilationist tendencies. It is evident, however, that all of them have sought to negotiate the impact of Western influences with much forethought, in keeping with the aesthetic of film-making each privileges. The pull of Westernization, and the concomitant lure of internationalization, are, of course, so strong that there is a clear danger of some of them falling prey to the pernicious influence of international glamour.

All six film-makers discussed here are innovative artists who are reaching out to new insights, straining after new wisdoms and illuminations. Their innovation has to be understood against the film traditions that they are seeking to unsettle and move away from. In the case of Chen, Zhang, and Tian, they were reacting against a sterile tradition characterized by escapism, romanticism, and propaganda, with little visual innovation or social interrogation. In response, they have attempted a personal cinema, reflective, interrogative, ushering in novel ways of seeing the world. Similarly, Kwan, along with other Hong Kong new wave film-makers, has rebelled against the outworn conventions and cheap commercialism that has characterized the Territory's mainstream cinema. Together, theirs was an attempt to capture the complex social reality of Hong Kong as it enters new cultural spaces and engenders new cultural modernities; their films aspire to an authorization of hope through social renewal. Similarly, Hou and Yang are reacting against Taiwan's mainstream cinematic habits, with their rigid conventionalism and puerile entertainments, to make cinema into a site in which the whole notion of Taiwaneseness and the ramifications of modernity could be purposefully articulated and discussed. The six film-makers on whose work we have focused can be described as innovative artists with compelling social visions, as articulate cultural voices driven by a common reformist impulse.

All film-makers are products of specific historical moments, of particular cultural geographies. The six that we have discussed in this book are no exceptions. It is important, therefore, that we consider their achievements, the driving centres of their work, in relation to the specificities of the social and cultural spaces that they inhabit. At the beginning of this essay, we alluded to the fact that many of the six artists discussed in this book are now in their forties. That is to say, their respective lives are works-in-progress. How they will evolve in the future, what new areas of experiences they would reclaim for cinematic exploration, the stylistic and formal innovations they would fashion, and the social visions they would institute, depend as much on their individual talents as on the contextual factors that press upon them. At this critical juncture in Chinese history, with the pull between national reunification and regional autonomy, between cultural reassertion and the yearning for an individual space, the new Chinese filmmakers provide visions of the private sphere through the public sphere of their cinema, which bears witness to the footprints of the Chinese as they move toward the twenty-first century.

Chen Kaige, Zhang Yimou, and Tian Zhuangzhuang will have to tread cautiously, not incurring the hostility of the officialdom; they will also have to be circumspect about the attractions, possibilities, and perils of transnationalization and the lures of Hollywood. Hou Hsiao-hsien and Edward Yang will have to fortify the space they have created for innovative and non-mainstream cinema, while continually pondering Taiwan's relationship with mainland China, particularly now that Hong Kong has been returned to Chinese sovereignty. Stanley Kwan, as well, will have to protect the integrity of his cinema, while staving off the pressures of commercialization. Now that Hong Kong is a part of China, it will be incumbent upon him to explore this new phase of history and the social forces it will release, to examine how they might affect cinematic communication and entertainment.

It is evident that Chinese cinema, during the last quarter century, has entered a new and exciting period in its development. The six film directors that we highlight in this book, in their diverse ways and with their diverse ambitions, represent some of the strengths of this new phase of Chinese cinema. In concluding this interim report, we hope that they, along with other equally gifted filmmakers, will continue to enrich Chinese cinema and expand its boundaries creatively in the years to come.

Selected Filmography

Chen Kaige (b.1952)

Farewell to Yesterday (Xiang zuotian gaobie, 1980)
Yellow Earth (Huang tudi, 1984)
The Big Parade (Da yuebing, 1986)
King of the Children (Haizi wang, 1987)
Life on a String (Bian zou bian chang, 1991)
Farewell to My Concubine (Ba wang bie ji, 1992)
Temptress Moon (Feng yue, 1996)

Zhang Yimou (b.1950)

Red Sorghum (Hong gaoliang, 1987)
Judou (1990)
Raise the Red Lantern (Da hong denglong gaogao
    gua, 1991)
The Story of Qiu Ju (Qiu Ju daguansi, 1992)
To Live (Huozhe, 1994)
Shanghai Triad (Yao a yao, yao dao waipo qiao, 1995)
Keep Cool (You hua haohao shuo, 1997)

Tian Zhuangzhuang (b.1952)

Our Corner (Women de jiaoluo, 1980)
Red Elephant (Hong xiang, 1982)
A Summer Experience (Xiatian de jingli, 1982)
September (Jiuyue, 1984)

On the Hunting Ground (Liechang zhasa, 1985)
The Horse Thief (Daoma zei, 1986)
Story-tellers (Gushu yiren, 1987)
Rock 'n Roll Kids (Yaogun qingnian, 1988)
Illegal Life (Feifa shengming, 1990)
Eunuch Li Lianying (Da taijian Li Lianying, 1991)
The Blue Kite (Nan fengzheng, 1993)

Hou Hsiao-hsien (b.1947)

The Boys from Fengkuei (Fenggui lai de ren, 1983)
A Summer at Grandpa's (Dongdong de jaiqi, 1984)
A Time to Live and a Time to Die (Tongnian
    wangshi, 1985)
Dust in the Wind (Lianlian fengchen, 1987)
Daughter of the Nile (Niluohe nu'er, 1987)
A City of Sadness (Beiqing chengshi, 1989)
The Puppetmaster (Xi meng rensheng, 1993)
Good Men, Good Women (Hao nan hao nu, 1995)
Goodbye South, Goodbye (Nanguo zaijian, nanguo, 1996)

Edward Yang (b.1947)

Desires (Zhi wang, 1982)(in series, *In Our Time*)
That Day, On the Beach (Haitan de yitian, 1983)
Taipei Story (Qingmei zhuma, 1985)
The Terrorizer (Kongbu fenzi, 1986)
A Brighter Summer Day (Guling jie shaonian sharen
    shijian, 1991)
A Confucian Confusion (Duli shidai, 1994)
Mahjong (1996)

Stanley Kwan (b.1957)

Women (Nuren xin, 1985)
Love Unto Waste (Dixia qing, 1986)
Rouge (Yanzhi kou, 1988)
Full Moon in New York (Ren zai Niuyue, 1989)
Centre Stage (Ruan Lingyu, 1991)
Red Rose White Rose (Hong meigui bai meigui, 1994)
Yang and Yin: Gender in Chinese Cinema (Nan sheng nu xiang, 1996)

Selected Bibliography

Abbas, Ackbar (1997), *Hong Kong: Culture and the Politics of Disappearance*, Minneapolis: University of Minnesota Press.

Bergeron, Regis (1984), *Le Cinema chinois, 1949–1983*, Paris: Harmattan.

Berry, Chris, ed. (1992), *Perspectives on Chinese Cinema*, London: British Film Institute.

——— (1993), '*Farewell to My Concubine*: At What Price Success?', *Cinemaya*, 20: 20–2.

——— (1994), 'A Nation T(w/o)o: Chinese Cinema(s) and Nationhood(s)', in Wimal Dissanayake, ed., *Colonialism and Nationalism in Asian Cinema*, Bloomington: University of Indiana Press, pp. 42–64.

Browne, Nick, Paul C. Piuckowicz, Vivian Sobchack, and Esther Yau, eds. (1994), *New Chinese Cinemas: Forms, Identities and Politics*, Cambridge: Cambridge University Press.

Chen Feibao, ed. (1988), *Taiwan dianying shi hua* (A history of Taiwan cinema), Beijing: Zhongguo dianying chubanshe.

Chen Kaige, Wan Zhi, and Tony Rayns (1989), King of the Children *and the New Chinese Cinema*, London: Faber & Faber.

Chen Ken (1988), 'Diwudai: Chuantou Zhongguo yinmu de youling' (The fifth generation: The spirit permeating Chinese cinema), *Dianying yishu*, 3: 17–23.

Cheng Jihua, Li Xiaobai, and Xing Zuwen (1963), *Zhongguo dianying fazhanshi* (History of the development of Chinese cinema), Beijing: Zhongguo dianying chubanshe.

Cheshire, Godfrey (1993), 'Time Span: The Cinema of Hou Hsiao-hsien', *Film Comment*, 29(6): 56–63.

Chiao Hsiung Ping, ed. (1988), *Taiwan xin dianying* (Taiwan's new cinema), Taipei: Shibao.

Chow, Rey (1995), *Primitive Passions: Visuality, Sexuality, Ethnography and Contemporary Chinese Cinema*, New York: Columbia University Press.

Clark, Paul (1987), *Chinese Cinema: Culture and Politics Since 1949*, New York: Cambridge University Press.

Dissanayake, Wimal, ed. (1988), *Cinema and Cultural Identity: Reflections on Films from Japan, India, and China*, Lanham, MD: University Press of America.

———, ed. (1994), *Colonialism and Nationalism in Asian Cinema*, Bloomington: Indiana University Press.

Eberhard, Wolfram (1972), *The Chinese Silver Screen: Hong Kong and Taiwanese Motion Pictures in the 1960's*, Taipei: Oriental Culture Service, Asian Folklore and Social Life Monographs.

Gladney, Dru (1995), 'Tian Zhuangzhuang, the Fifth Generation, and the Minorities Film in China', *Public Culture*, 18(1): 165–75.

Hitchcock, Peter (1992), 'The Aesthetics of Alienation, or China's "Fifth Generation"', *Cultural Studies*, 6(1): 116–41.

Hou Hsiao-hsien (1989), *Viewers' Guide: The Tenth Hawaii International Film Festival*, Honolulu: Hawaii International Film Festival.

Huang Jianye (Wong Kin-yip)(1995), *Yang Dechang dianying yanjiu* (A study of Edward Yang's films), Taipei: Yuanliu chuban gongsi.

Huang Ren (1990), 'Taiwan shehui de bianqian yu zhipian shiye de fazhan' (The transformation of Taiwan society and the transformation of its film industry), *Dangdai dianying*, 1: 82–91.

Jameson, Fredric (1992), *The Geopolitical Aesthetic: Cinema and Space in the World System*, Bloomington: Indiana University Press.

Jarvie, Ian C. (1977), *Window on Hong Kong: A Sociological Survey of the Hong Kong Film Industry and Its Audience*, Hong Kong: Centre of Asian Studies, University of Hong Kong.

Kaplan, E. Ann (1991), 'Melodrama/Subjectivity/Ideology:

The Relevance of Western Melodrama Theories to Recent Chinese Cinema', *East–West Film Journal*, 5(1): 6–27.

Kwan, Stanley (1993), 'Carrying the Past Lightly', *Cinemaya*, 19: 10–13.

Lau, Jenny Kwok Wah (1989), 'Towards a Cultural Understanding of Cinema: A Comparison of Contemporary Films from the People's Republic of China and Hong Kong', *Wide Angle*, 11(3): 42–9.

Lent, John A. (1990), *The Asian Film Industry*, London: Christopher Helm.

Li Cheuk-to (1990), *Bashi niandai Xianggang dianying biji* (Notes on Hong Kong cinema of the 1980s), 2 vols., Xianggang (Hong Kong): Chuangjian chubangongsi.

——— (1996), 'Popular Cinema in Hong Kong', in Geoffrey Nowell-Smith, ed., *The Oxford History of World Cinema*, Oxford: Oxford University Press, pp. 704–11.

Li He (1989), *Phantoms of the Hong Kong Cinema* (13th Hong Kong International Film Festival), Hong Kong: The Urban Council.

Li Wenbing (1987), 'Weile Zhongguo dianying de tongfei' (On the take-off of Chinese cinema), *Dangdai dianying*, 4: 6–14.

Lie Fu (1991), *Zhidian shi nian: 79–89 dalu dianying zongping* (A few pointers on the last decade: critical overview of mainland cinema in 1979–1989), Xianggang (Hong Kong): Guangyaxuan chubanshe.

Lin Niantong (1995), 'The Chinese Cinema in Its Third Period', trans. Terry Siu Han Yip, *The Humanities Bulletin*, 4: 132–41.

Liu, Jerry, ed. (1982), *The Hong Kong Contemporary Cinema* (6th Hong Kong International Film Festival), Hong Kong: The Urban Council.

Liu Wenfeng (1988), 'Bashi niandai Taiwan xin dianying yipie' (A glimpse of Taiwan new cinema of the 1980s), *Dangdai dianying*, 5: 97–103.

Logan, Bey (1995), *Hong Kong Action Cinema*, London: Titan Books.

Marchetti, Gina (1987), 'Hong Kong Independent Filmmaking: An Interview with Roger Garcia', *Afterimage*, 14(10): 16–17.

Passek, Jean-Loup, and Marie-Claire Quiquemelle, eds. (1985), *Le cinema chinois*, Paris: Centre Georges Pompidou.

Rayns, Tony (1989a), *The New Chinese Cinema: An Introduction*, London: Faber & Faber.

—— (1989b), 'The Terrorizer', *The 1989 East–West Center Film Tour Programme Notes*, Honolulu: East–West Center.

Semsel, George S., ed. (1987), *Chinese Film: The State of the Art in the People's Republic*, New York: Praeger.

Semsel, George S., Hou Jianping, and Xia Hong, eds. (1990), *Chinese Film Theory: A Guide to the New Era*, New York: Praeger.

Shao Mujun (1986), 'Chinese Film Amidst the Tide of Reform', *East–West Film Journal*, 1(1): 59–68.

Tian Zhuangzhuang (1989), 'Reflections', *Cinemaya*, 5: 14–18.

Yau, Esther C. M. (1987–8), '*Yellow Earth*: Western Analysis and a Non-Western Text', *Film Quarterly*, 41(2): 22–33.

—— (1996), 'China After the Revolution', in Geoffrey Nowell-Smith, ed., *The Oxford History of World Cinema*, Oxford: Oxford University Press, pp. 693–704.

Yip, June (1995), 'Taiwanese New Cinema', in Geoffrey Nowell-Smith, ed., *The Oxford History of World Cinema*, Oxford: Oxford University Press, pp. 711–13.

Zhang Jiaxuan (1989), '*The Big Parade*', *Film Quarterly*, 43(1): 57–9.

Zhang Xudong (1997), *Chinese Modernism in the Era of Reforms*. Durham and London: Duke University Press.

Zhang Yingjin (1990), 'Ideology of the Body in *Red Sorghum*: National Allegory, National Roots, and Third Cinema', *East–West Film Journal*, 4(2): 38–53.

Zheng Shusen (William S. Tay)(1996), *Wenhua piping yu huayu dianying* (Cultural criticism and Chinese cinema), Taipei: Maitian chubanshe.

Index

DOCUMENTS ILLUSTRATING THE CRISIS OF 1297–98 IN ENGLAND

edited for the Royal Historical Society

by

MICHAEL PRESTWICH

M.A., D.Phil., F.R.Hist.S.

CAMDEN FOURTH SERIES

VOLUME 24

LONDON
OFFICES OF THE ROYAL HISTORICAL SOCIETY
UNIVERSITY COLLEGE LONDON, GOWER STREET
LONDON WC1E 6BT
1980

ISBN 0 901050 56 3

Printed in Great Britain by Butler & Tanner Ltd
Frome and London

CONTENTS

ACKNOWLEDGEMENTS

This volume originated in a proposal by Professor E. B. Fryde to produce an edition of texts covering the period 1294–1298. At an early stage he was good enough to hand the project over to me; the decision to limit the period to the year of crisis, 1297–98, was mine, taken in view of the problems of selection from the considerable bulk of surviving evidence. Without Professor Fryde's initial inspiration and help, this collection would not have been possible. I have incurred many other debts. Dr J. H. Denton brought some of the most important texts in the volume to my attention, and most kindly lent me parts of his own work on the period while it was still in manuscript. The majority of the transcripts were read through by Dr P. Chaplais, who corrected innumerable errors with patience and kindness. Mr D. J. Corner and Mr H. P. King have also helped me with various textual problems. Without the financial assistance of the Travel and Research Funds of the University of St Andrews, the work for this edition could never have been undertaken. It is only thanks to the help and encouragement of my wife that the task has been completed.

Crown copyright material appears by permission of the Controller of H.M. Stationery Office. I am in addition grateful to the Dean and Chapter of Canterbury Cathedral, to the Registrar of the diocese of Worcester, to the British Library Board and the Bodleian Library for permission to print documents in their possession or care.

University of Durham   MICHAEL PRESTWICH

ABBREVIATIONS

(Introduction and text)

Acta Imperii	*Acta Imperii Angliae et Franciae, ab a. 1267 ad a. 1313*, ed. F. Kern (Tübingen, 1911).
B.L.	British Library.
C.C.R.	*Calendar of Close Rolls.*
C.P.R.	*Calendar of Patent Rolls.*
C. Var. Chanc. R.	*Calendar of Various Chancery Rolls (1277–1326).*
E.H.R.	*English Historical Review.*
E.H.D., iii	*English Historical Documents*, iii, ed. H. Rothwell (London, 1975).
Foedera	*Foedera, conventiones, literae et cuiuscunque generis acta publica*, ed. T. Rymer (Record Commission, London, 1816).
Guisborough	*The Chronicle of Walter of Guisborough*, ed. H. Rothwell (Camden Third Series, lxxxix, 1957).
Parl. Writs	*The Parliamentary Writs and Writs of Military Summons*, ed. F. Palgrave (Record Commission, London, 1827).
Reg. Winchelsey	*Registrum Roberti de Winchelsey, archiepiscopi Cantuariensis, 1294–1308*, ed. R. Graham (Canterbury and York Society, 1917–51).
T. R. Hist. S.	*Transactions of the Royal Historical Society.*

EDITORIAL NOTE

Many of the documents in this volume are taken from the memoranda rolls of the exchequer. For this year these are longer and contain more important material than normal. The relationship between the two rolls, King's Remembrancer's and Lord Treasurer's Remembrancer's, is complex. Neither is a direct copy of the other, and each contains some documents not included in the other. Items do not always follow in the same order in the two rolls. It is most likely that both were drawn up at the same time, independently, with the clerks often working from a single text. In this edition all the variant readings between the two rolls have not been noted, particularly in the case of Anglo-Norman spelling. Nor has one roll been consistently preferred to the other; where a document appears in both, I have used whichever version appears preferable, noting significant variant readings. The roll given first in the reference is that on which the edited text is based.

In transcribing the documents, I have attempted to normalize use of *u* and *v*, and *c* and *t*. In Anglo-Norman, *q'* has been given as *qe*. Deficiencies in the manuscript are marked ..., and sections in square brackets are editorial additions. The punctuation has been modernized, but the honorific .. indicating a name omitted, as in no. 40, has been preserved. All major abbreviations have been extended.

In giving references to documents in the Public Record Office, modern call-numbers have been given, as follows:

Ancient Correspondence	SC 1
Ancient Petitions	SC 8
Chancery Miscellanea	C 47
Parliamentary and Council Proceedings	C 49
Liberate Rolls	C 62
Patent Rolls	C 66
Chancery Warrants	C 81
Chancery Files	C 266
Exchequer Plea Rolls	E 13
Exchequer Accounts Various	E 101
Exchequer Particulars of Customs Accounts	E 122
Exchequer Extents and Inquisitions	E 143
Exchequer King's Remembrancer's Memoranda Rolls	E 159
Exchequer Miscellanea	E 163
Exchequer Treasury of Receipt Miscellanea	E 175
Exchequer Lord Treasurer's Remembrancer's Memoranda Rolls	E 368

Exchequer Receipt Rolls   E 401
Exchequer Warrants for Issue   E 404
Exchequer Jornalia Rolls   E 405/1
Duchy of Lancaster, Ancient Correspondence   DL 34
Assize Rolls   JI 1

INTRODUCTION

i. *The documents*

Although the crisis of 1297 has been very extensively studied, and the chief texts relating to the constitutional arguments subjected to careful analysis,[1] much of the evidence concerning the activities of Edward I and his officials has never been printed. The purpose of this volume is to illustrate, as far as possible, the salient problems that faced the English government in a year when it came under the most severe pressure. The chronological limits are provided by the king's decision to outlaw the clergy in February 1297, following their refusal to grant financial aid, and by his return from his expedition to Flanders in March 1298. The types of document included range from official ordinances and writs to petitions, private correspondence and notarial instruments.

The documents have been collected from various classes of record, largely in the Public Record Office, and they are intended as an illustrative selection rather than as a comprehensive compilation. The majority consist of royal letters issued under the privy seal. Although, regrettably, no registers of such letters survive, many of the originals sent by Edward I when he was in Flanders to his son and the government at home have been preserved. Privy seal letters sent to the exchequer were generally enrolled on the memoranda rolls of that department, and these have proved to be a most fruitful source. Memoranda, ordinances and writs issued by the exchequer, also recorded on the memoranda rolls, yield a great deal of valuable information on the major preoccupations of the royal administration, notably on such questions as taxation, the payment of fines by the clergy in return for royal protection, and the organization of seizures of wool and victuals. Letters and petitions, both originals and enrolled copies, help to demonstrate the reactions of Edward I's subjects to the demands made of them, although unfortunately there is no equivalent of the royal correspondence to illuminate the activities of the king's opponents. Notarial instruments, two originals and two enrolled copies, help to illustrate different aspects of the conflict between the

---

[1] In particular by J. G. Edwards, '*Confirmatio Cartarum* and Baronial Grievances in 1297', *E.H.R.*, lviii (1943), 147–71, 273–300; H. Rothwell, 'The Confirmation of the Charters, 1297', *E.H.R.*, lx (1945), 16–35, 177–91, 300–15; B. Wilkinson, *Constitutional History of Medieval England, 1216–1399* (London, 1948), i, 187–232; G. L. Harriss, *King, Parliament and Public Finance in Medieval England to 1369* (Oxford, 1975), pp. 49–74; J. H. Denton, 'A Worcester Text of the Remonstrances of 1297', *Speculum*, liii (1978), 511–21. An important unpublished discussion of the events of the year is D. Beddoe, 'Some Financial and Political Aspects of the Constitutional Crisis of 1297' (U. of Wales Ph.D. thesis, 1969).

crown and the clergy. Formal diplomatic documents have not been included in this collection, but some letters from Edward's allies, notably the count of Holland, shed light on the problems that the English faced in maintaining an elaborate coalition that had been created in 1294. Certain texts have been provided from the highly important, and until recently little known, Evesham chronicle, while an appendix gives the hitherto unprinted section of the Hagnaby chronicle, which, though not particularly well informed, is not reliant upon any of the better known narrative sources.

The one topic that has been almost completely excluded is that of Scotland. Edward I and his ministers paid remarkably little attention to Scottish affairs in the period up to the departure of the expedition to Flanders in August 1297, and there is no indication that the king himself began to take an active interest until after his return in 1298. Further, the great bulk of the texts relating to Scotland are already readily available in print.[2] Certain types of document, too, have not been included. Financial accounts and legal records are so bulky that they would have no place in a collection of this nature, although use has of course been made of the extremely valuable wardrobe book for the twenty-fifth year of the reign in annotating the documents.[3] Mention should also be made of the little known exchequer Jornalia Rolls,[4] which provide an invaluable supplement and extension to the series of issue and receipt rolls for this period. Some of the legal records have been published, notably the Lincolnshire assize roll for 1298,[5] and such texts lie outside the range of this selection.

While the majority of the documents in this volume have not been published previously, no volume dealing with the events of 1297 would be complete without the inclusion of the major texts, such as the series of letters dealing with the earls' protest at the exchequer, or the De Tallagio and the Confirmatio Cartarum. Such documents have been included, although it is only in the case of the baronial Remonstrances of late July that the version printed is substantially different from those used in the past. The register of Bishop Giffard of Worcester unexpectedly yielded a text of this document which, although related to that provided by the chroniclers Cotton and Guisborough, contains an additional clause as well as many minor changes in wording.

---

[2] *Documents illustrative of the History of Scotland, 1286–1306*, ed. J. Stevenson, ii (Edinburgh, 1870); *Calendar of Documents relating to Scotland*, ed. J. Bain, ii (Edinburgh, 1884), with a supplementary volume shortly to appear; H. Gough, *Scotland in 1298* (Paisley, 1888).
[3] B.L., Add. MS. 7965.
[4] E 405/1 (unless otherwise stated, all references to manuscripts are to documents in the Public Record Office, London).
[5] *A Lincolnshire Assize Roll for 1298*, ed. W. S. Thomson (Lincoln Record Society, xxxvi, 1944). Of less relevance to the crisis is *The Pleas of the Court of King's Bench, Trinity Term 25 Edward I*, ed. W. P. W. Phillimore (English Record Society, London, 1898).

Although the form for the tax of an eighth, authorized at the end of July, along with that for the ninth which ultimately superseded it, has been printed previously, it was considered worth including the version from the exchequer memoranda roll, which illustrates how, by means of cancellations and interlineations, the text was altered from the one tax to the other.

ii. *The king's aims*

In order to understand the events of 1297, it is necessary to appreciate Edward I's intentions. He had been at war with Philip IV of France since 1294, and although an elaborate system of alliances had been created in the Low Countries, Germany and Franche-Comté with the intention of launching a combined offensive, little had been achieved. The English had, however, maintained a precarious foothold in Gascony, despite Philip IV's declaration that the duchy was forfeit.[6] The English king had been diverted from his plans for continental warfare by the Welsh revolt of 1294–5, and by his Scottish campaign of 1296. At last, however, in 1297 he was free from such encumbrances, and in January the way was opened for a campaign in the Low Countries with the striking diplomatic success of the formation of an alliance with the count of Flanders.[7] This provided Edward with a convenient landing place for a campaign: as he was later to explain to the king of Germany, to land further north, in the territory of his ally the count of Holland, would involve the use of inferior and unfamiliar ports, as well as a long march south.[8]

The first essential for Edward was, however, to provide for his forces in Gascony. There, the year started disastrously with a major defeat at Bellegarde, in which the English seneschal, John de St John, was captured. At the parliament held in late February the question of reinforcements for Gascony was the central issue, with the king threatening, according to the chronicler Walter of Guisborough, that if the magnates did not go, he would give their lands to others who would. This led to the famous dispute between Edward and Roger Bigod, earl of Norfolk. As marshal, the earl claimed that he was only obliged to campaign with the king, and he begged to be excused since Edward himself was not proposing to go to Gascony.[9] Successful as Bigod's stand was, it did not mean that no support was given to the

---

[6] There is a large literature on these alliances; but see in particular F. Trautz, *Die Könige von England und das Reich, 1272–1377* (Heidelberg, 1961), and E. B. Fryde, 'Financial Resources of Edward I in the Netherlands, 1294–98: Main Problems and Some Comparisons with Edward III in 1337–40', *Revue belge de philologie et d'histoire*, xl (1962), 1168–87. For the war in Gascony, see the introduction by C. Bémont to *Rôles Gascons*, iii (Paris, 1906).

[7] *Foedera*, I, ii, 850–3.

[8] *Treaty Rolls*, i, ed. P. Chaplais (London, 1955), 183–4.

[9] *Guisborough*, pp. 289–90.

troops in Gascony. Large quantities of supplies were assembled, and on 5 April Edward declared that he would not leave the south-west until the fleet for the duchy had sailed. Some forty ships were employed in taking victuals and coin, though a few were not to reach Gascony.[10] The final instalment of money, 11,000 marks, arrived at Portsmouth on 23 May: four days later Edward had reached Arundel in the course of a journey east towards Canterbury.[11]

Edward was extremely cautious about revealing his plans to campaign in Flanders. Writing to the exchequer on 5 April, he suggested that victuals purveyed in Northamptonshire might be sent to Gascony or elsewhere, while his concern with the way matters were proceeding in the Low Countries is indicated by his irritation at the lack of news from his agents there.[12] A demand for naval service from the men of the Cinque Ports issued on 27 April, the fleet to assemble on 25 June at Winchelsea, was the first overt indication that a campaign was intended, but no mention was made of where the expedition was to go.[13] A demand on 7 May for a search to be made for the treaties which had been made in 1294 with the king of Germany and the archbishop of Cologne is indicative of the attention being paid to the organization of the great coalition of princes against the French.[14] When summonses were issued on 15 May for a muster at London on 7 July, they did not state where service was to take place.[15] The king's caution in declaring his plans extended to his correspondence with his officials: a privy seal letter of 15 May talked of no more than his hope of going overseas at the end of June, with no precise destination mentioned.[16]

It is possible that Edward hoped by means of this surprising secrecy to avoid some of the inevitable opposition to an expedition to Flanders, where there was no precedent for an English army fighting. However, in the Remonstrances drawn up by his opponents at the end of July this point was clearly made, and it was further pointed out that without knowing where the army was to go, it was impossible to make proper preparations.[17] It may be simply that the king was being deliberately careful not to disclose his intentions for security reasons, but it is still surprising that Edward, in view of his past record of consulting his subjects in parliament, should have been so chary of revealing his plans.

[10] Nos. 34, 165. Details of the fleet are given in B.L., Add. MS. 7965, fos. 90 seq., and in C 62/74, writ of 14 December.
[11] On 10 May Edward was at Chudleigh in Devon, and Ralph Manton was sent from there to London to fetch this sum of money (B.L., Add. MS. 7965, fos. 17v, 19v).
[12] No. 34.   [13] No. 49; C.C.R., 1296-1302, pp. 99-100.
[14] No. 55. It does not appear that the treaties were found.
[15] Parl. Writs, i, 282.
[16] No. 60.   [17] No. 98.

The short notice provided for the expedition to Flanders is also remarkable. Later, for the campaign against the Scots in 1300, the military summons for a muster at Midsummer was issued in December of the previous year, not in May. In 1297 victualling arrangements were still being made in June, when a seizure of meat was ordered: in 1300 purveyance was organized in January.[18] Certainly, some supplies already ordered and collected for Gascony could be diverted to Flanders, and with royal officials already overseas organizing the alliance and the king's dealings in wool, problems, once the force landed, would be lessened. It is still surprising that an expedition originally envisaged in 1294 should have been organized in such haste.

The muster at London which took place on 7 July was, from the king's point of view, a disaster. Bigod and Bohun, the Marshal and Constable respectively, refused to co-operate and draw up muster lists.[19] It was evident that the expedition would have to be postponed, but despite the failure of peace negotiations with the baronial leaders at the end of July, Edward determined to pursue his plans. Final preparations began with new financial arrangements being made. Privy seal writs to the sheriffs issued on 28 July requested all those who had agreed to serve the king to come to Winchelsea as soon as possible. Unlike the earlier summons, this made it clear that they were to go overseas, and that they would be paid wages.[20] By 5 August a substantial fleet had been organized, and the king was assured that, in view of the circumstances, adequate supplies of victuals should be available.[21] On 15 August proclamations were made in London, ordering all members of the royal household to go to Winchelsea without delay,[22] and finally, on 22 August, the king and his men embarked for Flanders. The final stages of preparation were characterized not by secrecy, but by a considerable propaganda effort on behalf of the king, most notably in the lengthy justification of his actions issued on 12 August. This stressed Edward's treaty obligation to the count of Flanders, and pointed out the dangers that would threaten England if his continental allies were defeated.[23] This was a strong argument, but there were also strong grounds for opposing the king's plans and the methods he adopted to implement them.

iii. *The opposition to the king: the laity*

There were many reasons for opposition to Edward I's plans and the expedients he adopted for their implementation, with the situation changing as the crisis developed. The question of military service was

[18] No. 72; *C.C.R., 1296–1302*, p. 374; *C.P.R., 1292–1301*, p. 487.
[19] For these events, see Edward I's letter of 12 August (no. 111).
[20] Nos. 94–97.   [21] No. 105.
[22] Nos. 114, 116.   [23] No. 111.

probably that which featured most obviously in the minds of the baronial and knightly classes in the early stages. The demand for service in Gascony outlined by the king at the Salisbury parliament had to be abandoned in face of the hostility expressed there, while the remarkably vague form of summons for the muster at London aroused deep suspicion. No mention was made of the form of obligation to which the king was appealing, whereas it was conventional to request men to attend in accordance with either the homage or fealty they owed to the crown. As the chronicler Pierre Langtoft explained, to perform a new kind of service would be tantamount to disinheritance. The case against overseas service was not, however, purely constitutional. Not only did the Remonstrances complain of the imprecise nature of the summons, making it hard to know what practical arrangements for the expedition should be made, but the document also stated that royal exactions had reduced the king's subjects to such a state of poverty that they could not perform any service for him.[24] This plea was more than mere rhetoric shaped by the requirements of scholastic theories regarding the rights of a prince over his subjects.[25] A letter from the earl of Arundel complained that he could only find men to go overseas with him if he rewarded them with land, which he was unwilling to do. The earl was unable to find anyone willing to lend him money on security of a lease of land worth £100 p.a.[26] Arundel did not in fact go with the king to Flanders. The Evesham chronicle suggests that the earl of Warwick was also in financial difficulties, stating that he came to the king complaining of his poverty. He was given money and as a result ceased his opposition to Edward.[27] However, although Warwick had his horses valued ready for the campaign, he too did not go.[28] A number of grants of permission either to alienate land, or to demise it for a term of years, made in July and August suggest that men were finding it hard to raise money for their expenses in the king's service, and that they could only recruit retainers by granting them lands.[29] A loan of £20 from

---

[24] M. C. Prestwich, *War, Politics and Finance under Edward I* (London, 1972), pp. 84–86. The fear of disinheritance is also expressed in the additional clause of the Worcester version of the Remonstrances (no. 98).

[25] For an argument which places the Remonstrances in the context of such theories, see Harriss, *King, Parliament and Public Finance*, pp. 61–2.

[26] No. 132.

[27] J. H. Denton, 'The Crisis of 1297 from the Evesham Chronicle', *E.H.R.*, xciii (1978), 576.

[28] N. B. Lewis, 'The English Forces in Flanders', *Studies in Medieval History presented to F. M. Powicke*, ed. R. W. Hunt, W. A. Pantin and R. W. Southern (Oxford, 1948), p. 311, n. 1.

[29] *C.P.R., 1292–1301*, pp. 292, 300, 302, 303, 305, 307, 312, 314. A different type of excuse for not going on the campaign was produced by Theobald de Verdun; he was ill, and his eldest son had recently died. Edward, however, ordered him to send his younger son (*Parl. Writs*, i, 295).

the wardrobe to John de Hastings was clearly of considerable assistance to a man who chose not to accept royal wages while serving in
Flanders.[30]

The inclusion in the summons to the muster at London of all those
holding land worth at least £20 p.a. broadened the basis of opposition
to Edward's military plans. Suggestions that this group, of knights
and gentry, were at least in part reconciled to the king by his offer
of pay after the failure of the London muster find little support in
these documents.[31] Replies to the writs sent to the sheriffs on 28 July
asking them to send those who had agreed to go on campaign to Winchelsea show that from three counties, only one man, a royal household knight, was prepared to enrol.[32] The wardrobe account book
contains a section listing squires who were not members of the royal
household, under their respective counties, and it seems probable that
these were the men who attended in response to these writs. A total
of only sixty-three men is recorded from the whole of England.[33]

The demands for military service, even when extended to the
twenty librate class, did not bear on so great a proportion of the popu-
lation as did those of taxation. Annual taxes had been negotiated in
parliament without great difficulty since 1294, although in that year
the earl of Gloucester had succeeded in persuading the king to reduce
the proposed rate at which the tax was to be levied.[34] In 1297 there
was considerable activity on the part of the exchequer and of royal
officials at a local level. The most recent tax to be granted was the
twelfth and eighth authorized on 29 November 1296. Substantial
sums were flowing in between late April and June, according to a
surviving receipt roll. The second instalment of the tax was due by
2 June, and the records suggest that matters were proceeding effi-
ciently. There were problems in Westmorland, where the collectors
failed to produce their records for the exchequer on time, but despite
the failure of the sheriff to take action against them, they paid £100
into the exchequer on 7 May.[35] On 7 June action was ordered against
the collectors of the previous tax, an eleventh and seventh, in Wiltshire; it was suspected that some receipts were being held back from
the crown.[36] It was not, however, until the judicial enquiry of 1298

[30] No. 106.
[31] Wilkinson, *Constitutional History*, i, 198–9.
[32] No. 94.
[33] B.L., Add. MS. 7965, fos. 73–4. See also M. R. Powicke, *Military Obligation in
Medieval England* (Oxford, 1962), pp. 111–12. He concludes that with the summons
of twenty librate men, 'over a hundred cavalry *may* have been added in this way'.
This estimate includes those serving in the retinues of magnates, whereas the sixty-
three listed in the wardrobe book were not part of any retinue.
[34] The Hagnaby chronicle, B.L., Cotton MS. Vesp. B. xi, fo. 56.
[35] *Lancashire Lay Subsidies*, ed. J. A. C. Vincent (Lancs. and Cheshire Record Society,
xxvii, 1893), pp. 191–5; *infra*, no. 47.
[36] No. 74.

that the bulk of cases of maladministration and corruption were to be discovered.[37] There are no signs of any extensive refusal to comply with the king's demands for the payment of these taxes, which had been duly granted in parliament, and the only complaint that was open to the opposition was that of impoverishment, to which royal taxation undoubtedly contributed.

A new element entered the argument with the new tax of an eighth and fifth authorized by royal writs on 30 July. The king claimed that the tax had been granted by the earls, barons, knights and the whole laity of the realm, but this was demonstrably false. The Westminster chronicler described the grant as being made *a plebe in sua camera circumstante*, which was probably no more than a pardonable exaggeration. It may have taken place in parliament, for parliament was in session on 22 July, but this was not an assembly for which any general summons was issued, and there can be little doubt that those primarily involved in the grant were the king's closest supporters, his officials, and the members of his household.[38] An element of doubt about the constitutional propriety of the tax may perhaps be detected in the way that the instructions for its collection described it as a *doun*, or gift; when the text was revised for the ninth properly granted later in the year, the phraseology was changed to *graunte e doun*.[39] There was clearly suspicion that if local men were appointed to make the assessment, as was normal practice, they would be too lenient. Accordingly, those appointed were from neighbouring counties.[40] Edward put great pressure on the exchequer to organize the tax with speed, but arrangements for its collection were rudely interrupted by the appearance of the recalcitrant earls, Bigod and Bohun, with their followers, at the exchequer on 22 August. They stated that neither they nor the community had consented to the tax, and claimed that to pay it would be tantamount to accepting servile status.[41] To the question of the weight of taxation had now been added a powerful constitutional argument. The earls' protest did not, however, halt the preparations. On 28 August letters patent were issued promising that no precedent would be made of the tax, and on 15 September knights were summoned to London to receive letters concerning the confirmation of the Charters and the collection of the eighth.[42] On 9 September the exchequer had even ordered the seizure of the goods of one of the collectors for Bedfordshire who had not taken up his duties.[43] Nevertheless, it does not appear that much was done by way of

---

[37] *A Lincolnshire Assize Roll for 1298*, pp. xlii–lii.
[38] Nos. 95, 93; *Flores Historiarum*, ed. H. R. Luard, iii (Rolls Series, 1890), 296.
[39] No. 96; Beddoe, 'Some Financial and Political Aspects of the Constitutional Crisis of 1297', pp. 22–3.
[40] *C.P.R., 1292–1301*, pp. 297–8.   [41] No. 126.
[42] *Foedera*, I, ii, 877; *Parl. Writs*, i, 58.   [43] No. 136.

assessment, much less collection, before 14 October, when the eighth was replaced by a properly granted tax of a ninth.

The other form of lay taxation to which the opposition objected in 1297 was the heavy export duty on wool, the *maltolt* of forty shillings a sack. This had been negotiated with the merchants in 1294, in lieu of a general seizure of wool.[44] This collection of documents does not reveal much about the tax, for it had been raised with little trouble since its introduction, and posed few new problems in 1297. Something is revealed of the practice of merchants whereby they handed over part of their wool as a pledge to the customs officials against future payment of the tax, since they often did not have sufficient means to pay the duty before the wool had been sold overseas.[45] In April, however, this practice was forbidden, a move perhaps intelligible in terms of an immediate need for cash outweighing the likely decline of exports.[46] One of the techniques of customs evasion is revealed in a letter of 2 April which forbade the export of spun thread and partly tanned hides, which did not pay duty, while a case that emerged while the king was in Flanders showed that smuggling was practised on an organized basis.[47] An interesting favour was granted to Aymer de Valence, who was allowed to export up to twenty sacks of wool without payment of duty. The matter was to be kept secret, lest others should demand similar favours.[48] There is no doubt that the magnates, as wool producers, were suffering a loss of income as a result of the tax.

The Remonstrances laid stress on the weight of the tax, which allegedly amounted to a fifth of the value of all the land. No mention was made of the manner in which the tax had been granted, and *De Tallagio* similarly ignored the constitutional question, merely demanding the abolition of the duty. A curious feature of the case presented in the Remonstrances is that it is assumed that a double rate of tax existed, with prepared wool paying five marks. Such had been the case when the *maltolt* was first introduced, but the system had proved unworkable, and was rapidly replaced by a single rate of forty shillings. Although one set of writs issued in 1295 does mention the double rate, the customs accounts show only the forty shilling duty, and this is the level of duty specified in the writs sent out in November 1297 ordering the suspension of the tax.[49] It seems probable that the

[44] E 159/68, m. 82. For a discussion of the *maltolt*, see T. H. Lloyd, *The English Wool Trade in the Middle Ages* (Cambridge, 1977), pp. 76–96.
[45] Nos. 71, 180.
[46] No. 45; Fryde, 'Financial Resources of Edward I in the Netherlands', 1182.
[47] Nos. 31, 199.
[48] No. 124. Compare the incident of the restoration of thirty sacks of wool to the earl of Lincoln (no. 65).
[49] Lloyd, *English Wool Trade*, p. 77; *infra*, nos. 173, 174.

Remonstrances were in error. There is no evidence to show that the earls and their associates had direct support from any merchants, and it clearly suited their case to show the duty at as high a rate as possible. The main objection was to the weight of the tax, and the essential demand was for its abolition.

The other issue regarding wool was that of the two seizures, one at Easter and the other at the end of July 1297. Unfortunately the ordinance relating to the first one has not survived, and the precise scheme is hard to elucidate. In a proclamation it was declared that all persons possessing wool were to prepare it for sale, and take it to specific towns by 21 April. A petition later stated that not only was all the wool not so taken declared forfeit, but that the king also seized all the supplies accumulated in the towns.[50] However, it is clear that at the outset wool in the hands of English merchants was not to be taken, but that John Droxford, Hugh Despenser and others of the council later extended the provisions to cover all wool. This was done without the king's knowledge.[51] Edward's ignorance of the operation is also shown by a letter to the dowager countess of Pembroke on 7 April, in which he stated that neither he nor those with him knew anything of the instructions for the collection of wool in South Wales.[52] The chronology of the decisions is not certain, but on 20 April Adam Bacon and Robert Dymmock came to Royston in Hertfordshire to seize the wool collected there, only to find that, contrary to the proclamation, none had been taken to the town, and it seems likely that the seizure had already been extended to English merchants by that date.

There was much resentment at the seizure, and considerable problems in implementing it. The vicar of Littleport's plea that he had never heard of the proclamation did him little good,[53] but the removal of wool to a franchise was a manoeuvre which had sufficient success for it to be necessary to order the sheriffs on 6 May to take steps against anyone who did this. The failure to give proper receipts was widespread, and trouble was caused by officials taking wool that had been handed to the customs officials as a pledge for future payment of duty. In the course of May the attitude of the government softened noticeably, perhaps as a result of the king's own intervention. Wool was restored to some favoured individuals and abbeys. The release of some men from custody, where they had been placed for concealing wool, was followed on 28 May by an ordinance permitting all those imprisoned to be freed, provided sufficient security was given.[54]

[50] C.C.R., 1296–1302, p. 111; infra, no. 208.
[51] Lloyd, English Wool Trade, pp. 87–8; G. O. Sayles, 'The Seizure of Wool at Easter 1297', E.H.R., lxvii (1952), 543–7.   [52] No. 37.
[53] Lloyd, English Wool Trade, p. 87; E 101/457/3.   [54] Nos. 63, 64.

The process of exporting the wool did not go smoothly. A letter from the customs officials at Boston testifies to the difficulties they faced in implementing vague instructions that did not specify where the wool was to be sent, and as late as 15 June the king was ordering the exchequer to see to the prompt export of the wool. Even then, some collected in Wales was never sent overseas, but was simply kept in store.[55] The total quantity that had been taken was not great. It is difficult to provide a definitive figure, as in using the exchequer memoranda rolls and the customs accounts there is a danger of counting the same wool twice, but the quantity of 2,333 sacks worked out by Lloyd is as accurate as can be hoped for. In some localities the prise had produced very meagre results indeed; the operations of Adam Bacon and Robert Dymmock in Cambridgeshire and Huntingdonshire yielded a paltry nine sacks and eight stones of wool.[56] Payment for the wool seized was, of course, dilatory. One record gives a list of payments due, covering most of the country, totalling £1,389, which were only agreed between October 1297 and the following February.[57] The debts from the seizure had not yet been paid off in full by the end of Edward I's reign.

Despite the considerable problems and meagre results of the Easter wool seizure, it was decided at the end of July to institute a further prise of wool. This was a part of the measures needed to finance the expedition to Flanders, and it was estimated that 8,000 sacks were needed to raise the money required for subsidies, together with the wages of troops and sailors. Merchants were appointed to carry out the forced purchase, while payment was promised out of the proceeds of the taxes on laity and clergy, and the measure can be seen as an attempt to anticipate revenue. The instructions in fact ordered the collection of 8,300 sacks in all, and no exemptions from the prise were laid down, save for a statement that the poor should not be afflicted. Later, however, it was stated that some alien merchants should not have their wool taken. Harsh as the measure appears, there is no reason to doubt the statement that it was adopted as the means of raising money least likely to affect the people of the realm.[58] There was, however, little constitutional justification for the prise. In 1294 Edward had negotiated a seizure of wool with the magnates, and had obtained their consent for it; in 1297, he was only able to defend his action with the remarkable statement that he should be as free as any man to buy wool in his own kingdom. The prise naturally featured in the earls' protest at the exchequer on 22 August, and it seems unlikely that much wool was collected after that date. In

[55] Nos. 56, 79, 201, 207.   [56] Lloyd, *English Wool Trade*, pp. 90–3.
[57] E 122/156/19. For a late repayment, see *C.P.R., 1313–18*, p. 252.
[58] Nos. 97, 120, 125.

12   DOCUMENTS ILLUSTRATING

Somerset and Dorset those appointed to take wool were unco-opera-
tive, vexing the exchequer with unnecessary questions. The prise was
finally abandoned on 15 November, when it was decided to leave wool
that had not been packed and sent to the ports in the hands of its
owners.[59] This seizure had been even less effective than that at Easter.
Letters patent promising payment to those whose wool had been taken
reveal some 525 sacks taken by nine of the fourteen commissions, and
the accounts suggest a total yield of a mere 798 sacks in all.[60] As a
means of raising money, the wool seizures clearly fell far below the
crown's expectations, while the dislocation they caused to the wool
trade was clearly very considerable indeed. It is likely that had there
been no seizures, the crown would have been better off as a result
of higher exports yielding more customs duty.

Wool was not, of course, the only commodity liable to compulsory
purchase in 1297. The seizure of foodstuffs must have caused far
greater hardship, and was perhaps even more open to abuse. A massive prise of 33,800 quarters of grain had been ordered in November
1296,[61] while in April 1297 a further 13,000 quarters were requested.
Early in June the king demanded 3,100 carcases of bacon, and 1,500
of beef.[62] Records show that the fleets sailing to Gascony carried a
total of 6,470 quarters of wheat, 10,524 quarters of oats, 954 quarters
of beans and peas, 571 tuns of flour and 2,500 stockfish. For Flanders,
4,893 quarters of wheat and 3,831 quarters of oats, barley and dredge
were brought from England, with further supplies being bought locally. Some of these supplies sent overseas had doubtless been collected
in 1296, but the sheriffs' accounts suggest that in the course of the
year 1297 itself at least 10,300 quarters of wheat, 6,700 quarters of
oats, 2,400 quarters of barley and malt, and 1,000 quarters of beans
and peas were taken by royal officials for the use of Edward's armies.[63]
As in the case of the taxes, the burden of prise was a cumulative one
over the whole wartime period. The year 1297 itself did not see the
king adopting new techniques of prise, so creating novel constitutional
problems.

[59] Nos. 111, 99, 168.
[60] C.P.R., 1292–1301, pp. 299–300, 310–11, 321–3, 332, 335; Lloyd, English Wool
Trade, p. 91. For further calculations of the yield of the prises, see J. de Sturler, Les
relations politiques et les échanges commerciaux entre le duché de Brabant et l'Angleterre au moyen
âge (Paris, 1936), pp. 193–4; Fryde, 'Financial Resources of Edward I in the Netherlands', 1183.
[61] E 159/70, mm. 119–20. For a discussion of the burden of purveyance, see J. R.
Maddicott, The English Peasantry and the Demands of the Crown, 1294–1341 (Past and
Present Supplement, no. 1, 1975), pp. 15–34.
[62] Nos. 50, 72.
[63] B.L., Add. MS. 7965, fos. 44–50, 89, 93, 96–7. E 101/6/18 contains indentures
with specific details of many shipments; see also Rôles Gascons, iii, clv–vi, notes. The
sheriffs' accounts are summarized in E 159/71, mm. 7–8d, 10, 13, 34, 50, 84d seq.,
and in C 62/74.

It is probable that the abuses of the system of prise caused most of the resentment. Legal records provide innumerable examples, such as the case in Kent where Richard of Rochester claimed that eleven men acting as royal bailiffs had driven off thirty of his sheep, since he would not hand over five quarters of wheat to them, because they had no royal warrant. It was alleged that Richard had raised the hue and cry against the eleven, and that he had forcibly recovered twenty-two of the sheep, though this he strongly denied.[64] Payment for goods taken was, of course, dilatory, and it is interesting to note that the Evesham chronicler specifically complained of the way in which tallies and receipts were used instead of cash.[65] In the atmosphere created by the concession of the *Confirmatio Cartarum* in the autumn the government had to respond to such complaints, and instructions issued on 23 November to royal clerks to buy and take grain in Kent stated that prompt payment should be made.[66]

Edward I's demands on his people by way of military service, taxation and prise caused opposition because of both their extent and their nature. The period since 1294 had seen an almost intolerable burden placed on England, while the expedients adopted at the end of July were of a highly questionable nature in constitutional terms, as were the king's attempts to compel men to serve him in Flanders. As far as the laity were concerned, the situation was further exacerbated by the existence of individual grievances against the king. By 1297 the two baronial leaders, Bigod and Bohun, had well-known reasons for resenting Edward I. Bohun had been humiliated as a result of his dispute with the earl of Gloucester in 1290, while Bigod was so hard pressed by the exchequer to pay the debts he owed to the crown that he made public protest in parliament in 1293. Both men found their hereditary positions as marshal and constable respectively being severely eroded by Edward, and following their refusal to co-operate with what they clearly regarded as the unconstitutional muster at London were deprived of their functions, though they were still accorded the titles by royal officials.[67] Edward I's personal hostility to Bigod is indicated by the instructions he issued to prohibit his brother John Bigod, a cleric, from being taken back into royal protection even if he paid the required fine.[68] The king's action in taking up the complaints of the men of Bohun's liberty of Brecon on 13 July is another indication of the personal character of the dispute between

[64] E 13/21, m. 64d.
[65] Denton, 'The Crisis of 1297 from the Evesham Chronicle', 575–7.
[66] No. 172.
[67] Nos. 89, 91. In their letter describing the events of 22 August at the exchequer, the treasurer and barons described Bigod as earl marshal, but only accorded Bohun his territorial title of Hereford (no. 126).
[68] No. 10.

Edward and the earls.[69] John de Ferrers was another baronial leader who had a clear private motive for opposing the king, for his father had been effectively disinherited by Edward in the aftermath of the Barons' Wars.[70] Robert FitzRoger, one of those who appeared at the exchequer on 22 August with the earls, had been compelled under duress to go to Gascony in 1295.[71]

One of the complaints in the Remonstrances related to Edward I's treatment of the holders of franchises, who were not permitted the rights of their ancestors. While this might apply in a general sense to the process of the *Quo Warranto* enquiries, it was the king's attitude to the Welsh marcher lords that was probably more relevant to the situation in 1297. Both Bigod, with his lordship of Chepstow, and Bohun, as earl of Hereford and lord of Brecon, were major marcher lords. The Evesham chronicle lists among those present at a meeting near Montgomery, where grievances against the king were discussed, these two earls, together with the earls of Arundel and Warwick, John de Hastings and Edmund Mortimer.[72] In 1294 Mortimer and Arundel had been charged with refusing to allow royal tax assessors into their liberties in Shropshire, and it is worth noting that both men, like FitzRoger, were compelled to go to Gascony in 1295.[73] In 1297 there were a number of disputes regarding the marcher franchises. The dowager countess of Pembroke complained of the way in which royal bailiffs had transgressed on her rights in Walwynscastle.[74] In May the king, following complaints from Mortimer's Welsh tenants, requested them to bring their case before him in parliament, ordering Mortimer to attend in person, and forbidding him from molesting his men.[75] There was trouble over the question of the king's right to take fines from the clergy within franchises; Hastings protested over this issue.[76] Such instances may not represent a wholesale assault on the liberties of the marcher lords, and it was possible for the king to conciliate Arundel, Warwick and Hastings to some extent. Yet in the tense and suspicious atmosphere of 1297 it is easy to imagine that the import of the king's actions could well have been misinterpreted and exaggerated.

There were, therefore, many strands to the lay opposition to

[69] No. 90.
[70] K. B. McFarlane, *The Nobility of Later Medieval England* (Oxford, 1973), p. 254.
[71] *Book of Prests of the King's Wardrobe for 1294–5*, ed. E. B. Fryde (Oxford, 1962), p. xlviii, n. 5.
[72] Denton, 'The Crisis of 1297 from the Evesham Chronicle', 576.
[73] J. F. Willard, *Parliamentary Taxation on Personal Property, 1290 to 1334* (Cambridge, Mass., 1934), p. 32; *Book of Prests*, p. xlviii, n. 5.
[74] No. 37.
[75] *C.C.R., 1296–1302*, p. 107.
[76] Nos. 89, 108. For a further discussion of the significance of the marcher lordships in 1297, see R. R. Davies, *Lordship and Society in the March of Wales, 1282–1400* (Oxford, 1978), pp. 267–9.

Edward I in 1297. The difficulty of identifying the men involved with Bigod and Bohun has meant that more attention has been paid to the general issues than to the personal: the only reliable list of any length is one of Bigod's own household. More knowledge of the identity of those actively involved with the earls might provide a fuller picture of individual dissatisfaction with decisions the king had taken. However, there is no doubt that the succession of demands for personal service, taxes and goods over the years since the outbreak of war in 1294, culminating with the arbitrary measures of late July 1297, were at the heart of the hostility which many of Edward's subjects felt towards their ruler.

iv. *The opposition to the king: the clergy*

In the case of the laity, it seems likely that it was the scale of Edward I's taxes, rather than their nature, that caused most resentment. In the case of the clergy, however, principles emerged at an early stage in the crisis. The issue was the well-known one of the papal prohibition on the payment of taxes to secular authorities, as set out in the bull *Clericis Laicos*, promulgated in 1296.[77] The archbishop of Canterbury, Robert Winchelsey, acted at first with considerable caution, only issuing mandates for the publication of the bull shortly before an ecclesiastical council met at St Pauls on 13 January 1297.[78] This council was called to give an answer to the king's demand for taxation made at the Bury St. Edmunds parliament in the previous November. Despite the threat made on the king's behalf by Hugh Despenser, to the effect that the clergy would be deprived of their lands, the tax was refused. On 12 February the king duly issued instructions for the lay fees of the clergy, with all their goods and chattels, to be taken into his hands.[79] The decision to outlaw the clergy had in fact been taken earlier, on 30 January, and one of the royal justices, John de Metingham, had proclaimed that the remedies of the law would no longer be available to the clergy.[80] On 13 February Despenser informed the exchequer authorities that they were not to permit clergy to plead unless they could produce royal letters of protection.[81] Such protections were available to those who agreed to pay as a fine the sum that they would have paid in taxation, had a clerical fifth been

[77] For a full analysis of Edward I's dispute with the clergy in 1297, see the important discussion in J. H. Denton's forthcoming study, *Robert Winchelsey and the Crown.*

[78] *Councils and Synods*, ed. F. M. Powicke and C. R. Cheney (Oxford, 1964), ii, 1149, n. 6.

[79] *Bartholomaei de Cotton, Historia Anglicana*, ed. H. R. Luard (Rolls Series, 1859), pp. 314–15; *Guisborough*, pp. 286–8; *C.C.R., 1296–1302*, p. 14.

[80] 'Annales Prioratus de Wigornia', *Annales Monastici*, ed. H. R. Luard (Rolls Series, 1869), iv, 530.

[81] No. 1.

granted. The northern clergy, lacking Winchelsey's leadership, made such a grant, receiving protections on 18 February *en bloc*.[82] For the southern province, however, the story was to be a long one of royal threats and individual submissions.

The clerks in the royal administration naturally came to terms quickly with the king, many receiving protections before arrangements had been made for the exchequer to issue them. It is striking that many of the early submissions were made by clergy in the southwest, where the king was. It was not until 1 March that arrangements were in hand for bannerets to be appointed to receive fines, along with the sheriffs, in all the counties of England, making it much easier to purchase the king's peace. Among these men were John Lovel, John de Segrave, Henry Tieys and Robert FitzRoger, all later to emerge as close associates of Bigod and Bohun in their resistance to the king.[83] Clearly there was as yet no unity between secular and ecclesiastical opposition. The collection of the fines from the clergy did not proceed altogether smoothly. The date for payment of the money was postponed, and the sheriffs and bannerets were ordered to recruit assistants on 20 March.[84] By 2 April pressure was being put on recalcitrant clerks with instructions for the sale of their goods which had been confiscated by the crown, but the severity of the edict was reduced by the crown's emphasizing the exclusion of growing crops and the tools required for their cultivation.[85] On 11 April the order for the sale of goods was repeated in a privy seal letter to the exchequer, with an illuminating emphasis on the king's need for money, which was such that it did not matter if the goods were sold for less than their worth, as long as the money was raised quickly. Two days later the king stressed that the clergy should not be permitted to buy back their own possessions.[86]

A different tone entered the king's correspondence on 14 April, when he stated that he had heard that the clergy were more willing to come to terms.[87] This must have been the result of the decision of the ecclesiastical council which met in mid-Lent. An impressive royal delegation had threatened an appeal to the pope against any action taken by Winchelsey and his bishops that was directed at the king, his officials and his subjects.[88] It was decided that individuals should be permitted to follow their own consciences, and as a result many more came forward to receive royal protection.[89] Edward allowed an extra three weeks before the sale of goods should take place, but also instructed his officials to take a harsher attitude to

[82] *C.P.R., 1292–1301*, p. 237.
[83] No. 5; *C.P.R., 1292–1301*, pp. 235–40, 260–86.
[84] No. 20. [85] No. 30.
[86] Nos. 40, 42. [87] No. 43.
[88] No. 23. [89] *Cotton, Historia Anglicana*, p. 323.

those who came late to pay their fines than to those who were prompt. On 26 April the exchequer issued instructions to the effect that if payment was not made by 23 May then the clergy would have to buy new protections, as the old ones would be rendered invalid.[90]

Some idea of the pressure placed upon the clergy is given by the notarial instrument recording events at Canterbury Cathedral Priory on 27 February, when the granary, cellar, larder and guesthouse were locked and sealed, as part of the measures for the sequestration of clerical property. The event was sufficiently noteworthy for Bartholemew Cotton to include it in his chronicle. Then, on 6 March, the notary was recalled to view the state of the granary, where for want of proper care the grain was rotting and overheating.[91] Another notorious incident was the seizure of Archbishop Winchelsey's horses at Maidstone, where it seems that horses belonging to the prior of Canterbury were taken as well. Royal clemency extended only to allowing the archbishop's lay squires to take back their own mounts. The priory was placed under some financial pressure, with Prior Eastry being forced to make application to Rome for relief by borrowing funds.[92] Even in the north, where the clergy had initially complied with the king's demands, there was some trouble. News of the hostility of the Carlisle clergy to payment of the fifth reached the king by the end of March, and Alexander le Convers, a royal clerk, was sent to deal with the matter. At the beginning of May the sheriff of Yorkshire was ordered to deal with a group of canons of York who were resisting collection of the tax.[93]

Negotiations between the king and the archbishop eased the crisis. The Evesham chronicle tells of discussions at Salisbury in March,[94] but it was not until 12 June that a softening of the king's attitude can be detected, with the order to permit Winchelsey use of his houses, allowing him to travel once more: he had been residing at Chartham, near Canterbury.[95] There was no relaxation of the process of collecting clerical fines, however, for on 14 June clerks were appointed to oversee their speedy collection. Account was to be rendered by 8 July.[96] It was the fiasco of the muster at London which made it imperative for Edward to come to an understanding with the archbishop, and this was reached by 11 July, when orders were issued for the restitution of his lands and chattels. On 14 July Winchelsey

[90] Nos. 43, 48.
[91] Nos. 6, 9; Cotton, *Historia Anglicana*, p. 322. At the abbey of La Roche, the sealing up of the granary was avoided only by means of bribery (JI.1/672, m. 7d).
[92] Nos. 13, 46; Cambridge University Library MS. Ee. v, fos. 79, 83.
[93] Nos. 27, 29, 35, 53.
[94] Denton, 'The Crisis of 1297 from the Evesham Chronicle', 571–2.
[95] No. 76; *Guisborough*, p. 288; *Historia Anglicanae Scriptores Decem*, ed. R. Twysden (1652), pp. 1965–6.
[96] No. 78.

was present when fealty was sworn to the young prince Edward.[97] This was not, however, quite the end of the story of the outlawry of the clergy. On the very day that the chancery was authorizing the restitution of Winchelsey's lands, the exchequer was issuing writs concerning the failure of various Welsh marcher lords to provide information on the submission of the clergy and to account for the money received in fines: an interesting indication of sympathy among the secular opposition for the plight of the clergy. The bishop of Llandaff submitted as late as 18 July, paying a fourth, rather than the usual fifth. It was still necessary for instructions to be sent out at the beginning of August stressing that the king had no intention that spiritualities should be seized to the king's use, but it seems improbable that by this date much was being done by royal officials in respect of the clergy's goods.[98] Winchelsey's reconciliation with Edward, and the decision to allow individuals to follow their own consciences, had ensured that this dispute would no longer dominate affairs in the way that it had done since February.

In financial terms, the grant of protections to the clergy in return for payment of fines had been most successful. The total receipt of £23,174 was almost exactly the sum that the king had originally demanded by way of collection.[99] The one incident in which clerks declined to co-operate in the matter was the refusal of the sheriff of Devon's clerks to render account for clerical fines when representing their master at the exchequer.[100] One unusual problem was presented when friends of clerics paid fines on their behalf, without their authorization or knowledge. This could result in a double payment. In other cases, however, such as that of the bishop of Lincoln, the willingness of the royal authorities to accept payment from well-wishers meant that potential difficulties in individual cases were avoided.[101]

Arguments over clerical taxation, however, did not end with the payment of fines for clerical protection. Edward was so hard pressed for money that he raised the question of a new grant with Winchelsey and some of the bishops, the grant to be in return for the confirmation of the charters. On 10 August the Canterbury convocation met to discuss the matter, and it was agreed, as Winchelsey must have expected, that no grant could be made without papal consent.[102] Edward's response was not to repeat the threat of outlawry, but simply to issue an ordinance on 20 August for the collection of either a fifth

---

[97] These events are fully described by Rothwell, 'The Confirmation of the Charters, 1297', 27–8.

[98] Nos. 89, 92, 100.

[99] Prestwich, *War, Politics and Finance under Edward I*, p. 257, gives the total as £22,810, but to this should be added £364 shown by E 401/1651 to have been received between 9 February and 9 April.

[100] E 368/69, m. 71.   [101] No. 32; *Guisborough*, p. 288.   [102] No. 109.

on all clerical possessions, or a third on temporalities. Edward could not claim consent for this, but he found justification in arguments drawing on canon law, stressing the state of necessity in which the realm was placed.[103] By this time, of course, Boniface VIII had withdrawn considerably from the stern line taken in *Clericis Laicos*, most notably in giving the French clergy permission to make a grant to Philip IV in the bull *Coram Illo Fatemur*, of 28 February. If Edward hoped, however, to avoid a new clash with the church in England, he was mistaken. Renewed threats of excommunication of royal officials were countered by royal renewal of the procurations directed against Winchelsey that had been promulgated on 24 March. A highly dramatic scene took place in Canterbury cathedral on 1 September, with the royal proctor, Hugh of Yarmouth, reading out his procuration in the middle of a sermon preached by Winchelsey himself.[104] It seems, however, that little was done to try to collect the new tax. There is no record of the appointment of collectors, and it may be that in the absence of Edward's dominating presence the royal ministers took a less aggressive attitude than they had done earlier in the year. It seems that with the drawing up of the *Confirmatio Cartarum* on 10 October the issue was quietly dropped. Once news came through from Scotland of the defeat of the English forces at Stirling Bridge the clergy voted new taxes which naturally superseded the arbitrarily imposed third or fifth.

While the moral issue facing the church, with the conflict of allegiance to king and pope, was very different from the problems confronting the laity, it would be wrong to distinguish too sharply between the ecclesiastical and secular opposition to Edward I. The clergy were, for example, as much affected by prises as the rest of the king's subjects, as is shown by the reaction of those who gathered at a manor belonging to the Hospitallers near Hertford, when an official of the marshalsea tried to seize grain for the king's horses.[105] There was a personal antagonism between king and archbishop just as there was between king and earls. Winchelsey had been the choice of the Canterbury chapter, not of king or pope, as archbishop. In 1295 he had not taken his oath of fealty in the form demanded by Edward, and the king made exceptionally heavy financial demands, asking for debts of almost £3,500 to be paid off in the course of three years.[106] The crisis between church and state was not, however, an inevitable conflict between personal enemies holding incompatible views. It was the result of the oppressive burdens necessitated by Edward I's over-ambitious military policies, and of the archbishop's

---

[103] No. 119.
[104] No. 133.   [105] No. 57.
[106] Prestwich, *War, Politics and Finance under Edward I*, p. 237.

natural desire to defend the privileges of the clergy in accordance with
the dictates of Boniface VIII.

v. *Royal administration and finance*

The demands that the king made on his administration in 1297 were
enormous. An army had to be raised for Flanders, with a fleet both
for that expedition and for taking supplies to Gascony. Taxes, clerical
fines and victuals had to be collected against a background of mount-
ing political unrest. How do the records suggest that the king's
ministers and officials dealt with such a massive burden of work?

The central departments of chancery, exchequer and wardrobe
appear to have operated with surprising efficiency under this considerable pressure. It was only in the matter of the Easter prise of
wool that plans seem to have been thought out hurriedly and in-
competently. There was, too, some confusion as the methods of collecting clerical fines evolved, with the exchequer officials being left
in some uncertainty, following the appointment of the bannerets, as
to whether they should continue to perform this task or not.[107] There
are occasional indications of a shortage of manpower, as when the
king stated that he did not have anyone with him to send to deal
with the question of the Carlisle clergy, and asked the exchequer to
attend to the matter.[108] An attempt had to be made early in July to
restrict the scope of exchequer business so as to free the officials for
essential matters. Lengthy speeches by attorneys were forbidden in
order to speed up business.[109] As the year proceeded, there was a
marked alteration in the tone of the king's letters to the exchequer.
Satisfaction with their actions, as indicated for example on 8 March,
was replaced by a growing impatience, particularly with regard to
setting up the tax of an eighth.[110] In general, despite the king's suspi-
cions, his orders appear to have been quickly implemented. A privy
seal letter of 15 May sent from Loders, near Dorchester, was acted
upon on 20 May. Instructions issued at Lenham in Kent on 12 June
were followed up on 14 June,[111] and many similar examples could
be given.

If the exchequer could be relied upon to implement royal instructions, the sheriffs and local officials could not. On 21 March letters
were issued in strong terms expressing the king's astonishment that
the prise of victuals had not been properly carried out, with supplies
not taken to the seaports as requested.[112] Towards the end of April
the arrest of the collectors of the twelfth and eighth for Westmorland
was ordered, but the sheriff was unable to carry out his orders; his

[107] No. 16.
[109] No. 84.
[111] Nos. 60, 62, 76.

[108] No. 27.
[110] Nos. 12, 101, 104.
[112] No. 21.

excuse that he could find no one to value lands and chattels, since all knights and free tenants were engaged in the defence of the Borders, seems rather implausible.[113] The surviving returns to the military summons of 28 July suggest no enthusiasm on the part of the sheriffs to carry through Edward's policies.[114] Cases of bribery and corruption began to come to light in 1297. In March enquiries were ordered into abuses of the coastguard system in Hampshire, and in June into extortion by a clerk appointed to take grain for the king in Gloucestershire. In November there was the case of Richard of Louth, accepting bribes in Kent while purveying victuals.[115] It was not, however, until 1298 that the evidence really began to accumulate on the way in which matters had gone wrong in the counties, with the setting up of the judicial enquiries of that year as one of Edward's measures for defusing a critical situation. The surviving records of the justices show that there had been extremely widespread corruption and malpractice, notably in the collection of prises and taxes. It was all too clear that the king's often-expressed intention that the poor should be spared had rarely been put into effect.[116] An ordinance produced by the council in February 1298 also provides evidence of the way things had been going wrong at the local level. This dealt with the problem of sheriffs' clerks who gave false, fictitious and frivolous replies to royal writs, a matter to which the sheriffs, even if literate, paid little attention. It used to be the custom to punish the sheriff for the actions of his subordinates, but it was now decided to make the clerks themselves responsible for their actions. The ordinance was soon to be put into effect in the case of the sheriff of Devon's clerks who had refused to co-operate over the question of clerical fines.[117]

Yet the surviving evidence does not suggest a complete breakdown of administration even at the local level. There is no evidence to support Guisborough's statement that the earls and their allies prevented any royal officials from entering their lands to take prises.[118] The novel procedure of collecting clerical fines went surprisingly smoothly, with the co-operation of at least some of those laymen who were later to oppose the king. The tax of a twelfth and eighth, collected mainly in the course of 1297, was better organized than the taxes on moveables which had preceded it. The assembly of the fleet for Flanders seems to have caused little difficulty, and the supplies collected for

---

[113] No. 47.   [114] No. 94.

[115] H. Rothwell, 'The Disgrace of Richard of Louth, 1297', *E.H.R.*, xlviii (1933), 259–64; *infra*, nos. 11, 75.

[116] *A Lincolnshire Assize Roll for 1298*; a full list of the surviving rolls from this enquiry is given by Rothwell, 'The Disgrace of Richard of Louth', 261.

[117] *Statutes of the Realm* (London, 1810), i, 213; E 368/69, m. 71.

[118] *Guisborough*, p. 290. They did not co-operate, however, over the payment of clerical fines in the liberties of the Welsh Marches.

the expedition were adequate. It was only in the matters of the wool prises and the recruitment of twenty-pound landholders that results fell badly below expectations. This was probably more the result of opposition to the king's plans by his subjects than of administrative incompetence, despite such examples as that of the wool seized in Lancashire and taken to Chester. The sheriff's officials found that there were no customs men there, so the wool had to be taken overland to York and then by water to Hull.[119]

A crucial question was plainly that of the loyalty of the administrative officials. There are very few indications to suggest that the events of the year put any great stress in this respect on the staff of the central departments. An odd incident in July suggests a short-lived argument, probably over the issue of hearing private pleas in the exchequer. One of the barons of the exchequer, John de Lisle, was summarily dismissed by the king, only to be reinstated soon afterwards. Royal officials were not much affected by divided loyalty over the outlawry of the clergy; the only royal clerk who appears to have opposed Edward's policy was John de Craucombe, archdeacon of the East Riding, who took exception to the payment of the fifth granted in the northern province.[120] Such royalist bishops as Anthony Bek of Durham or Walter Langton of Coventry and Lichfield, the treasurer, naturally fully supported the king. There was likewise no question mark over the support given to the king by the laymen who served him in his council and his household, men like Hugh Despenser, who did much to supervise the wool policy, or the steward of the household, Walter de Beauchamp. There are few indications that the king's ministers even questioned his policies. Hugh Cressingham in Scotland was certainly highly critical of a request that he return £2,000 sent him by the exchequer, in view of the gravity of the situation in the north,[121] but it was left for the opposition to make the point forcibly that it was unsafe for the king to go abroad while the English position in Scotland was so insecure. Edward did admit on the eve of his departure that the council had misgivings over the projected campaign, but he was not a man to be shifted easily from his resolve.[122]

One of the points that must have alarmed the council regarding the proposed campaign in Flanders was that of finance. English armies had been campaigning continuously since 1294, and the reserves of cash built up in that year had not lasted long under this constant pressure. Wardrobe expenditure in the year from November 1294 reached £138,255, and in the next year stood at £83,648. Nor

[119] E 159/70, m. 88d; Fryde, 'Financial Resources of Edward I in the Netherlands', 1182, n. 6.
[120] No. 54. Craucombe had been sent as a royal envoy to Rome in 1294 (*C.P.R., 1292–1301*, p. 105).
[121] No. 88.   [122] No. 98; *Treaty Rolls*, i, 134.

were these complete figures of royal expenditure, for they excluded what was spent on foreign alliances and much of the costs of the operations in Gascony.[123] The king's alarm over the financial situation was indicated in March 1297, when he asked the exchequer to provide him with details of what income that department expected to receive, and when. Unfortunately no reply is recorded, and there is no contemporary estimate of income and expenditure available.[124] However, there are some indications of the position. Wardrobe expenditure from November 1296 to November 1297 stood at £119,519, as against receipts of £106,356. This level of deficit is confirmed by a list of wardrobe debts totalling between £12,000 and £13,000.[125] Nor at this period was all expenditure channelled through the department of the wardrobe. There was in addition, for example, a total of £27,333 sent to Gascony by the exchequer,[126] while Walter Langton's receipts in the course of his diplomatic mission which began in June 1296 and continued in 1297 totalled £34,726, and were not fully accounted for in the wardrobe in the year starting in November 1296.[127] £5,188 of the revenues from Scotland were used to pay a subsidy to the count of Bar.[128] There is no way in which it is possible to produce a definitive figure for royal expenditure in 1297 in view of the manner in which the accounts were drawn up, but it is evident that it stood at a very high level.

Nor is it possible to calculate Edward I's income in 1297 with precision, although it is clear that receipts did not match the king's financial obligations. The receipt and issue rolls of the exchequer are incomplete for this period, although some figures can be provided. The tax of a twelfth and eighth yielded £17,070 at the exchequer between late April and mid-September, all but £2,444 of it before 7 June.[129] As already shown, clerical fines raised £23,174, while other income from the church included substantial profits from the confiscated alien priories. The receipt roll for the Easter term recorded the receipt of £39,566.[130] A different source, the Jornalia Roll, shows that £15,986 came in from all sources between 25 June and 18 July.[131]

[123] The figures of wardrobe expenditure are conveniently summarized in T. F. Tout, *Chapters in the Administrative History of Medieval England*, vi (Manchester, 1933), 80–1. For a fuller discussion of the costs of war in this period, see Prestwich, *War, Politics and Finance under Edward I*, pp. 171–5.

[124] No. 16.

[125] Tout, *Chapters*, vi, 80–1; E 101/354/5. This contains two books, which give slightly different totals.

[126] B.L., Add. MS. 7965, fo. 17; E 405/1/11.

[127] Langton's account is printed by G. Cuttino, *English Diplomatic Administration, 1259–1339* (2nd edn., Oxford, 1971), pp. 224–50.

[128] E 405/1/11 (1 June).

[129] *Lancashire Lay Subsidies*, p. 195.

[130] J. H. Ramsay, *A History of the Revenues of the Kings of England*, ii (Oxford, 1925), 88. [131] E 405/1/11.

There was a clear determination to try to raise all possible revenue, as is shown by the commissions set up on 12 March to levy all debts owed to the crown. The measure was followed up on 4 July with the appointment of clerks to assist in the task. It seems unlikely, however, that much was achieved in this way. The Lincolnshire assize roll of 1298 contains only one case which definitely relates to the collection of such debts, and there was certainly no marked increase in the sums paid into the exchequer by the sheriffs to suggest that they were successful in obtaining payment of sums in arrears.[132] The exchequer records in no way contradict the impression provided by the wardrobe account of a government whose revenue was inadequate. While there was almost £5,500 in cash in the exchequer on 25 June, the figure by 18 July had fallen to a mere £700.[133]

The calculations used to justify the prise of wool at the end of July 1297 clearly demonstrate the gravity of the financial situation by that date. For the subsidies to the duke of Brabant and the king of Germany, together with the wages of the expedition to Flanders, it was estimated that 75,500 marks were needed.[134] It is easy to see why the king resorted to the arbitrary measures of the prise and the imposition of the taxes on laity and clergy. A simpler, and less politically offensive, measure would have been to borrow money, rather than impose fresh taxes on an overburdened people, but it was not possible for Edward to obtain credit on the required scale. No company of Italian merchants had yet emerged to take the place held by the Ricciardi of Lucca until 1294, and it has rightly been pointed out that had they not failed, Edward might well not have had to adopt such high-handed measures in 1297.[135] Some money was borrowed, but not on the massive scale that was needed. Forced loans from Italians in 1297 yielded nearly £3,000.[136] The bishop of Ely, in a vulnerable position since he had not settled his accounts for the period when he had been keeper of the wardrobe, advanced some money.[137] The most substantial loan received in the year was that of 7,000 marks worth of tin from the earl of Cornwall, but this was used to repay some citizens of Bayonne, not to provide funds in an immediate sense.[138]

[132] Nos. 15, 85; *A Lincolnshire Assize Roll for 1298*, pp. xl–xli. The appointment mentioned there of Richard of Hetherington on 14 June was not related to this measure, but was for the collection of clerical fines. Details of cash receipts at the exchequer are given by M. H. Mills, 'Adventus Vicecomitum, 1272–1307', *E.H.R.*, xxxviii (1923), 340. Although there was a rise as compared with 1296, the level of receipts from the sheriffs was still lower than it had been in 1295.
[133] E 405/1/11. [134] No. 97.
[135] R. W. Kaeuper, 'Royal Finance and the Crisis of 1297', *Order and Innovation in the Middle Ages*, ed. W. C. Jordan, B. McNab, T. F. Ruiz (Princeton, 1976), pp. 103–10.
[136] R. W. Kaeuper, 'The Frescobaldi of Florence and the English Crown', *Studies in Medieval and Renaissance History*, x (1973), 48–9.
[137] Nos. 2, 145. [138] *C.P.R., 1292–1301*, p. 316.

Some funds were borrowed in the Low Countries. John Botetourt, Richard de Havering and John de Hustwayt raised some small sums early in the year, while more substantial loans were made to Walter Langton in the course of his embassy.[139] However, Edward's complaint of 20 August that he had found little by way of *chevisaunce*, or loans, seems amply justified, and the anxiety of some of the letters he wrote to the exchequer earlier in the month was most understandable.[140] Once he arrived in Flanders, Edward was to find his financial difficulties still more acute.

vi. *The constitutional arguments*

It is not part of the purpose of this introduction to provide a fresh analysis of the whole question of the ultimate constitutional significance of the crisis of 1297, for to do that would involve discussing documents and events ranging much more widely than the confines of the year itself. The documents printed here do, however, provide some indication as to the way in which the arguments between king and opposition proceeded in 1297, in the immediate circumstances of the time. It is worth bearing in mind G. O. Sayles' wise note of caution, when he remarked of the crisis of 1297 that practical politics 'in times of great upheaval are likely to treat legal considerations as irrelevant and discardable'.[141]

Both Edward I and his opponents in 1297 clearly recognized the importance of propaganda. Initially, the king seems to have been more concerned to prevent the views of Winchelsey and his supporters gaining widespread currency than with presenting his own side of the case. A writ, which only survives in a chronicle, records a general prohibition by the king on 27 February of the issue of sentences of excommunication which affected the dignity of the crown in any way. This was a direct attack on *Clericis Laicos* which included the excommunication of all those involved in unauthorized taxation.[142] The bannerets who were appointed to receive the submissions of the clergy were also ordered to enquire into such excommunications, and into those who 'tell news whereby discord may arise between the king and the prelates, earls, barons and others of the realm'.[143] As early as 4 March there was news of the arrest of a clerk, probably Walter de Maidstone, for the alleged forgery of papal bulls, and later Adam de Berdeseye was held for making transcripts of them, presumably for circulation. Three men were arrested at Lancaster for a similar

---

[139] E 405/1/10; Fryde, 'Financial Resources of Edward I in the Netherlands', 1175-6; Cuttino, *English Diplomatic Administration*, pp. 228, 248; *infra*, no. 58.
[140] *Treaty Rolls*, i, 134.
[141] Sayles, 'The Seizure of Wool at Easter 1297', 543.
[142] No. 7.
[143] *C.P.R., 1292-1301*, p. 239.

offence, and clerks were also arrested in Devon, Cornwall and East Anglia for publication of a papal letter.[144]

As the crisis proceeded, so the king made increasing efforts to counter opposition by attempting to explain and justify his actions. Whereas in April no reason for the prise of grain was given, that of meat in June was justified in terms of the war.[145] By the end of July, still more attention was being paid to the need to persuade the people of the necessity for new taxes and the prise of wool. The financial calculations of royal expenditure on the alliance and on wages for the proposed expedition were known beyond the confines of the exchequer, for the Evesham chronicle contains a passage which is clearly based on them.[146] On 8 August those appointed to take oaths from the taxers of the eighth were being asked to see that the people were approached in the most pleasant and courteous manner to explain the king's need for the tax. Four days later the king's elaborate apologia for his conduct was prepared for publication, and evidence for messengers taking it to the counties of England survives in the accounts.[147] There was probably more royal propaganda that has not survived. The Hagnaby chronicle contains a lengthy and highly exaggerated list of the military aid promised by Edward's allies, and it seems likely that this was the result of an attempt to whip up enthusiasm for the forthcoming campaign.[148] Further, Edward did not confine his attempts to persuade men to support him to England: letters of encouragement and explanation were also sent to his beleaguered supporters in Gascony.[149]

In contrast to the king's rather frenzied efforts, the opposition merely produced one major document in the period prior to Edward's departure on 22 August. This was the Remonstrances, written in French for popular consumption, and, as the Evesham chronicle shows, produced in the course of the abortive negotiations at the end of July. Wilkinson's suggestion that this document may have originated with the knights finds no support there; the document is said to summarize the arguments put forward by the earl of Hereford.[150] The number of variant readings in the surviving texts suggest that the Remonstrances circulated widely; Edward I's letter of 12 August referred to 'certain articles for the common profit of the people and the realm' receiving publicity. The recently discovered Worcester ver-

[144] Nos. 8, 51; *C.C.R.*, *1296–1302*, pp. 25–7.
[145] Nos. 50, 72.
[146] Denton, 'The Crisis of 1297 from the Evesham Chronicle', 578. The figures are not quite accurately reported by the chronicler.
[147] Nos. 104, 111.
[148] Appendix, p. 200.
[149] *Treaty Rolls*, 1, 133–4.
[150] No. 98; Denton, 'The Crisis of 1297 from the Evesham Chronicle', 577; Wilkinson, *Constitutional History*, i, 193–5.

sion interestingly lays greater stress on the fact that the complaints
were those of the community of both clergy and laity than do the
texts preserved by chroniclers.[151]

There has been much discussion of the nature of the arguments
used in 1297, and of the constitutional issues they were designed to
resolve. In particular, attention has centred upon the question of the
opposition's desire to 'vindicate the ancient political principle of
government by consent',[152] and more recently upon the king's use of
'the argument and phraseology of the plea of necessity, which had
for the first time been extensively employed in political controversy'.[153] The documents in this collection do not provide much
new information on this topic, for the discussion largely depends on
analysis of the major texts yielded by the crisis, and not on the day-
to-day administrative correspondence.

The question of consent by the community of the realm for war
taxation and other impositions appears to have emerged only at a
late stage in the crisis. The Remonstrances contained a general protest
at the way in which the laws and customs of the land were not being
upheld, and while Edwards argued that this might well refer, among
other things, to the imposition of taxes and prises,[154] the additional
final clause which appears only in the Worcester version of the text
does not suggest that the opposition was attempting to define the consent necessary for future taxes at that stage. Rather, it was simply
concerned to abolish any possible precedent created by the wartime
taxes. The king was of course to promise that the eighth was not to be
so used, in letters authorized on 24 August, but by that date so limited
a concession was insufficient to pacify his opponents.[155] The arbitrary
nature of the measures introduced at the end of July made the question of establishing the proper means for obtaining consent more important, but it was only with the drafting of *De Tallagio*, probably
after the king had sailed for Flanders, that a clear demand for consent
to taxation emerged.[156] Even then, there was no question of consent
for the *maltolt*; the request was simply for its abolition. With the *Confirmatio Cartarum* itself, the principle of assent by all the realm for the
common profit was at last clearly enunciated.[157] This covered aids

[151] No. 111; Denton, 'A Worcester Text of the Remonstrances of 1297', 518–19; see
no. 98. Note in the third paragraph the insertion of *ausi bien des clers com de lays*.
[152] Wilkinson, *Constitutional History*, i, 208.
[153] Harriss, *King, Parliament and Public Finance*, p. 70.
[154] Edwards, '*Confirmatio Cartarum* and Baronial Grievances in 1297', 161.
[155] Nos. 98, 131.
[156] No. 151.
[157] No. 155. This clarity did not, of course, extend to definition of the consenting
body, and it may be that the phrase 'common assent of all the realm' was deliberately
imprecise. Harriss, following Gaines Post, argues that the rôle of representatives in
assenting to taxes was a very limited one (*King, Parliament and Public Finance*, pp. 52–

and prises, together with the ambiguous *mises*, but as far as the *maltolt*
was concerned, the wording of the *Confirmatio* is a little obscure. G. L.
Harriss has suggested that while grammatically the text requires
common assent by the greater part of the community of the realm,
this in practice amounted to no more than a demand that the merchants should give their consent as part of the assent of the whole community. In his view, the *Confirmatio* did not 'seek to remove the right
of consent from merchants to parliament'. Harriss further distinguished between the *maltolt* as a temporary subsidy on wool, and the
more permanent customs duties.[158] However, the writs issued late in
November abolishing the *maltolt* make such a complex interpretation
seem unnecessary. They stated quite categorically that the *maltolt* or
any other custom was not to be taken in future without the will and
common assent of the community. No mention was made of 'the
greater part' of the community, and the precedent that should be followed for the future was clearly intended to be that of the Ancient
Custom, granted at the instance of the merchants in parliament in
1275. There was no distinction made between customs and subsidies.[159]

To what extent were the arguments conducted within a framework
provided by canon law, and in particular that of the doctrine of
necessity? There can be no doubt of the importance of this in
Edward's dealings with the clergy. It was the doctrine of necessity
which provided Boniface VIII with the means of withdrawing from
the stringent views set out in *Clericis Laicos*. The position in France,
where by appeal to necessity Philip IV was able to receive financial
support from the clergy, had an obvious relevance to affairs in England. Edward I's justification for the imposition of fresh clerical taxes
on 20 August was evidently couched in terms derived directly from
current views on the rights of a ruler in a case of urgent necessity.
The term necessity also appeared in the procuration directed against
Winchelsey on 1 September, though not in that of 24 March. The
terminology used was curiously archaic, not suggesting a great fami-
liarity with scholastic theories.[160] The protection granted to the northern clergy in February 1297, making it clear that they had acceded

3). For a different view of the powers of representatives, which seems more plausible,
see E. A. R. Brown, 'Representation and Agency Law', *Viator*, iii (1972), 329–64,
especially 363. From the inclusion in *De Tallagio* of knights, burgesses and other freemen
in the clause regarding taxation, it would seem that the opposition probably expected
representatives to participate in the grant of taxation.
[158] Harriss, *King, Parliament and Public Finance*, p. 425.
[159] *Infra*, nos. 173, 174. For a further discussion of the constitutional issues regarding
the *maltolt*, see Lloyd, *English Wool Trade*, pp. 95–6.
[160] Nos. 119, 133. Appeal to necessity was also made by the king on 19 August when
he forbade the bishops to excommunicate ministers taking prises (*Foedera*, I, ii, 875;
C.C.R., *1296–1302*, p. 124).

to the king's demands for a tax in view of the 'machinations and invasions of enemies', can certainly be seen as fitting the case that the clergy might pay aids if the kingdom was faced by an urgent necessity.[161]

Was the debate with the secular opposition conducted within a similar framework? The one letter which makes it clear that the writer considered a state of necessity to exist was that sent by Hugh Cressingham to Philip de Willoughby at the exchequer on 10 July, and which referred solely to matters in Scotland. There is no reason to suppose that Edward I accepted this view.[162] Although the king had made reference to the 'certain and urgent necessity' in 1294 when announcing the institution of the *maltolt*,[163] he did not use the terminology of necessity in any precise way in 1297. The justification he issued for the eighth on 8 August is particularly remarkable. It stressed that the money was needed for the king's 'great business', and the defence and salvation of his allies. It pointed out that the king was risking his own life on behalf of his subjects, and the final plea was put in feudal terms, not employing doctrines of Roman or canon law. Edward's subjects should 'do their duty toward their lord with good will, as good and loyal people ought, and are bound to do toward their liege lord in so great and high an affair'.[164] It was not easy for the king to appeal to the necessity in which the realm was placed when he was not proposing to defend the country from an aggressor, but rather to launch an expedition overseas in support of his allies. The broadest defence of his policies, of course, came in the letter of 12 August, but there was no specific statement here of his right to tax the country if a state of necessity existed. He simply stressed that he could not defend the realm without taxes, and pointed out that he had used the money for the common profit. The argument can be seen in terms of the developing scholastic doctrines of the just war, but it is hard to see the plea as being 'in effect an *ex post facto* assent to the plea of necessity'.[165] It is unfortunately not easy to distinguish between a technical argument constructed according to the views of legal theorists, and a straightforward exposition of the practical problems of the situation, but the letter of 12 August seems to fit the latter better than it does the former. These were arguments intended for general consumption, and it must be doubted whether many of those who heard them would set them in the context of the complex and involved theories of the commentators and glossators of Roman and canon law.

[161] *C.P.R.*, *1292-1301*, p. 237.
[162] No. 88.
[163] *Cotton, Historia Anglicana*, p. 245.
[164] No. 104.
[165] No. 111; Harriss, *King, Parliament and Public Finance*, p. 65.

Underlying the Remonstrances, G. L. Harriss has perceived certain of the principles expounded by Aquinas. The baronial case, however, seems to be more based on practicalities than on ultimate rights and wrongs. The justice of Edward I's case against Philip IV was not questioned, but the matter of the reliability of the Flemings was raised, with some justification, as events were to show. While it is true that a plea of necessity could be countered by the argument that no king should impoverish his subjects, it seems that the view that Edward's taxes were insupportable had a basis in fact, and was inspired by problems such as those faced by the earl of Arundel, rather than by any theorist. The protest of the earls at the exchequer on 22 August, as reported, does not fit into the framework of argument as to whether or not there was a state of urgent necessity, with its emphasis on the fact that to pay an arbitrarily imposed levy would be tantamount to accepting servile status.[166] Finally it is worth noting, in discussing this question of necessity, that the French monarchy did not find the plea to be a particularly effective one when dealing with the laity.[167]

There is unfortunately little material to show how the discussions leading to the settlement of the *Confirmatio Cartarum* went. It is evident that the king gave the authorities in England a very free hand to settle the dispute, and there is no evidence to suggest that he took any part in the debates between his departure on 22 August and the issue of the *Confirmatio* on 10 October under the authority of his son Edward. Edward's absence probably facilitated rather than hindered matters. The negotiations took place under a clear threat of civil war, and were concluded in the unsettled atmosphere of genuine emergency following the news of the English defeat at Stirling Bridge, which probably came on about 24 September.[168] There has been much discussion of the nature of the document which appears to set out the baronial position, the *De Tallagio*. Its authenticity was sharply attacked by Edwards, and cautiously defended by H. Rothwell.[169] The recent discovery by J. H. Denton of a form of pardon to the earls, John de Ferrers and their associates, has put a new complexion on the discussion. This text, surviving in the Evesham chronicle, closely parallels the fifth clause of *De Tallagio*, and gives weight to the view that that document was a genuine product of the baronial opposition. Further, it seems possible that, with Reginald de Grey and the rest

---

[166] No. 126; Harriss, *King, Parliament and Public Finance*, pp. 161–2

[167] For difficulties in the 1290s, see Brown, 'Representation and Agency Law', 357–9; for the later 'skeptical and parochial reaction to royal assertions of "necessity"', see J. B. Henneman, *Royal Taxation in Fourteenth Century France* (Princeton, 1971), pp. 321–4.

[168] The fullest discussion of these negotiations is by Rothwell, 'The Confirmation of the Charters, 1297', 177–81.

[169] Edwards, '*Confirmatio Cartarum* and Baronial Grievances in 1297', 273–300; Rothwell, 'The Confirmation of the Charters, 1297', 300–15.

of the council in England being in no position to conclude a firm agreement with the opposition, *De Tallagio* and this draft pardon were sent to the king in Flanders along with the *Confirmatio Cartarum*, as Guisborough's chronicle suggests.[170] There can, however, be no doubt that the king never gave his approval to the *De Tallagio*: the *Confirmatio* was the document which effected the eventual compromise between Edward and his opponents.

The one document printed in this volume relating to the period of the settlement of the issues which has not been previously published is the very full list of Bigod's household. This was either a list prepared so that Bigod's men could receive royal protections during the period of negotiations, or, though this is less likely, it was produced with the intention that each of those with Bigod should receive an individual pardon. With the inclusion on the list of John de Segrave, Alan la Zouche, Robert FitzRoger and John Lovel, it becomes clear to what extent the protest at the exchequer on 22 August had been dominated by Bigod's men: of those named by the exchequer officials as being present, only Henry le Tieys was not a member of Bigod's retinue.[171]

The version of the *Confirmatio* itself given in this volume is not identical in all respects with that issued by the king at Ghent on 5 November. It may even be a draft version, but the differences are of no great significance, and certainly do not help to reveal the stages through which the negotiations went. Curiously, although the *Confirmatio* was a wholly separate document to the Charters themselves, even being distinguished by being in a different language, the exchequer itself could later describe it as consisting of articles added to Magna Carta. This almost certainly had been the intention of the *De Tallagio*, which with its absence of preamble was clearly meant, as Walter of Guisborough considered, to be tacked on as an addition to Magna Carta.[172]

For all its undoubted importance as a statement of the constitutional position, with its emphasis on consent for taxation levied for the common profit of the realm, the *Confirmatio* did not mark the end of the conflict. In immediate terms it had done nothing to redress the many individual grievances, particularly regarding prises of wool and foodstuffs, that had done much to exacerbate the situation in 1297. The king's chief contribution to the settlement of the crisis was perhaps the institution of a large-scale judicial enquiry into the maladministration that had undoubtedly taken place at a local level during the years of emergency. He had, in his letter of 12 August,

[170] Denton, 'The Crisis of 1297 from the Evesham Chronicle', 565–7; *infra*, no. 152.
[171] No. 154.
[172] Nos. 151, 155. *Guisborough*, p. 311. The problem of regarding the *Confirmatio* as an *addicio* is discussed by Rothwell, 'The Confirmation of the Charters, 1297', 181, n. 3.

promised to make amends for the impositions he had placed on the realm, and this enquiry was the means typically chosen to make good this promise. Edward had throughout expressed a desire to ensure that the poor should not suffer as a result of his exactions, and there is no reason to doubt that, as well as being a politically wise move, the judicial enquiry was prompted by the king's very real concern for the realm.[173] It is interesting to note, however, that there are no indications that Edward felt any personal remorse for the policies adopted during the period of war, in contrast to Philip IV, whose will drawn up in March 1297 promised full restitution to all those who had suffered from the currency manipulations which had been a major source of war finance.[174]

vii. *The campaign in Flanders*

Edward I displayed a remarkable determination and single-minded purpose in the period up to his embarkation on the *Cog St. Edward* on 22 August. Nothing would deflect him from his planned campaign, even his own recognition in the letter of 12 August that there was a danger of the most perilous and grave conflict that had ever occurred in England breaking out.[175] His correspondence after his arrival in Flanders again bears witness to this quality of determination, though it was qualified by a greater understanding of the difficulties facing him. The surviving letters show a surprising lack of concern with the progress of events at home.

Edward's first problem on landing was not his enemies, but the dispute between the men of Yarmouth and the Cinque Ports, which flared up into what was probably the most bitter fighting of the campaign. The king took hostages from both sides in a successful attempt to restore peace, but it was hardly an auspicious start to the expedition. The wardrobe itself, the nerve centre of the administration, had almost been destroyed when the general conflagration threatened the ship containing the records and equipment, but someone had the sense to cut the mooring rope, allowing it to drift out of reach of the flames.[176] News of the king's allies was not good; a substantial force had been defeated by the French at the battle of Veurne just before the English arrival. The forebodings of the opposition about the unreliability of the Flemings were justified in part when there were rumours of unrest among the townspeople of Bruges, and the king

---

[173] No. 203.
[174] E. A. R. Brown, 'Royal Salvation and Needs of State', *Order and Innovation in the Middle Ages*, pp. 369–70. Although Edward I sent for a copy of his will in 1297, an act which may reveal something of his state of mind, he did not make a new will (no. 117).
[175] No. 111.
[176] No. 134; Prestwich, *War, Politics and Finance under Edward I*, p. 143.

was forced to move to Ghent.[177] A letter from Damme reported a riot in which some thirty or forty locals were killed by English troops, and the count of Holland complained that his merchants had suffered at the hands of Edward's men.[178] But if the English displayed an aggressive tendency towards their allies, they could not afford to do so with regard to the French, given the inadequate size of their army. Like later English soldiers in Flanders, they dug themselves in, with the assistance of local workmen, though miners from the Forest of Dean were also sent for, and they deceived the enemy into thinking that the army was a substantial one by the ruse of sending footmen forward bearing cavalry banners.[179]

The support of the allies was vital to Edward, and the surviving letters testify to some of the problems that the coalition faced. The most important of those whose support Edward had bought with promises of massive subsidies was Adolf of Nassau, king of Germany. Edward placed much reliance on John, lord of Cuyk, who was also in receipt of subsidies, as an intermediary. On 18 September the German king had expressed his willingness to campaign, but on 15 October John was writing in guarded terms, noting that Adolf did not seem to have sufficient forces with him, but that he was expecting reinforcements.[180] When Edward negotiated a truce with the French it was laid down that the Germans might break it, provided proper notice was given. Edward was clearly hopeful that Adolf would come to his assistance. On 16 October he wrote to the exchequer asking it to send money for the subsidies to the duke of Brabant and the king of Germany, and expressing his concern lest the alliance should fall through because he could not keep the financial terms of the agreements.[181] In fact, Adolf did not appear, and Edward had certainly given up hope that he would come by 27 November when he wrote to his son announcing an extension of the truce, in which no mention was made of the German ruler. In contrast to the letter of 16 October, there was no thought of possible victory, merely of his hope of obtaining the best possible peace terms.[182]

There has been extensive controversy over the rôle of Adolf of Nassau: was he bribed by the offer of French subsidies to abandon, secretly, the English alliance? The arguments largely hinge on the reliability of a French memorandum on the war which lists the king of Germany as one of Philip IV's allies. The document is a curious one, containing many errors. It was certainly written after 1304, and

[177] *The Chronicle of Bury St. Edmunds, 1212–1301*, ed. A. Gransden (London, 1964), p. 144.
[178] Nos. 149, 157.
[179] No. 182; Lewis, 'The English Forces in Flanders', p. 315, n. 2; *Chronicle of Bury St. Edmunds*, p. 143.   [180] Nos. 142, 158.
[181] No. 159.   [182] No. 176.

it seems possible that it may be a historical memorandum drawn up in the late 1330s, when France was again threatened by a massive coalition. It does not actually name the king of Germany concerned, and a tempting theory, though one not without difficulties, is that the author was confused between Adolf of Nassau and his successor, Albrecht of Habsburg. Albrecht certainly was an ally of the French, and he is not listed in the text. Albrecht's opposition to Adolf provides a perfectly adequate explanation for the king's inactivity in 1297: the king could not afford to go on campaign with Edward I because of rebellion at home. And if Adolf had indeed reached agreement with the French, it made little sense for him to keep the fact secret.[183] Whatever the truth in this complex question, there was certainly no suspicion in the English camp that Adolf might have betrayed their cause, and Edward never recriminated against the German king, although his dislike of Albrecht of Habsburg, who succeeded to the throne in 1298, is certainly attested.[184]

Edward's relations with another of the allies, John, count of Holland, are revealed by the letters surviving in English archives. John's father, Florence, had been murdered in the previous year, as a result of his pro-French leanings, and there is some suspicion of English involvement in the murder, given the favour that Edward showed to one of the knights responsible, John de Renesse. Edward took a rather high-handed attitude towards John. The latter had been betrothed to the English king's daughter, Elizabeth, since 1281, and the marriage finally took place on 7 January 1297, but Edward was unwilling to allow his daughter to go to Holland, treating her virtually as a hostage. By 18 October John's correspondence had become very bitter, resenting the prevarications of his father-in-law over this matter, and taking grave exception to the threatened return of Count Florence's murderers to his territory.[185] The coalition was also marred by a minor dispute with the duke of Brabant over the date of his proposed knighting by Edward I.[186] The English king does not seem to have been as diplomatic as might have been expected towards the allies he had sailed to protect in their time of danger.

[183] This memorandum is printed by F. Funck-Brentano, 'Document pour servir à l'histoire des relations de la France avec l'Angleterre et l'Allemagne sous le règne de Philippe le Bel', *Revue Historique*, xxxix (1889), 326–48; and in *Monumenta Germaniae Historica, Constitutiones*, iii, 632–5. The fullest discussion in English of the alleged bribery of Adolf of Nassau is by G. Barraclough, 'Edward I and Adolf of Nassau', *Cambridge Historical Journal*, vi (1940), 225–62; but for a more balanced recent survey, see Trautz, *Die Könige von England und das Reich, 1272–1377*, pp. 149–72.

[184] P. Chaplais, 'Some Private Letters of Edward I', *E.H.R.*, lxxvii (1962), 85.

[185] No. 160. For the announcement of the murder in 1296 to Edward I, see *Acta Imperii*, nos. 111, 112. The alliance with Holland is discussed by Sturler, *Les relations politiques et les échanges commerciaux entre le duché de Brabant et l'Angleterre au moyen âge*, pp. 181–6.

[186] No. 164.

Edward was severely embarrassed by a lack of funds during his stay in Flanders. The most striking indication of his difficulties is the loan of 4,000 *livres tournois* he borrowed on 3 October from a group of merchants of Asti upon security of jewels worth 7,015 *livres tournois*. Repayment was specified as either 4,300 *livres* by 1 January 1298, or 4,600 *livres* by 1 April. It is rare to find an interest rate made as explicit as this, while the scale of the charges Edward was asked to pay is a good indication of the state of English credit in the Low Countries. In the event, Edward had to employ the Italian company of the Frescobaldi to come to his rescue, redeeming the jewels for £1,290. The original loan had been worth £1,000. Another Italian, Albisso de Fifanti, lent 930 *livres parisis* to Edward, at a cost in interest of £34 5s. 8d.[187] A debt that the king owed to a group of citizens of Ypres was not paid off on time by the exchequer in England.[188] By early February Edward was informing the exchequer of his effective bankruptcy, stating that he could not return home until money was sent to discharge his obligations to his Burgundian allies, and to deliver him and his men from Flanders. In the event, it was again the Frescobaldi who came to the king's rescue, advancing the sums necessary for his disentanglement. This firm was soon to take the place once held by the Ricciardi. A striking piece of evidence of its relationship with the crown is a royal order forbidding the diversion of funds from the customs which had been promised to them, even though the money was badly needed in Scotland.[189]

A letter sent on 30 January 1298 to John de Lisle testifies to the financial difficulties facing the government at home, with the demands for funds both in Flanders and Scotland. Arrears of lay and clerical taxes were to be collected, and the importance of having sufficient financial means to face the enemies of the realm was stressed.[190] Stronger evidence is provided by the affair of the ransom of John de St John, seneschal of Gascony. He had been captured at Bellegarde, and his ransom fixed at £5,000. There was the greatest difficulty in raising this. Thomas Paynel, St John's attorney, found Italian companies unwilling to accept royal security, insisting in spite of considerable pressure on receiving security from monastic houses. Even this was not easily obtained, several communities resisting the king's demands. In the end the matter was successfully concluded, and St John released, long before the majority of those who had been

---

[187] No. 206; Fryde, 'Financial Resources of Edward I in the Netherlands', 1178–9; B.L., Add. MS. 7965, fo. 29.
[188] No. 185.
[189] Fryde, 'Financial Resources of Edward I in the Netherlands', 1175–6; *infra*, no. 189.
[190] No. 192.

captured by the French in Gascony. The weakness of the king's credit had, however, been very clearly demonstrated.[191]

In a letter about his daughter Mary's affairs, sent some time before his departure for Flanders, Edward had expressed some concern lest in his absence abroad his orders might not be carried out properly.[192] This fear does not seem to have been justified. The bulk of the surviving writs sent by the king to the government at home under the charge of Reginald de Grey relate to requests made by those present in the army, and appear to have been properly implemented. Actions of novel disseisin were halted, debts owed to men on campaign were to be levied by the exchequer on their behalf, and in general the king tried to ensure that no one would suffer loss to their possessions because they had chosen to accompany him overseas.[193] The practice of granting pardons to prisoners in return for service, first used on a large scale in 1294, is illustrated by the example of Scots imprisoned at Berwick being permitted to go to Flanders,[194] and by a petition for such a pardon, complete with striking extenuating circumstances to which the king was likely to be extremely sympathetic.[195] Of considerable interest is a letter asking the authorities to take action against one of Roger de Mowbray's retainers who had failed to come on the campaign as he had contracted to do. The practice of retaining men in this way was certainly common at this time, but this is a unique example of the threat of legal action in a case where the terms of the indenture were not adhered to. Edward presumably felt particularly strongly in this case, given the severe problems that there had been in recruiting men for the Flemish campaign.[196] The king's letters also show a proper respect for the observance of the truce agreements, especially in demanding restitution of goods in the case of merchants who had suffered loss during the cessation of open hostilities.[197]

In retrospect, Edward I was very fortunate in 1297, even though he did not achieve a victory over Philip IV akin to his triumphs over the Welsh and the Scots. In a letter to the treasurer and barons of the exchequer he had stressed that it was above all on the matter of Gascony that his honour depended, and in the course of the negotiations that followed the campaign of 1297–98 he was able to recover

[191] Nos. 190, 197, 198, 205; *Rôles Gascons*, iii, clxvi.

[192] No. 103.

[193] Nos. 166, 167, 171, 175, 183. No. 187 suggests that there might be some delay on occasion in implementing the king's wishes with regard to those in his service.

[194] No. 162.

[195] Nos. 137, 138.

[196] No. 135. For surviving indentures of retainer dating from 1297, see G. Barraclough, *The Earldom and County Palatine of Chester* (Oxford, 1953), p. 36; N. Denholm-Young, *Seignorial Administration in England* (Oxford, 1937), pp. 167–8; *Calendar of Documents relating to Scotland*, ii, nos. 905, 981, 1004.

[197] No. 195.

possession of the duchy.[198] Some of the fears expressed by the opposition at home had been justified: the Flemings had proved unreliable, and, above all, the Scots at the battle of Stirling Bridge had taken advantage of Edward's absence abroad. Yet, partly because that defeat aroused patriotic feelings in a way that Edward's propaganda earlier had failed to do, the threat of civil war never materialized. It may seem that the king's decision to set out on campaign overseas at a time when England was in political turmoil was foolhardy, yet criticism of the king would surely have been far more bitter if the expedition, to support which such unpopular measures had been taken, had not taken place. It is also possible that in the king's absence it was easier to reach some form of settlement at home. The king may have been unwilling to yield, and according to Guisborough hesitated for three days before granting the *Confirmatio*,[199] but his ministers clearly found it easier to effect what proved to be a surprisingly satisfactory compromise. The concessions that were made did not provide a major check to the crown in the future, although the events of 1297 certainly were a substantial setback for Edward I's more arbitrary tendencies. The conclusion of the crisis reinforced the tradition of government by counsel and consent which the king himself had done much to foster earlier in the reign. It was in the matter of the clergy that fundamental principles were most at stake, with Winchelsey's stand against royal taxation. Yet even here, successful as the archbishop was in establishing the privileged position of the clergy, Edward I was able to solve the problem of taxing the church with the aid of a compliant pope, willing to share the profits of papal taxes with the crown. As far as the laity was concerned, the objections were more to the measures of prise, taxation, and military service themselves, than to the principles underlying them, though in the resolution of the crisis constitutional definition became necessary. The crisis was one which sprang out of the immediate circumstances and needs of war, and was not the product of a widespread and fundamental dissatisfaction with the manner of the king's government.

[198] No. 159. The peace negotiations are summarized by F. M. Powicke, *The Thirteenth Century* (2nd edn., Oxford, 1962), pp. 650–4.
[199] *Guisborough*, p. 313.

TEXT

1. *Exchequer memorandum, 13 February 1297*

Memorandum quod tertiodecimo die Februarii venit hic coram venerabili patre Waltero de Langetone, Coventr' et Lychef' episcopo, thesaurario, Philippo de Wylughby cancellario de scaccario, Johanne de Cobham, Petro de Leyc' et Johanne de Insula, baronibus de eodem scaccario assidentibus eis venerabili patre Antonio Dunolm' episcopo, Johanne de Drokenesford' custode garderobe regis et aliis fidelibus ipsius regis, Hugo le Despenser proferens prefatis thesaurario et baronibus breve regis sub privato sigillo in hec verba:

Edwardus dei gratia rex Anglie etc., thesaurario et baronibus de scaccario suo, salutem. Mandamus vobis firmiter iniungentes quod ea que dilectus et fidelis noster Hugo le Despenser vobis ex parte nostra duxerit iniungenda credatis confidenter et studeatis efficaciter adimplere. Et hoc nullatenus omittatis. Dat' sub privato sigillo nostro apud Brandone Ferye'[1] ix die Februarii, anno xxv.

Et huius brevis auctoritate predictus Hugo iniunxit prefatis thesaurario et baronibus quod nullus clericus admittatur ad placitandum in scaccario, nec aliquod breve pro aliquo clerico inde emanet, nec aliquod placitum motum in eodem scaccario ad sectam alicuius clerici ulterius exequatur, nisi profferant hic litteras patentes domini regis de protectione sua, nec licet alicui clerico sive sit de scaccario sive non aliquid sit forisfactum nullum inde sibi fiat remedium nisi ut supra etc., set si aliquod placitum motum sit in scaccario inter laicum querentem et clericum defendentem seu fuerit movendum, admittatur et exequatur modo debito secundum quod lex et consuetudines scaccarii predicti exigunt etc. ad sectam laici querentis. Nunciavit insuper[a] prefatus Hugo dictis thesaurario et baronibus ex parte regis quod religiosi aliegene quorum possessiones capte fuerunt in manu regis et iuxta extentam earundem factam per certum finem hic per annum regi reddendum eisdem committuntur, habeant breve pro negotiis suis domos suos tangentibus et prosequi possunt in scaccario ea que eos contingere dinoscuntur et eo modo per scaccarium eis succuratur sicut[b] prius fieri solebat et quod si quid capiatur de bladis huiusmodi religiosorum, habeant breve de scaccario de restitucione inde habenda.

E 368/68, m. 22d.

[a] *word interlined.*
[b] *MS.* sicus.
[1] Brandon Ferry, Suff.

2. *Edward I on behalf of the bishop of Ely, 13 February 1297*

Rex omnibus ad quos presentes littere pervenerint, salutem. Sciatis quod pro utilitate regni nostri recepimus die confectionis presencium litterarum nomine mutui a venerabili patre domino W. dei gratia Eliensi episcopo mille libras sterlingorum in pecunia numerata per manus thesaurarii et camerariorum nostrorum apud Westm', solvendas eidem vel suo certo attornato has litteras ad scaccarium nostrum apud Westm' deferenti quam cicius commode potuerimus, et super hoc fuerimus requisiti. Et si contingat quod dictus Elyensis episcopus habuerit seu receperit litteras obligatorias venerabilis patris W. Coventr' et Lich' episcopi, thesaurarii nostri, seu dilectorum et fidelium nostrorum Hugonis le Despenser et Johannis de Berewik' de predicta summa milium librarum nomine nostro dicto episcopo Eliensis solvenda, quod presens littera nostra sit penitus irrita et inanis. In cuius rei testimonium has litteras nostras fieri fecimus patentes. Teste P. de Wylugby, tenente locum thesaurarii nostri apud Westm' xiii die Februarii, anno regni nostri vicesimo quinto.[1]

E 368/68, m. 23d.

3. *Edward I to the keepers of the customs at Boston, 18 February 1297*

Rex custodibus custume apud Sanctum Botolphum, salutem. Cum nuper pro debitis, in quibus Taldo Janyan et sociis suis mercatoribus de societate Friscobaldorum Alborum tenemur, tam per breve de scaccario nostro quam per thesaurarium nostrum vobis districte esset iniunctum quod in partem solucionis debitorum illorum dictos mercatores ccc saccos lane sue usque ad partes transmarinas libere et licite absque aliqua custuma exigenda ab eisdem transducere permitteretis, dum tamen facerent vobis litteras suas patentes numerum saccorum et custumam inde provenientem distincte et aperte continentes, ac iidem mercatores ut ex relatu eorundem accepimus iam lanas suas usque ad summam cc saccorum tantum ad partes predictas vehi fecerint. Vobis mandamus firmiter iniungentes quod eosdem mercatores illos c saccos lane qui supersunt de summa predicta usque ad partes Brabant', Flandr', Holand' vel Zeland' libere transducere permittatis in forma predicta, recipientes ab eisdem litteras suas patentes numerum saccorum et custumam inde emergentem continentes. Et

[1] This document is immediately followed in the roll by the receipt dated 1 October 1297 (no. 145). For a similar loan to this one made by Reginald de Brandon on 18 February 1297, repayable at Easter, for which he received letters of obligation from Walter Langton, the treasurer, see E 159/70, m. 17.

nos vobis inde in compoto vestro debitam allocationem habere faciemus; illud quod in premissis feceritis dicto thesaurario et baronibus de scaccario nostro quamprimum poteritis constare faciatis. Teste W. Coventr' et Lich' episcopo xviii die Februarii, anno xxv^{to}.[1]

E 159/70, m. 110.

4. *Edward I to Richard of Louth, William Trussel and Robert de Segre, 18 February 1297*

Rex dilectis et fidelibus suis Ricardo de Luda, Willelmo Trussel vice-comiti Kanc' et Roberto de Segre, salutem. Cum dilectus clericus noster magister Petrus Amarici persona ecclesie de Pecham[2] in comitiva venerabilis patris W. Coventr' et Lich' episcopi thesaurarii nostri profecturus sit ad partes Flandrie,[3] vobis mandamus quod de capcione bladorum ipsius magistri Petri de ecclesia sua predicta ad opus nostrum in nullo vos intromittatis. Et si quid de bladis suis ad opus nostrum cepistis id eidem sine dilacione restitui faciatis. Teste W. Coventr' et Lich' episcopo xviii die Februarii, anno xxv^{to}.

E 159/70, m. 119d.

5. *Exchequer memorandum, 20 February 1297*

Memorandum quod xx° die Februarii, anno presenti, ordinatum fuit in scaccario per venerabilem patrem W. de Langeton', Coventr' et Lich' episcopum, thesaurarium, Hugonem le Despenser, justiciarium foreste citra Trentam, Johannem de Berewik', Johannem de Drokenesforth', custodem garderobe regis, Johannem de Metingham, justiciarium regis de banco, Gilbertum de Roubery et barones de scaccario et alios de consilio regis eis assidentes, quod protectiones fiant de sigillo scaccarii omnibus clericis volentibus facere finem in forma

---

[1] Similar instructions were issued on the same date to the keepers of the customs at Hull, permitting the Frescobaldi to export 134 sacks 8 stones of wool, the remaining part of a total of 250 sacks (E 159/70, m. 110). Earlier, on 4 December 1296, the Fresco-baldi had been granted 400 marks out of the customs at Boston in payment of debts, and permission to export 100 sacks of wool to Brabant or Holland, with respite of payment of customs until Easter (E 159/70, m. 100d). For licences to the Spini to export 84 sacks from Boston and 16 sacks from London, and the Frescobaldi for 500 sacks from Newcastle, with the customs duty being used to pay off the crown's debts to them in part, see E 159/70, m. 113d.

[2] Peckham, Kent.

[3] Pierre Emerik received royal protection for a year, as he was going overseas with the treasurer, on 17 February 1297, and a further protection on 18 February, as a result of paying his fine for the clerical fifth (*C.P.R., 1292–1301*, pp. 235–6). See also no. 186.

provisa, et similiter brevia clausa vicecomitibus de terris et tenementis, bonis et catallis suis ea occasione captis in manum regis sibi
restituendis, quousque super hoc sciatur voluntas regis. Ita quod
singuli duo*a* pro singulis protectionibus duo solidi recipiantur et alii
denarii quos continget recipere pro aliis brevibus clausis dictum
negocium tangentibus cedant regi in comodum et per aliquem clericum ad hoc iuratum colligentur et liberentur in thesauro regis. Et
eodem die predictus J. de Drokenesforth*b* assignavit Walterum de
Palacio cappellanum ad recipiendum denarios ad opus regis pro
protectionibus predictis, et ad reddendum inde compotum ad
scaccarium.

E 159/70, m. 10d; E 368/68, m. 23d.

6. *Notarial instrument, 27 February 1297*

Presens publicum instrumentum inspecturis pateat manifeste, quod
anno videlicet a nativitate domini millesimo ducentesimo nonagesimo
septimo, intrante indictione decima, die Cinerum, vicesima septima
die scilicet mensis Februarii, officiis et ostiis officiorum infra septa
prioratus ecclesie Christi Cantuarie et ipsius monasterii inventorum,
ut vulgariter dicebatur, sequestratis et sub sequestro positis dicto die
per quemdam Johannem Dymmok,*c* serenissimi principis domini
Edwardi dei gratia regis Anglie illustris ut dicebatur nuntium ad hoc
missum, et de precepto ac mandato ipsius regis septa monasterii sepe-
dicti ac ipsum monasterium una cum vicecomite Kancie et alia comitiva, ut asserebatur, ingredientem circa horam tertiam, omniaque et
singula officia de quibus inferius fit mentio tam infra claustra eiusdem
monasterii quam extra, ut prima facie apparebat, sigillo quodam inferius descripto sequestri nomine consignantem, et monachis ipsius
ecclesie alimenta vite necessaria esculenta precipue et poculenta
quibus ipso die vesci debebant, ut asserebant, penitus denegantem,
ecclesiastice privilegio postposito libertatis, quod satis erat eodem die
in instanti per totam civitatem Cantuariensem publicum et notorium
et publice divulgatum; quidam ipsius monasterii monacorum, quibus
precipue ipsius prioratus committebantur post priorem negotia dis-
ponenda, perpendentes et coniecturantes verisimiliter huiusmodi
sevitiam et violentiam potius ad eorum personarum, ut dicebant, con-
fusionem quam rerum suarum seu possessionum subventionem seu
subsidium adquirendum commissam, in non modicum ipsorum et
ecclesie sue predicte posse verti obprobrium atque dampnum, si eam
conniventibus oculis pertransirent, non audentes tamen ut dicebant

---

a Sic in MS.   *b MS.* Drokenesfortd.   *c MS.* Dynnok.

propter metum regium in presentia dicti nuntii sicut premittitur sequestrantis aliquam vocare personam per quam sevitie et violentie factum huiusmodi in futuram posset redigi memoriam vel reduci; immediate post prandium dicto die, me infrascriptum notarium in suum predictum monasterium convocarunt, rogantes diligenter ut dicta sequestra sic apposita inspicerem, et super in hac parte inventis eis publicum facerem instrumentum. Ductus igitur secrete et non palam, propter insidias regalium ministrorum circummorantium, per fratrem Ricardum de Clyva dicte ecclesie monacum de officio ad officium ostiatim, et primo per medium claustri quoddam ostium ducens ab ipso claustro in quoddam cellarium et aliud ostium a parte exteriori, in quo cellario liberationes corradiorum, ostium maioris cellarii ubi esculenta et poculenta conventus, ostium lardarii ubi totum coquine instaurum, ostium hospitalarie ubi hospites solebant recipi, necnon ostium granarii ubi annone instaurum reponebantur ut dicebatur, vidi, inspexi et repperi clausa et signata in medio singule serrure impressione cuiusdam sigilli parvi rotondi in viridi cera impressi, habentis in medio imaginem quasi leonis rapacis infra binum quadratum nodatum et in angulis se complectens et in circumferencia has litteras *ci repos. Demum ductus ut prius versus portam curie monacorum[a] ego infrascriptus notarius vidi quemdam Ricardum vocatum de Celeby portantem quandam virgulam nomine officii janitoris qui dicebat ita se nominari, et ibidem loco janitoris esse positum ex parte dicti domini regis ac etiam constitutum.

Et ego Henricus de Tychefeld' clericus Wintoniensis diocesis, apostolica publicus auctoritate notarius, prefata sigilla ad modum sequestri sub unius impressionis forma singulis officiis premissis imposita et impressa, prefatumque janitorem sic constitutum ut supra fit mentio, vidi, repperi et diligenter inspexi, anno indictione et die prefatis inter horam nonam et vesperarum, presentibus religiosis viris fratribus Waltero suppriore, Johanne de Welles cellerario, Johanne coquinario et Ricardo de Clyve et aliis monachis pluribus ecclesie memorate ad quorum omnium rogatum et instantiam premissa omnia ut superius continetur in publicam formam redegi meoque signo et nomine roboravi.

Canterbury, Dean and Chapter Archives, Chartae Antiquae, x 3.

7. *Edward I to the prelates of the province of Canterbury, 27 February 1297*

Edwardus dei gracia etc., venerabili in Christo patri episcopo etc., salutem. Intellecto quod venerabilis pater Robertus Cantuariensis

---

[a] *Followed by* vidi, *cancelled.*

archiepiscopus contra ministros nostros clericos et laicos et maxime contra illos quos in protectionem nostram susceperimus quasdam excommunicationum sentencias proponebat, promulgavit et per suam provinciam faceret promulgari, quod si late et promulgate essent in corone et dignitatis nostre lesionem et preiudicium redundaret, eidem archiepiscopo prohibuimus ne aliquas huiusmodi sentencias promulgaret seu facere promulgari. Et quia nostra exheredatio et tocius regni subversio possit verisimiliter ex hoc sequi, vobis similiter prohibemus ne aliquas sentencias, que in corone vel dignitatis nostre lesionem et preiudicium possint cedere, quoquomodo pretextu alicuius mandati vobis a quocunque directi vel dirigendi, denunciari seu publicare aliquatenus presumatis. Teste meipso apud Clarind'[1] xxvii die Februarii, anno regni nostri xxv[to].[2]

Bodleian Library, MS. Laud Misc. 529, fo. 84v. Printed in Denton, 'The Crisis of 1297 from the Evesham Chronicle', 571.

8. *Edward I to Philip de Willoughby and John Droxford, 4 March 1297*

Edward par la grace de dieu etc, a ses chiers clerks Phelip de Wyleghby e Johan de Drokenesford, saluz. Nous avoms bien entendu ceo qe vous avez fait e ordene a faire de celuy qui est encuse contrefesour des bulles,[3] sicome vous nous mandastes, la queu chose nous tenoms assez aperte. Et nous semble qe vous en avez overe bien e aviseement de quei nous nous tenoms mult bien apaiez, e vous savoms bon gre. Et vus maundoms qe saunz nul delay faciez prendre en nostre meyn quantquil ad e sun corps metter en sauve garde a nostre Tour de Loundres, tant qe nous en eoms autre chose ordenee. Et nous faciez savoir par vos lettres au plus tost qe vous porrez quantque vous aurez fet de ceste chose, e du cuoyn ausint, dunt nous vous mandastes. E metez peyne de enquerre de touz ses compaynouns del un fait e del autre endreit des queux nous voloms qe soit feit ausi come de luy meismes en touz poynz. Donees de souz nostre prive seal a Clarendone le iiii iour de Marz, lan de nostre regne vintisme quint.

E 159/70, mm. 118, 15d; a version with some omissions is in E 368/68, m. 32.

[1] Clarendon, Wilts.
[2] There is no surviving chancery enrolment of this writ; its authenticity is therefore somewhat suspect.
[3] Probably Walter de Maidstone (no. 51; *C.P.R., 1292–1301*, p. 403). Orders for the seizure of his goods were issued on 14 March 1297 (E 368/68, m. 88).

9. *Notarial instrument, 6 March 1297*

Pateat universis presens instrumentum publicum inspecturis quod
cum nuper quedam certa officia infra septa prioratus ecclesie Christi
Cant' de mandato, ut dicebatur, domini Edwardi dei gratia regis
Anglie illustris sequestrata fuissent prout alibi per instrumentum mei
notarii infrascripti monachis eiusdem ecclesie confectum plenius continetur, propter quod quidem sequestrum et eius violentiam quedam
certa summa frumenti inferius expressa in granario ipsius prioratus
deposita et ex parte dicti domini regis inter cetera sequestrata putre-
dini et quasi perditioni totaliter exposita ac etiam in materiam fere
ignitam conversa, ut prima facie videbatur, frater Stephanus de Sand-
wico, monacus ecclesie predicte et granetarius prioratus eiusdem,
quamquam tamen tunc ut dicebat a suo in hac parte ministerio per
dicti regis ministros exclusus, perpendens nihilominus verisimiliter sibi
et conventui dicti monasterii, ad quorum sustentacionem et victum
ipsum bladum servabatur, ut asseruit, dampnum, gravamen, periculum non modicum et preiudicium imminere, volensque propter hoc
sibi super huiusmodi violentia evidens imposterum testimonium
perhiberi, rogavit me infrascriptum notarium ut dictum bladum et
eius qualitatem ceteraque pericula ipsum ob violentiam huiusmodi
contingentia inspicerem et viderem. Accedens igitur ad dictum
granarium, inveniensque clausum ostium et serratum, ascendi in
quoddam solarium ad capud ipsius granarii et per quandam fenes-
tram una cum dicto monaco prefatum granarium introspiciens vidi
et inspexi dictum bladum ad centum summas frumenti videlicet esti-
matum, per medium domus late dispersum per quosdam operarios
tunc ibidem presentialiter existentes, expressos inferius, et ipsum bladum dirigentes etiam ad ventandum eo quod erat ita calidum in pal-
pando quod in eo bene calefieri frigida posset manus, et fumus quasi
exibat ab eo. Item ibidem in presencia mei notarii et monachi preno-
tati accesserunt quidam duo cives Cant', Adam videlicet dictus Beel
et Simon Bartholomei ad granarium antedictum, ipsius ut dicebatur
ex parte dicti domini regis custodiam tunc habentes, et ostium
ipsius granarii cum clavibus quas secum portarunt aperierunt, et
prefatos operarios qui ob causam ventandi dictum bladum inibi
erant clausi dimittentes exire, prefatum ostium̃ reclauserunt, in-
consulto granetario memorato. Actum in granario antedicto,
anno a Nativitate Domini millesimo ducentesimo nonagesimo
septimo, indictione decima, mense Martii, die sexta, hiis operantibus
ut predicitur tunc ibidem, videlicet Johanne de Neugate, Philippo
Bommere, Henrico garcione pistrine, Henrico Roolp, Gilberto
Molendinario, Johanne Molling', Willelmo Puppe, Hamone de May-
destane et Ricardo de Scoutinge, quos tamen non audebat tunc

dictus granetarius propter metum regium ut dicebat in testimonium invocare.

Et ego Henricus de Tichefeld clericus Wintoniensis diocesis apostolica publicus auctoritate notarius predictum bladum sic putrefactum vidi et palpavi, dictosque custodes intrare et exire ut premittitur, et ipsos operarios operantes circa ipsum bladum similiter vidi et omnia premissa prout superius conscribuntur ad rogatum dicti granetarii in publicam formam redegi, meoque signo et nomine roboravi.[1]

Canterbury, Dean and Chapter Archives, Chartae Antiquae, C. 169.

10. *Edward I to the barons of the exchequer, 6 March 1297*

Edward par la grace de deu etc. Nous vous mandoms fermement enioignauntz qe, si Johan Bygod frere le conte le mareschal viegne a vous por avoir protection ou pur faire sa fin, soiez avisez qe pur nul fin ou purchaz qi il porra faire, ou pur chose qui peust avenir ne ly delivrez nule maniere de seisine des terres ne des tenemens qui furent soens e qui sont lay fye, einz faciez retenir en nostre mein tote la temporaute quil ont denz nostre roiaume tant qe vous eez sur ce especial mandement de nous meismes. Don' desuz nostre prive seal a Clarendone le vi iur de Marz, lan de nostre regne xxv.[2]

E 159/70, m. 15; E 368/68, m. 31.

11. *Letters patent, 7 March 1297*

Quia ex gravi querela plurimum de comitatu Suth' tam pro se quam pro ceteris de communitate eiusdem comitatu rex accepit quod collectores denariorum ad sustentacionem custodie maris in comitatu Suth' faciendam, non racione contribucionis sed violencia gravissime extorsionis homines eiusdem comitatu deprimunt et molestant, capiendo de quibusdam pro viginti solidatis terre qualibet septimana vii d., et de aliis secundum maius et minus ad voluntatem suam, et iuxta quod maiorem favorem erga eosdem collectores habent et denarios inde provenientes pro maiori parte penes se detinent, et sibi ipsis appropriant, et eciam quosdam alios de huiusmodi contribucione omnino in pace dimittunt in depauperacionem tocius populi regis, et impedimentum et defraudacionem custodie predicte; rex assig-

---

[1] For this document, see C. R. Cheney, *Notaries Public in England* (Oxford, 1972), p. 70.

[2] John Bigod was granted royal protection on the testimony of Alan Plukenet on 4 April 1297 (*C.P.R., 1292–1301*, p. 273). On 7 April the sheriff of Lincolnshire was ordered to restore his lands to him (*C.C.R., 1296–1302*, p. 25).

navit Johannem Randolf et Henricum de Gildeford ad inquirendum modis omnibus quibus rei veritas melius scire poterit et inquiriri qui huiusmodi pecuniam extorserint, vel qui pecuniam de contributoribus eiusdem comitatus ad predictam custodiam faciendam levaverint et penes se detinuerint, et sibi ipsis appropriaverint vel aliquid inde defraudaverint, et quantum et de quibus personis vel qui racione parcendi vel gravandi pecuniam fraudulenter acceperint, et quantum huiusmodi occasione ceperint. Et mandatum est eisdem Johanni et Henrici quod ad certos diem et locum quos ad hoc providerint et vocatis coram eis collectoribus predicti comitatu, et omnibus aliis quod predictum negocium contingit, inquisicionem illam facere in forma predicta. Mandatum est eciam vicecomiti predicti comitatu quod ad certos diem et locum quos ei scire faciant coram eis tot et tales probos et legales homines de comitatu predicto per quos rei veritas in premissis melius sciri poterit et inquiriri. In cuius rei testimonium etc. T. P. de Wileghby etc., vii° die Marcii anno xxv^{to}.

E 159/70, m. 66d.

12. *Edward I to the barons of the exchequer, 8 March 1297*

Edward par la grace dieu etc. Nous avoms bien entendu les lettres qe vous nous envoyastes par le porteur de cestes, par les queles vous nous maundastes coment vous aviez ordine pur resceyvre les fyns de ceux de la clergie,[1] e avoms encharge nostre chaunceler qil tiegne mesmes cele ordinaunce devers lui, kar il nous semble qe la fourme est bone, par quoi nous voloms qe vous la tiegnez e en facez solum ceo qe vous verrez qe bien soit. E vous maundoms si le clerk le counte de Hollaunde soit passe; qe vous nous facez savoir ou e qaunt e tut coment il passa e, sil ne soit uncore passee, nous faciez savoir kaunt il devera passier, e le achaisoun pur quoy il est demorrez. Doneez sutz nostre prive seal a Langeford[2] le viii iour de Marz lan de nostre regne xxv.

E 368/68, m. 32; E 159/70, m. 15d.

13. *Edward I to the deputy treasurer and barons of the exchequer, 9 March 1297*

Edward par la grace dieu etc. Come aucuns chivaux qui sunt as valletz

---

[1] Presumably the memorandum of 20 February 1297 (no. 5). The instructions issued to the bannerets and sheriffs for the taking of clerical fines, on 1 March 1297, appear to have only been sent to the exchequer on 13 March (no. 16; *C.P.R., 1292–1301*, p. 240).   [2] Langford, Wilts.

larchevesqe de Caunterbirs soient arestez a Maydenstan en noun de nous, a ceo qe nous avoms entendu;[1] nous, lur voillauntz faire especial grace in cele partie a ceste foiz, vous maundoms qe les chivaux, qe les valletz lays poessent pruver estre lur propres, facez deliverer a mesmes les valletz ensemblement ove les garsouns qe ceux chivaux gardent a cest foiz de nostre grace. Doneez sutz nostre prive seal a Brummore[2] le ix iour de Mars, lan de nostre regne xxv.

E 368/68, m. 32; another version in E 159/70, m. 15d.

14. *Edward I to the deputy treasurer and barons of the exchequer, 9 March 1297*

Edward par la grace [de] dieu roi Dengleterre, seigneur Dirlande e ducs Daquitaine, au tenant le lieu le tresourier e as barons del escheqer, salutz. A la requeste de nostre foial e loial Johan sire de Cuyk vous mandoms qe vous faciez regardier coment aucunes vedues demorantes a Loundres, qui sont acustumees a herberger marchandz de Brabant qi y vienent, sont taxees. Car il nous ad mande qe eles ne porroient en nule maniere suffrir a paier solonc ce qe hom les ad taxees, eynz leur covendreit aler en Brebant e lesser du tot la vile de Londres, par quei nous voloms qe vous enquergez coment eles sont assises e si vous troefsetz qe eles en soient grevees autrement qe eles deverount, qe vous en eyez tieu regard, e faciez la chose en tieu manere redrescer, come vus veretz qi face a faire par reson. Don' souz nostre prive seal a Brommore le ix iour de Marz, lan de nostre regne xxv.

E 159/70, m. 11.

15. *Ordinance for the collection of royal debts, 12 March 1297*

Pur ceo qe viscountes e lour souz baillifs, taxours e quilleurs ne unt leve ne lever ne volent les dettes le rey, ne les deniers sourdauntz des taxours e des eides grauntez au rei countre leur serment, a graunt damage au rei e a grant peril du reaume, est ordine qe certeines gentz aillent es countez Dengleterre a seurveer e examiner les fetz des

---

[1] For this incident of the seizure of Winchelsey's horses, see *Reg. Winchelsey*, pp. 216–17. The seizure of two horses belonging to the prior of Christ Church, Canterbury (no. 46), presumably took place at the same time.
[2] Breamore, Hants.

viscountes e des autres avantdiz en ceste forme, cest asaver qe, en les countiez ou triding seunt allent de triding en triding pur eese du poeple auxi en haste com il purrount. E es countez ou triding ne sount point, seit le counte partie en quatre ou en cink parties ou en plus ou en mains, solom la grandour e la petitsce du counte, e la aillent de partie e pur eese du poeple sicom desouz est dit. E facent venir devant eus viscountes, e les baillifs de meismes le triding ou de partie de counte qui ore sunt e qe unt este ces treis aunz prochein passez, e ausy les chiefs taxours ou lun de eaux e aukuns de seus taxours de mesmes le triding ou partie du counte, e sis prodes hommes de checun hundred ou wappentak denz triding, ou partie de counte, a certeyns jour e liu auxi bien denz fraunchises com de hors. E illoques veient les nouns de touz ceaux qui dettes deivent au rey, auxi bien par sou-mounses del eschequer, estretes e brief com des eides avauntditz e tute manere des autres dettes. E qe les viscountes e baillifs e les taxours seyent garniz de aveir illoques tutes les estretes des dettes avantditz e en presence du viscounte, baillifs e taxours seient les sis hommes de checun hundred ou wappentak iures e examinez de checun noun dettur, sil eit de quay la dette le rey poet estre leve, e en qui defaute e laschesce demoert qe celes dettes sount taunt arere. E de ceo qe serra trove qe peut estre leve hastivement e qe nest leve, seit le viscounte charge quil le eit a Loundres denz les viii iours apres la mi Quarreme, e quil eit le remenant de ceo qe poet estre leve lende-mayn de la cluse Pasque, e des deniers qe les ditz taxours avereient leve a porrunt lever seient chargez de fere le venir al eschequer de iour de nuit saunz certein iour aveir sour forffaiture de quant quil porrount forfaire au rey. E des tutes choses seit fete certeine remem-braunce entre les dites gentz qui serrount assignez de par le rey e les viscountes e les taxours apertement e distincteaument. E en cele remembraunce seit escrite la somme des dettes qe sount levees e qe porrount estre levees. E certeine signe mis en les estretes des viscountes sur checun neun, issi qe parmy cele somme e cele signe peussent les viscountes estre charges. E cele remembraunce eient, ou enveient, as barouns del eschequier lendemayn de la cluse Pasque desouz lour seaus. E si viscountes, sous viscountes, receyvours des viscountes, chiefs taxours, chiefs baillifs des fraunchises, de triding e de hundred seient attainz quil eient respite la dette le rey, ou desporte a lever la ou ele poet estre levee pur douns ou pur faveur ou autre manere, ou dautre trespas par quey il eient deservi la prisone, seient mis a la prisone e puis seient mainpris par bone e suffisaunte mainprise de estre al eschequer a la quinzeine de Paske a fere leur fins. E si autre petitz gentz, souz baillifs, bedeaus, e autres ceaus seient attaynz de trespas, seient enprisounes sil eient deservi e facent fin illoqes en counte solum richesce e solom la quantite de trespas. E la ou

prisonement ne gist mye seient touz ceauz amercies solom la quantite du trespas.[1]

E 159/70, m. 109.

16. *Edward I to the deputy treasurer and barons of the exchequer, 13 March 1297*

Edward par la grace dieu etc. Nous vous chargeoms[a] especiaument qe les Gascoins qi vienent a vous pur receivre lur paiementz a nostre escheker faciez deliverer en si corteise manere e en si douce qil se tiegnent apaiez. Estre ce nous vous mandoms e comandoms fermement enioignantz en la foi qe vous nous devez qe vous mettez peine de purveer en totes maneres les quinze mil mars dont nous vous avoms mande avant ces houres par Johan de Drokenesford nostre clerk, de quei nous voloms qe les set mil e cinc cent mars seent en deners, e les autres set mil e cink cent mars en ble, outre cele somme qe fu ordine a seynt Eymun,[2] e qe ausi tost se face lune somme come lautre, car autrement tendrums nous tot le remenant a nient, pur ce qe nous lavoms ia fait a saver e promis a nos gentz de Gascoigne. E voloms qe le dit Johan demurge a Londres tant qe il viegne tot[b] la somme entiere, e lacres[c] ausint ovesqe li. Dont nous vous chargioms derechief qe a entre vous de ne demerge mie la defaute qe la somme entiere

[a] *E 159/70 reads* chagions.
[b] *E 159/70 reads* quil vienge tota.
[c] *E 368/68 reads* lautres.

[1] Appointments of clerks were duly made on 12 March 1297, as follows:

Cumb., Westm., Lancs.	Adam del Crokedayk
Yorks.	Hasculf de Cleseby & J. de Meinhull
Lincs.	Lambert de Trikingham
Cambs., Hunts., Norf., Suff.	John de Kirkeby
Midd., Essex, Herts.	Henry de Durham
Kent, Surrey, Sussex	David le Graunt
Hants, Som., Dorset	John de London
Devon, Cornwall	Philip Deverdon
Wilts, Oxon., Berks.	John de Foxle
Beds. & Bucks.	Richard de Kerstan
Northants. & Rutland	Roger de Hegham
Warw., Leics., Salop., Staffs.	William de Pershore
Glos., Worcs., Heref.	Nicholas de Warwick
Notts. & Derbs.	Henry Spigurnel

E 159/70, m. 109.

Payment of expenses to Nicholas de Warwick, William de Pershore, Henry de Durham, Richard de Kerstan, John de Kirkeby and David le Graunt are recorded on the Jornalia Roll (E 405/1/10) between 12 and 15 March.

[2] Bury St Edmunds, Suff.

e lacres ne se facent,[a] car nous nentendoms partir de Plymue[1] vers ou nous aloms de iour en autre tant come nous veoms la flote sigler ou soveauns qe ele[b] seit preste a sigler. E nous faciez savoir par vos lettres lestat del escheker, e ce qe vous en biez faire, e de combien nous nous pooms fier de aveir de vous e dedenz queu temps, issint qe nous seoms pleinement avisez au plus tost qe vous porrez. E nous enveoms a vous e al avantdit Johan suz nostre petit seal lordinance e le poer qe nous avoms bailez as baneretz les quex nous avoms enveez en divers contez. E vous mandoms qe de iours de paiement e des autres choses qe vous verrez qe seient a mander lour facent les avisez e lour mandez, e qui vous entendez qe mieux seit pur nostre profit e pur deners lever ove tot la haste qe hom porra, car le bosoign est chescun iour greignur[c] qe autre. Et de ceo qe nous avoms entendu qe vous ne savez mie si vous devez prendre finz de ceux de la clergie sicome vous feistes avant ce qe les banerets furent assignez parmi les contez, sachiez qe nostre volunte est qe tutes foiz se facent les fyns ausi bien al escheker e a la chancelerie come aillours. Donez desuz nostre prive seal a Bremmore le xiii iour de Mars, lan de nostre regne xxv.

E 159/70, m. 15d; E 368/68, m. 32.

17. *Edward I to the deputy treasurer and the barons of the exchequer, 13 March 1297*

Edward etc. au lieu tenaunt nostre tresourier e as barouns del eschequier, saluz. Nous vous enveoms deus pere de lettres les queles vindrent de Cardoyl,[2] escrites a .. levesqe de Cestre nostre tresourier, e les queles nous feismes overir en aventure si nules noveles en feussent contenues. E pur ceo qe la respounse des dites lettres apartient a vostre place, vous maundoms qe vous en faciez ceo qui vous verrez qe face a faire. Don' souz nostre prive seal a Brommore le xiii iour de Marz.

E 368/68, m. 9d.

18. *Edward I to John le Bretoun and the sheriff of Middlesex, 14 March 1297*

Rex dilecto et fideli suo Johanni le Bretoun et vicecomiti Midd', salutem. Cum assignaverimus vos ad recogniciones prelatorum et aliorum

---

[a] *E368/68 reads* qe la somme entiere ne la crus se facent.
[b] *E 159/70 reads* le.   [c] greignur *omitted in E 368/68.*

---

[1] Plymouth, Devon.   [2] Carlisle, Cumb.

clericorum quorumcumque protectionem nostram hiis diebus non habencium, et eam habere volencium in comitatu predicto, capiendas nomine nostro prout in forma per nos et consilium nostrum inde provisa, vobis nuper commissa plenius continetur; vobis mandamus in fide et dilectione quibus nobis tenemini firmiter iniungentes quod prelatis et aliis clericis quibuscumque qui coram vobis huiusmodi recogniciones fecerint, vel citra crastinum medie quadragesime que iam instat sint facturi; scire faciatis quod medietate summe pecunie recogniciones suas contingentis ad scaccarium nostrum apud Westm' ad eandem diem vel die Lune proximo post sine ulteriori dilacione satisfaciant, et illis qui huiusmodi recogniciones a predicto crastino in antea coram vobis facere contigerint quod medietatem summe nobis per ipsos recogniture ad dictum scaccarium nostrum a tempore sue recognicionis solvi faciant sine mora, alioquin terras et tenementa, bona et catalla eorum omnia que certis de causis nuper in manum nostram capi fecimus et pretextu huiusmodi recognicionum de gratia nostra speciali iam eisdem concessimus restitui ut nostis incurrantur. Et scire faciatis baronibus de scaccario nostro apud Westm' ad alterum dierum predictorum quot et quibus prefixeritis hec predicta et summam quemlibet eorum contingentem sub sigillo vestro distincte et aperte, hoc sicut commodum nostrum et totius regni nostri diligitis nullatenus omittentes. Et habeatis ibi hoc breve. Teste P. de Wylugby etc. xiiii die Martii, anno xxv°, per breve de privato sigillo.[1]

E 368/68, m. 90.

19. *Edward I to the deputy treasurer and the keeper of the wardrobe, 15 March 1297*

Edward etc., a nos chiers clerks e foiaux Phelip' de Wileghby, tenaunt le lieu nostre tresourier, e a Johan de Drokenesford gardein de nostre garderobe, saluz. Nous vous maundoms qe touz ceaux qui nous deivent le servise de muer nos estours faciez somondre e venir devant vous a Loundres por resceivre nos estours les queux nous y enverroms procheinement, e pur faire sour ceo le servise quil deivent, sicome nostre feal e loial William de Carleton vous dirra plus pleinement de par nous.[2] Endreit des trente mile mars en deniers, e des trente mile marchees de bliez, dount nous vous avoms chargez avaunt ces houres

[1] Similar writs were issued to all the other bannerets and sheriffs appointed to take fines from the clergy.
[2] See no. 22 for the summons of those who owed falconry service.

pur enveer en Gascoigne,[1] uncore vous enchargeoms quantqe nous
pooms qe vous ensouveregne en tieu maniere qe nous nen failloms
mie. Car si rien en fausist, e nous tendrioms a deceu, e nos gentz qui
sount en Gascoigne a trahiz. Dons souz nostre prive seal a Ringwode[2]
le xv iour de Marz, lan xxv.

E 159/70, m. 18.

20. *Edward I to John Lovel and the sheriff of Oxfordshire and Berkshire,
20 March 1297*

Rex dilectis et fidelibus suis Johanni Lovel et vicecomiti Oxon' et
Berk', salutem. Licet nuper vobis mandaremus quod recogniciones
prelatorum, religiosorum et aliorum clericorum iuxta concessionem
bonorum suorum in defensionem regni et ecclesie Anglicane con-
vertendorum, et pro protectione nostra habenda admitteretis, et quod
de singulis summis iuxta predictas recogniciones thesaurario et
baronibus nostris de scaccario apud Westm' constare faceretis, et illas
ibidem liberaretis. Nos tamen tum propter pecunie indigenciam[a]
variam et necessariam que nobis et regno nostro ad presens incumbit,
tum propter misas et expensas dictorum clericorum parcendas, pre-
sertim cum expensarum gravitatem non evaderent, si soluciones suas
ad scaccarium nostrum ad mediam quadragesimam singulatim facere
deberent, volentes quod denarii qui nobis debentur seu debebantur
per formam recognicionum antedictarum penes vos leventur, et vobis
liberentur in forma subscripta. Vobis mandamus quod certum fidelem et discretum hominem, pro quo vos, Johannes respondere
volueritis loco vestri substituatis, dummodo vos, Johannes, circa predictas recogniciones intenderitis, qui una cum te, vicecomes, predictos
denarios de singulis clericis recognitos seu recognoscendos de bonis
eorundem seu plegia suorum quos coram vobis invenerint statim post
recognitiones inde factas seu faciendas et etiam denarii qui in cancel-
laria nostra seu ad scaccarium nostrum de huiusmodi clericis recognitos qui nobis in summonicionibus seu brevibus nostris venerint omni
celeritate et expedicione quibus fieri poterit levari facere, et denarios
una tecum recipiat, et sub sigillo suo et tuo in certo et securo loco
iuxta vestri omnium circumspectionem absque aliquo diminucione
vel subtractione et absque hoc quod aliquid inde penes vos in manibus
vestris remaneat in presentia, et per visum utriusque vestrum ad opus

[a] *MS*. indigenciciam.

[1] See no. 16 for the question of supplies for Gascony. The doubling of the quantities
of grain and money mentioned there is presumably an error.
[2] Ringwood, Hants.

nostrum deponantur. Et quod tu, vicecomes, singulis solventibus litteram tuam facias patentem cum tibi constiterit de singula solucione
veraciter esse facta, super qua quidem littera nos eis acquitancie ad
scaccarium predictum fieri faciemus cum illam quesierint seu illam
habere voluerint. Et quod medietatem omnium denariorum de
huiusmodi recognicionibus proveniencium absque omni dilacione
seu excusacione quacumque habeatis coram prefatis thesaurario et
baronibus nostris apud Westm' citra diem dominicam in Ramis Palmarum[1] nobis ibidem solvendam. Et vos in execucione huiusmodi
mandati nostri ita circumspecte vos habeatis ut effectio et effectus
circa premissa per vos fideliter impensuri perfecti evidenciam emine-
ant et ut nostra indignacio in vobis locum non repereat per viam vestri
demeriti cuiuscunque. Teste P. de Wylugby, tenente locum thesaurarii nostri apud Westm' xx die Martii, anno regni nostri xxv[to].[2]

E 159/70, m. 109d.

21. *Edward I to John de Gillingham and the sheriff of Essex and Hertfordshire,
21 March 1297*

Rex dilectis et fidelis suis Johanni de Gillingham et vicecomiti Essex'
et Hertf', ad blada capienda ad opus nostrum in comitatibus predictis
assignatis, salutem. Miramur vehementer et indignamur inaniter
super tanta vestra negligencia et tarditate, cum totiens vobis scrip-
simus et demandavimus quod dicta blada nostra nuper per vos ad
opus nostrum in comitatibus predictis capta cariari faceretis versus
partes maritimas, apud Vasconiam transducenda, secundum quod
pluries vobis iniunximus, de quo modicam, vel fere nullam expeditionem huiusque fecistis. Et ideo vobis mandamus, sicut pluries vobis
mandavimus, quod super forisfacturam corporum et terrarum
vestrarum omni celeritate quam poteritis de die et nocte dicta blada
in maiori quantitate cariagii qua fieri poterit versus predictas partes
maritimas, ubi naves inde melius et citius impleri et onerari poterunt,
cariari faciatis tam per aquam quam per terram, secundum quod
melius ad commodum nostrum videritis expedire. Ita siquidem quod
naves quas ad dicta blada ad dictas partes Vasconie transducenda
providistis in adventu nostro apud Plummue, qui in proximo erit, deo
volente, prompte existant et parate ad velum explicandum, cum
tempus prosperum se optulerit et oportunum versus partes supra-
dictas. Et vos, Johannes, sitis tunc apud Plummue[3] ad certificandum

[1] Palm Sunday, 7 April.
[2] Similar letters were issued to the other bannerets and sheriffs appointed to receive
clerical fines (E 159/70, m. 109d).
[3] Plymouth, Devon.

nos de summa bladorum, etiam de navium fretagiis, cariagiis et aliis custubus circa eadem blada appositis. Et hoc nullo modo omittatis, sicut de vobismet ipsis et vestris extunc gaudere volueritis. Teste P. etc. xxi die Martii, anno xxv[to].[1]

E 159/70, m. 119d.

22. *Edward I to the sheriff of Yorkshire, 22 March 1297*

Rex vicecomiti Ebor', salutem. Precepimus tibi in fide qua nobis teneris, firmiter iniungentes quod visis presentibus, omni dilacione et excusatione omissis, scire facias Alicie filie Galfridi de Gersingham, que tenet de nobis sex bovatas terre per servicium custodiendi austurcos nostros errentes in Lonesdale[2] quousque firmi fuerunt, vel heredibus vel tenentibus terre et tenementa predicta, si ipsa mortua fuerit, quod omni festinacione qua poterit vel poterint veniat vel veniant coram dilectis et fidelibus nostris Philippo de Wylugby tenente locum thesaurarii nostri et Johanne de Drokenesford custode garderobe nostre, apud Westm', ita quod sit vel sint ibidem ad ultimum in crastino dominice in Ramis Palmarum,[3] sub pena ammissionis terrarum et tenementorum predictorum, paratus aut parati ad faciendum servicium predictum. Et habeas ibi nomina eorum per quos eis scire feceris et hoc breve. Teste P. de Wylugby etc. xxii die Marcii anno etc. xxv. Per breve de privato sigillo. Ad quem diem non retornavit brevem. Ideo alias a die Pasche in quindecim dies etc.[4]

E 368/68, m. 90d.

23. *Procuration directed against the archbishop and clergy of the province of Canterbury, 24 March 1297*

Magister Iterius de Engolisma clericus regis protulit ad scaccarium die Jovis xxix die Augusti, anno xxv[to], quoddam instrumentum in hec verba:
    In nomine domini amen. Per presens publicum instrumentum

---

[1] Similar writs were sent to the sheriffs of Oxon. & Berks., Surrey & Sussex, Hants., Som. & Dorset, Glos., Devon, Cornwall, Wilts. The prise of grain in question was that ordered on 29 November 1296, when a total of 27,000 qu. of wheat, 5,000 qu. of barley, 16,000 qu. of oats, 1,600 qu. of beans and 600 qu. of peas had been demanded from seventeen counties (E 159/70, m. 119).

[2] Lonsdale.

[3] 8 April.

[4] Writs concerning similar services relating to hawks were issued on the same day to the sheriffs of Oxon. & Berks., Norf., Wilts, Kent, Cornwall, Notts. & Derbs., Lincs. (E 368/68, m. 90d). See also no. 19.

omnibus appareat evidenter quod ix kalendas Aprilis, anno ab incarnatione domini millesimo ducentesimo sexto, indictione decima,[1] in presencia venerabilium patrum dominorum R. dei gratia Cantuariensis archiepiscopi totius Anglie primatis, R. Londoniensis, O. Lincolniensis, R. Herefordiensis, R. Norwicensis, T. Exoniensis, W. Bathonensis et Wellensis, T. Roffensis[2] et D. Menevensis[3] episcoporum, et mei notarii publici, et testium subscriptorum, discretus vir magister Iterius de Engolisma, illustris regis Anglie clericus procurator eiusdem litteratorie destinatus, prout infra patet quoddam procuratorium dicti regis sigillo signatum, publice legi fecit. Cuius tenor talis est:

Edward par la grace de dieu, roi Dengleterre, seigneur Dirlaunde et ducs Daquitaigne, as honourables pieres en dieu Robert par la meisme grace ercevesqe de Caunterbiry, e a ses suffragans, e a toutz autres prelatz de nostre reaume, qui serront a ceste mie quarresme assemblez a Loundres, saluz. Pur ceo qe par aukunes evidentes resouns e presumptions, e pur aukunes volentez qe nous avoms vewes de vous deficenables, semble a nous qe par vous, ou par aukuns de vous, purroient estre ordinees par aventure a la dite assemblee aukunes choses en preiudice de nous e de nostre reaume de fet, come ce ne peussez, ne ne devez feire de droit. Nous, pur eschuire qe ce ne puisse a grevaunce de nous estre fait, fesoms e establissoms nostre certein procureur Iter de Engulesme nostre clerk a faire procuracion ou appelacion de vous, ou de chescun de vous, a la Pape, e a proposer tuttes e chescunes choses e resons pur nous e pur les noz, qui sont de nostre foi e a nostre pees e suz nostre protection, e pur toutz nos aherdauntz, sicome nous freioms si nous fuissoms illeoqes present, e en propre persone, e avoms ferm e estable e averoms qant qe serra fait par nostre dit procureur, ou purra estre fait en les choses avantdites, e ceo signifioms a vous e a chescun de vous e a toutz autres a ques cestes chose avantdites.[a] E ceo signifioms a vous e a toutz autres a queux cestes choses apartienent, ou purrount apartenir, par cestes presentes lettres sealees de nostre seal. Donees a Wimburne Menstre,[4] le vintisme iour de Marz, lan de nostre regne vintisme quint.[5]

Quo procuratorio lecto, dominus procurator quamdam procurationem et appellationem in scriptis interposuit in hec verba:

In dei[b] nomine amen. Cum serenissimus princeps dominus Edwardus dei gratia rex Anglie, dominus Hibernie et dux Aquitanie, attendens ex quibusdam causis evidentibus ac presumtionibus factis

[a] There is no indication in the manuscript of an omission at this point.
[b] MS. die.

[1] 24 March 1297.　　　　[2] Rochester.　　　　[3] St David's.
[4] Wimborne Minster, Dorset.
[5] Edward's letter of 20 March is calendared in *C.P.R., 1292–1301*, p. 244.

et dictis voluntarie et iuridissonie, dicto quia regi ac regno suo et eius incolis gravibus plurimum et preiudicialibus, et ex eo potissime quod vos venerabilis pater domine R. dei gratia Cantuar' archiepiscope, et quidam vestri suffragenei aliique prelati et clerici vestri provincie Cantuar', vobis in hac parte adherentibus, publice comminati fuistis et molliti contra fidelitatis vestre debitum, ius regni absorbere; conspiciensque ex hiis et aliis causis probabilibus et veresimilibus coniecturis sibi et regno suo, eiusque incolis posse fieri de facta preiudicium infuturum, michi Iterio de Engolisma clerico mandaverit suo suorum sibique adherentium nomine ad sedem apostolicam procurare, et etiam appellare. Ego predictus Iterius tam dicti regi procurator, ne vos pater predicte vel quivis predicti regni, episcopus aut prelatus, vel alter quispiam superiori vestra, vel cuius ius vice nomine, auctoritate vel mandato contra dominum regem predictum ipsiusque regnum aut eius incolas, aut adherentes eidem, cuiuscumque eminencie status dignitatis etiam episcopalis seu condicionis existant, vel quorumcumque sibi adherentium, preiudicium per vos, vel per alios vel alium quomodolibet attemptetis, vel faciatis, coniunctim vel divisim, aliqualiter attemptari mandando, monendo, citando, statuendo, ordinando vel diffiniendo, declarando, denunciando, publicando, suspendendo, excommunicando, interdicendo aut exequendo, seu quicquam aliud in iudicio vel extra iudicium attemptdando, pro ipso domino rege et suis, qui de sua fidelitate et pace consistunt, et omnibus aliis qui protectionem suam regiam impetraverunt vel in postremum impetrabunt, iusticiariis, consiliariis, clericis et ministris aliis quibuscumque, quocumque nomine censeantur ad sacrosanctam sedem apostolicam in hiis scriptis provoco et appello et appellos peto.

Acta fuerunt hec London' in aula venerabilis patris dicti domini London' episcopi, ix Kalendas Aprilis anno et indictione predictis, presentibus venerabilibus viris domini Philippo de Wileghby, decano Lincoln', magistro Johanne de Derby, decano Lich', Petro de Leycestr', Walteri de Thorp canonicis eiusdem loci, magistro Johanne Lovel, canonico Wellensis, domini Hugoni le Despenser, Rogero Brabazon, Willelmo le Bereford, Johanne de Cobham, militibus, Johanne de Insula et aliis testibus ad hec rogatis.

Et ego Walterus le Norreys filius quondam Roberti Lawys de Killum, Eboracensis diocesis, sacrosancte Romane ecclesie et sacri imperii et alme urbis prefecti publicus auctoritate notarius, et in registro felicis recordàtionis, domini Honorii pape quarti, centesimo x⁰iiii, capitulo de anno primo pontificatus sui registratus, predictis omnibus sic actis et habitis coram dictis prelatis una cum dictis testibus presens interfui, et ea sic fieri vicidet audivi, ac ea omnia predicta ad instanciam dicti magistri Iterii de Engolisma procurationis dicti

domini regis scripsi, et hanc publicam scripturam et formam redegi, meoque signo consueto, signavi, rogatus.[a][1]

E 159/70, m. 117

24. *Edward I to John Droxford, keeper of the wardrobe, the deputy treasurer and barons of the exchequer, 25 March 1297*

Edward etc. a nostre chier clerk Johan de Drokenesford gardein de nostre garderobe, e au lieu tenant nostre tresorier e as barons del escheker, salutz. Nous vous mandoms fermement enioignauntz en la foi e la loiaute qe vous nous devez, qe tant come les terres e les biens de ceux de la clergie sont en nostre mein, faciez treere par tot pur lamener tot la ble qe vous porrez pur enveer en Gascoigne outre tot ceo qe en est purveu sanz aver regard a nule summe. E qe ceste chose seit mise en oeuvre hastivement e sanz nule manire delay e parfaite au plus tost qe vous porrez, issi qe nous en eoms quant qe nous porroms tant come les choses sont en nostre mein. E de ceux blez e dautres, qi hom porra bonement purchacer, faciez charger la nief qi est apele La Rose de Sandwyz e autres vesseaus tieux come vous verrez qi bosoignables y serront.[2] E vous, avauntdit Johan, tant come vous demorez a Londres faciez enquerre quantes niefs des Portz e de Jernemue[3] ou daillours chargez de ble sen irront en Gascoigne de celes dont nous vous mandasmes nadguerres par nos lettres e quantes serront assignez daler a Burgh'[4] e a Bleyves[5] e quantes a Bayon,[6] e de combien e de que manere de blez chescune serra chargeez e de quez lieux, e quant moueront. E de ces choses nous faciez savoir la certeinete quant vous serrets venuz. E si par aventure aucune de celes niefs ne soit avant quant vous departirez de Londres vers nous, si lessez aucun de vos deriere vous pur nous aviser de la chose meintenant apres ceo qe la nief serra mue. De tottes ces choses nous faciez savoir

[a] *A sign like a large cursive* y *is inserted in the manuscript at this point.*

[1] Walter le Norreys was paid 13s. 4d. on 3 April for his work in writing this instrument. Alan of Kent and John de Borham, with two tabellars, received £6 for going to various bishoprics to make similar procurations (B.L., Add. MS. 7965, fos. 15v, 16v). Following this document, the manuscript continues with details of further procurations made on 1 September (no. 133).

[2] Details of the cargo carried by the *Rose* of Sandwich and seven other ships from the Cinque Ports are given in a writ of *allocate* to the sheriff of Kent. They carried in all some 2,200 qu. of wheat, some of it ground, 1,166 qu. of barley and 1,540 qu. of oats to Bourg and Blaye (C 62/74, writ of 14 December). The *Rose* had returned by September (no. 143).

[3] The Cinque Ports and Yarmouth.

[4] Bourg-sur-Gironde, *dép.* Gironde.

[5] Blaye, *dép.* Gironde.

[6] Bayonne, *dép.* Basses-Pyrénées.

par vos lettres sauntz delay ce qe vous en biez faire. E vous chargeoms
touz ensemble e chescon par soy qe vous seiez tendries des choses
desusdites, e numeement dattrere du ble quantqe vous porrez solonc
ce quil est avauntdit, sicome vous amez e desirez nostre honeur, e
la sauvacion de nos bones gentz e des lieux qe nous avoms en
Gascoigne. Don' suz nostre prive seal a Gillingham le xxv iour de
Marz, lan de nostre regne xxv.

E 159/70, m. 18d.

25. *Robert FitzRoger and the sheriff of Hertfordshire to the chancellor, 28*
March 1297

Au chancelier nostre seyngur le rey, par Roberd le Fiz Roger e le
vescounte de Hertford. Fet a remembrer que le joedi procheyn apres
la my quareym lan del regne le rey Edward vintime quint, vynt Saher
chapeleyn de Renggesbury[1] nient benefice devaunt les avantdiz
Robert e le vescounte e fist fyn e reconysaunce pur protectioun nostre
seignur le rey aver. En temoyngne de quele les dit Robert e vescounte
a ceste bille unt mis lour seals.[2]

SC 1/26/189. Original.

26. *Edward I to the deputy treasurer and barons of the exchequer, 29 March*
1297

Edward par la grace de deu etc. Nous vous mandoms e chargioms
a la foi qe vous nous devez e sicome vous aimez lonnour e le profit
de nous e la sauvacioun de nos bone gentz e des biens qe nous tenoms
en Gascoigne, qe les vivres qe serront enveez en Gascoigne ensemblement les deniers e les autres choses dont nous avoms maunde sovent
a vous e a Johan de Drokenesford avant ces houres,[3] faciez purveer
e aprester en totes les bones manieres e ove tote la haste qe vous porrez
de touz costez. Car il ne nous sovient mie qe nous eussens unques
bosoigne qe plus grant haste demandist, ne de quei nous feussons a

[1] Ringsbury, Herts.
[2] Large numbers of protections under the great seal to clergy who paid, or promised
to pay, fines to obtain royal protections are listed in *C.P.R., 1292–1301*, pp. 260–86,
and in *C. Var. Chanc. R.*, pp. 42–53. In addition, files of bills or receipts from the clergy
survive in C 81/1660B, C and D. There are also exchequer receipt rolls, E 401/165
and E 401/1653, detailing a total of £23,174 received from the clergy. For the enrolment
of Saher's protection, dated 8 April, see *C.P.R., 1292–1301*, p. 278. For further examples,
see nos. 36, 39, 41.
[3] See in particular the letters of 13 and 15 March (nos. 16, 19).

si grant meschief de cuer. Don' desuz nostre prive seal a Shirburne en Dors' le xxix iour de Marz, lan de nostre regne xxv.

E 159/70, m. 19.

27. *Edward I to John Droxford and the barons of the exchequer, 30 March 1297*

Edward par la grace de deu etc. Pur ce qe nous avoms entendu qe ceus de la clergie del evesche de Cardoil sont relest a faire sicome les autres de nostre reaume qe font nostre gre, vous mandoms qe hastivement veues ces lettres enveez y certeynes gentz de qi vous vous fiez qi mettent sur eus tel reddeur e teu destresse come hom ad fait as autres avant quil firent nostre gre e plus avant si faire le peusset, car il ont plus grant maugre e greinor duresse deservis puis quil sont venuz contre lur promesse qe ceus qui point nen promistrent. E sachez si nous eussoms ou pres de nous quant cestes lettres furent faitz gentz covenables qui nous y peussoms aver enveer, nous le eussoms fait e les eussoms enformes en tieu manere quil eussent fait reddement nostre comandement e nostre volonte en cele busoigne, mais pur ce qe nous ne les avoms mis a ore, nous enchargioms vous si qe vous en faciez tant qe nous nous peussoms tenir apaiez.[1] E des blez e des deners pur la bosoigne de Gascoigne dont nous vous avoms sovent fiez mande, vous chargioms especiaument qe vous empensez tant e qe vous y mettez teu consail e teu diligence qe nous ne failloms mie de rien qe nous vous en eoms mande avant ces houres. Car si les choses ne se feissent, qe ia deu ne veule, nous nous tendroms a deceuz e a desheritez e nos gentz qui sont en Gascoigne a trahiz e a perduz sanz recoverir. Don' suz nostre prive seal a Crukuerum[2] le xxx iour de Marz, lan de nostre regne xxv.

E 159/70, m. 19.

28. *Edward I to the sheriff of Kent, 31 March 1297*

Precipimus tibi firmiter iniungentes quatenus totam pecuniam provenientem de balliva tua quam ad presens penes te habes, excepta pecunia illa quam super proximo profro tuo ad scaccarium nostrum solvere teneris, et eciam omnes denarios quos per preceptum nostrum levavisti de bonis et catallis Roberti archiepiscopi Cantuar', una cum

---

[1] For the implementation of the orders regarding the Carlisle clergy, see the letter of 6 April (no. 35).
[2] Crewkerne, Som.

pecunia proveniente de finibus protectionum, habeas ad predictum scaccarium nostrum die Jovis proxima ante Ramos Palmarum proximo futur'[1] nobis solvenda, et hoc sicut teipsum et tua diligitis, nullatenus omittas. Teste P. de Wylugby etc., xxxi die Marcii anno xxv°.

E 368/68, m. 91d.

29. *Credence of Alexander le Convers to the exchequer, late March or early April 1297*

Ce est la creaunce Alisaundre le Convers endreit des busoignes de la clergie del eveske de Cardoil, ce est asaver qe touz les lays feez de touz clercks beneficez en la dite evesche ausi bien des abbes, prioures, persones, come des autres beneficez qi qe il seient, horsprys les terres le eveske e de ces gents lays e de ces tenants non*[a]* beneficez seyent prys en la meyn le Roy, e ce seit fet par tot des tenements tenuz en fee ou a terme de vye ou a terme de auns. E touz les biens e les chateus soient ausi par tot seisiis qe en ceus tenementz seyent trovez e tous les avantdites biens e chateus seient vendus horspris ceaux qe serront del acord le evesqe de faire gre le roy, sicome ceaux del arcevesqe de Everewyk ount fait.[2]

E 368/68, m. 26.

30. *Edward I to the deputy treasurer and barons of the exchequer, 2 April 1297*

Edward par la grace de dieu roi Dengleterre, seigneur Dirlande e ducs Daquitaine, au lieu tenant nostre tresorier e as barons del escheker, saluz. Nous vous mandoms qe vous faciez enveer briefs de nostre escheker parmy touz les contez Dengleterre as viscontes e as autres selonc ce qe vous verrez qe seit a faire qe hastivement veues les lettres facent vendre touz les biens moebles qui sunt pris en nostre meyn des clercs qui ne averont mie fait nostre gre avant qe celes lettres vendront, sauve tantsoulement les gaigneres e les choses qui covenent por les gaignages, e quil respoignent des levees duement a nostre escheker. Et sachiez qe ausint le forsoms nous faire la ou nous aloms. E ce qe

---

[a] *MS.* nec.

[1] 4 April.
[2] For this matter, see the letter of 30 March (no. 27), and that of 6 April (no. 36). The clergy of the York diocese were granted royal protection on 18 February, following their grant of a fifth (*C.P.R., 1292–1301*, p. 237).

vous en aurez fait nous facez savoir au plus tost qe vous porrez.[1] Don' desous nostre prive seal a Coleoumbe[2] le secund iour Daveril, lan de nostre regne vintisme quint.

E 159/70, m. 19d.

31. *Edward I to the collectors of customs, 2 April 1297*

Rex custodibus custume London', salutem. Intelleximus quod quidam mercatores tam de regno nostro quam aliunde in defraudationem eiusdem custume nostre, lanas suas filare et alii coria sua depilare et quodamodo superficialiter tannare et postea per medium scindi faciunt ut sic dicte lane sub colore dicti filacii, et coria sub colore dicte tannationis, et decisionis incustumabilia videantur, et absque solucione dicte custume nostre inde nobis facte, cum dictis filacio et coriis ad partes transmarinas transeunt, ad dampnum nostrum non modicum. Nos huiusmodi malicie et defraudationi obviare volentes, vobis mandamus quod eandem custumam quam de lanis et coriis integris et non tannatis hucusque ad opus nostrum cepistis de filacis et coriis tannatis et decisis decetero capiatis. Teste P. etc. secundo die Aprilis, anno xxv^{to}.

Consimili modo mandatum est custodibus custume apud Novum Castrum,[3] Hul',[4] Sanctum Botolphum,[5] Jernemutam,[6] Gipwicum,[7] Sandwicum[8] et Suth'.[9] Teste etc. ut supra.

E 159/70, m. 110.

32. *Edward I to the barons of the exchequer, 3 April 1297*

Baronibus pro abbate de Tavystok.^{a} Monstravit regi idem abbas quod licet quedam recognitio cuiusdam certe summe pecunie coram Gilberto de Knovill' vicecomite Devon' pro protectione regis habenda nuper facta fuerit regi ex parte sua, quidam tamen amici sui de recognitione predicta ignorantes quandam recognitionem de quadam pecunie summa ad opus regis pro eadem protectione habenda nomine ipsius abbatis coram baronibus in scaccario iam fecerunt. Rex igitur

---

^{a} *Marginal heading.*

[1] Exchequer writs ordering the sale of clerical goods were duly issued on 8 April (no. 38).
[2] Cullompton, Devon.
[3] Newcastle-upon-Tyne, Northumb.
[4] Hull, Yorks.
[5] Boston, Lincs.
[6] Yarmouth, Norf.
[7] Ipswich, Suff.
[8] Sandwich, Kent.
[9] Southampton, Hants.

mandat baronibus quod inspectis rotulis de huiusmodi recogni-
tionibus et etiam extractis prefati vicecomitis de huiusmodi recogni-
tionibus eis liberatis si eis constare possit ita esse; tunc habita consideratione ad recognitiones predictas eidem abbati inde fieri faciant
remedium quod convenit in hac parte. Teste rege apud Plympton'
iii die Aprilis, anno xxv.[1]

E 159/70, m. 23; E 368/68, m. 38.

33. *Edward I to the sheriffs, 4 April 1297*

Rex vicecomiti etc. Precipimus tibi quod baronibus de scaccario
nostro apud Westm' in crastino clausi Pasche[2] precise certifices qui
sunt prelati, religiosi et clerici beneficiati quicumque in balliva tua
quorum beneficia valorem xl solidorum attingunt et ultra, et que sunt
nomina ipsorum, et in quibus ecclesiis beneficiati vel de quibus benefi-
ciis possessionati existunt, et qui ultra diem Pasche proximo futurum
protectionem nostram habuerunt et qui non, et qui laicum feodum
habuerunt et qui non. Et omnia bona et catalla, terras et tenementa
illorum qui protectionem nostram non habuerunt salvo in manum
nostram teneas et custodias in forma qua alias tibi precepimus donec
aliud tibi preceperimus. Et hoc nullo modo omittas. Teste etc., quarto
die Aprilis etc.[3]

E 368/68, m. 92d.

34. *Edward I to John Droxford, the deputy treasurer, barons and chamberlains
of the exchequer, 5 April 1297*

Edward par la grace de dieu rey Dengleterre, seigneur Dirland e ducs
Daquitaine, a nostre chier clerc Johan de Drokensford, gardeyn de
nostre garderobe, au lieu tenant nostre tresurier, as barons, e as
chaumberlains del escheker, salutz. De ceo qe nous avoms entendu
qe vous avetz fait mander en Kent e en Essex, Surr' e Sussex ou les
clerks lercevesqe ount blez pur attreere de meisme le ble sur la mer
ceo qe hom purra pur enveer en Gascoigne, sachietz qe nous nous

---

[1] A chancery protection was issued to the abbot of Tavistock on 4 April 1297, on
the testimony of Gilbert de Knovill (*C.P.R.*, *1292–1301*, p. 271). A similar incident of
double payment of the fine for protection occurred in the case of the prior of Plympton.
A letter on his behalf was sent to the exchequer on 15 April (E 159/70, m. 23d). Two
further cases, one detailed, *ibid.*, m. 25d.

[2] 22 April.

[3] The following day writs in almost identical terms were issued, the date for the
returns being extended to 29 April (E 159/70, m. 96d).

tenoms bien appaiez, e vous mandoms qe des blez des meismes les clerks, e des autres qui nount fait nostre gre, facietz treere a la mer, e enveer en Gascoigne desorendeit quant qe vous purretz, mes de ceaux qui ount fait nostre gre, vous chargeoms qe leur blez, e toutz leur autres biens faciet par tot sauver, e garder a leur oes, qe nul ne prenge rien contre leur bon gre. E faciet saver as viscontes e as nos autres ministres qe chescon endreit de soy le face en meisme la manere si qe ceaux qui sont en nostre protection se pussent loer, e quil pussent aparcevoir quil ont fait qe sages, de ceo quil unt fait nostre volunte. E de ceo qe nous avoms entendu quil vous semble bon qe nous faceoms nostre prise de blez en les parties de Northampton, en aventure si nous en eoms a faire cest estre pur enveer en Gascoigne ou pur mesner dailleurs solonc ceo qe nos bosoignes demanderont, il nous semble qe vous estes molt bien avisetz, e voloms qe des maintenant vous enveez en les contez de Nichole,[1] Northampton, Rotel',[2] Leycestre, Notingham, Derby, Everwyk[3] e Northumbr' certeines gent e penibles pur prendre y de ces blez a nostre oes, ce quil porront sauve resnable sustenauntz as gentz, e santz trop grever le poeple, e pur meisme le ble faire venir as plus eesetz portz des contez avantditz au plus tost quil porront, si qe le ble y demoerge en bone garde e sauve, e soit tot prest e bien apparaille pur mettre en vesseaux quant il nous plerra, mais quil nel mettent en nul vesseal tant qe nous eoms mande, quen part nous les voudroms enveer.[4] E endreit des deniers pur ceste bosoigne de Gascoigne, dont nous vous avoms soventefoitz mande avant ces houres, vous chargeoms uncore si especiaument com nous pooms, qe vous y mettez tot la peyne, e tot le bon conseil qui vous porrez si qe nous nen failloms mie sicome vous aimetz la sauvacion de nos bones gentz qui sont en Gascoigne, e des lieux qi nous tenoms celes parties, e sicom vous voletz deliverer nous meismes hors de prison. Car sachietz nous ne bioms a partir des parties de Plimmuth tant qe la bosoigne de Gascoigne soit bien arraiee, e qe la flote soit avant. E en droit des niefs de Norff', e Suff', Dessex', de Londres e de Kent, vous mandoms qe vus les facieez haster quant qe vous porretz, e qe nous sacheoms quantes irrent a Burgh'[5] e a Blayves[6] e quantes a Bayone,[7] e de comben eles serront chargeetz de tottes maneres de choses. E de la baleyne, que vous, devantdit Johan, nous enveiastes, vus savoms bon gre, car ele nous vient tot apoint, e nous enmangeames molt bien. E pur ceo qe nous avoms mervaille de ceo[a] qe nous navoms uncore eu nule certeynes noveles de nos gentz de dela, puis qe mons'

---

[a] de ceo *repeated in MS.*

---

[1] Lincoln.
[3] York.
[5] Bourg-sur-Gironde, *dép.* Gironde.
[7] Bayonne, *dép.* Basses-Pyrénées.

[2] Rutland.
[4] For this purveyance, see no. 51.
[6] Blaye, *dép.* Gironde.

Johan Sauvage en vynt, vous mandoms qe vous mandetz a mons'
Robert de Burghersh e a ceaux de Sandwyz, e en chargetz le gardein
e ceaux de Loundres ausint qe, sitost come il averont nule novele quil
la nous facent savoir, e quil hastent le message vers nous quantquil
porront. Don' soutz nostre prive seal a Excestre le v iour de Averill,
lan de nostre regne xxv.

E 159/70, m. 120d.

35. *Edward I to the sheriff of Cumberland, 6 April 1297*

Rex vicecomiti Cumbr', salutem. Cum venerabilis pater J. Karl' episcopus in ultimo parliamento nostro apud Sanctum Edmundum nobis
tam per se quam pro toto clero episcopatus sui, iuxta promissum et
concessionem quas ei prius fecerant quintam partem bonorum
suorum sicut prelati, religiosi et ceteri clerici de provincia Ebor' in
certo loco deponendam ad defensionem ecclesie et regni nostri gratanter concessisset, propter quod eidem episcopo et clericis suis eiusdem episcopatus pro se, hominibus, terris, redditibus et possessionibus
suis litteras nostras de protectione fieri fecimus gratiose. Et modo intelleximus quod dicti clerici predicti episcopatus tanquam rebelles
et dicti promissi, ad quod iuxta fidelitatis debitum perficere et com-
plere sunt astricti, nullatenus meminentes, dictam concessionem
bonorum suorum quam per predictum episcopum nobis promiserunt
ingrate nobis facere contradicunt in dampnum et periculum totius
regni nostri maximum. Nos huiusmodi contradictionem et rebellionem
quas contra protectionis nostre favorem et gratiam ingratius excercent
gravius puniri volentes, dictam protectionem nostram preter quam
erga dictum episcopum et homines suos laicos irritamus et evacuamus
omnino, tibi sub omni eo quod nobis forisfacere potes districte preci-
piendo quod per visum et in presencia dilecti clerici nostri Alex' le
Convers, quem ad partes tuas mittimus, et cui super hoc precepto
nostro et illud tangentibus, prout ex parte nostra tibi exponet, redeun-
tiam adhibeas, omnia laica feoda dictorum clericorum predicti episcopatus quorumcumque, una cum omnibus bonis et catallis in eisdem
inventis in manum nostram capias et ea salvo custodias, ita quod nec
ipsi nec aliquis pro eis ad ea manum apponant, donec aliud inde tibi
precepimus. Inhibentes autem ne dicti clerici dicti episcopatus
actiones suas qualescumque versus quoscumque in curia nostra coram
te seu aliis ministris nostris exponentes ad aliquid audientiam admit-
tantur seu expediantur. Et quod omnes et singuli eorum laicis omnibus
et singulis de eis conqueri seu versus eos prosequi volentibus responde-
ant et responsales fiant quousque in forma aliorum clericorum de

provincia Ebor' concessionem suam faventium et prosequentium per
sufficientes emendas pro contradictione et rebellione predictis facienda
voluntati nostre humilius se reformaverint et benevolenciam vestram
graciosus impetraverint. Et scire facias dictis clericis dicti episcopatus
et plene et aperte significari quod nisi super predicta concessione
quam per predictum episcopum nobis fecerunt firmiter tenenda et
facienda in forma qua ceteri clerici de predicta provincia Ebor' concesserunt citius et celerius se conformaverint, nos eos[a] extra pacem
nostram omnino eici faciemus. T. de Jus' apud Westm' vi[to] die Aprilis
anno xxv[to].[1]

E 159/70, m. 110d.

36. *Bogo de Knoville to the chancellor, John de Langton, 6 April 1297*

Provido viro et amico suo si placet domino J. de Langeton cancellario
domini regis vel domino cancellario de scaccario, Bogo de Knovill'
ad recognitiones cleri in comitatu Salop' una cum vicecomite eiusdem
comitatus recipiendas assignatus, salutem et sincere dilectionis aug-
mentum. Sciatis quod prior de Bromfeld' concessit ad defensionem
regni et sancte ecclesie et pro protectione sua habenda quintam partem bonorum suorum temporalium et spiritualium iuxta taxationem
decime sibi alias a clero concesse, unde vos si placet protectionem
illam et brevia clausa ipsam contingentia eidem priori fieri precipere
velitis. In cuius rei testimonium has litteras meas vobis transmitto
patentes. Datum apud Salop' vi die Aprilis, anno regni domini nostri
regis xx quinto.[2]

C 81/1694/22.

37. *Edward I to Joan de Valence, countess of Pembroke, 7 April 1297*

Edward par la grace de dieu, roy Dengleterre, seigneur Dirlande
e ducs Daquitaine, a sa chiere taunte e feale Johane de Valence,
contesse de Pembrok, saluz. De ce qe vous avez entendu qe les
leynes e les quyrs des contes de Gales sont assemblez a le chief vile
de chescun conte, sicome a Estrugoil,[3] Kaerdif[4] e Breghenok,[5] e

[a] eos *repeated in MS.*

---

[1] For the affair of the Carlisle clergy, see Edward I's letter of 30 March to the exchequer (no. 27) and Alexander le Convers' credence to the exchequer (no. 29).
[2] It appears that the Prior of Bromfield had already received royal protection on
23 March (*C.P.R., 1292–1301*, p. 270). For other examples of clergy requesting royal
protection, see nos. 39, 41. A large number of these documents survive: see no. 25,
n. 1.   [3] Chepstow, Mon.
[4] Cardiff, Glam.   [5] Brecon.

voudriez qe les leynes e les quyrs de vostre conte de Pembrok feussent
ausint cariez e assemblez a Pembrok; vous feisoms savoir qil ne sovient
mie a nous ne a ceux qui sont ore pres de nous ce qe est ordene de
ceste busoigne, mais a nostre parlement quant nous serroms venuz
a Londres, ou nous averoms ceux qui sont assignez e se entremettent
de tieu chose, porrez vous enveer aucun des voz, e lors en feroms nous
ce qe nous porroms en bone maniere. E endroit des demaundes qui
vous sont faites por les dettes vostre seigneur, por les queles Eymer
vostre fuiz ad trove meinprise a nostre escheker, sicome vous nous
avez mande, nous vous enveoms nos lettres escrites a ceux del
escheker, par les queles nous leur mandoms quil vous sueffrent en pees
endroit des dites demandes, e quil ne vous facent nule part destreindre
countre la forme de la meinprise avantdite, e qe sil vous eient fait
faire destresce par cele encheson qe sanz delay la fecent mander
relesser.[1] E endroit de vostre fraunchise du chastel Gaweyn[2] dont nos
baillifs de Haverford vous fount aucune duresce e damage sicome vous
nous mandastes par vos lettres, si voloms qe vous enveez a nostre dit
parlement aucun des voez, si vous veez qe ce soit a faire, e nous feroms
mander nos ditz baillifs si vous volez quil y soient aussint, e issi oie
vostre pleinte e lour response, en feroums volontiers por vous
quantque nous porroms par reson. Don' desouz nostre prive seal a
Ilstinton'[3] le vii iour Daveril, lan de nostre regne xxv.

SC 1/47/92. Original. Calendared in *Calendar of Ancient Correspondence
concerning Wales*, ed. J. G. Edwards (Cardiff, 1935), pp. 212–13.

38. *Edward I to the sheriff of Norfolk and Suffolk, 8 April 1297*

Rex vicecomiti Norff' et Suff', salutem. Precipimus tibi quod omnia
bona et catalla prelatorum, religiosorum et aliorum clericorum
quorumcumque beneficia xl *s.* et ultra habentium in balliva tua,
mobilia in manum nostram ad nostri preceptum quibusdam de causis
nuper per te capta, exceptis bladis in terris eorum nunc crescentibus
et hiis quibus necessario indigetur pro earundem terrarum cultura,
qui post instantem diem Pasche protectionem nostram non habuerint,
vel finem pro eadem non fecerint; sine dilacione vendicioni facias
exponi per visum cuiuslibet dictorum clericorum cuius dicta bona
fuerint, vel eorum ballivorum seu alicuius alterius fidelis hominis de
visneto illo, in quo dicta bona inventa fuerunt, si ambo abesse

---

[1] A privy seal letter to the exchequer was issued on 8 April, ordering the distraint
on Joan to be relaxed if the letters of Aymer de Valence giving security for the debts
could be found at the exchequer (E 159/70, m. 23).
[2] Walwynscastle. For the background to this complaint see J. R. S. Phillips, *Aymer
de Valence* (Oxford, 1972), pp. 251–2.
[3] Ilsingston, Devon.

contigerint. Et quod inde fiat cirographum inter te seu ballivos tuos quos ad dictam vendicionem miseris, et dictos clericos seu eorum ballivos, seu alium fidelem hominem de visneto illo, in quo dicta bona existunt. Ita quod omnes denarios inde provenientes habeas coram baronibus de scaccario nostro apud Westm' absque omni mora seu excusatione nobis solvendos. Et nichilominus easdem terras et tenementa dictorum clericorum, qui protectionem nostram post diem predictum non habuerint, vel finem pro eadem non fecerint, in manum nostram teneas et salvo custodias donec aliud inde tibi preceperimus, proviso siquidem quod tunc prefatos barones nostros certifices, de quibus et cuiusmodi bonis et catallis et de quibus clericis et per quorum visionem dictos denarios levaveris. Et habeas ibi hoc breve. Teste J. de Cobeham etc. viii die Aprilis, anno xxv.

E 159/70, m. 110d; E 368/68, m. 92d.

39. *John Lovel to the chancellor, John Langton, 9 April 1297.*

A sire Johan de Langeton, chaunceler nostre seygnur le rey, Johan Lovel saluz. Pur ceo que nagueres pus devant moy a Oxenford que Thomas vicar' de Mercheham en le conte de Buk' vint a la fey nostre seignur le rey e sa fyn fist au double de quil dona au dyme, par quey ieo luy ay done cestes lettres overtes pur la protection aver. Donez a Oxenford le ix iour Davery lan du regne nostre seygnur vintyme quint.

E 163/2/6, no. 47. Original, with fragment of seal attached.

40. *Edward I to the deputy treasurer and barons of the exchequer, 11 April 1297*

Edward par la grace de dieu etc. au .. lieu tenant nostre thresorier e as barons del eschequer, saluz. Endreit de ceux de la clergie qui nauront nostre gre fait avant ceste Pasque procheinement avenyr, dont nous vous avoms mande avant ces houres; vous mandoms derechiefs pur ceo quil ont failly a leur seignur lige e a leur nation propre e au roiaume en plus grant bosoigne quil unkes eurent, qe des meintenant santz nule manere dexcusation ou de delay faciez vendre parmy les countes quant quil y ad de leur moeble seisi en nostre meyn, sauve tant seulement ceo quil en covendra pur les gaignages e qe les viscontes respoignent des levees a le escheker deins le plus court terme quil porrunt. Car nous voloms mieuz pur le bosoign de deners que nous avoms orendreit e pur aucunes autres reisons ausint qe les choses soient vendues pur meins qe eles ne valent qe nous attendissiens tant qe plus avant quant par avienture nous naveriens mye si grant haste ne tant

a bosoigner de deniers come nous avoms ore. E pur lavantdite busoigne faire, enveiez tieux gentz qui diligeaument e apertement en facent nostre comandement, e qui nul nesparnient pur amyste ne en autre manere. Doneez desouz nostre pryve seal a Plympton'[1] le xi iour Daveril, lan de nostre regne xxv.

Et memorandum quod dominus rex mandavit baronibus breve predictum xvii die Aprilis anno predicto quo die illud receperunt. Item dominus rex mandavit quandam billam in predicto brevi inclusam cuius tenor talis est:—

E pur ce qe moltz diverses noveles de dela nous vienent de iour en iour es parties ou nous sumes, de qui nous ne pooms savoir nule certeinete, si en avoms grant merveille, e vous mandoms fermement enioinantz se vous puyssez novele savoir des parties de Holland', de Brebant, de Flandres, de Bar ou de nul de nos aliez, ou de nos autres amys de dela, ou de .. levesque de Cestre e de nos autres gentz qui sunt celes parties, par marchaundz ou par mariners ou par lettres ou en autre certeyn manere, que vous la nous maundez pleinement par vos lettres od tote la haste qui vous porrez, de nuytz e de iours. Et de ceste chose vous soviegne bien si come nous nous fioms de vous, si qe vous la fournissez diligeaument, e nomeement apres ce qe Johan de Drokenesford serra parti de Londres.

E 368/68, m. 27.

---

41. *The sheriff of Rutland to the chancellor of the exchequer, 11 April 1297*

A sire Phelippe de Wylugby, chaunceler del eschekere nostre seygnour le rey, Geffray Russel, vescounte de Rotel, saluz e honours. Sachez, sire, ke Johan parsone del eglise de Billeforde en le counte de Northampton' ad fet sa fyn pur sis mars, ceo est a saver au double de ceo ke il dona dereyn, de queus sis mars il moy ad trove bone surete, pur ceo ke il ne poyt suffisaunte surete trover en la counte de Northampton' pur la protection nostre seygnour le rey aver. En testmoynaunce de quel chose ieo ay mis moun sel. Done a Ocham[2] le Jeudy absolut, lan du regne nostre seynour le rey Edward vintime quint.

Northampton' protectio et breve.[a]

E 163/2/6, no. 65. Original.

[a] *Note added in a different hand.*

---

[1] During his stay at Plympton, the king underwent a blood-letting operation, the discomfort of which was eased by the playing of a harpist (B.L., Add. MS. 7965, fo. 54v).

[2] Oakham, Rutland.

42. *Edward I to John Droxford, and to the deputy treasurer and barons of the exchequer, 13 April 1297*

Edward par la grace de dieu etc., a nostre chier clerk Johan de Drokenesford' gardein de nostre garderobe e au lieu tenant nostre tresorier e as barons del escheqer, saluz. Quant a ceux de la clergie qui nauront nostre gre fait avant ceste Pasque, dont nous vous avoms mande qe vos faciez vendre hastivement touz leur biens e touz leur moebles en nostre mayn seisis, sauve tantsoulement les gaignages e sauve ce qi vous enverrez en Gascoigne, sicome plus pleinement est contenu es lettres qui sour ce vous avoms enveez; nous eumes obliez iusques a ore de faire vous savoir nostre volunte sour un pointe qui sensuite. Ce est asavoir qe vous mandez expressement a touz ceux qui de la dite vente se entremettront quil soient bien avisez sicome il voelent eux meismes garder de greif damage qe eux nule rien des ditz biens e moebles ne vendent a ceux a qui il feurent, ne a nuls autres par qui les choses pussent revenir en leur meyn, ny a leur profit en nule manere, tant quil soient venuz a nous meismes e eient fait nostre gre, ou tant qe nous en eoms autre chose comandee. Car puis quil verront qe les choses se vendront par aventure pur meins qe eles ne valent, porreit estre qe eux meismes mettroient peine de les achater devant autres pur avoir ent aucun avantage. La queu chose nous ne voudriens en nule manere tant quil eussent fait chose de quei nous vous tenisseoms appaez. Donees desouz nostre prive seal a Plympton le xiii iour Daveril, lan de nostre regne vintisme quinte.

E 368/68, m. 27d.

43. *Edward I to the deputy treasurer and barons of the exchequer, 14 April 1297*

Edward par la grace de dieu etc., a lieu tenaunt nostre thresorier e as baruns del escheker, saluz. Pur coe qe nous avoms entendu qe ceux de la clergie ount plus graunt volente communeaument a faire nostre gre, e quil vienent al escheker plus espressement qil ne soleynt, si voloms bien puys quil en sont mieuz avisez e le volent fere de bone volente, coment qe nous eoms avaunt ces hores maunde qe tuz les biens e les mobles de ceux qui ne eussent nostre gre fet avaunt cest Paske feissent venduz a nostre oeps, sauve les gaynages e coe qui hom enverreit en Gascoigne, qe le terme leur en seit esloigne taunt sulement par trays symaines prescheinement suiantz ceste meisme Pasche, issint quil peussent entre cy e la faire nostre gre sil neent a bien feit, e qe de autres qe nel auraunt fayt denz cel terme peussoms comander plus avaunt nostre volunte. Pur la queu chose nous vous maundoms

qe entre cy e la receyves les fins de ceus qi faire les voudront par devaunt vous e qe vous maundet hastivement pur coe qe la chose est hastive qe hom le face ausint parmy les countez e qe tant dementers hom sursiete de la vente qe nous en eumes commandee. Issint tutes veies qe les choses seisiez en nostre meyn y demoergent taunt qe nostre gre en seit fait, ou qe nous en eoms autre chose ordenee.[1] E vous maundrums qe endreit del evesqe de Nichole,[2] faciez coe qe nostre cher clerc Johan de Drokenesford gardeyn de nostre garderobe vous dirra de par nous.[3] Don' desouz nostre prive seal a Plympton' le xiiii iour de Averil, lan de nostre regne xxv.

Et memorandum quod breve istud venit baronibus die veneris in septimana Pasche anno predicto.

E 368/68, m. 27d.

44. *Edward I to the barons of the exchequer, 15 April 1297*

Edward par la grace de deu etc. Ia soit ce qe nous eoms attryez qe ceux de la clergie eient terme pur finer e pur faire nostre gre iesques a la fyn de troys symeynes suiantz ceste meisme Pasque sicome nous vous avoms plus pleinement mande par nos lettres ; vous fesoms a saver qe nostre entention est e voloms e mandoms qe ceux qe averont la terme de la dite Pasque le quel nous lour eumes premerement assignez sicome bien savez e qui entre cy e la fyn des avantdits troys symaynes veudront faire nostre gre, ne soient mie de bone condicion ne de si graciouse come les autres qe le ont fait avant ces houres, einz doynent aucune chose plus qe les autres e tote foiz qui plus demorrunt e plus tardifs serront de fair lur fyn plus doygnent, car il ne est mie reson qe ceux qe plus ont attenduz seient receuz si passaument come les autres, e dautre part, si hom le fesoit ce serroit mal ensample. E pur ce faites saver hastivement a touz ceux qe se entremettent de par nous parmy les contez qe chescun endreit soy en soit bien avisez e le face en ceste meismes manere e qe apres dites troys symaynes passees nule tieu fyn ne seit receu de nuly tant qe nous eoms autre chose comandee. Don' desouz nostre prive seal a Plympton' le xv iour Daveryl, lan de nostre regne xxv.[4]

E 159/70, m. 23; E 368/68, m. 38.

[1] Letters implementing these instructions were issued on 22 April by the exchequer (E 368/68, m. 92).
[2] Lincoln.
[3] According to *Guisborough*, p. 288, the bishop of Lincoln's friends, without his authorization, arranged for the sheriff to raise the fine from his estates. Receipts of £150 from the sale of the bishop's goods are recorded on the receipt roll (E 401/1653).
[4] Instructions in these terms were duly issued to the bannerets and sheriffs responsible for collecting the fines (E 159/70, m. 96).

45. *Hugh le Despenser to Philip de Willoughby, 15 April 1297*

A sun chier amy sire Phelippe de Wilugby, chaunceler del escheker nostre seignur le rey, Hughes le Despenser, saluz e chieres amistez. Jo vous pri de par mey e maunke de par le dit nostre seignur le rey, qe as tuz custumiers e gardeyns de la nuvele custume au port ou passage ou le coket seyt, hastivement saunz delay facez fere brefs le rey desouthes le seel de lescheker qe nuls custumier desore gage ne plegge resceyve pur la custume des leynes qe deivent passer, mes qi unkes weille leyne passier, hastivement einz qe la leyne passe payes a custume ou qe celes leynes qe sount a passer demorgent en arrest iekes taunt qe la custume seit pae. E ceste lettre vous serra garaunt. Escrit a Odyham,[1] le xv iour de Averil.

E 368/68, m. 27d.

46. *Edward I to the barons of the exchequer, 18 April 1297*

Baronibus pro priore ecclesie Cristi Cantuariensis.[a] Rex mandat baronibus quod si idem prior per recognitionem coram eis factam habeat protectionem regis sigillo scaccarii signatam, tunc duos equos suos quos vicecomes Kancie ab eodem priore nuper cepit apud Maydenstan' cum idem prior ultimo versus regem apud Sar' esset in veniendo, et qui in custodia eiusdem vicecomitis adhuc existunt ibidem ut dicitur, eidem priori sine dilacione restitui faciant prout idem prior equos illos suos esse et ab eo captos fuisse et detentos rationabiliter dicere poterit coram eis. Teste rege apud Plympton' xviii die Aprilis, anno xxv.[2]

E 159/70, m. 23d.

47. *Edward I to the sheriff of Westmorland, 26 April 1297*

Edwardus dei gratia rex Anglie, dominus Hibernie et dux Aquitanie, vicecomiti Westmorland', salutem. Precipimus tibi quod capitales taxatores et collectores duodecime nobis in comitatu predicto a laicis concesse ponas per manucaptionem duodecim hominum sufficientium, qui ipsos manucapiant quod erunt in propriis personis suis

---

[a] *Marginal heading.*

---

[1] Odiham, Hants.
[2] These two horses were presumably taken at the same time as those of the archbishop: see no. 13.

coram baronibus de scaccario nostro apud Westmonasterium in octabis Ascensionis Domini[1] una cum omnibus denariis qui nobis debentur de arreragiis predicte duodecime in comitatu predicto et rotulis taxationis eiusdem duodecime nobis ibidem absque omni ulteriori dilacione reddendis. Et interim omnia bona et catalla mobilia eorum per sacramentum proborum et legalium hominum de comitatu predicto appreciari, et omnes terras et tenementa eorum extendi facias, videlicet quid et quantum valeant per annum in omnibus exitibus, salvis serviciis dominorum feodi. Et de appreciacione eorundem bonorum et de extenta terrarum et tenementorum predictorum prefatis baronibus nostris ad diem supradictam constare facias et ea per predictam manucaptionem eis liberes inde respondendo ad voluntatem nostram. Exponens siquidem et scire faciens precise prefatis taxatoribus et collectoribus quod, nisi omnes denarios supradictos ad dicta diem et locum habuerint, bona et catalla, terre et tenementa eorum supradicta nobis erunt forisfacta et corpora eorum ad voluntatem nostram ut preceptorum nostrorum contemptores et inimicorum nostrorum fautorum complices et adiutores qui extunc nullius gratie remedium in nobis reperient. Et tu ipse eisdem taxatoribus et collectoribus cum omni diligencia et adiutorio quibus poteritis ad dicta arreragia levanda celeriter assistas. Et scias quod per excusationem sinistram seu per aliquam simulatam responsionem a debita punicione tibi infligenda non evades quin ad corpus tuum omnia bona et catalla, terras et tenementa tua ita graviter capiamus quod tua punicio exemplum aliis erit terroris precepta nostra exequendi alias contempnendi vel exequi retardandi si te tardum vel remissum in premissis aliquatenus invenerimus. Teste J. de Cobeham apud Westmonasterium xxvi[to] die Aprilis, anno regni nostri vicesimo quinto.

Dorse

Willelmus de Cumbe est clericus et nullum habet laycum feodum et tamen non fuit inventus in balliva mea post receptionem huius brevis. Johannes de Helton' taxator et collector xii[e] et viii[e] in comitatu Westmorland' non fuit inventus in balliva mea post receptionem huius brevis et non erat aliquis in balliva mea per quem terras suas et catalla extendere potui et appreciare, quia omnes milites et libere tenentes sunt in comitatu Cumberland' ad defendendum marchiam inter Angliam et Scotiam ex adventu Scottorum. Et ideo executio huius brevis non potuit ·ad presens.

E 143/4/3. Original.

[1] 30 May.

48. *Edward I to John Engayne and the sheriff of Northampton, 26 April 1297*

Rex dilectis et fidelibus suis Johanni Engayne et vicecomiti North' ad fines clericorum in eodem comitatu admittendos assignatis, salutem. Mandamus vobis in fide et dilectione quibus nobis tenemini quod statim visis letteris istis per totum dictum comitatum, [in] burgis, civitatibus et villis mercatoribus et in quolibet hundredo eiusdem comitatus puplice et aperte proclamari faciatis quod omnes et singuli prelati, religiosi et clerici eiusdem comitatus protectionem nostram habentes solvant vobis ad opus nostrum omnes denarios per quos finem fecerunt pro predicta nostra protectione habenda, tam de solucione prime medietatis quam secunde citra festum Ascensionis Domini proximo futurum,[1] ita quod cum vicecomes sis in propria persona tua coram baronibus de scaccario nostro apud Westm' in crastino Ascensionis Domini et omnes illos denarios, una cum omnibus denariis quod vos ambo vel unus vestrum seu alius nomine vestro ad hoc per vos deputatus receperitis seu receperit habeas sub salvo et securo conductu nobis tunc ibidem una cum rotulis eorundem finium ab ultimo solvendis, exponentes siquidem et scire facientes in eadem proclamatione dictis clericis precise quod nisi plenam solucionem fecerint citra predictum festum Ascensionis Domini de omnibus denariis quos nobis debent nomine finis supradicte, dicta nostra protectio quam eis graciose concessimus pretextu aliorum ingratitudinis cassa, irrita erit et vacua. Ita quod ex tunc nullo modo eis valebit quousque novem finem pro eadem protectione rehabenda vobiscum fecerint. Et scias tu vicecomes quod ex tunc a debita punicione tibi infligenda de cetero non evades, quin ad corpus tuum et omnia bona et catalla, terras et tenementa etiam capiamus si in executione precepti nostri te tardum vel remissum invenerimus, et in illum qui ad nostrum commodum et honorem nullum habet respectum nec periculum regni nostri aliquo modo considerat. Teste J. de Cobeham', xxvi die Aprilis.

Consimili modo mandatum est omnibus aliis banerettis et vicecomitibus assignatis ad predictos fines admittendos. Teste ut supra.

E 159/70, m. 96d.

49. *Edward I to the barons and men of Winchelsea, and to Stephen de Pencester, warden of the Cinque Ports, April 1297*

Le roi *a ses chiers e feals barons e prodes hommes*[a] de son port de Winchelse, saluz. Pur aucunes grant busoignes e especiales[b] qui

---

[a] ... [a] *Passage interlined, written over* as barons *struck out.*
[b] e especiales *interlined.*

---

[1] 23 May.

touchent nous e vous e nos autres feals de nostre roiaume, vous mandoms en la fei qe vous nous devez, fermement enioinantz qe tot le
servise qui nous est deu des nefs de vostre port avandit *a*eez encontre
nous*a* a Winchelse lendemein de la seint Johan le Baptist prochein
avenir[1] prest e apparaille *b*e bien garnie*c* daler de illoeke adunke*c* en
nostre servise la ou il nous les froms donkes asavoir. *d* Issi qe par defaut
de vostre servise avantdit les dites bosoignes ne seient targees en nule
manere etc.

Le rei a son chier e feal mons' Estevne de Pencestr' gardein des Cink
Portz*e* ou a son leu tenant, saluz. Pur ce qe pur aucunes grant busoignes*f* qui touchent nous e nostre roialme avoms mande as nos chiers
e feals barons e prodeshommes de ditz Cink Portz qe tot le servise
qe nous est due*g* de leur nefs eent encontre nous a Wynchelse lendemein de la seint Johan le Baptist prochein avenir[1] prest e apparaille
e bein garny daler*h* de illoke en nostre servise la ou nous les feroms
donkes asavoir; vous mandoms en la fei e en la loiaute qe vous nous
devez fermement enioin[an]tz qe vous*i* a les avantditz barons e
prodeshommes santz nule delai, de la nostre part facez fermement
en[i]oindre qe le dit servise de leur nefs eient prest ancountre nous
a iour e lieu avantnomez, prest e apparaille e bien garni daler en
nostre servise solom le fourme qui nous sur ce les avoms mande. Issi
qe par defaute de cel servise ne soient les dites bosoignes en nule
manere destourbees etc.[2]

SC 1/14/92, draft privy seal letters.

50. *Ordinance for the prise of grain, April 1297*

Ordene est qen chescun counte ou ble deit estre pris, seit le ble pris
par le viscounte e par [le clerk] qui y serra assigne de par le rei, e
pur sauver le povre poeple des volunterines prises que plusurs [qui

a···aPassage interlined, written over eez prest et apparaille *struck out.*
b···b Passage interlined.
c adunke *struck out, subsequently marked stet.*
d E ce *struck out.*
e salu *struck out.*
f e especiales *struck out.*
g des nefs *struck out.*
h daler *struck out, then repeated.*
i les a *struck out.*

[1] 25 June 1297.
[2] The summons of service from the Cinque Ports, and the order to Pencester to see
to the matter, were issued formally in letters close under the great seal on 27 April
1297 (*C.C.R., 1296–1302*, pp. 99–100). For a reference to the performance of the service,
see the letter of 5 August (no. 105). The period of service lasted from 26 July to 9
August (B.L., Add. MS. 7965, fo. 103).

se] feseient ministres le rei soleient feire, veut le rei qe les chiefs taxours de dusime en chescun [counte] qui bone conoissaunce ount de chescun poeir seient appelez a la prise, ordener e prendre de chescun [solom] son poeir, sauve leur resnable sustenaunce e sauntz trop grevier le poeple, iesqes a la somme ... a prendre en le counte. E fet a saveir qe des blez des ercevesques, evesques, religieux e autres ... unt la protectioun le rei, generale ou especiale, par gree quil unt fet au rei entre autres clerks ... pris, mes seient sauvez e gardiez au mieux qe hom poet. E des ercevesqes, evesqes, religieux [e] autres clerks qui ne unt mie la protectioun le rei e qui biens sount seisiz en la mein le rei ... toutz leur blez pris al oes le rei, a la summe avauntdite parfaire, sauve la necesseire sustenau[nce] ... le gaignage. E seit la mesure de furment prise par mesure reese, issi ne pur quant qe xxi ... seient pris pur vynt quartiers. E orge, feves, poys e aveine seient mesurez sicome homme ... tieu manere de ble vendu e achate en villes marchaundes en pays. E seit lordenaunce ... endentee entre les taxours e le viscounte e le clerk, issi qele ne seit chaungee par viscounte ... autre. E les viscountes e les clerks en chescun counte facent taille a toutz ceaux qui [blez il] prendront, du noumbre des quartiers e du pris.[a] E en chescun wappentak ou hundred ... seit fet un taille endente e laenz seient escrites tuttes les dites tailles destincteaument ... partie de cele endenture qe demorra vers ceaux du wappentak ou del hundred ... les seaux du viscounte e du clerk, e a la partie qe demorra vers le viscounte e le clerk ... mis les seaux de quatre prodes hommes du wappentak ou del hundred. E cele part ... viscounte e le clerk al eschequier lendemeyn de seint Michel prochein avenir. E cel ... iour seit assigne a ceaux qui bliez serront pris a receivre leur deniers al eschequier ... comencent a faire batre le ble a graunt espleit de iour en iour. E les viscountes ... ove les clerks assignez auxi bien ceaux qui baillies ne se ioygnent mie a l... ceaux qui baillies se ioygnent a la mier, facent carier ceaux bliez as plus p[roche] portz des countiez ou les bliez serront pris, a plus tost quil purront, si qe ... ceaux bliez y demoergent en bone garde e sauve e sauntz enpirement, e seient ... apparaillie pur mettre en vesseaux quant il plerra au rei, mes quil ... en nule vesseaux taunt qe le rei en eit maunde quen part il les vodra faire ... viscountes chescun en sa baillie troefsent les coustages a les sousditz bliez ... illeoques sicome sous est dit, sauvement gardier taunt qe le rei sur ce ... volunte, e de ceo auront allowaunce sur leur acounte al eschequier ... eit cest ordenement ove lui en escrit souz le seal del eschequier.[1]

[a] MS. reads du ble, but pris, as in m. 119, is clearly intended.

[1] Further instructions were issued later, for a third of the wheat to be ground and bolted, and put into tuns, the rest to be put in sacks. The manuscript is unfortunately

E 159/70, m. 120, faded and torn on right margin. The words in brackets are taken from the ordinance of 29 November 1296, *ibid.* m. 119, which starts identically with this one.

51. *Pledges for Adam de Berdeseye, Easter term 1297*

Willelmus de la Puntfeld', Elias de la Breche de comitatu Kantie, Ricardus filius Thomas de comitatu Dors', Johannes de Bermondeseye de comitatu Surr', Johannes de Horneby de comitatu Lanc', Ricardus de Claghton de comitatu Lanc' et Thomas de Schepeleye de comitatu Ebor' venerunt coram baronibus et manuceperunt habere corpus Ade de Berdeseye ad prisonam regis deliberari pro scriptura transcriptorum falsarum bullarum[a] pro quibus Walterus de Maidenestan in prisona regis apud Turrim London' detinetur,[1]

[a] bullarum *repeated in MS.*

badly damaged. The same membrane, 120, gives details of the quantities to be purveyed, and of the clerks appointed to assist the sheriffs, as follows:

Beds. & Bucks.	1,000 qu. wheat	Clerk
	500 qu. oats	Reginald de Gatecoumbe
	300 qu. barley	
	200 qu. beans & peas	
Lincs.	1,500 qu. wheat	Clerk
	500 qu. barley	Richard de Hetherington
	1,000 qu. oats	
	500 qu. beans & peas	
Northants.	1,000 qu. wheat	Clerk
	500 qu. oats	John de Everdon
	200 qu. beans & peas	
Rutland	200 qu. wheat	Clerk
	100 qu. oats	John de Everdon
Warw. & Leics.	1,000 qu. wheat	Clerk
	500 qu. oats	John de Everdon
	100 qu. beans & peas	
Notts. & Derbs.	500 qu. wheat	Clerk
	500 qu. oats	Thomas de Boyvill
Yorks.	2,000 qu. wheat	Clerk
	2,000 qu. oats	Robert Beaufey
Northumbr.	100 qu. wheat	No clerk, the sheriff to act by himself
	300 qu. oats	(John de Kirke's name deleted as clerk)
Totals	7,300 qu. wheat	
	800 qu. barley	
	5,400 qu. oats	
	1,000 qu. beans & peas	
Grand total	14,500 qu. grain	

The Jornalia Roll (E 405/1/11) shows that on 2 May these clerks received payment of 40s. each to cover their expenses. On 25 May further instructions were issued for the grain to be taken to London, by land or sea (E 159/70, m. 120d).

[1] For details of a case brought against Walter de Maidstone involving the alleged possession of coinage dies and the counterfeiting of coin while he was controller of the silver mines in Devon, see E 368/69, m. 47. He was probably the man referred to in

coram rege vel justiciariis sive baronibus de scaccario vel aliis ministris regis ad faciendum voluntatem regis. Et per istam manucaptionem predictus Adam deliberatur a prisona predicta.[1]

E 368/68, m. 53.

52. *Edward I to the barons of the exchequer, 1 May 1297*

Edward par la grace de deu etc. Nous vous mandoms fermement enioygnantz qe les vi Bayoneys qui vienent a Londres pur receyvre par de sa les deniers qe nous lour devoms, recevez bel e corteisement e lour faciez teu gre pur leur despenses e pur lour missions quil se tiegnent bien appaiez, e leur soiez di bel acueil e faites savoir au conestable de la Tour e au Gardien de Londres qe eux ensy seient si qe les Bayoneis se peussent loer de vous e de eux quant nous vendroms a Londres, car il sont de autre condicion qe gueres autres de lour pais quant a ceste venue de ore. Don' souz nostre prive seal a Neuton Ferrers[2] le primer iour de Mai, lan de nostre regne vintisme quinte.

E 159/70, m. 24; E 368/68, m. 38d.

53. *Edward I to the sheriff of Yorkshire, 1 May 1297*

Rex vicecomiti Ebor', salutem. Ex relatu quorumdam fidedignorum nostrorum intelleximus quod cum prelati, religiosi et ceteri clerici de provincia Ebor' omnium eorum assensu quintam partem bonorum suorum ad ecclesie sancte et regni nostri defensionem gratanter concessissent, et inter eos statuissent omnes denarios de eadem quinta provenientes colligi et in certis locis infra predictam provinciam deponi ad dicte defensionis expedicionem maturius et securius inde faciendam, magister Johannes de Crauecombe, archidiaconus Estridingg', Thomas de Corbigg', Robertus de Forda, Rogerus de Marnham canonici ecclesie Ebor' et quidam alii concanonici eiusdem ecclesie

the writ of 4 March 1297 (no. 8). In March 1299 he was pardoned (*C.P.R., 1292–1301*, p. 403). He had been released from the Tower on 20 August 1297 and handed over to the bishop of London in accordance with clerical privilege (*C.C.R., 1296–1302*, p. 56). His innocence on the coinage charge seems fairly clear from the verdict of local jurors, but he was fined £200, presumably over the issue of the papal bulls (E 368/69, mm. 47, 115).

[1] A similar case is referred to in the Liberate Roll (C 62/74, m. 4), in which the sheriff of Lancashire received an *allocate* for 9s. spent on the case of Robet le Bel, chaplain, Walter de Mundham and Edmund his brother. They were arrested at Lancaster by John Russel, who had come from London for the purpose, and who returned south with them.

[2] Newton Ferrers, Dorset.

a voto fideli et concessione gratuita indecenter divertentes predictam quintam partem bonorum suorum concedere eandemque de eis collegi et in dictis locis deponi ingrate contradicunt in dampnum et periculum totius regni nostri. Et ideo tibi precipimus quod statim visis litteris istis singulas personas predictorum magistri Johannis et aliorum concanonicorum predicte ecclesie Ebor' in propria persona tua una cum aliis fidedignis nostris quos ad hoc tecum assumas, adeas ipsos que coram te super hoc aggrediari et ad rationem ponas qui eorum concessionem predicte quinte eiusque collectionem et in locis predictis depositionem ratificare voluerunt, et qui non. Et si qui eorundem concessionem et collectionem dicte quinte eiusdem que in dictis locis depositionem in forma supradicta aliquatenus fieri denegaverint, tunc omnes terras, bona et catalla eorundem in manum nostram capias et seisias. Ita quod nec ipsi nec aliquis per ipsos ad ea manus apponent donec aliud inde tibi precepimus. Et si firme vel redditus de terris eorundem interim pervenerunt seu pervenire debent, illos sine dilacione ad opus nostrum levari facias. Et scire facias baronibus de scaccario nostro sine dilacione omnium concanonicorum predictorum super hoc responsum, et quorum terras et tenementa, bona et catalla una cum valore eorundem bonorum in manum nostram ceperis, occasione supradicta. Et habeas ibi hoc breve. Teste J. de Cobeham apud Westm' primo die Maii, anno regni nostri vicesimo quinto.

E 159/70, m. 110d.

54. *Edward I to the barons of the exchequer, 6 May 1297*

Edward etc. Endreit de ceaux qe unt treit lour leynes ou quirs deinz la fraunchise seint Cuthbert de Dureme ou en autres fraunchises a qui qe eles soient por les chose esloigner de nostre meyne countre la fourme del ordeynement qe en est fait, si voloms qe les viscontes environ celes fraunchises enquergent sour ce le plus sotivement e le plus diligeaument quil porront. E de ceaux quil en troveront coupables e qe unt terres e tenementz dentz les viscontez dehors les boundes de la dite fraunchise quil preignent tantost en nostre meyn totes leur terres e leur tenementz e quant quil unt, issint qe eux ne nul de par eux ny mette la meyn tant quil eient fait a nous pleyne restitutioun de tot ce quil averont ensi esloignez, ou au meyns de la value. E des autres qe averont mesmes teux trespas fait e ne eyent terres ne tenementz dehors la fraunchise qe les viscuntes par dehors les bundes de la dite fraunchise les facent bien geitier e pregnent lour cors e sauvement les gardent, issint quil ne seient delivres en nule manere tant

quil eient sor ce porchace nostre gre e qe nous en eoms comaunde nostre volunte. E qe les viscuntes mettent tote la peine e le conseil quil porront qe nul ne pusse issi par mer ne par terre tant quil en eent fet nostre volunte. E nostre entencioun est qe les viscuntes seient avisez quil ne mettent nul chaleng par auctorite de ceste maundement a nule chose qe seit nee e murie e totes foiz demorant denz les boundes de la fraunchise avantdite. E qe les viscontes nentrent denz les bondes de meisme la fraunchise por prendre ceux qe se recettent ne por nul autre execucioun fere qui appent a cest busoignes, mais par dehors en facent selonc ce quil est avauntdite. Por la queu chose nous vous maundoms qe ceste busoigne facez faire le plus avisement e le plus en haste qe vous porrez. Donez desouz nostre prive seal a Plympton' le vi iour de May, lan de nostre regne vintisme quint.[1]

E 368/68, m. 40; E 159/70, m. 25.

55. *Edward I to the treasurer and barons of the exchequer, 7 May 1297*

Edward par la grace de deu etc. Pur ce qe nous ne trovoms mie devers nous ne nous ne savoms ou est lescrit le rey Dalemayne sele de son seal de lalliance qe est entre ly e nous,[2] ne celi ausint qe le ercevesqe de Coloyne nous fist ou deust aver fait de lalliance qe fust entre nous e ly, ne nous ne trovoms homme pres de nous qe nous en sache de rien aviser, car il dient qe il ne les ount mie receus ne unkes ne vindrent en lur garde; vous mandoms fermement enioignantz qe hastivement saunz nule manere de delay faciez sercher diligeaument meismes les escritz par tot en nostre tresourie e aillours ou vous verrez qe bien soit. E si vous les peussez nule part trover si les nous faciez enveer de iourz e de nutz od tote la haste qe vous porrez. *E nous faciez saver par vos lettres le plus pleinement qe vous porrez quantqe*[b] *vous ensaverez.*[a] Car si nous ne les eussoms meyntenant nous en averoms grant ennuy e grant damage. Don' souz nostre prive seal a Sutton[3] le vii iour de May, lan de nostre regne xxv.

E 159/70, m. 24; an inferior version is in E 368/68, m. 38d.

---

[a]...[a] *Omitted in E 368/68, m. 38d.*
[b] *Followed by* qe *in MS.*

---

[1] A writ in pursuance of this order, issued to the sheriff of Yorkshire in June, is in E 159/70, m. 122.
[2] For the English articles of the treaty, see the facsimile in P. Chaplais, *English Medieval Diplomatic Practice, Part II* (London, 1975), plate 6. Edward's ratification of the treaty is in *Treaty Rolls*, i, 98–100.
[3] In Plymouth.

56. *The keepers of the customs at Boston to the treasurer and barons of the exchequer, 9 May 1297*

A nobles siers e lors treschers seignurs, a thresorier e barouns del escheker nostre seigneur le rey, les gardeyns de la custume nostre seignur le rey a la Seint Botouf, saluz, honeurs e reverences. Sachez sires qe nous resceumes la lettre nostre seigneur le rey desuz son prive seal a la Seint Botouf le merkedy le utyme ior de May au soir, de la quele lettre nous vous enveoms le transcrit enclos denz ceste lettre. E vous requestoms sil vous plet ke vous nous [voillez] certifier de acune poinz de meime la lettre que sont dotous e oscure a nus. Cest asaver qe de ceo qe nostre seignur le rey nous mande qe nous seoms prestement purveu de suffisaunte navye pur envoier iesques en Flaundres ou en Brabant les leynes e les quirs que a nous vendront a son oes, e qe nous les enveoms hastivement tot les sacs qe a nous vendrunt e qe nous les facoms livrer illoqes a ceus qui sont assignez resceyvors de par nostre seignur le rey, sicum vous porrez plus pleynement veer par lavauntdit transcript. E pur ceo sires quil i ad plusurs havenes en Flandres e en Brabant, e nous ne savoms a quel haven neefs freeter ne queus miuz sunt rescyvors de la par le rey ne en quele viles il demorgent ne queus persones escrire ne cyrograffe fere de les avantdit leynes e quirs. Dont, sil vous plet, vous nous voillez hastivement certifier par bref e apertement ceo que nous en devoms fere en les avandit choses. Sachez sire qe il ny ad nule leynes uncore venuz a le Seint Botouf for les leynes que William Hauward lessa illoques en nostre garde. Dont, sil vous plet, nous vous voillez mander si nous devoms cele leynes passer avant ceo qe plus nous veiynt. E sachez, sires, qe nule navye ne veint a la Seint Botouf for de la outre e de cele navye ne pouns rien aver sanz certeyn frecte e a certeyn haven. Dont sil vous plet nous voillez mander garant par bref le rey de alluance de custage quil coveint mettre en neefs freiter e en autre custages qe apendent a les avantdit leynes e quirs passer. E pur dei, sires, sil vous plet, haster le portur de ceste lettre a retourner a nous pur le hastive mandement nostre seignur le rey.[1] Escrit a Seint Botouf le ix iour de May.

Endorsement

[a]En Brebaunt ... au port de Andwerp. E Elis Russel est recevoir de le ... e demoert en meismes la ville de Andwerp. E a li serront les leines envees e cirograf fet cuntre li.

[a] *Above the first line is the word* Flaundr', *struck out.*

[1] On 14 May exchequer writs were issued to the customs collectors at Hull, Boston, Ipswich, Yarmouth, Sandwich, Southampton, Bristol, London and Newcastle, ordering them to elect, together with the urban authorities, a man experienced in the business of wool and hides, to be responsible for exporting the wool to Brabant, and ordering them to have the wool shipped as soon as possible (E 159/70, m. 101).

Les leines, qe Willame Haward lessa en la vile de Seint Botouf en vostre garde, seient hastivement enveez en Brebaunt au dit port, issi qe nule defaute seit trovee en vous. E si tost come autres leines vous vendront, hastivement seient envees au dit port solom le bref le rei du prive seal.

E tuttes les leines qe vendront a la Seint Botouf al oes le rei seient envees a Brebaunt au dit port e livrees au dit Elis.

Frettez niefs au mieux qe vous purrez, e le cust qe vous y mettrez par resun vous serra allouwe sur vostre acount.

SC 1/47/173. Original, holed for filing.

57. *Edward I to the deputy treasurer and barons of the exchequer, 11 May 1297*

Edward etc. au lieu tenaunt nostre tresorier e as barouns del escheker, salutz. Nous avoms entendu qe Adam de Brai, gardein de nos chevaux qui sont a Hertford',[1] envea ne ad gueres un de ses valetz iusqes a un manoir pres de Hertford' qui est del Hospital, pur prendre y aveynes pur la sustenaunce de nos chevaux avantditz, a qe un frere del Hospital qui lors estoit a meismes cel manier fist la refuite des dites aveynes tot vite, de quei nous ne feimes mie molt grant force. Car nostre entencion est qe ceux del Hospital e du Temple e les autres qe ount fait fraunchement nostre gre eent lour choses bien e en peis a faire ent lur profit, e qe hom nen preigne rien encontre lour gre,[2] mes pur ce qe puis y vindrent aucuns chapeleyns e diaknes ausint e donoient sentence sour touz ceux qe teux prises y firent e qui sy entremettent en despit de nous e de nos, sicome le dit Adam ou aucuns de suens vous porra plus pleynement mostrer. Vous mandoms qe hastivement enveez y aucun certein homme qui enquerre la certeinete de la dite sentence en touz poinz, e ceux qe vous en trovez copables faciez venir devant vous a nostre escheker e lour faciez trover bon meinprise e sufisante de ester ent a nostre agard quele houre qe nous lour feseoms saver sour ce nostre volunte. E volums qe la dite meinprise se face en totes manieres devant vous a nostre escheker e ne mie aillours. De autre part nous vous mandoms qe vous facez mander a bailif de Hertford' quil seit en aide a noz gentz qe ont nos chevaux

---

[1] Adam de Bray had charge of a number of royal horses, at one time totalling 53, at Hertford between 22 February and 28 May 1297 (B.L., Add. MS. 7965, fo. 27). As clerk of the marshalsea he was again to be in trouble for taking prises illegally in 1311 (*Chronicles of the Reigns of Edward I and Edward II*, ed. W. Stubbs, Rolls Series, 1882–3, i, 200).

[2] The king had forbidden the taking of corn from the Hospitallers on 7 March (*C.C.R., 1296–1302*, p. 19).

en garde celes parties, coment il eent aveynes e autres choses dount
nos chevaux ... [peuvent] estre sustenuz, e vous meismes pernez garde
qe ensi soit, e lour faciez aveir aucuns deners pur ... mieux suffeire
e pur meinz grever le pueple. Car le temps dort ne doune mie qe
ceux chevaux ... moergent pur defaute. E ce qe vous avez fait de
ceux qui doneient la sentence avantdite nous faciez saver par vos
lettres au plus tost qe vous porrez. Don' desouz nostre prive seal a
Cheddeleye¹ le xi iour de May, lan de nostre regne xxv.

E 159/70, m. 24d.

58. *Receipt from Richard de Havering and John de Hustwayt, 18 February
1297, with royal order for payment, 14 May 1297*

Willelmus Russel vadlettus Willelmi Waughan de Salop' protulit
coram baronibus xiiii die Maii quandam litteram obligatoriam in hec
verba:

Universis pateat per presentes quod nos Ricardus de Havering' et
Johannes de Hustwayt, illustris regis Anglie clerici, recognoscimus nos
mutuo recepisse de Willelmo Russell vadletto Willelmi Waughan de
Salop' centum marcas sterlingorum pro quibusdam prefati domini
regis arduis negotiis expediendis in partibus transmarinis, videlicet
ad quandam summam decem milium librarum turronensis nigrorum
quas idem dominus rex a diversis mercatoribus suis in predictis partibus mutuare fecit per quamdam commissionem ipsius domini regis
quam domino Reginaldo de Ferre et nobis inde fieri fecit.² Ad quarum
quidem centum marcarum solucionem dicto Willelmo aut eius attornato has litteras deferenti in scaccario dicti domini regis apud Westm'
infra quindenam Pasche proximo futuro faciendam, dictum
dominum regem bonaque sua virtute prefate commissionis obligamus
per presentes. In cuius rei testimonium has litteras nostras eidem fieri
fecimus patentes. Dat' apud Andwerpe³ xviii die Februarii, anno
domini milesimo ducentesimo nonagesimo sexto.⁴

Pretextu cuiusdam littere mandatum est Ade de Rokesle et Johanni
de Cantuar' custodibus custume nostre London' in hac forma:

¹ Chudleigh, Devon.
² The Jornalia Roll (E 405/1/11, m. 5) reveals that the purpose of these loans was
to pay 10,000 *livres tournois* to John, count of Holland. The entry records repayment
at the exchequer of £10 to Thomas Holpit on 2 July 1297.
³ Antwerp, Belgium.
⁴ For an example of a similar receipt, made out by John Botetourt, William de Carleton and John de Hustwayt for £20 borrowed from Roger de Seaford, see E 159/70,
m. 98. For a discussion of loans made by English merchants in the Low Countries,
see Fryde, 'Financial Resources of Edward I in the Netherlands', 1176–7. To the
references given there should be added the Jornalia Rolls (E 405/1/10 and E 405/1/
11).

Edwardus dei gratia etc. Mandamus vobis quod de pecunia proveniente de custuma predicta habere facere Willelmo Russel vadletto Willelmi Waughan de Salop' c. marcas quas dilecti clerici nostri Ricardus de Havering et Johannes de Hustweyt ad negotia nostra in partibus transmarinis expedienda a predicto Willelmo mutuo receperunt, recepta tamen prius ab ipso Willelmo littera obligatoria predictorum Ricardi et Johannis quam inde habet. Et nos illas c. marcas in compoto vestro proximo ad scaccarium nostrum allocari faciemus. Teste P. de Wylughby, tenente locum thesaurarii nostri apud Westm' xiiii die Maii, anno regni nostri vicesimo quinto.[1]

E 368/68, m. 94.

59. *Edward I to Henry Newark, archbishop-elect of York, 14 May 1297*

Rex dilecto sibi in Cristo electo Ebor', salutem. Cum inter nos et clerum vestre diocesis felici consideratione statuissetis et concessissetis ad quintam partem bonorum vestrorum et suorum in certo loco depondendam, et quandocumque ad ecclesie sancte et regni nostri defensionem de eadem indigeretur, prompta in denariis inveniretur, quod hucusque fieri differtur, de quo miramur, cum debita executio gratanti voto sapientis debeat corespondere, et eo celerius ne sub inde tarditatis periculum intensius posset imminere,[a] vobis mandamus quod omnes denarios de predicta quinta provenientes seu proventuros in domo Sancti Leonardi Eboracensis que pro nobis et vobis securior et competentior locus videtur, absque omni dilacione omnino adunari et deponi faciatis. Et de summa denariorum in dicto loco depositorum, seu deponendorum, thesaurario et baronibus nostris de scaccario apud Westm' absque mora constare faciatis. Et hoc nullo modo omittatis sicut dicte ecclesie et regni nostri defensionem nostrumque honorem iuxta voti nostri gratam affectionem quam merito habemus recomendatam diligitis et a periculo penitus salvari volueritis remittatisque ibi tunc hoc breve. Teste P. de Wileghby tenente locum thesaurarii nostri apud Westm' xiiii de Maii, anno regni nostri vicesimo quinto.

Consimile breve mandatum est episcopo Karl'. Teste ut supra.

E 159/70, m. 101.

[a] *MS.* imienere.

[1] For another method of payment, see the case of John Schirle of Hampshire, who lent William de Carleton and John de Hustwayt £40 in Brabant, which was then credited to him in accounting for a sum of £56 which he owed at the exchequer. The writ was dated 23 May 1297 (E 368/68, m. 96).

60. *Edward I to John Droxford and the barons and chamberlains of the exchequer, 15 May 1297*

Edward par la grace de deu etc. Nous vous avoms mande avant ces hures par nos lettres qe vous enveiastez en les contez de Nicole, Norhampton', Rotel', Leyc', Notingh', Derb', Everwyk' et Norhumbr' certeines gentz e penibles pur prendre y de ble a nostre oes, ce qe il porreint sauve resnable sustenaunce as gentz e saunz trop grever le puple, e pur meismes le ble faire venir a plus eesez portz des ditz contez a plus tost quil porreient, les queux choses vous avez mises en oevre despuis a ce qe nous entendoms.[1] E pur ce qe nous meismes bioms passer la outre si dieu plest bien tost apres les oytaves de la nativite seint Johan le Baptiste procheinement avenir[2] ove les gentz darmes de nostre reaume qui nous porroms bonement aveir ovesqe nous a cele houre, par quei il nous covendra grant foison de blez e de vivres pur la sustenance de nous e de noz pur ceu voyage; vous mandoms qe hastivement e sauntz nul delay faciez mander par lettres de nostre escheker le plus chargeaument e le plus especiaument qe vous porrez a tuz ceux qui se entremettent de prendre les blez avantditz qe entour la prise de meismes ces blez, mettent tota la haste e la dilegence quil porrount. E qe meismes les blez facient bien aparailer e mettre en bons vesseaus al plus en haste quil porront. E qe le ble seit en teu manere eskipez e atirrez en toutz poinz qe nous le croissoms bon e freis quele houre qe nous en eioms a fere. E pur meismes les blez faciez assigner certeins veseaus solonc ce qe vous verrez qe mieuz seit e sicome la bosoigne le demande, mais tut seit le ble ensi eskipe e mis en vesseaux; nous voloms qe vous avisez apertement tuz ceux qe se entremettent de la dite bosoigne qe les vesseaus ne se moevent nule part des portz ou il serrunt chargiez tant qe nous en eoms comande plus avant nostre volunte, e prenez*[a]* bone garde qe totes ces choses seient faites en la manere avantdit. E nous faciez saver par vos lettres au plus tost qe vous porrez ce qe vous en avez fait. Don' desuz nostre prive seal a Ludres[3] le xv iour de May, lan de nostre regne xxv. E nous vous mandoms qe hastivement enveez un penible clerk en le conte de Kent e qe meismes le clerk ensemblement ove le visconte de meisme le conte facent purveer en les parties de Sussex e de Wynchels' cleyes e pountz e autres choses qui covienent pur chevaux eskiper ove tote la foison quil porront. E a ceste chose faire lur faitez aveir lettres de poer e quantqe mester lur serra, e faciez tant

---

[a] *MS.* pernez.

[1] This prise was authorized by the king on 5 April (no. 34), and duly organized by the exchequer (no. 50).
[2] 31 June.
[3] Loders, Dorset.

qe ceste bosoigne seit mise en oevre e sespleite en la meylore manere
e au plus en haste qe vous porrez.[1] E vous remandez par vos lettres
au plus tost qe vous porrez ce qe vous en averez fait.

E 159/70, m. 25.

61. Edward I to John Botetourt, 15 May 1297

Rex dilecto et fideli suo Johanni de Botetourte, salutem. Mandamus
vobis quod visis litteris omni dilacione postposita obligacionem
archiepiscopi Coloniensis[a] de serviendo nobis cum mille hominibus
equitibus armatis de ferro per dimidium annum contra regem
Francie, quam vos de partibus Holandie attulistis, per aliquem de
vestris de quo confidetis, tenenti locum thesaurarii nostri de scaccario
transmittatis.[2] Et hoc nullo modo omittatis. Teste P. de Wileghby etc.,
xv die Maii, anno xxv. Per breve de privato sigillo. Et mittitur per
Johannem le Cok nuncium scaccarii xvi die Maii ad horam nonam.

E 159/70, m. 101d.

62. Letters patent of Edward I, 20 May 1297

Rex omnibus ad quos presentes littere pervenerint, salutem. Sciatis
quod assignavimus vicecomitem nostrum Kancie et dilectos clericos
nostros Alexandrum le Convers et Petrum de Cicestr' vel unum
eorundem clericorum quociens ambo interesse non poterunt, ad quedam victualia pro nobis et aliis nobiscum profecturis versus partes
transmarinas, et ad meremium et alia necessaria ad pontes et clayas
pro eodem passagio nostro in singulis boscis quorumcumque fuerunt
in comitatu predicto capienda et providenda, et ad alia facienda que
eis ex parte nostra plenius sunt iniuncta. Ita quod predicti vicecomes
et clerici nostri vel unus eorundem clericorum omnia et singula que
ad opus nostrum sic capient per sacramentum fidedignorum appreciari et tallias de precio eorundem illis quorum predicte res fuerint
faciant, ut precium illud simul cum omnibus custibus in premissis
omnibus capiendis, providendis, faciendis et cariandis apponendis de
garderoba nostra solvi faciamus. Et ideo vobis mandamus quod eisdem vicecomiti et clericis nostris vel uni eorundem clericorum in

---

[a] MS. reads Coloni eum.

[1] Alexander le Convers and Peter of Chichester were duly appointed to act with the
sheriff of Kent in this matter (no. 62).
[2] For this matter, see the letter of 7 May (no. 55). The agreement with the archbishop
is printed in Treaty Rolls, i, 105.

premissis omnibus intendentes sitis et respondentes, consulentes et auxiliantes, quociens per ipsos vel unum ipsorum ex parte nostra fueritis requisiti. In cuius rei testimonium has litteras nostras fieri fecimus patentes. Teste P. de Wylugby, tenente locum thesaurii nostri, xx die Maii, anno regis Edwardi vicesimo quinto, per breve de privato sigillo.[1]

E 159/70, m. 101d.

63. Edward I to the sheriff of Warwickshire, 24 May 1297

Precepimus tibi quod, accepta sufficienti securitate, pro qua tu ipse respondere volueris a Willelmo de Copston de Coventr', Ricardo le Brochere de eadem, Willelmo de Shepeye de eadem et Richero de Weston de eadem, captis et detentis in prisona nostra Warr' pro lanis per ipsos concelatis contra formam proclamacionis quam per te in eodem comitatu nuper inde fieri fecerimus, prout in inquisicione coram dilecto nobis Johanne de Crokesle super huiusmodi concelamento nuper in dicto comitatu ad mandatum nostrum facta, et ad scaccarium nostrum retornata est compertum quod parati erunt ad voluntatem nostram ad satisfaciendum nobis pro de concelamento predicto et de valore bonorum et catallorum suorum ea occasione in manum nostram captorum, si ea habere debeamus, racione concelamenti predicti, tunc ipsos Willelmum, Ricardum, Willelmum et Richerum a prisone predicta, si dicta occasione detineantur in eadem. Et scire facias baronibus de scaccario nostro apud Westm' a die Sancti Trinitatis in quindecim dies, que bona et catalla pretextu huius precepti nostri eis liberaveris, et quantum valeant, et securitatem quam ab eis ceperis in forma predicta. Et habeas ibi tunc hoc brevem. Teste J. de Cobeham etc. xxiiii die Maii, anno xxv^{to}. Per rotulum memorandorum de eodem anno.[2]

E 368/68, m. 43.

64. Ordinance of 28 May 1297

Memorandum quod xxviii die Maii etc. venit hic dilectus et fidelis regis Hugo le Despenser et exposuit Philippo de Wylugby tenente locum thesaurarii et baronibus ex parte domini regis quod rex de gracia sua speciali wult et concessit quod omnes illi qui coram hiis

---

[1] This writ was issued as a result of the instructions contained in the privy seal writ of 15 May (no. 60). See no. 121 for a financial agreement between Alexander le Convers and Peter of Chichester.

[2] Four similar writs on behalf of other merchants follow in the roll. A general ordinance dealing with this problem was issued on 28 May (no. 64).

qui deputabantur in singulis comitatibus huius regni ad arestandum lanas et coria salsa ad opus regis iuxta ordinacionem inde factam sint convicti quod lanas et coria sua concelarunt et ad certos locum et diem ad quos ea cariasse debuissent secundum formam proclamacionis quam rex in singulis comitatibus predictis per vicecomites eorundem comitatuum inde fieri fecerat pro eiusmodi transgressione terras et tenementas, bona et catalla eorum omnium ex precepto ipsius domini regis in manu sua capta existunt; quandocumque veniant hic et inveniant sufficientem securitatem quod parati erunt ad voluntatem regis ad satisfaciendum ei de transgressione predicta et de valore bonorum et catallorum suorum captorum in manum regis occasione illius transgressionis, si rex ea causa debeat ea habere; tunc per securitatem illam habeant brevia vicecomitum de quorum balliva existant quod bona et catalla sua capta in manu regis pro huiusmodi transgressione restituant eisdem et quod illi qui capti sunt et detenti in prisona pro transgressionibus consimili, prout supradicitur ad sectam illius qui pro eis hic prosequi voluerit habeant brevia vicecomitum in quorum custodia imprisonentur, quod capiant ab eis securitatem in forma predicta, et extunc eos a prisona deliberent, si alia occasione non detineantur in eadem, et terras et tenementas, bona et catalla sua eis restituant et vicecomites illi scire faciant hic ad diem eis prefigendum securitatem quam inde ceperint etc.[1]

E 368/68, m. 44.

65. *Edward I to Adam de Guildford, John Atte Wood, Henry le Berchey and Henry Grinegone, 29 May 1297*

Rex dilectis suis Ade de Gildeford, Johanni Atte Wode de Wycumbe, Henrico le Berchey et Henrico Grinegone de Aylesbury, salutem. Quia dilecto et fideli nostro Henrici de Lacy comiti Linc', qui in obsequio nostro in partibus Vasconie moratur hiis diebus, graciam volumus facere specialem, vobis mandamus quod triginta petras lane ipsius comitis per dilectionem et fidelem nostrum Johannem de Mitford iuxta ordinacionem factam de lanis in regno nostro ad opus nostrum arestandis, arestatas et vobis per eundem Johannem liberatas custodiendas, predicto comiti sine dilacione et diminucione qualibet liberetis ad faciendum inde commodum suum pro voluntate sua. Teste J. de Cobham etc. xxix die Maii etc., per J. de Insula.

E 368/68, m. 43.

[1] On 31 May exchequer writs were sent to all sheriffs, instructing them to release all those held in prison for concealing wool and hides, by mainprise of four lawful men (E 159/70, m. 43d).

66. *Edward I to John Droxford and the barons of the exchequer, 30 May 1297*

Edward par la grace de deu etc. Pur ce qe nous avoms entendu qe un Restor Bonaventur' de la companie de Spine passa ne ad gueres la outre en capinage hors del port de Seint Botolph' en defaute des gardiens du passages celes parties; vous mandoms qe hastivement, veues ces lettres, faciez chastier les gardiens du passage du dit port en tieu maniere qe autres preignent ensample de garder les passages en due maniere. Et au plus tost qe vous porrez nous faciez saver par vos lettres ce qe vous en aurez fait. Don' desuz nostre prive seal a Lewes le xxx iour de Mai, lan de nostre regne xxv.[1]

E 159/70, m. 25d.

67. *Exchequer ordinance concerning wool exports, probably made in May 1297*

E voet le rey qe tuttes ses leynes propres qui passees ne sount, de quei nule coustume nest due, demoergent par de cea, si qe nules ne passent la outre, taunt quil en eit autre chose ordene. E qe tuttes les leynes qui autres averont a passier qui quil soient, passent tuttes foiz sauntz destourbance, paiant la coustume, e qom haste le passage quanqe hom purra fors qe des leynes le rey propres. E face a remembrier qe home deit escrire a touz les custumers Dengleterre que il ne soeffrent nule leyne que seit au rei propre passer mes la facent enveier a Lundres, e quil certifiount as barons del eschequier quan des sakes de leines sount passez outre a leur portz des leines le rei propres einz ces houres, e ausint de quirs. E quil certifiount les ditz barons deinz[a] leur lettres quantz sakes de leyne seont passiez a leur portz, de qyqe ces seit, paiaunt la custume, cest a saver del iour quil aveient e receivent de congie de passier ieskes a iour qe cestui brif leur vendra, e auxissint de quirs. E que les chamberleyns le rei serchint hastivement estreittement toutz les remembranz quil unt de totes les pais que unt este faites, par de la ou de cea a nul des aliennes le rei ou autre pur le rei qe de la seit, issint qe riens ne seit obliez quil neint serchie a leur peril, e que celes remembranz, oveskes totz manier descriz quil eient de pais, ou des covenances ou daquitances de nuli autre, fait quil valier peut seurement seient liverez en garderobe par bon endenture e qe laeniz

---

[a] *MS.* veniez.

[1] For the ordinance appointing guardians of the ports, made on 1 March 1297, see *C.C.R., 1296–1302*, p. 86. Another version, with slight changes, is enrolled on E 159/70, m. 98. For the unlicensed departure from the realm of two other Italian merchants, see E 159/70, m. 61d.

demoerge e passier oveske le rei, e iea le meins que sire Johan de Ber-
wik eit le transescrist oveskes luy.

E 159/70, m. 98d.

68. *The treasurer to Edward I, probably May 1297*

Excellentissimo principi et domino suo domino Edwardo regi Anglie,
devoti sui thesaurarius etc, fidele semper servitium cum omni
reverencia et honore; mandavit nobis vestra serenitas quod si
Gerardus de Sesenaco, procurator Pandulphi de Sabello et Jacobi de
Sabello, ut asseruit, coram nobis sufficiens procurationem ostenderet
per quod procuratorium haberet recognitionem pro dictis Pandulpho
et Jacobo coram nobis faciendum, sicut alii de clero regni vestri
faciunt pro pace vestra habenda, tunc recognitionem quam procurator predictus coram nobis in forma predicta facere vellet, reciperemus
et vos inde certioraremus, super quo sciat vestra dominatio quod per
sufficientem manucaptionem vobis ad scaccarium vestrum inventam,
ratione insufficientie procuratorie predicti, dictus procurator finem
fecit vobiscum pro predicto Pandulpho per xlvii marcas pro protectione vestra habenda, et pro predicto Jacobo per xxvi marcas pro
eodem. Breve vestrum nobis super hoc directum vobis remittimus presentibus interclusum. Valeat dominatio vestra per tempora longiora.[1]

E 368/68, m. 38d.

69. *Edward I to Henry Newark, archbishop-elect of York, 1 June 1297*

Rex dilecto sibi in Cristo H. electo Ebor', salutem. Cum iuxta nostre
circumspectionis decretum et vestri ac cleri vestre diocesis consensum
pecunie deposicionem de quinta parte bonorum vestrorum et ipsius
cleri provenientis, quam ad ecclesie sancte et regni nostri defensionem
gratanter concessistis, in domo sancti Leonardi Ebor' fieri decre-
veritis, et nos per litteras vestras intelleximus quod dicta pecunia in
loco predicto citra festum sancte Trinitatis plene deponatur, nos ad
ipsius ecclesie et dicti regni inimmicorum propulsionem, ad quam ex
corde procedere nitimur, huiusmodi pecunia indigentes; vobis mandamus in fide et dilectione quibus nobis tenemini quod dicta pecunia
iuxta vestrum mandatum in loco predicto plenarie deponatur. Mandavimus enim vicecomiti nostro Ebor' quod dictam pecuniam per
visum Johannis Dymmok' servientis de scaccario nostro, quem ad

[1] Pandulf and James de Sabello received protections for three years on 3 June 1297
(*C.P.R., 1292–1301*, p. 250).

partes vestras misimus, citra octabas sancte Trinitatis usque London'
faciat cariari. Et si aliquem vestre diocesis rebellem et solucionem
dicte pecunie resistentem inveneritis, tunc nomen illius baronibus de
scaccario nostro sine dilacione significetis, ut contra ipsum tanquam
inimicorum nostrorum complicem et fautorem iusta et debita punicione procedatur. Scientes autem quod intencionis nostre non fuerit,
nec vestre fuerit credimus, quod ulli beneficiato, cuius valor beneficii
ad xl. solidos vel utra se extenderet, in dicta concessione parceretur,
cum nulli beneficiato alibi infra regnum nostrum super hoc parcatur,
unde vestram diligenciam circumspectius interponatis, ut iuxta concessionem nostram saltim vestram dicta pecunia colligatur et deponatur in forma supradicta. Teste P. de Wileghby, tenente locum thesaurarii nostri apud Westm' primo die Junii, anno regni nostri xxv^to.[1]

E 159/70, m. 114d.

70. *Edward I to John Droxford, the deputy treasurer and barons of the exchequer, 2 June 1297*

Edward par la grace de dieu roy Dengleterre, seigneur Dirlande e
ducs Daquitaine, a nostre chier clerk e foial Johan de Drokensford
gardeyn de nostre garderobe, au lieu tenaunt nostre tresorier e as
barouns del eschequier, saluz. Nous vous maundoms qe desorena-
vaunt recevez a nostre dit eschekier les fyns des .. ercevesqes, ..
evesques, .. abbez, .. priours e autres gentz de religioun, e de dames
vedues qui fins voudront faire pur le servise darmes quil nous deyvent.
E sur ce leur assignez le plus bref terme qe vous porrez bonement.
Don' souz nostre prive seal a Canterbir' le ii iour de Juyn, lan de
nostre regne vintisme quint.[2]

E 159/70, m. 42d.

71. *Hugh le Despenser to John de Lisle and John de Baukwell, 3 June 1297*

A ses chiers amys Johan del Isle e Johan de Baukwelle ou a lun de
eux, Hughe le Despenser, saluz. Pur ce qe nus avoms entendu qe Willame de Upton', marchaunt, mist en gage a Loundres cink saks de

---

[1] A writ in pursuance of these instructions was issued on the same date to the sheriff
of Yorkshire, and similar writs to the bishop of Carlisle and the sheriff of Cumberland
(E 159/70, m. 114d). On 3 June Dymmock received 40s. as expenses at the exchequer
(Jornalia Roll, E 405/1/11).
[2] Exchequer writs to the sheriffs were issued on 4 June, requesting that fines for service
should be paid by 7 July (E 159/70, m. 42d). The original summons had been issued
on 15 May (*Parl. Writs*, i, 282).

leyne por la custume de cele leyne e des autres leynes e qe cele leyne est peus areste, tut eyt il la custume pae. Vus maundoms de par le roy qe, si issint soyt, dunke ceux cink saks de leynes au dyt marchaunt facez liverer. E ceste lettre ws serra garaunt. A dieu soez. Escrit a Cantwarbere le iii iour de Jun.

Et pretextu huius littere mandatum est Adamo de Rokeslegh', Johanni de Cantuar' et Albredo de Fiscampo, custodibus custume apud London', quod, accepta a predicto Willelmo custuma illa pro qua dicta lana invadiata fuit, si prius inde non satisfecerit, et similiter custuma de predictis quinque saccis lane debita, tunc eosdem quinque saccos eidem Willelmo restituant. Teste etc.

E 368/68, m. 40.

72. *Letters patent of Edward I, 5 June 1297*

Rex omnibus ad quos presentes littere pervenerint, salutem. Cum negocium presentis guerre inter nos et regem Francorum existentis, ob quod nos ad partes transmarinas in brevi transfretare intendimus, domino concedente, tam arduum et vigens existit, nosque et singulos de regno nostro in tantum contingit, quod in capcione victualium pro nobis et nostris nobiscum profecturis, nulli parcere possumus ista vice; assignavimus vicecomitem nostrum Bed' et Buk' ad providendum et capiendum tam a personis ecclesiasticis quam aliis potentibus infra comitatus predictos, a quibus melius fieri poterit, cc bacones et c carcos' boum salsatos, salvo singulorum sustentacione decenti, per racionabile precium, ad opus nostrum et per visum et testimonium dilecti clerici nostri Reginaldi de Gatecoumbe. Ita quod iidem vicecomes et clericus noster de baconibus et carcos' predictis sic capiendis et de precio eorundem tallias sigillis eorundem vicecomitis et clerici sigillatas faciant omnibus a quibus capient hec predicta, et nos precium illud eis in garderoba nostra solvi faciemus. Et ideo vobis mandamus quod eisdem vicecomiti et clerico nostris, vel uni eorum, in premissis intendentes sitis, et respondentes, consulentes et auxiliantes, cum per eosdem vel unum eorum ex parte nostra fueritis requisiti, sicut commodum nostrum, totiusque regni nostri, diligitis, et honorem. In cuius rei testimonium has litteras nostras fieri fecimus patentes. Teste P. de Wileghby, tenente locum etc., apud Westm' quinto die Junii, anno etc. xxv[to]. Per ipsum regem, nunciante W. de Bello Campo et J. de Drokenesford.[1]

E 159/70, m. 121.

[1] Similar writs were issued to the following counties, specifying the quantities of victuals and the supervisors of the prise as follows:

73. *Edward I to the deputy treasurer and barons of the exchequer, 7 June 1297*

Edward etc au lieu tenaunt nostre tresorier e as barons del eschekier, saluz. Come nous eoms entendu qe Geffredyn de Sarzane, procuratour mestre Geffred de Vezan, est pris e tenu en nostre prisoun a Nichole pur ceo quil dit a un baillif, qui vint nadgueres a seint Botulf de par le viscounte de Nichole pur feire prises illoqes a nostre oes des bliez e dautres choses quil se gardast en tieu maniere quant a tieu chose feire quil nen feust excomengiez; vous faisoms a savoir qe pur lamour lavauntdit mestre Geffred nous voloms feire grace au dit Geffredin en cele partie, en tieu maniere qe, si celi mestre Greffred meinpreigne devaunt vous le dit Geffredyn de le feire venir devaunt nous a la quinzeine de la Trinite procheinement avenir, pur feire nostre volunte sour la busoigne avauntdite, qe adonqes par lettres de nostre eschekier faciez deliverer le dit Geffredyn sauntz delai solonc la meinprise desousdite.[1] Donees desouz nostre prive seal a Canterbir' le vii iour de Juyn, lan de nostre regne xxv.[2]

E 159/70, m. 24.

Lincs.	300 bacons	100 beef carcases	Richard de Hetherington		
Northants.	200 ,,	100 ,, ,,	John de Everdon		
Rutland	100 ,,	50 ,, ,,	,, ,,		
Warw. & Leics.	200 ,,	100 ,, ,,	,, ,,		
Notts. & Derbs.	200 ,,	100 ,, ,,	Thomas de Boyvill		
Yorks.	400 ,,	300 ,, ,,	William de St. Quintino, Robert Beaufey		
Northumb.	200 ,,	100 ,, ,,	Two good men of the county		
Cambs. & Hunts.	200 ,,	100 ,, ,,	,,	,,	,,
Oxon. & Berks.	200 ,,	100 ,, ,,	,,	,,	,,
Essex & Herts.	200 ,,	100 ,, ,,	,,	,,	,,
Surrey & Sussex	200 ,,	100 ,, ,,	,,	,,	,,
Wilts.	100 ,,		,,	,,	,,
Kent	200 ,,	100 ,, ,,	,,	,,	,,
Som. & Dorset	200 ,,	50 ,, ,,	,,	,,	,,
Total	2,900 ,,	1,400 ,, ,,			

Writs were also issued on 5 June 1297 ordering the victuals to be taken to the same ports as the grain ordered earlier, in the case of the counties where clerks were appointed to supervise the prise. In the case of the other counties, the supplies were to be taken to Winchelsea (E 159/70, m. 121). On 23 June writs were issued hastening the process under threat of imprisonment (E 159/70, m. 107d). Payments to messengers taking these writs of 5 June are recorded under 6 June in the wardrobe book (B.L., Add. MS. 7965, fo. 112).

[1] The mainprise is duly recorded in E 159/70, m. 6od.

[2] On the previous day fourteen minstrels had played before the image of the Virgin Mary in the cathedral crypt, in the presence of the king (B.L., Add. MS. 7965, fo. 55v).

74. *Edward I to William de Brumbelschete and Richard de Aylsetone, 7 June 1297*

Rex dilectis et fidelibus suis Willelmo de Brumbelschete et Ricardo de Aylseton', salutem. Quia intelleximus quod principales taxatores et collectores undecime nuper nobis a laycis concesse in comitatu Wiltes' diversas summas pecunie de diversis hominibus eiusdem comitatu receperunt pro predicta undecima, que ad nos pertinebant, et quas in rotulis suis de taxatione eiusdem undecime quos libera-verunt ad scaccarium nostrum nondum plenarie apposuerunt, set eas pro magna parte penes se hucusque detinuerunt, et eas sibi ipsis appropriaverunt ad dampnum nostrum non modicum, assignavimus vos ad diligentem inquisicionem super hoc faciendam, videlicet quod et quantum et de quo seu de quibus singillatim receperunt, et quod in rotulis suis predictis non apposuerunt. Et ideo vobis mandamus quod ad certos diem et locum quos ad hoc provideritis predictam in-quisicionem capiatis in presencia Willelmi Malin quem ad partes vestras mittimus. Et inquisicionem illam distincte et aperte factam habeatis coram baronibus de scaccario nostro apud Westm' quam pri-mum fieri poterit, sub sigillis vestris et sigillis eorum per quos facta fuerit, mandavimus enim vicecomiti nostro comitatus eiusdem quod ad certos diem et locum quos ei scire facietis, venire faciat coram vobis tot et tales tam milites quam alios liberos et legales homines de comi-tatu predicto, per quos rei veritas melius sciri poterit in premissis. In cuius rei testimonium has litteras nostras fieri fecimus patentes. Teste J. de Cobeham apud Westm' septimo die Junii, anno regni nostri vice-simo quinto.

E 159/70, m. 43d.

75. *Edward I to John de Everdon and the sheriff of Gloucestershire, 7 June 1297*

Rex dilectis et fidelibus suis magistro Johanni de Everdon' et vice-comiti Gloucestr', salutem. Quia intelleximus quod Ricardus le Hos-tage, clericus ad capiendum blada ad opus nostrum in eodem comi-tatu nuper assignatus, recepit de abbate Glouc' sexaginta solidos et unum firmaculum aureum, de elemosinario eiusdem domus quatuor marcas, de magistro operibus eiusdem domus quadraginta solidos, de camerario eiusdem domus sexaginta solidos, de priore de Lant[hony] unam bursam de serico et quadraginta solidos, de magistro Thom' de Scok' quadraginta solidos, de priore de Horsleye quadraginta solidos, de priore de Stanlegh'[1] unam marcam, de abbate sancti

[1] Stanley, Glos.

Augustini Bristoll' quadraginta solidos, de tribus villanis apud Nimdesfeld[1] novem solidos, de abbate de Teukesbur' quadraginta solidos,
de abbate Wynch[combe] sexaginta solidos, de custode ecclesie de
Chiltham quadraginta solidos, de Nicholo de Assaldon' dimidiam
marcam, de vicario de Northlegh'[2] dimidiam marcam, de abbate
Cirecest' sexaginta solidos, de Waltero clerico decem solidos, ut in
donis sinistris ad parcendum eis super capcionem predictorum bladorum suorum propter quod providencia nostra de transmissione
eorundem bladorum ad partes Vasconie facienda perperam erit
recordata ad dampnum nostrum et regni nostri periculum non modicum. Assignavimus vos ad diligentem inquisicionem super hoc faciendam, videlicet quid et quantum predictus Ricardus recepit de predictis abbate et aliis et quibuscumque aliis hominibus predicti comitatus occasione supradicta. Et ideo vobis mandamus quod ad certos
diem et locum quos ad hoc provideritis, inquisicionem illam capiatis.
Et tu, vicecomes, ad eosdem diem et locum venire facias coram prefato
magistro Johanne et te sufficientem inquisicionem tam de militibus
quam aliis liberis et legalibus hominibus de comitatu tuo per quos
rei veritas melius scire poteritis in premissis. Et inquisicionem illam
distincte et aperte factam habeatis coram baronibus de scaccario
nostro apud Westm' quam primum fieri poterit sub sigillis vestris et
sigillis eorum per quos facta fuerit. In cuius rei testimonium has litteras nostras fieri fecimus patentes. Teste J. de Cobeham apud Westm'
septimo die Junii, anno regni nostri vicesimo quinto.

E 159/70, m. 43d.

76. *Edward I to the barons of the exchequer, 12 June 1297*

Edward par la grace de deu etc. Ia soit ce qe les manoirs lercevesqe
de Cantebir' seient en nostre mein, sicome vous savez bien, ne mie
par ce nous voloms bien qe meismes lercevesqe eit leesement e le covert
des meisons parmy les maneirs avantditz taunt solement quele hure
qe li plerra, issint totes voies qe les issues, les biens e les profitz des
dits maneirs seent levez entierement a nostre oes e demoergent en
nostre mein tant qe nous en eioms autre chose ordine. Dont nous vous
mandoms qe par lettre de nostre escheker faciez saveir de par nous
a ceux qui sont gardeins des avantditz maneirs de par nous qe leesement e le covert des meisons parmy meismes les maneirs tantsolem-
ment sueffrent audit[a] ercevesqe en la manere avantdite. Don' desuz

---

[a] *E 368/68 has* avauntdit.

---

[1] Nympsfield, Glos.
[2] Northleach, Glos.

96   DOCUMENTS ILLUSTRATING

nostre prive seal a Lenham le xii iour de Juyn, lan de nostre regne
xxv.[1]

E 159/70, m. 26; E 368/68, m. 50d.

77. *Letters patent of John de Clavering, 13 June 1297*

Omnibus Christi fidelibus ad quos presentes littere pervenerint,
Johannes de Clavering[2] miles, salutem in domino. Noveritis me teneri
domino Johanni de Drokenesford custodi garderobe domini regis
Anglie illustris in sex libris sterlingorum quas mutuo recepi ab eodem;
solvendis eidem domino Johanni vel suo certo attornato has litteras
ostendenti in eadem garderoba ad festum nativitatis sancti Johannis
Baptiste proximo sequentem sine dilacione ulteriori. Et ad hoc obligo
me, heredes et executores meos et omnia bona mea mobilia et immo-
bilia ubicumque fuerint inventa districcionibus et cohercionibus
senescalli et marescallorum hospicii domini regis qui pro tempore
fuerint. In cuius rei testimonium sigillum meum presentibus est
appensum. Dat' apud Westm' xiii die Junii anno regni regis Edwardi
vicesimo quinto.

E 101/684/79, no. 17. Original, with seal attached.

78. *Ordinance for the collection of clerical fines, 14 June 1297*

Fait a remembrier qe le clerk qui irra au counte preigne bone meinprise du viscounte quil respoigne a la quinzeine de la seint Johan[3] des
arrirages des clerks qui ount fins fetz, de qui il ad la somounse, e qui
taille ne lui moustrent, nautre aquitaunce, e ceaux qui unt lay fie, e
nule aquitaunce ne moustrent, seit leve de leur lays fiez, e de leur
chateaux e de leur meinperneurs ceo qe serra ariere. E ceaux qui ne
unt nul lay fie seit leve de leur meinperneurs sil seint trovez, e eient
de quey, ou des biens meismes ces persones trovez hors de seintweire.
E ceaux qui naveront mie fetez pleine fin du quint pur lentier de la
taxacioun de leur eglises, facent lever ceo qe remeint outre la fin fete
auxi come la fin, en la fourme sousdite, e mette en roulle les nouns
de ceaux, e la somme que fait de la fin quil deussent avoir feitz. E
de toutz beneficiez qui ne unt mie feitz fin, ne protectioun ne unt,
e unt lai fie, seit sen, si le viscounte eit pris leur terres e leur biens

[1] An exchequer writ implementing these instructions was issued on 14 June (E 159/
70, m. 104).
[2] John of Clavering was son of Robert FitzRoger, who was one of those who accompanied Bigod and Bohun in their protest at the exchequer on 22 August (no. 126).
[3] 8 July.

en la mein le rei, par comaundement que lui fu feit de par le roi,
e quant e queux biens e a qui mayns ceaux biens sount puis devenuz.
E sil eit nul desporte, seient leur terres e leur chateaux temporaux
meintenaunt seisiz en la main le rei. E face estendre les terres e priser
les biens e les chateaux ore trovez, e auxi enquerge si tieux beneficiez
eient a nuly terre vendue, ou donee, ou leur chateaux qi poeient adonqe
aveir este trove en ceaux tenementz aloigne ou aliene puis la date
du brief qe vint au viscounte pur seisir, e celes terres face seisir en
la mein le rei, ove toutz les chateaux qui ore serront trovez en celes
terres, e ceaux biens e chateaux meintenaunt vende a mieux qom poet,
pur le rei. E enquerge come bien celes terres valent par an, e le pris
des chateaux ore trovez, e auxi aloeignez puis le dit temps. E face a
savoir as barouns del eschequier les nouns de ceaux issi desportiez,
e la value de leur terres, e le pris de leur biens. Endreit des beneficiez
qui ne unt mie protection, ne lai fie, ne unt ne possession de lai tene-
ment, ne biens temporaux, seit feit ceo qe le rei ordonera a faire de
eaux, outre ceo qe le rei ad avaunt ces houres ordene e comaunde.
E meisme le clerk surveie tuttes les somonses que les viscountes unt
des dettes le rei, e face lever hastivement celes dettes, issi que le
viscounte eit toutz les deniers que purront estre levez de tuttes ces
dettes, a quinzeine de la seint Johan, par lavaundite meinprise. E
ensement face lever hastivement tuttes les fins des religieux aliens du
poeir le rei de Fraunce que sount ariere, e les arrerages del quinzime
e disme solom les estreites liverees au dit clerk.[1]

E 159/70, m. 108.

[1] Appointments of clerks were duly made on 14 June 1297, according to E 159/
70, m. 108, as follows:

Beds. & Bucks.	Reginald de Gatecoumbe
Kent	Roger de Norton
Heref.	Thurstan de Hamslape
Som. & Dorset	Richard de Clare
Norf. & Suff.	John de St Ivone
Hants & Wilts.	John de London
Northants & Rutland	Richard de Kerstan
Surrey & Sussex	Thomas de Hustweyt
Essex & Herts.	Henry de Lisle
Lincs.	Richard de Hetherington
Warw. & Leics.	John de Batlesford
Notts. & Derbs.	Thomas de Boyvill
Glos. & Worcs.	Robert Dymmok
Devon & Cornwall	William de Aulton
Oxon. & Berks.	John de Everdon
Salop & Staffs.	William de Coventry

On the same day, according to E 368/68, m. 47, writs were issued to the sheriffs of
twenty-four counties, asking them to assist various clerks. In the majority of cases, the
names are the same as those above, with the addition of Yorks., William de St Quintino
& Robert Beaufey; Northumb., Adam of York. In six instances, however, different
clerks are named to those in the E 159/70 list: Lincs., Ralph Paynel; Norf. & Suff.,

79. *Edward I to Hugh le Despenser, John Droxford and the barons of the exchequer, 15 June 1297*

Edward par la grace etc. Nous vous mandoms qe meintenant veues ces lettres faciez enveer par bons e hastifs messagers en touz les lius Dengleterre ou nous avoms coket, e mandez as gardeyns de nostre novele custume qe totes les leynes qe sont ia venuz as portz e qe vendront, facent hastier de passer quanquil porront.[1] E leur mandez ausint quil vous facent savoir a plus en haste quil porront la somme de leynes e des quirs ausint en teu manere qe vous le sachez a cest seyn Johan procheynement avenir, ou dens les octaves a tot le plus tard, issint qe nous e vous y puyssums estre plus pleinement avisez qant nous serroms a Loundres. Donez desouz nostre privee seal a Chetham le xv iour de Juyn, lan de nostre regne xxv.

E 368/68, m. 50; E 159/70, m. 26.

80. *Edward I to Robert of Basings, 21 June 1297*

Rex dilecto et fideli suo Roberti de Basinges, salutem. Meminimus nos xix° die Martii proximo preterito prioratum de Lewes cum omnibus terris et tenementis, bonis et catallis pertinentiis ad eundem capi fecisse in manum nostram pro arreragiis et finis quem Johannes de Aveneu nuper prior eiusdem loci aliegena et de potestate et dominio regis Francie fecit nobiscum pro prioratu suo rehabendo ad voluntatem nostram[2] et iuxta formam ordinacionis status religiosorum de potestate et dominio eiusdem rege Francie existentium infra regnum nostrum per nos et consilium nostrum factam, et vobis eodem die predictum prioratum cum terris et tenementis et catallis eiusdem commisse custodiendum quamdiu nobis placeret, ita quod de exitibus inde provenientibus salva racionabili sustentacione prioris et conventus eiusdem loci nobis responderetis ad scaccarium nostrum in partem solucionis arreragiorum illius finis. Et quia idem prior nuper diem clausit extremum, ut accepimus, et dilectus et fidelis noster Johannes de Warenna comes Surr' coram nobis et consilio nostro custodiam vacacionis prioratus predicti, qui de fundacione et patronatu

---

Richard de Kerstan; Essex, Henry de Dunholm; Northants, John de St Ivone; Warw. & Leics., John de Gildon'; Oxon. & Berks., John de Batlesford. The Jornalia Roll (E 405/1/11), recording payment of 20s. to each of these clerks on 18 June, is in agreement with E 159/70 in eleven cases, but no mention is made of Richard de Hetherington, Thomas de Boyvill, William de Aulton, John de St Ivone or John de London.

[1] On 20 July instructions were sent to the customs ports ordering the export of the king's wool: the ships were to be organized in convoys for fear of enemy attack (E 159/70, m. 122d).

[2] Robert of Basings' instructions to take the priory into his hands are enrolled in E 368/68, m. 4d.

eiusdem comitis et antecessorum suorum existit, per nos petiit si reddi habendum in forma qua ipse et antecessores sui semper hactenus habere consueverunt in omnibus vacacionibus eiusdem domus. Nos petitioni eiusdem comitis in hac parte ammittere volentes, reddidimus eidem comiti custodiam predicti prioratus sic vacantis cum omnibus pertinentibus ad eundem, habendam in forma qua idem comes et antecessores sui in huiusmodi vacacionibus hactenus habere consueverunt. Et ideo vobis mandamus quod predictum prioratum cum omnibus pertinentibus ad eidem comiti liberetis in forma predicta. Teste P. de Wileghby etc. xxi die Junii, anno xxv^{to}. Per ipsum regem in pleno parliamento suo apud Westm', die Jovis proximo ante festum sancti Johannis Baptiste anno predicto.[1]

E 159/70, m. 103.

81. *Edward I to the deputy treasurer and barons of the exchequer, 22 June 1297*

Edward par la grace de dieu etc., au .. lieu tenaunt nostre tresorier e as barouns del eschequer, saluz. Nous vous mandoms fermement eniognantz qe par lettres de nostre eschekier faciez mander hastivement a toutz les viscountes de nostre reaume qe par leur baillifs, e par autres bones gentz de qui il se fient, e pur les queux il voudront respondre, facent espier e enqueire le plus diligeaument e le plus sotivement quil porront, quantz e queux clers beneficiez sont denz leur baillies, qui eent quarante souzez de rente de seinte eglise e outre, seit en personage, vicarie, ou en autre manere, e qui ne ont nul lay fee ne biens temporaux fors soulement benefice de seinte eglise, e ne ent mie unkore nostre protection purchacee. E facez enioindre de par nous as avantditz viscontes par les dites lettres qe toutz les biens e chateaux qui sont a tieux clers beneficiez denz leur baillies qui ne unt mie nostre protection purchacee, sicome est avantdit, quele houre qe meimes les biens e les chateaux serront trovez hors de seintwerre, preignent en nostre mein sauntz delay, e les vendent a mieux quil porront pur nostre profit, e du pris e de les deniers respoignent a nostre dit eschequier, au plus en haste quil porront, ^{a}e quil vous remandent hastivement ceo quil en auront fait.^{a} E de toutz les clers beneficez qui auront lay fee, e nount mie nostre protection, facent en meisme la manere ovesqes totes les autres penances pur ceo avant ordenees.

^{a}$\cdots$^{a} *Passage interlined.*

[1] 20 June 1297. A further reference to this parliament, dated as taking place in the quindene of the nativity of St John the Baptist (24 June), is in E 159/71, m. 6. See also no. 93.

Don' desouz nostre prive seal a Westmoustier le xxii iour de Juyn, lan de nostre regne vintisme quint.[1]

E 159/70, m. 121d.

82. *Edward I to Hugh Cressingham, treasurer of Scotland, 25 June 1297*

Rex dilecto et fideli suo Hugoni de Cressingham, thesaurario suo Scotie, salutem. Mittimus vobis per Johannem de Burwelle, Galfridum le Hurer et Alanum de Walton', servientes nostros, MM libras pro negociis nostris in partibus Scocie inde expediendis, prout melius et commodius esse videritis faciendum, quas super vos poni fecimus ad scaccarium nostrum Westmon' de prestito; vobis mandantes quod eadem duo milia librarum de exititus regni Scocie per vos recipienda, restitui faciatis ad idem scaccarium Westmon' citra gulam Augusti proximo futuro. Et hoc nullatenus omittatis. Teste P. de Wileghby etc. xxv[to] die Junii anno xxv[to].[2]

E 159/70, m. 107.

83. *Edward I to the sheriff of Kent, 27 June 1297*

Rex vicecomiti Kanc', salutem. Cum de obvencionibus nuper vobis in subsidium terre sancte concessis in diocese Cantuar' plura adhuc arreragia nobis debeantur et magna et quamplures qui in arreragiis illis nobis tenentur dilecto nobis in Cristo priori sancti Gregorii Cantuar' et magistro Johanni Hardy clerico quibus arreragia illa levari mandavimus et recipere solvere contradicant, sentencias excommunicacionis vel suspensionis in ipsos latas aliqualiter non verentes, per quod levacio et collectio predictorum arreragiorum ad dampnum nostrum non modicum retardatur; tibi precipimus in fide et dileccione quibus nobis teneris firmiter iniungentes quod tu in propria persona tua cum predictis priore et magistro Johanne vel ministris suis arreragia predicta de bonis et catallis eorum qui nobis ea debent in comitatu tua et quorum nomina iidem collectores nostri tibi scire facient, omni dilacione postposita levari, et eisdem ad opus nostrum solvi facere. Ita quod iidem collectores arreragia illa habeant ad scac-

---

[1] Exchequer writs instructing the sheriffs to take this action were issued on the same day, 22 June (E 159/70, m. 121d).

[2] Payment of £2,000 to Hugh Cressingham was authorized by means of a *liberate* writ on 10 June (*Documents illustrative of the History of Scotland*, ii, 174). The payment on 25 June is recorded in the Jornalia Roll (E 405/1/11). Cressingham's reply to Philip de Willoughby is given below (no. 86). The £2,000 was taken north with an escort of ten horse and sixteen footsoldiers, at a cost of £19 19s. 0d. (B.L., Add. MS. 7965, fo. 22v).

carium nostrum apud Westm' sine dilacione nobis solvendis ibidem. Et scias quod si te remissum vel negligentem in huiusmodi execucione facienda reperiri contigerit, nos eadem arreragia de terris et tenementa, bonis et catalla tuis in quantum sufficienti levari faciemus et nichilominus graviter ad te capiemus. T. P. de Wileghby etc., xxvii die Junii, anno xxv^{to}.[1]

E 159/70, m. 104d.

84. *Exchequer memorandum, 2 July 1297*

Memorandum quod die Martis secundo die Julii, anno regni regis Edwardi xxv^{to}, idem dominus rex precepit Philippo de Wilughby, tenenti locum W. de Langeton' Coventr' et Lich' episcopi, thesaurarii regis, et baronibus de scaccario quod placita ad idem scaccarium decetero non teneantur donec aliter preceperit sive ordinaverit, preter placita ipsum regem specialiter tangencia quoad denarios levandos, et huiusmodi placita fiant et teneantur cum omni celeritate quam fieri poterunt, absque ulla cautela et cavillacione facienda in placitando. Et quod in placitis que in scaccario ex necessitate et loci consuetudine debent placitari decetero nullus narrator audiatur, set rei veritas per partes plano ore et sine solempnitate et cavillacione seu cautela placiti ostendatur.

Item eodem die rex precepit quod Johannes de Insula unus baronum de eodem scaccario amoveatur ab officio baronum, et quod in obsequio regis nec alibi moretur, nec coram justiciariis de banco seu aliis justiciis vel ministris regis quibuscumque audiatur decetero in nulla causa, donec rex aliud dederit in mandatis.

Die Mercurii sequenti mane convenerant predictus Philippus de Wilugby cancellarius regis de eodem scaccario et tenens locum predicti thesaurarii ibidem et barones predicti et idem Johannes per eosdem fuit licensatus iuxta formam prenotatam.

Postea die Jovis proxima ante festum sancte Margarete virginis, videlicet xviii die Julii predicto anno xxv^{to}, venit ad scaccarium Johannes de Drokenesford, custos garderobe regis, et nunciavit prefatis baronibus ex parte regis quod predictus Johannes de Insula ad pristinum statum quem habuit in scaccario in officio baronum admittatur. Ita quod occasione prioris precepti domini regis prefatis baronibus facti, sicut supra continetur, prefatus Johannes de Insula in nullo occasionetur vel dampnum incurrat, set quod officium illud in omnibus excerceat, sicut prius facere et exercere consuevit.

[1] Similar writs were issued to the sheriffs of Sussex, Essex and Norfolk. It is unlikely that much money was received by the crown from this source (W. E. Lunt, *Financial Relations of England with the Papacy to 1327* (Cambridge, Mass., 1939), pp. 456–7).

E 368/68, m. 50d. The first paragraph is printed by G. O. Sayles, *Select Cases in the Court of King's Bench, Edward I*, i (Selden Society, 55, 1936), cv, n. 3.

85. *Exchequer ordinance, 4 July 1297*

Ordine est que celui qui deit aler es countez pur les dettes le rei hastivement levier, face venier au certein jour devaunt luy le viscounte du counte e touz les ballifs e souz baillifs, auxi bien denz fraunchise com dehors, de meisme le counte, e de cescon hundred e wappentak deus les plus prodeshomes e plus leaux e plus suffisauntz del hundred ou du wappentak e illoeques face le viscounte, baillifs e suz baillifs e les homes avauntdites iurier qe leaument presenteround e verite dirrount e frount de quanque home lour enchargera de par le rei, e apres face demander les somounses le viscounte e totes les autres estreites de dettes le rei a lui liverez, e celes somounses e estreites, ensemblement ove les estreites qe il portera ove lui del eschequier, face lire e opposier par ordre de noun en noun, e les nounes que sont afoirer face afoirier, e par leur serment e par autres bones e leaux solom ceo qe il verra que mieuz seit a fair pur le rei, enquerge des chescon que dettes deit au rei ou il ad terres e chateaux, en queles viles e dedenz quel hundred e wappentak auxi bien dedenz fraunchise com dehors, e meintenaunt livre en estreite a les deus homes avauntdites e as baillifs de meismes le hundred ou wappentak tote les dettes dewes en leur hundred ou wappentak, e les charge e enioigne de par le rei seur forfetur de terres, tenemenz, biens e chateux e de vie e membre qe hastivement e leaument saunz avier regard a nuli persone face levier de dettes de chescon homme qe les devera qe quil seit, e les assigne bref iour de la face faire a viscounte du conte. Issi que lui e le viscounte eient les deniers au dit eschequier lendemain de la goule aust a pleus tart. E si celui issi assigne de par le rei troefse viscounte, baillifs, souzbaillif, denz fraunchis ou dehors, seient de fie ou autrement, ou les deus homes avauntdites, ou nul autre quil chargera de ceste bosoingne, necligent, lache ou feynt en lexecution faire maintenant face prendre terres, tenemenz, biens e chateaux quanque il ad en la main le rei e son corps face*a* enveier hastivement a la tour le Londres a demorier yloques e receivre ceo qe le rei en vodra ordiner.[1]

E 159/70, m. 108d.

a Face *repeated in MS.*

[1] Appointments were duly made on 4 July 1297 as follows:

Cumb., Westm., Lancs.	Adam de Crokedayk
Norf. & Suff.	John de St Ivone

86. *Edward I to Nicholas Fermbaud, constable of Bristol castle, 5 July 1297*

Edward par la grace de dieu, rey Dengleterre, seignur Dirlaund e ducs Daquitaigne, a son feal e loal Nichol Fermbaud son conestable de Bristeud, saluz. Nous vous maundoms qe vous ressevet de nostre feal e loal Wauter de Beauchamp, seneschal de nostre hostel, un chivaler quil vous baudra de par nous. E vous chargeoms qe vous le facet sauvement gardier au dist chastel, e le plus priveement qe vous porret, taunt qe vous en eet autre maundement de nous. E le custages qe vous y mettret vous feroms duement allouer sur vostre acounte. Don' sout nostre prive seal a Westmoster le quint ior de Juyl, lan de nostre regne vintisme quint.[1]

E 101/6/4.

87. *Edward I to the abbot of Reading Abbey, 7 July 1297*

Rex dilecto sibi in Cristo abbati de Redingg', salutem. Cum inter cetera que nostram exorant regiam dignitatem in hoc prerogativa quod incole regni nostri quorum servicio indigemus nobis nostrisque negotiis et serviciis insistere et intendere debent, non obstante alicuius

Essex & Herts.	Henry de Dunholm
Salop & Staffs.	Thomas de Warberge
Northants & Rutland	Roger de Hegham
Surrey & Sussex	Henry de Guildford
Hants & Wilts.	Willam Inge
Som. & Dorset	John de Godele
Cambs. & Hunts.	Henry de Staunton
Beds. & Bucks.	John de Motteford
Devon & Cornwall	Ralph de Odiham
Notts. & Derbs.	Henry Spigurnel
Warw. & Leics.	John de Sutwell
Oxon. & Berks.	Richard de Bereford
Hereford	William de Wodeford
Glos.	Roger de Suthcote
Northumb.	Robert de Benton
Kent	Roger de Bellafago
Lincs.	Roger de Norton

E 159/70, m. 108d.

Payments to cover expenses were made by the exchequer on 8 July, and the record of these adds the name of John de Sheffield, appointed to Yorkshire (Jornalia Roll, E 405/1/11, m. 5).

[1] This writ is entered on Fermbaud's particulars of account, which state that the knight in question was Ralph de Monthermer, earl of Gloucester. He was imprisoned in Bristol from 10 July to 22 July, as a result of the king's displeasure at his marriage without licence to Joan of Acre, countess of Gloucester. The king's anger was soon remitted, and Ralph, with his wife, did fealty on 2 August. All the estates were restored, save Tonbridge and the Isle of Portland, which they presumably retained for reasons of security. By September Ralph and his wife were allowed to stay in the outer bailey of Windsor castle, which the king lent to them (M. Altschul, *A Baronial Family in Medieval England: the Clares, 1217–1314*, pp. 157–8; *C.C.R., 1296–1302*, p. 63).

alterius servicio sub federe promissionis vel scripti cuiuscumque inde facto, et nos servicium Willelmi Melkesop' servientis vestri pro quibusdam negotiis nostris celeriter expediendis ad presens optinere volentes;[1] vobis mandamus quod dictus Willelmus pretextu dicti servicii nostri penes vos in nullo sit perdens vel gravatus in ipsum pro eo aliquatenus occasionetis seu occasionari permittatis, qualicumque modo seu causa servicio vestro fuerit astrictus. Teste P. de Wilegby tenente locum thesaurarii nostri apud Westm' vii die Julii, anno nostri xxv[io].

E 159/70, m. 108.

88. *Hugh Cressingham to Philip de Willoughby, 10 July 1297*

Egregio viro domino suo si placet et amico domino Philipo de Wileghby, domini regis thesaurarii locum tenenti et scaccarii Westm' cancellario, suus Hugo de Cressingham, salutem et prosperos ad vota successus. Litteras vestras nuper michi porrectas et in se continentes duo milia librarum michi de prestito mitti, de quibus litteras meas patentes vobis destinandas fieri et eadem duo milia librarum vobis citra gulam Augusti solvi et remitti petebatis, per Johannem de Burewelle et Galfridum le Hurer de London' tercio die Julii apud Berewicum recepi, unde in isto urgentis necessitatis articulo pro negociis regiis que rebus se habentibus ut nunc; tale iuvamen voluerunt et adhuc necessarie requirunt, dominacionem vestram non modicas ad grates assurgo. Advertentes, si placet, quod, ut michi videtur, nec decet nec oportet me litteras meas patentes vobis de dictis denariis facere vel destinare, quod discretioni vestre non displiceat, cum per rotulos vestros et rotulos camerarii dicti scaccarii satisfeci de eisdem denariis ut de prestito de thesauro facto oneratus. Ceterum et quia de mandato vestro est quod dicta pecunia circa gulam Augusti sit restituta; hoc nullo modo posse fieri firmiter credatis quod, si placet, moleste non feratis, tum propter quoddam mandatum regium michi per breve suum nuper directum per quod est michi finaliter iniunctum ut omnes denarios de quibuscumque exitibus terre et regni Scocie provenientes domino meo J. comiti de Warenna quandocumque et quotienscumque sibi placuerit solvi faciam, nullis exceptione vel mentione factis ad aliquam solucionem de predicta pecunia vobis ut aliis aliunde faciendum, tum pro eo quod nulli vicecomitum, ballivorum vel ministrorum domini regis infra eadem terram et regnum constitutorum aliquos denarios de exitibus balliarum suarum hiis diebus propter multa diversa continua et cotidiana pericula que iminent

[1] On 30 July William Milksop was appointed one of the taxers and collectors of the eighth (*C.P.R., 1292–1301*, p. 298).

levare possunt, quod deus advertat; qui vos incolumes diu conservet. Scriptum apud Boulton'[1] x die Julii.[2]

E 159/70, m. 29d.

89. *Edward I to Roger Bigod, earl of Norfolk, 11 July 1297*

Rex dilecto de fideli suo Rogero le Bygod, comite Norff' et marescallo Anglie, vel locum suum tenenti, salutem. Cum diu est vobis mandaremus quod omnia laica feoda archiepiscoporum, episcoporum, religiosorum et aliorum clericorum quorumcumque, protectionem nostram non habentium, una cum omnibus bonis et catallis in eisdem laicis feodis inventis, quibusdam de causis in manum nostram caperes, seisires et salvo custodires, ita quod nec ipsi nec aliqui per ipsos ad ea manum apponerent, donec aliud a nobis haberetis in mandatis, et quod de nominibus eorundem protectionem nostram non habentium barones de scaccario nostro certificaretis, super quo eisdem baronibus nichil huiusque significatis, nec ipsos aliquatenus certificastis, de quo quamplurimum admiramur. Vobis mandamus, sicut alias mandavimus, in fide et dilectione quibus nobis tenemini, quod statim, visis litteris istis, omnia laici feoda predictorum archiepiscoporum, religiosorum et aliorum clericorum quorumcumque quadraginta solidatas beneficiorum ecclesiasticorum, et ultra, habentium, tam in personatu et vicaria quam alia modo quocumque, qui nostram protectionem non optinuerunt, una cum omnibus bonis et catallis in eisdem inventis, et ceteris bonis suis cum extra sanctuarium reperta fuerunt in manum nostram capiatis et vendicioni exponatis et de denariis inde provenientibus, vobis ad scaccarium nostrum de die in diem respondeatis, et quod quilibet eorum cuilibet laico de eo conquerenti fiat responsalis. Et quod nullus eorundem prelatorum, religiosorum et aliorum clericorum coram vobis suggerencium, vel de aliquo seu aliquibus conquerentium in querela sua aliquo modo admittatu, donec protectionem nostram optinuerint, et vobis illam ostenderint. Scire facientes eisdem quod nisi citra talem diem ad curiam nostram venerint, et protectionem nostram impetraverint, nos ad eos gravius capiemus, ut ad illos qui a fide et dilectione nostra ingrate se diverterunt. Et quid super hoc feceritis, prefatis baronibus nostris una cum nominibus tam illorum quadraginta solidatas beneficiorum ecclesiasticorum et ultra habentium, nostram protectionem optinencium quam non optinencium, absque omni mora constare faciatis. Et ita vos habeatis in ista execucione facienda ut nulla dissimulacio seu remissio diligencie vestre reperiatur, per quod in-

---

[1] Bolton, Northumb.   [2] Written in reply to no. 82.

dignationem nostram incurrere debeatis. T. P. de Wileghby etc. xi die Julii, anno xxv^{to}.

Consimili modo mandatum est Henrico de Lancastr', Johanni de Hastinges, vel eorum locum tenentibus, et vicecomiti de Glamorgan. T. ut supra.

E 159/70, m. 103.

90. *Letters patent of Edward I, 13 July 1297*

Edwardus dei gratia rex Anglie, dominus Hibernie et dux Aquitanie, omnibus ad quos presentes littere pervenerint, salutem. Quia intelleximus quod gentes comitis Hereford' de Breghenogh' per ipsum comitem et ministros suos iniuste et contra earum consuetudines quibus hactenus usi sunt gravantur multipliciter et vexantur, nos nolentes quod predicte gentes vel alii subditi nostri indebite pergraventur, damus dilectis et fidelibus nostris Waltero Haclutel' et Morgano ap Mereduth' vel eorum alteri plenam tenore presencium potestatem audiendi clamores omnium illorum de predictis partibus de Breghenogh' qui de predicto comite vel ministris suis querelam duxerint deponendam, et eosdem querelantes defendendi et manutenendi quousque eisdem inde factum fuerit iusticie complementum ^{a}necnon eiectos de terris suis ibidem per ipsum comitem ad pacem nostram admittendi et ipsos in eisdem terris^b prout iustum fuerit reponendi.^{a} In cuius rei testimonium has litteras nostras fieri fecimus patentes quamdiu nobis placuerit, vel donec aliud super hoc ordinandum duxerimus duraturas. Teste meipso apud Westmonasterium xiii die Julii, anno regni nostri vicesimo quinto. Irrot'.$^{c\,1}$

C 266/4/11, copy or draft for enrolment. Calendared from the Patent Roll in *C.P.R.*, *1292–1301*, p. 293.

91. *Fealty performed to Edward, son of Edward I, 14 July 1297*

De fidelitate facta Edwardo filio regis Edwardi.

Memorandum quod die Dominica proxima ante festum sancte

$^{a...a}$ *Passage interlined.*
^{b} *Followed by* reponendi *struck out.*
^{c} Irrot' *added in a different hand.*

---

[1] For the earl of Hereford's response, see *Calendar of Ancient Correspondence concerning Wales*, p. 101. Two of his officials summoned the tenants of Brecon, and gave them a charter granting them all the laws and usages of their ancestors. This is dated by Edwards as 1321–2, but the mention of Morgan ap Maredudd supports a date of 1297. See also Davies, *Lordship and Society in the March of Wales, 1282–1400*, pp. 269, 290.

Margarete anno regni regis nunc vicesimo quinto,[1] ipso rege apud Westm' existente, convocatisque ibidem archiepiscopis, episcopis, abbatibus, prioribus, comitibus, baronibus et aliis magnatibus huius regni in presencia ipsius regis infra palacium suum Westm', ex assensu et voluntate ipsius regis et magnatum predictorum ipsi magnates, videlicet venerabiles patres R. de Winchelese Cantuar' archiepiscopus, totius Anglie primas, magister Henricus de Newerk Ebor', frater W. de Hothum Dublin' electi, A. de Bek Dunelm', O. de Sutton Lincoln', W. de Luda Elyens', R. de Walpol Norwic', R. de Gravesende London', W. de March' Bath' et Wellens' episcopi; W. de Bello Campo comes Warr', J. de Hastinges, W. de Breouse, Th. de Berkle, G. de Geynville, A. de Valence, H. le Despenser et alii magnates videlicet quilibet eorundem per se fecerunt fidelitatem Edwardo filio domini regis Edwardi regis nunc, et iuramentum inde prestiterunt corporale in hac forma, videlicet:

Qe nous serroms feaux et leaux a Eadward fuiz Edward roy Dengleterre, e foy e leaute ly porteroms de vie e de membre e de terriene honur encountre totes gentz e apres le mort son piere por rey e seigneur ly tendroms, si dieus nous eyde e les seintz.

Postea secundo die sequenti R. Bygod comes Norff' et marescallus Anglie, H. de Boun comes Hereford' et constabularius Anglie et alii magnates regni et omnes adermanni civitatis London' et alii concives eiusdem civitatis et quamplures de regno fidelitatem fecerunt in forma memorata.

E 368/68, m. 58. Printed in *Lancashire Lay Subsidies*, pp. 200–1.

92. *Edward I to the barons of the exchequer, 18 July 1297*

Edward par la grace de deu etc. Il vous deyt bien sovenir comment nous comandasmes nadgueres qe tote la temporaute leveske de Landa,[2] pur ce qe nous le tenismes hors de nostre pees, feissez prendre e tenir en nostre meyn tant quil eust fait nostre gre sur la desobedience quil nous avoit faict. E pur ce qe nostre volunte est qe de la dite temporaute e de ses autre biens, sauve glebes, dismes e offrendes sont levez a nostre oes iusques au quart pur la desobedience avantdite, vous mandoms qe vous en facez tant lever e nyent plus a ceste fiz. E pur ce qe lerceveske de*a* Cantebir' nous ad priez pur le dit evesque, e nous meismes avoms sa persone recomendeit pur le bien qe nous y avoms entendu, si voloms qe sil y ad rien levez de soen a nostre oes par cele

---

a de *repeated in MS.*

[1] 14 July, 1297.
[2] Llandaff.

acheison, del houre qe nous y meismes la meyn iusques au temps qe nos lettres del escheker sur ce serront venues a ceus qe se entremettent de par nous qe ce le soit pleinement alowez en le quart avantdit, si qe nous ne eyoms de ce qe serra levez en le meen temps e de ce qe uncore fait a lever iusqe le quart. E voloms qe le dit evesqe quant le quart serra levez eit deliverance e ioysse de tot le remenaunt sanz plus demander ent par lencheison avauntdit. Pur quei nous vous mandoms qe cestes choses faciez faire, sicome est avantdit. Don' suz nostre prive seal le xviii iour de Juyl, lan de nostre regne xxv.

E 159/70, m. 33.

93. *Exchequer memorandum, 22 July 1297*

Memorandum quod xxii die Julii domino rege agente hic apud Westm' in parliamento suo,[1] concordatum fuit per ipsum regem et consilium suum quod omnes qui servicium suum fecerunt in exercitibus Wallie annis quinto et decimo et quorum nomina inseruntur in rotulis marescalcie eorundem exercituum quamquam scutagium ab eis exigatur pro pluribus feodis quam servicium fecerunt tunc respectum habeant de exactione totius illius scutagii donec rex inde aliud duxerit ordinandum. Quia omnes qui servicium fecerunt in dictis exercitibus clamant esse quieti de toto scutagio quod ab eis exigitur etc. per servicium quod ibidem fecerunt etc.

E 368/68, m. 51.

94. *Edward I to the sheriffs of Devonshire, Herefordshire and Lancashire, 28 July 1297, with endorsements and replies*

Edward par la grace de dieu roi Dengleterre, seigneur Dirland e ducs Daquitaine, au visconte de Deveneshire, saluz. Nous vous mandoms fermement eniognantz qe hastivement, veues ces lettres, faciez crier parmy vostre baillie qe touz ceux qui nous ont grante de passer oveque nous la outre a cest passage, e touz ceux ausint qui ont prestement mounture e armoure e qui nous porront servir a nos gages a ceu voyage, viegnent a Wynchelse le plus en haste quil porront. Car nous aloms ovendroit vers celes parties de iour en autre tant come nous pooms. Pur la queu chose nous vous chargeoms derechef qe ceux de vostre baillie faciez haster dy venir en totes les bones maneres qui vous porrez. E nous faites savoir hastivement ce qui vous en avez fait.

[1] For this parliament, see also no. 80.

Donees desouz nostre prive seal a seint Auban[1] le xxviii iour de Juyl, lan de nostre regne vintisme quint.

Endorsement

Ieo ay fete la criee parmy ma baillie solom la tenur du bref, mes ieo ne treofs nul qe se conusse qe graunte eyt de passer ove le roy, ne qe veoillent ses gages prendre de aler y cele veage.

C 47/2/16/2. Original.

Endorsement to a similar writ to the sheriff of Herefordshire

Le executioun de cesti bref ay fet entierement soloms ceo que plus pleynement est contenu en meme le bref, mes ieo ne treofs nul homme ke purveu seyt de passer fors taunt soulement sire Miles Pychard chevaler.[2]

C 47/2/16/3. Original.

Endorsement to a similar writ to the sheriff of Lancashire

Le retourn de cesti bref est en un escrowe atache a cesti bref.

C 47/2/16/4. Original.

Reply by the sheriff of Lancashire

Ie ay fete la crie parmy le cunte de Lancastr' en chekon luy de counte qe touz ceus qe unt promys au rey de aler of ly en ce veage, e touz ceus qe unt armure e mounture e pount servir le rey a ses gages veignent ausi hastivement cum il pount a Wynchelse solum ce qe est contenu en ce bref. Apres quele crie me vynt un bref par sire Henr' de Percy e sire Robert de Clyfford, del quel io vous envey le trans-escrist, ensemblement of le transescrist du bref nostre seigneur le rey, qe me vynt, qe ie fuse entendaunt a eus, qe sunt atachez a ce bref, e ia tardeys io ay comaunde qe touz ceus qe unt promys au rey de passer of luy seunt a son passage hastivement a Wynchelse.[3]

SC 1/31/186. Original.

[1] St Albans, Herts.

[2] Miles Pichard was a knight of the king's household. He had received payment for his summer robes at Sandwich on 7 June, and his horses were valued for the Flemish campaign on 14 August. He was accompanied by two squires (B.L., Add. MS. 7965, fos. 66v, 122v).

[3] The account for the non-household contingents in the royal army in Flanders fully supports the evidence of these replies to the summons. A section listing squires with their county of origin reveals only one from these three counties, Roger Freman from Hereford, and he was only taken on the pay roll on 1 October 1297 (B.L., Add. MS. 7965, fos. 73–4).

95. *Edward I to the knights, free tenants and whole community of Northumber-land, 30 July 1297*

Rex militibus, libere tenentibus et toti communitati comitatus North-umbr', salutem. Cum comites, barones, milites et totius laici regni nostri, extra civitates, burgos et dominicas nostras, octavam partem omnium bonorum suorum mobilium, et cives, burgenses et alii probi homines de omnibus et singulis civitatibus et burgis eiusdem regni nostri de quorumcumque tenuris aut libertatibus fuerint, e de omnibus dominicis nostris, quintam partem omnium bonorum suorum mobilium, exceptis hiis que in forma taxationis predictarum octave et quinte sunt excepta, nobis concesserint pro confirmacione magne carte celebris memorie domini H. regis patris nostri de liber-tatibus Anglie, et eciam pro confirmacione carte eius patris nostri de foresta a nobis habendis. Nos, ut octava et quinta predicte ad minus dampnum et gravamen populi dicti regni nostri leventur et colligan-tur providere volentes, assignavimus dilectos et fideles nostros Rober-tum de la Fierte et Adam de Crokedayk vel alterum ipsorum, quociens ambo altero eorum causa neccessaria prepedito, interesse non poterunt, ad dictas octavam et quintam in comitatu predicto assi-dendas, taxandas, levandas, colligendas et nobis solvendas iuxta for-mam in quodam rotulo, quem eisdem Roberto et Ade fecimus liberari, continentem. Et ideo vobis mandamus quod predictis Roberto et Ade vel uni eorum, ut predictum est, in premissis sitis in-tendentes, respondentes, consulentes et auxiliantes in forma predicta, prout ipsi vobis scire facient ex parte nostra. In cuius rei testimonium has litteras fieri fecimus patentes. Teste meipso apud Westm' xxx die Julii, anno regni nostri vicesimo quinto. Et predicti Robertus et Adam sunt de comitatu Cumbr'.[1]

E 159/70, m. 123d.

96. *Form of taxation for the eighth and fifth, 30 July 1297, with alterations for the ninth of 14 October 1297*

Octava et quinta bonorum temporalium regi a laicis concessis de ter-mino Trinitatis anno xxv^{to}.

Ordene est par la counsail qe le doun que est ore grante au rey par les lays du roiaume deit estre taxe e leve en la fourme qe senswit.

---

[1] Similar writs for all other counties were issued, together with writs to the sheriffs, on the same date (E 159/70, m. 123d). These writs are calendared from the Patent Roll in *C.P.R., 1292–1301*, pp. 297–9.

Cest a savoir primes qe en chescun counte seient deus chivaliers[a]
chief[b] taxours e quillours, ou un chyvalers e un serjaunt, les plus leaux
qe home purra trover, qui ne seient mie du counte meismes ou il serrount assigne, ne terres neient en meismes[b] le counte e qe ceaux
taxours e quillours en les countez ou il serrount mis par bone foi e
bone examinacioun facent eslire de chescun ville du counte quatre
ou deus loiaus hommes, ou meins ou plus, solom ce qe les villes sount
meindres ou greindres, des queux homme se purra mieuz fier, e les
queus peussent estre poussauntz de respoundre de leur feitz en temps
avenir, e suffisauntz pur asseer totes les gentz de la ville dount il serrount. ᶜE si tieux ne serront trovez, donk seient autre tieux esleuz des
plus procheines villes des plus loiaux e des plus suffisauntz.ᶜ E qe celes
gentz des villes ensuit esleuz seient iurez qe leaument asserrount e
taxerount toutz les biens de chescune des villes ou il frount la taxacioun quil averount avoient[b] en chaump ou en mesoun ou ailleurs
le iour de la nativite nostre Dame ᶜseint Michelᶜ prochein avenir
passe[b], e par bon e leal pris les priserount, e leaument mettrount en
roulle totes les parceles e les summes de meismes ceaux biens ensuit
prisez e assis sauntz nule desporter ou fraude faire par nule maniere
de colour, de parente, de favour ou damiste. ᶜE cel roulle desouz leur
seaux livrent as chief taxours et retiegnent le transcrit devers eaux
desouz les seaux des chiefs taxours pur lever les deniersᶜ. E les deus
chiefs asseours e taxours sousditz apres le dit serement resceuz des ditz
hommes de villes, aillent de hundred en hundred, de ville en ville
ausi avaunt come faire le purrount a veer e enquerre qe les biens
ᶜde chescuny seientᶜ bien e leaument seient assiz e taxez e prisez solonk
ce qe par dreit e reson estre deverount par les avauntditz hommes
de ville. E enquerrount si nul des villes eit nul bien esloigne qe ne
seit assis e taxe entre ses autres biens au iour sousnome. E, sil seit trove
qe nul eit nuls biens esloigne qe ceaux biens seient taxez auxi avaunt
come les autres. E sil troefsent qe ceaux des villes ou nul de eaux eient
riens concele, ou par doun ou par favours meins biens taxe, ceaux
le acressent e parfacent solom leur descrecioun en la plus leale maniere
quil poount al oes le rei, ᶜe le mettent en un nouveau roulle par liᶜ.
E facent a savoir au tresorier e as barouns del eschequier ᶜles nouns
de ceaux qui issi auront trespasse countre leur serment. E la taxacioun
des biens de ceaux des viles seit feit par aucuns leaux gentz de leur
visne qui ne seient de leur affinite, les queux les chevaliers chiefs
taxours a ceo assigneront par bon serment e leal. E la taxacioun des
biens des chiefs taxours e quillours seit reserve a tresorier e as barons
del eschequier.ᶜ E si tost come la taxacioun des biens serra faite en

---

[a] *Words underlined are so treated in the text, these being the sections of the form of taxation
for the eighth that were to be cancelled and replaced by the interlined words and passages so as
to adapt the text to the needs of the ninth.*

[b] *Word interlined.*   ᶜ....ᶜ *Passage interlined.*

la fourme sousdite, les chiefs taxours e quilleurs facent lever e quillir
le utime e le quint en la fourme que leur est baille de par le roi, *hastivement a paer al Escheqer as iours assignez.* E ceste taxacioun seit
fete ausi bien des biens as clerks come des lais, le queux biens ne seient
mie annex a leur eglises. E ensement seient taxez en ceste taxacion
les biens as vileins des ercevesqes, evesqes, religieux e de toutz autres
clerks qui quil seient. E fet a savoir qen ceste taxacion serront forspris
armure, mounteure, jueaux e robes as chivalers e gentiz hommes e
de leur femmes, e leur vesseal dor e dargent e darreim. E tutes citiez
e burghs, petiz e grauntz, du reaume quiquil seient e de quiqunqe
tenure ou franchise, e tutes les demeynes le roi seient taxez au quint.
E en cytez, burghs e viles marchaundes serrount forspris en la taxacion
une robe pur le home e un autre pur la femme, e un lit pur ambedeus
e un anel e un fermail dor ou dargent, e un ceynt de saie quil usent
touz les iours, e ausint un hanap dargent ou de mazre dount il beivent.
E les biens des meseaux la ou il sount governez par soverein meseal
ne seient taxez ne prisez, e sil*b* sient meseaux governez par mestres
sein, seient leur biens taxes com des autres gentz. E les biens de nul
ne seient taxe *al noefime* sil namountount a v. souz *noef souz.* E
facent les taxeurs*c* tauntost comencier deus roulles de la taxacion qe
en serra faite, en les queus roulles seient contenuz les nouns de chescun
qui serra taxe, e la somme dount il serra chargee del utime e du quint.
E lun roulle siwe touz iours lautre en escripture. E de ceaux deus
roulles quant la taxacion serra parfete e bien e leaument en la furme
sousdite entree, lun roulle demurge vers les taxeurs e lautre seit enveie
tauntost desouz leur seaux au tresorier e as barons del eschequier.
E que E*d* les taxeurs ne leur clerk rien*d* ne preignent pur chapitres
liverier ne pur tailles faire ne pur nul autre chose qe a la dite bosoigne
fere apent. E qe les chiefs taxeurs preignent la moneye le roi par counte
saunt paisier tiel com court en reaume. E seit envee en chescun counte
aucun bon e leal qui seit iure le rei a sourveir, espier, enquer e examiner si mester seit que la dite taxacion seit fete e leve bien e leaument
en al furme sousdite, e qe le pueple ne seit a tote greve, nen autre
manere damagee par viscontes ou autres ministres le rei, fors qe soulement de par le graunt del doun avauntdit. E deivent le chiefs taxeurs
e quillurs aver les roulles del quinzime chescons del counte ou il serrount assignez, e ausint un transescrit de la furme de cest ordeinement
de le transescrit del serment quil deivent faire. E pur cest *graunte
e* doun ensuit done fet*d* au rei a cest foiz ad nostre seigneur le rei
conferme la graunte chartre e la chartre de la foreste pur ly e pur
ses heires.

<hr>

a...a *Passage interlined.*   *b* e sil *supplied from 'Parl. Writs', i, 54–5, 62–3.*
c *The words* ne a sil namountenent *are interlined at this point.*
d *Word interlined.*   *e* *The words* ne a   sil namountenent *are interlined at this point.*

Sacramentum taxatorum

Ceo est le serment as taxeurs. Cest asaver qe bien e leaument e a lur poer e a lur ascient taxerount les biens a prodeshomes du reaume, e le utime e le quint quillerount en la forme que baille lur est, solonc ceo que leur est enioint de par le rei e pur rien ne levrount ne pur amur ne pur haine ne pur faveur ne pur doun ne par promesse que leaument nel facent saunt nuli esparnir, e que rien ne prendrount de nuli qui biens il deverount taxer ne par eaux ne par autres. E que leaument ferront la taxacion e la somme enbreverount e le noun de chescon e leaument le presenterount au tresorier e barons del eschequier. E que ceaus qui desouz eaux les biens taxerount front faire autil serment. E les clerks qui escriverount les roulles facent fere le serment qe leaument inbreverount les nouns e la somme de touz e que nule fraude ne frount par quay le rei seit perdaunt, ne autre eit damage e qe rien ne prendrount pur encheison de cel office, ne pur taille ne pur autre chose forspris manger e beivire.[1]

E 159/70, m. 123.

97. *Exchequer memorandum, late July 1297*

Pur ce quil covient en totes maneres qe nostre seigneur le roy por sauvete de ly e de touz ses aliez e de tut son reaume tiegne leaument ses covenaunces quil ad fait ovesque ses aliez par dela. E celes covenaunces sont iceles quil covent quil passe hastivement a grant poer. E si tost come il seit passe pardela, covenaunt est quil deit paer au rey Dalemaigne saunz delay a sa venue la outre trente mile mars,[2] e au duk' de Brabant vint cink mille e cink centz mars.[3] E covient quil eit busoignablement por son passage cest assaver por eide fere a ses bones gentz qui passeront e por gages paer as gentz des armes e gentz de pie e por mariners e autres despenses de son hostel xx mille mars outre tot ce qe vendra al escheker des issues du reaume entre

---

[1] The form for the taxation of the eighth and fifth is printed in *Parl. Writs*, i, 54–5, from the Patent Roll. It is translated in *E.H.D.*, iii, 473–4. That for the ninth is printed in *Parl. Writs*, i, 62–3, again from the Patent Roll. This version, however, has been printed in order to show the way in which the clerk attempted by means of interlinings and cancellations to transform the form for the eighth into that for the later ninth.

[2] This is the one reference to this obligation, which was not recorded in the formal agreements made with Adolf.

[3] This sum was presumably a calculation of the balance owing to the duke. In February 1297 the king acknowledged a debt of 40,000 *livres tournois* owed to him, and in addition he was assigned £25,000 out of the custom as a loan (*C.P.R.*, *1292–1301*, p. 134). He received *liberate* writs early in February totalling £14,000. For details of payments made to him, see B. D. Lyon, 'Un compte de l'échiquier relatif aux relations d'Édouard I d'Angleterre avec le duc Jean II de Brabant', *Bull. de la commission royale d'histoire*, cxx (1955), 67–93.

cy e le passage. Dont la summe totale est des choses seusdites quil
covient qe le rey eit ovesqe ly de dreite necessite ovesqe les autres
deniers qe vendront al escheqer entre cy e le dit passage lxxv mille
e d mars. E nostre seigneur le rey e son conseil unt enpense, parle
e conseillee coment e en quele manere e des queux choses la dite
summe se porra faire au meindre grevaunce de poeple, e meindre
damage de eux. E avis leur est qe le rey ne porra par voye meillure
hastivement aver la dite summe si noun par achat de tant de summe
des leynes des clerks e des lays en la forme qe sensuit. Cest assavoir
qe len face eslire des meilleurs marchauntz Dengleterre e des plus
leaux qui sachent achater leynes e qe ceux marchauntz seient assignez
en diverses countez qui achatent des leynes des ercevesques, evesques,
abbes, priours e touz autres clerks e autres gentz pusauntz de reaume
mesmes iusques a noumbre de viii M sacs de leynes par tel pois, come
autres marchauntz achateront mesmes tieux leynes en mesmes pays
ou les leynes serront issint achatees. E si les dites gentz respoignent
as marchauntz le rey e ses autres gentz a ce assignez quil ne voillent
leur leynes vendre, respondu lour soit par les marchauntz le rey e
ses autres gentz quil covient quil le facent^a si grant busoigne come
le rey ad ore a fere pur ly e por le commun profit de tot le reaume,
mes qe lour leynes serront en tieu manere prisees e paetz quil serront
gardez de damage e qe les marchauntz le rey facent avoir a chescun
bone lettre de rey de taunt dargent come serra convenu entre eux
e le vendour. E facent lour lettre demeigne ou taille a ceux de qui
il achateront endementiers taunt quil aient fet venir les dites lettres
le rey de la chauncelerie. E veut le rey qe les clerks e lays de queux
leynes serront issint a ses oes issi achatez, seient hastivement issi paez
del doun qe est ore a ly grante des clerks e des lays por confermer
la grant chartre e la chartre de la foreste. E qe a chescun de eaux
seit alowe en la somme de la leyne taunt come aferra a ly paer del
doune avauntdit. E ce qe ly serra plus duz e qe demorra seit pae en
deniers de mesme le doun, sicome est desusdit. E veut le rey qe la
leyne de nul poure homme seit a son oes ensint achatee. E ceux marchauntz meismes qui achateront les dites leynes les facent venir par
eides des viscontes as plus procheins portz des countez ou il irront
si come en la lettre patente que les ditz marchaundts le rey unt^a plus
pleinement est dit. E facent ausint passer les leines outre au plus en
haste quil porront en nule manere sauvement e en bon cunduit. E
aukuns de mesmes les marchauntz ou autres sages e leaux qui a ce
serront esluz e qui ensachent entremettre passent ovesques les leynes
outre bien enfurmez de touz les achatours del pris, du poys, e del achat
de celes leynes, ovesques queux il passera ou passeront en tieu manere

---

^{a} *There is an erasure at this point in E 159/70.*

qe eux les peussent deliverer par dela solom ce qe les evesque de Cestre[1] e Johan de Berewyk lour dirront pleynement, quant eux y vendront, mes quil ne deschargent mie avaunt quil eient lour avisement e sachent bien lour volunte. E les viscontes des countez ou les leynes serront achatez facent les custages de cariage e autres choses qe covient desques as portz. E puis les custoumiers en ordeinent e aquitent le passage e hastivement les ditz leynes facent passer de iour en iour si come leur vendront en la manere susdite. E qe les custumiers seient bien avisez del noumbre des saks quil averont receuz e passez.[2]

E 368/68, m. 63; E 159/70, m. 115. Printed in *Parl. Writs*, i, 344. Translated in *E.H.D.*, iii, 474–6.

98. *The Remonstrances, late July 1297*

Ces sunt les monstrances qe le .. erceveles, eveskes,[a] countes, barons e tote la comunalte de la terre monstrent a nostre seygnur le rey, e humblement ly priunt, come a seignur, qe il voylle qe il seyent entendutz, redrecees e amendees al honur de dyeu e de seynt eglise e de ly[b] e a salvacion de tout son peple e de la terre.[c]

En primes chef[d], il semble a tote la comunalte de la terre qe le gar-

[a] *Other versions include* abbes, priours *at this point* (*Edwards, 'Confirmatio Cartarum and Baronial Grievances in 1297', 170–1*), *where a text based on the three main chronicle versions, by Cotton, Guisborough, and Knighton is provided. The best version of the Guisborough text is, however, that given by Rothwell in his edition of the chronicle* ('Guisborough', pp. 292–3), *and this has been used in providing variant readings from this chronicler. Only significant differences are noted.*

[b] *Other versions have* com a seignur, qe cestes choses voille redrescer e amender al honur de lui

[c] e de la terre *only in this MS.*

[d] chef *only in this MS.*

[1] Walter Langton, bishop of Coventry and Lichfield, was frequently styled bishop of Chester. See no. 205.

[2] Letters patent appointing men to conduct this prise were issued on 30 July 1297. The quantities requested from various counties were as follows, according to E 159/70, m. 115:

Yorks.	1,500 sacks
Lincs.	1,500
Notts. & Derbs.	1,000
Northants & Rutland	600
Cambs. & Hunts.	200
Beds. & Bucks.	350
Oxon. & Berks.	600
Norf. & Suff.	400
Warw. & Leics.	400
Essex & Herts.	300
Wilts. & Hants	300
Som. & Dorset	300
Glos. & Worcs.	800
Surrey	50

The appointment of merchants is also given in *C.P.R., 1292–1301*, pp. 299–300.

nissement qe fet lur fut par le bref nostre seyngnur le rey [a]de venir
a chivaus e armes pur passer ove luy la outre[a] ne fus asez suffiant,
pur ceo qe il ne aveyt nul lyu[b] especefie ou il deveyent aler, kar solom
le lyu lur covenyt il fere la purveaunce, e pussent aver seu[c] le quel
il deussent la ferre service ou nun.

E pur ceo qe dit est comunalment qe nostre seygnur le rey vus passer
en Flaundres, avis est a tote la comunalte, ausi byen des clers com
de lays,[d] qe la ne deyvent il nul servise, pur ce qe eus ne lour prede-
cessours ne lor auncestres unkes en cele terre servise ne firent. E tut
fust qe il deussent[e] servise la ou ayllours, il ne avereyent pas poer de
ferre le, pur ce qe il unt este taunt greve de diverses tayllages, aydes
e prises,[f] de furment, aveyne, breyse, leynes, quirs, boefs, vaches e
chars salees, saunz nul dener paer dount il ceo deussent aver soustenuz
e meyntenuz.

Estre ceo il dyent qe ayde ne poient il ferre pur la poverte qe il
unt pur les tayllages, aydes, prises e mises avauntdites, kar il unt a
peyne dount il se poent sustiner, ne se poent, ne qe ne poent lor terres
gaynner.[g]

E pur ce qe tote la comunalte est mut greve[h] de ceo qe il ne sunt
par menetz solom le leys e les usages de la terre, par les queus eus
e lur auncestres[i] soleyent estre menetz, ne il ne un unt lur fraunchises
les queles il soleyent user e[j] aver, mes sont mis hors voluntrivement,
par quey il ceo sentent durement grevetz.

Estre ceo qe clers e lays se sentent durement grevetz de ceo qe il
soleynt estre menetz solom le poyns de la graunde chartre, le queus
poyns sount de touz le plus treslessez, la quele chose est trop graund
damage a poeple [k]e graunt peryl a ceus qe ne les volunt gardir.[k] Par
quey il prient qe cestes choses seyent redrecees al honur de dieu e
de seynte eglise e[l] de lui e a salvacion du poeple.

E pur ce qe la comunalte de la terre volent honur e sauvete a nostre
seyngnur le rey, si com il deyvent voler, ne lor semble pas qe honur[m]
serreyt a lui ne prou de passer en Flandres si il ne feust plus asseure

---

[a . . . a] de venir . . . la outre *only in this MS.*
[b] nul certayn lu *in other versions.*
[c] *Knighton reads* aviser; *two MSS. of Guisborough have* aversne *and* aversue *respectively.*
[d] ausi byen des clers com de lays *only in this MS.; Cotton has* de la terre.
[e] il issint qils dussent *in other versions.*
[f] *Cotton has* diverses talliages et diverses prises.
[g] *Cotton has* sustenir ne lur terres gaynger; *the best version is Guisborough, with* sustenir
e multz en sunt qe nount pas lur sustenaunce, ne lur terres gayner.
[h] *Guisborough has* se sentent durement grevez.
[i] *Cotton has* auncestres avaunt eus.
[j] user e *only in this MS.*
[k . . . k] e graunt . . . gardir *omitted in Cotton.*
[l] *Other versions have* par quoi ils prient a nostre seignur le roy qil voille qe cestes choses
soient redresses al honur de lui e a salvacioun du people.
[m] honur *only in this MS.; other versions read* ceo.

pur luy e pur ces genz[a] [b]qe il ne entendent qe seyt uncore.[b] E ausi pur la terre de Eschoce qe ceo comence lever contre luy taunt com il est en terre, e byen entendunt qe il ceo freyent en plus mauveyse manere si il susent[c] qe il feust la mer passe, e ne pas soulement eus, mes autres terres veysines qy ne sunt pas uncore de tut byen afermes.[d]

E ausi se sentunt il mutz grevez[e] de la male toute de leynnes qe est sy grevouse a chescun sake quarante soutz de la leyne entierre, e de la leyne brusee du sake v. mars, pur ceo ke la leyne de Engleterre est a poy la meyste de la value de tote la terre par an, e amounte la male toute par an a poy a quynt de la value de tote la terre par cele prise.

Estre ceo tote la comunalte se sente mult greve del assise de la foreste, qe nest pas garde ausi com ele soleyt estre sca en arerre, ne la chartre de la forest nuldour, mes hem fet voluntrifs attachemens e grevos rancons[f] hors dassise autrement qe hom ne soleyt ferre.[g]

E pur ceo qe divers talliages, aydes, prises e mises avauntdites qy unt este parmi le reume par les queus les clers e les lays se doutent mout qe eus e lor successours e lor heyrs pussent entrer en grant servage, par ceo qe il serreyent autrefietz trovez en roule, priunt il a nostre seyngnur le rey ke de ceo lur feyt aquitaunce, qe apres ces houres ne furent treyt a exaumple a desheritaunce de seynte eglise e de eus e de lor heyrs e a pardurable servage de tut le poeple.[h]

County of Hereford and Worcester Record Office, Bishop Giffard's Register, fos. 413v-414r. Printed in Denton, 'A Worcester Text of the Remonstrances of 1297', 520-1.

99. *Edward I to William de Luton and his associates, after 30 July 1297*

Rex Willelmo de Luton' et sociis suis ad emendum lanas in comitatu Somers' et Dors' assignatis salutem.[1] Visa et lecta lettera vestra thesaurario et baronibus nostris per vos transmissa, tenens locum thesaurarii et dicti barones fuerunt quamplurimum admirati, quod cum

---

[a] ses genz des Flaundreisses *in other versions.*
[b...b] qe il ... uncore *omitted in Guisborough.*
[c] *Guisborough has* si ils fussent seure.
[d] *The preceding paragraph forms the last clause in all other versions.*
[e] *Other versions have* Estre ceo tote la communaute de la terre se sentent durement grevez.
[f] e grevos rancons *omitted in Cotton.*
[g] *In all other versions this paragraph is placed before the preceding one.*
[h] *The final paragraph is unique to this MS.*

---

[1] William de Luton had been appointed together with John de Malplash, Thomas Tylly and John le Chanu to collect wool in Somerset and Dorset on 30 July 1297 (*C.P.R., 1292-1301,* p. 300).

super hiis lanis emendis per nos tradita vobis fuerit certa forma; vos non servantes eandem thesaurario et baronibus questiones voluntarias et inutiles facitis in hac parte. Quia vero predictis questionibus nulla facienda est responsio, vobis firmiter iniungendo mandamus quod formam predictam firmiter observantes super quod vobis iniunctum est exequandum indilate. T. etc.

E 159/70, m. 116.

100. *Credence brought by John Droxford to the exchequer, and writ to the sheriffs in pursuance, 1 August 1297*

Johannes de Drokenesford custos garderobe regis tulit baronibus ad scaccarium per breve regis sub privato sigillo de credencia, quod irrotulatur in hoc termino sancte Trinitatis quandam cedulam in hec verba:

Endreit des glebes qe sount duwerre des eglises, e des dimes pure e des offrendes, les queus choses sount clerement despiritualte, si voet le rei qe si nul de ses ministres en eit rien leve a son oes, qe ceaux qui sen tienent agrevez facent saveir au rei les nouns des ministres qui tieux choses ount fetes, e la manere des feitz, e le roi fera les choses redrescier en due manere.

Per quod mandatum est singulis vicecomitibus Anglie per breve de scaccario in hec verba:

Rex vicecomiti Cumbr', salutem. Licet nuper tibi precepissemus quod laica feoda et omnia bona et catalla beneficiatorum ad valorem quadraginta solidorum et supra, qui nostram protectionem adhuc non haberent, in manum nostram statim cum bona et catalla illa extra sanctuarium reperta essent, caperes et eadem bona et catalla vendicioni exponeres et de denariis inde provenientibus, in exitibus eorundem laicorum feodorum, nobis de die in diem ad scaccarium nostrum responderes; intencionis nostre tamen non extitit, nec adhuc existit, quod de terris et tenementis que sunt gleba, sive dos ecclesiarum, meris decimis et oblacionibus et aliis rebus que sunt mere spirituales, ad opus nostrum aliquid caperetur. Et ideo tibi precipimus quod de gleba sive dote ecclesiarum, decimis, oblacionibus et aliis huiusmodi rebus mere spiritualibus, ad opus nostrum capiendis, in nullo te intromittas. Teste J. de Cobeham apud Westm' primo die Augusti, anno xxv. Per ipsum regem.

E 159/70, m. 107d.

101. *Edward I to the barons of the exchequer, 1 August 1297*

Edward etc. Nous vous mandoms qe par vos lettres e par le portur de cestes nous faciez saver hastivement si les brefs e lordeinement del eyde des lays seent uncore enveez avant ou nun, e sil ne seient uncore avant, adonqe nous faciez asaver quant vous entendez qe les choses porront estre delivres. E nous mandez ausint ce qe est fait del ordinance des leynes. Don' de suz nostre prive seal a Lovesham[1] le primer iour Daugst, lan de nostre regne xxv.

E 159/70, m. 36.

102. *The deputy treasurer and barons of the exchequer to Edward I, in reply to the king's letter of 1 August*

Au treshaut prince seigneur honeurable sir E. par la grace de dieu roi Dengleterre, seigneur Dirlande e ducs Daquitaine, soens . . lieu tenaunt son tresorer e ses barons de son eschekier, leau service ove tutes maneres de reverences e de honeurs. Nous maunda vostre hautesce qe par nos lettres, e par le portour de cestes, vous feissoms a savoir hastivement si les briefs e lordeinement del ayde des lays soient uncore enveez avaunt ou noun. E ensement ceo qe est fait de lordenaunce des leynes, sur queu chose sache vostre seignurie qe les briefs e lordeinement des leynes sont enveez avant. E les briefs e lordeinement del ayde sont en fesaunt, e serront feitz dedeinz ces treis iours prestz de enveer avant. Bone vie e longe vous doint nostre sauveour e encresse toutz iours vos honeurs.

E 159/70, m. 36.

103. *Edward I to the deputy treasurer and barons of the exchequer, 2 August 1297*

Edward etc. au lieu tenaunt le tresorier e as barouns del eschequier, saluz. Nous avoms entendu qe Marie, nostre chier fille, par defaute des vyns qui ele deust avoir receuz de nous a Southampton' dont ele est ariere de quatre termes, ad fait achatier vyns par la sustenaunce de son houstel, iusqes a la montance des vyns qui lui faillent, dont ele sest endette de une somme des deniers, dont nous vous mandoms qe vous facez venir devaunt vous au plus tost qe vous porrez ceaux a qui les deniers sont deuz, e mettez peyne qe les plus riches facent paement as autres creaunzeurs qui ne se poent suffrir. Car nous enten-

[1] Lewisham, Kent.

doms qe les choses sont en plusures petites parceles dues a moulz de poures gentz qui en sont mult grevez. E peus pernez terme a ceaux qui averont le paement faite le mieuz qe vous purrez, ou si vous ne puissez meillure voye prendre, fetes tant vers eux touz qil vus grauntent un terme du paement, du quil vus ne leur faillez mye. Issint quil sen tiegnent du tut a nous e qe nostre fille ne soit mespressee e quil ne coveigne mye qe ele enpense desoremes par nostre defaute, car si nous soussiens qe la coupe feust vostre, nous nous entendriens molt a maupaez. Dautre part nous vus chargeons fermement eniognantz que vus ly faciez des ore enavant avoir prestement a ses termes les vyns quele deit prendre de nous par an pur la sustenance de sun hostel saunt nul debat, ou au meyns la value, si home ne peus le vin avoir ensemblement les deners quele deit receivre a nostre eschequer, si que ele se peusse tenir appaee. Car peus qe nous serroms la outre, peut estre qe autres enpenserent petit, si ceo ne veint de nous meismes. E pur ceo vus chargeoms derechef qe vous ly soyez bones attornez e bons amys e qe vus ne ly faillez mie mesmement endreit de ces choses. Don' sous nostre prive seal a Orpigton'[1] le ii iour de Aust, lan de nostre regne xxv.

E 159/70, m. 34.

104. *Edward I to the deputy treasurer and barons of the exchequer, 4 August 1297, with appointment of clerks to take oaths from the tax assessors, and their instructions, 8 August 1297*

Edward par la grace de dieu etc. Nous vous mandoms fermement enoignauntz qe les briefs e lordeinement del eide des lays faciez enveer avaunt au plus en haste qe vous purrez apres ceo qe les choses serront prestes. E enchargiez tieux gentz qui sachent beau parler au pueple e qui sachent bien e sagement mener la beusoigne. E nous remaundez par vos lettres e par le portour de cestes ceo qui vous en aurez fait. Donees desouz nostre prive seal a Sevenoke,[2] le quart iour Daugst, lan de nostre regne xxv.[3]

Pretextu cuius mandati assignati sunt clerici *et alii* in comitatibus subscriptis ad capiendum sacramentum de taxatoribus superius assignatis, *in comitatibus ubi morantur,* et ad informandum eosdem qualiter loqui debeant ad populum, per quandam formam super hoc or-

---

a...a Passage interlined.

---

[1] Orpington, Kent.
[2] Sevenoaks, Kent.
[3] See no. 107 for the exchequer's reply to this letter.

dinatam per barones et Johannem de Drokenesford custodem garderobe regis, *ut patet inferius. Et isti assignati,* videlicet Henricus
Spigornel in comitatibus Notingh', Derb', Warr' et Leyc' et North',
et Rogerus de Norton' in comitatibus Roteland' et Linc'. Et Hum-
fridus de Waledone et Johannes de Crokesle vel unus eorum in comitatibus Norff' et Suff'. Et Magister Ricardus de Clare in comitatibus
Suth', Wilt', Somers' et Dors', Devon' et Cornub'. Et magister Thur-
stanus de Hamslape in comitatibus Glouc', Wygorn', Hereford,
Salop' et Staff'. Et Johannes de Lythegreynes in comitatibus Ebor'
et Northumbr'. Et Vincentinus de Hulton' in comitatibus Cumbr',
Westm' et Lanc'. Et Rogerus de Southcote in comitatibus Bed', Buk',
Oxon' et Berk'. Et taxatores illi de comitatibus Cant' et Hunt', Essex'
et Hertf', Kanc', Surr', Sussex', et assignati in aliis comitatibus
venerunt ad scaccarium et fecerunt sacramentum ibidem et ibi receperunt commissiones et formas etc.

Et predicti assignati habent litteras regis patentes in hec verba:
Edwardus etc. omnibus ministris et fidelibus suis ad quos presentes
littere pervenerint, salutem. Sciatis quod assignavimus dilectum et
fidelem nostrum Henricum Spigornele ad capiendum sacramentum
in diversis comitatibus de taxatoribus et collectoribus octave et quinte
nobis a laicis concessarum, prout in litteris nostris patentibus, quas
idem Henricus habet penes se, eisdem taxatoribus et collectoribus
liberandas plenius continetur, et alia facienda prout ei iniunximus.
Et ideo vobis mandamus quod eidem Henrici sitis intendentes, respondentes et auxiliantes, prout idem Henricus ex parte nostra vobis
plenius exponet in premissis. In cuius rei testimonium has litteras
nostras fieri fecimus patentes. Teste J. de Cobeham apud Westmon'
viii die Augusti anno xxv^to.

Consimiles litteras habent alii clerici et alii superius assignati in
comitatibus supradictis.

Tenor forme predicte talis est *ad informandum* taxatores. Ceaux
qui prendront le serment des taxours les enfourmeront de dire au
poeple des countiez ou il sount assignez en la plus beale e la plus cur-
teise manere quil sauront ou porront qe nostre seigneur le roi sest apar-
ceu qe son pueple est moult chargee des plusurs eides quil lui unt
sovent e fraunchement graunte e fait pur son reaume e son pueple
avauntdit defendre encountre ses enemis, de quei il les mercie, taunt
come il poet, tut soient a ceo conuz, e se tient tenu a faire chose qen
aleggaunce e perpetuel profit puisse tourner a eaux e a lour heyres.
E ad graunte a la requeste des ercevesques, evesqes, abbez, priours,
countes e barons a confermer la graunt chartre e la chartre de la
foreste en toutz leur pointz. E pur cest graunt les ditz ercevesqes,
evesqes, abbez, e priours unt graunte au rei eide de la clergie. E les

*... * Words interlined.

ditz countes e barouns pur le graunt, e le confermement des dites
chartres e pur le grant beusoign qe le rei ad ore aparmeimes pur lui
e son pueple, e ses aliez defendre e sauver, unt graunte au rei pur
eaux e pur le pueple le utime e le quint, soulom la fourme de ceo
ordeine. E quil dient au pueple quil facent cest chose leement e de
bone volente depuis qe le rei mette son cors, e quant quil ad e tut
son aveir e quant quil prent de son reaume, pur sauvete de eaux e
de son reaume. E semble a nostre seigneur le rei qe plus ne purreit
il pur eaux faire qe mettre son cors e sa vie en aventure pour eaux,
come pur ceaux quil eyme leaument e les voet gardier e meintenir
en honeur a tut son poeir si avaunt come son cors demeine le purra
suffrir ou suffire, de quei il voeillent natureaument aveir regard e faire
leur deveir devers leur seigneur de bone volente, sicome bones gentz
e leaux deivent e sont tenuz a faire a leur lige seigneur a si grande
e si haute beusoigne e ovesqes ce prier pur lui qe dieux lui dount par
sa grace si bien faire e overir en son viage qe ceo soit al honeur de
dieu e de lui e de tut son reaume.

E 159/70, m. 124. The letter of 4 August is also given on m. 36. The
last section, from 'Tenor forme predicte talis est . . .', is printed, with
minor omissions, in Rothwell, 'The Confirmation of the Charters,
1297', 31–2, and is translated in *E.H.D.*, iii, 476–7.

105. *An official to Edward I, 5 August 1297*

Sire, il yad a Wynchelese cxix niefs a vos gages, e niefs venent communement de iour en iour quant il fet beau temps . . . ou del est, mes
quantes niefs vendront, e quant e de quieux lieux ieo ne le say mye
dire. Autres niefs y ad il en le port . . . Winchelese xlvi qui ne sont
mie uncore as gages por ce qe eles font lour service qe du vous est
des ports, e le remenan[t] des niefs del servise, ce est assaver de lvii
niefs, sont uncore a Dovere e a Sandwyz en venaunt vers Winchelesce
qe peu le houre qe eles revindrent de Flaundres ou eles passerent por
conduyt fere a sire Johan de Berewyk par vostre comandement, eles
ne aveyent peus nul temps covenable a venir a Wynchelesce, mes eles
sont totes prestes de venir, a ceo qe hom dit. Sire, les niefs qe deivent
porter chevaux se apparaillent forment e bien, la dieu mercy, de iour
en autre, e si hom seust certeynement ou vous est assentuz qe vos chevaux propres, dexters e palefreys, passeront, ou en les passagers de
Dovere ou en bones niefs autres, hom les freit especialment apparailler
par la vewe Adam de Ryshon' de denz bref temps, issi qe totes ceux
choses serreient prestes tost apres vostre venue a Wynchelese. Sire,
endreyt de vitailles por passauntz, enteng ieo al eide de dieu qe vous
averez assez solom la seson e solom le temps de la porveaunce des

vitailles. Sire, noveles ne vous say ieo nules hore dire qe a dire seient. Escrites a Wynchelese le v iour Daugst.

SC 1/21/176. Original or transcript, slightly torn.

106. *Letters patent of John de Hastings, 5 August 1297*

Pateat universis per presentes quod ego Johannes de Hastingg' miles teneor domino Johanni de Drokenesford' custodi garderobe regis in viginti libris sterlingorum quas die confeccionis presencium de garderoba regis michi mutuo fecit liberari solvere in garderoba predicta in octabis assumpcionis beate Marie proximo venturis. In cuius rei testimonium sigillum meum presentibus est appensum. Dat' London', v die Augusti anno regni regis Edwardi vicesimo quinto.

E 101/371/21, no. 6. Original.

107. *The deputy treasurer and barons of the exchequer to Edward I, 5 or 6 August 1297*

Au treshaut prince e leur trescher seigneur, honurable sire E. par la grace de dieu roy Dengleterre, seigneur Dirlaund e ducs Daquitayne, soens .. lieu tenant son .. tresorier e ses barons de son escheker, loiau servise e tote manere de reverence e de honeur. Sire, nous receumes vostre mandement y cest lundy a vostre escheker qe les brefs e lordeynement del ayde des lays feissoms enveer avant au plus en haste qe nous peussiens, e qe nous enchargissiens tieux gentz qui seussent beau parler au poeple, e qui seussent bien e sagement mesner la busoigne. Nous feisoms a savoir a vostre seigneurie qe nous mettroms loiale peyne quant qui en nous est de fournir vostre mandement au mieuz e le plus en haste qe nous porroms. E entendoms certeynement qe ove leyde de dieu la busoigne serra preste y ceo Meskerdi[1] au plus tard. Nostre seigneur vous sauve e vous doint bone vie e longe.[2]

SC 1/17/41, draft or transcript; a copy is also in E 159/70, m. 36.

108. *Edward I to the barons of the exchequer, 10 August 1297*

Edward par la grace de deu etc. Pur ce qe nous avoms entendu qe vous mandastes ne ad gueres par bref de nostre escheker as baillifs

[1] 7 August.
[2] This letter was written in reply to the king's letter of 4 August (no. 104).

mons' Johan de Hastinges de la franchise de Bergeveny de faire saisir
en nostre meyn les terres e tenemens, biens e chateux des clers qui
ne eurent mye nostre protection purchacee, sicome nous ordinasmes
a faire par aillurs denz nostre reaume, par ount le dit Johan nous
ad fait mostrer qe meismes le mandement porra grantement torner
en preiudice de li e de sa dite franchise, la quele chose nous ne vodrions
mye; vous mandoms qe memes le mandement, si vous leez fait, faciez
redresser sanz delay en due manere e surseer ent endreit de la dite
franchise quant a ore. Don' desuz nostre prive seal a Odymere[1] le
x iour Daugst, lan de nostre regne xxv.[2]

E 159/70, m. 36.

109. *Archbishop Winchelsey, the bishops and clergy of the province of Canterbury to Edward I, after 10 August 1297*

Il vous membre sire, coment moustre e offert fust ne ad geres al ercevesk e partie des eveskes dunk present, ce est a saver de Loundres,
Nicole, Norwiz, e Baa, de par vous ke le clergye vous feyst un regard
pur les chartres de communes franchises e de la foreste renoveler, e
de adrescer lestat de seynt eglise, e a cel houre vis fut al ercevesk e
as autres eveskes avaundiz ke ceo serreyt ben a fere, mes il ne poeyent
nent graunter saunz les autres prelaz e le clergye. Dount le ercevesk
fet un assemble de prelaz e de la clergie ore al jour seynt Lorenz al
novel Temple de Loundres, e ount cetes choses debatu communement
par touz le degrez de clergie. E chekun degre bailla al ercevesk en
presence del eveskis soun respouns en escrit. Dounc tut lour avysement
en les avantdytes choses est ke eus [ne purr]eyent rens graunter de
bens de seynte eglise pur les chartres renoveler, saunz conge le pape
[par mous] des resouns. Des autres adrescemenz de le estat de seynte
eglise fut avys memes ceo a [tres touz] mout poy exceptez, mes eus
espeyrent ke par bone resounz ke serrount moustrez a le pape [legere-
ment] averont le conge. E prient si vous plest pur commun prou e
pes de seynte eglise e de tut le [reaume], voillez sufrir ke [il puis]sent
hastivement a le pape enveyer par commun conseil de voz e [de] lours,
ou tut par eus pur les choses avantdites.

SC 1/31/98. Original or copy, slightly damaged. A copy is given in
Reg. Winchelsey, i, 189–90, from which the words in brackets are taken.
Printed in *Councils and Synods*, ii, 1171–2.

[1] Udimore, Sussex.
[2] An exchequer writ setting out arrangements for the collection of money from clerical
fines in Hastings' lordship was duly issued on 14 August (E 159/70, m. 103d). The
initial order to take all the lay fees of the clergy there into the king's hands had been
issued on 22 June, along with similar instructions for other marcher lordships (*C.C.R.*,
1296–1302, p. 41).

110. *Edward I to the deputy treasurer and barons of the exchequer, 11 August 1297*

Edward etc. au . . lieu tenant nostre tresorier e as barons del eschekier, saluz. Nous vous mandoms fermement enoignauntz qe vous sachiez le plus certeinement e le plus tost qe vous porrez ce qui les marchandz e les autres gentz qui nadgueres feurent enveez en divers countiez pur achatier leynes a nostre oes, sicome vous bien savez, ont feit de cele busoigne, e ceo qui est fait ausint del eide des lays qui se deit lever a nostre oes a ceste foiz deinz nostre reaume. E vous chargeoms en la foi e la loiaute qe vous nous devez qe lune beusoigne e lautre e nomement la beusoigne des leynes faciez hastier e esploiter en tuttes les maneres qe vous saurez e porrez, issint qe nous puissoms aparcevoir qe vous y aurez mys diligeaument vostre entente. E au plus en haste qe vous purrez, nous faciez savoir come avaunt les dites beusoignes sount espleitees e faites en toutz pointz e quant vous entendez qe le passage des dites leynes se purra faire e estre prest, selonc lordenaunce qui en est faite. Car il covendreit en tuttes maneres qeles passassent a nostre passage. E pur ce qe nous avoms grante busoign de deniers pur les beusoignes qui nous covendra mener a cest voiage, vous chargeoms especiaument sicome nous nous fioms de vous e sicome vous avez lonur e le profit de nous e de nostre reaume, e lavancement de nos beusoignes, qe vous mettez tutte la peyne e la diligence qe vous purrez de lever deniers a nostre oes ove tutte la foison e la haste qe vous unkes purrez, e enveez gentz par tut pur les faire venir a nostre eschekier hastivement, issi qe nous eyoms prestement avant nostre passage quant qe vous puissez puchacier, selonc ceo qe nous vous feroms a savoir procheinement, e quele houre qe nous le enverroms querre. Donees desouz nostre prive seal a Odimere[1] le xi iour Daugst, lan de nostre regne vintisme quint.

E 159/70, m. 36.

111. *Letters patent of Edward I, 12 August 1297*

Pur ceo qe le roy desire touz iours la pees e la quiete e le bon estat de tutes les gentz de sun reaume, e nomement qe, apres sun passage qil bye ore fayre al honur de deu, e pur recoverir sun dreit heritage, dunt il est par graunt fraude deceu par le roi de France, e pur le honur e le commun profit de sun reaume, tutes encheisouns, par queles la dite pees ou quiete pussent estre en nule manere trobleez, soient du tut hostees, kar acunes gentz purroient dire e fere entendre au puple

[1] Udimore, Sussex.

aucunes paroles noun verroies, des queles le meisme puple purroit
estre mu de eux porter envers lur seyngnur lige autrement qe faire
ne dussent, come endroit de coe qe le conte de Hereford' e le conte
mareschal se aloygnerent nadguers de lui, ou endroit des autres
choses, lui rois sur ceo e sur lestat de lui e de sun reaume e coment
les busoygnes du reaume sunt alees a une piece, fait asavoir e voet
qe tuz ensachent la verite, la quele senseut. Nadguers, quaunt graunt
partie de gentz darmes Dengleterre, les uns par priere, les autres par
somounse du roi, vindrent a Lundres, le roi, voillaunt purveer a la
deliveraunce de meisme les gentz e a aleggaunce de lur despens e de
lur deseses, maunda au ditz contes, com a conestable e mareschal Dengleterre, quil venyssent a lui a certeyn iour pur ordiner la deliveraunce
des dites gentz, au queu iour le dit conte de Hereford' e mons' Johan
de Segrave, qui escusa le conte mareschal par maladie, vindrent au
roi, e en lur presence e par lur assent fust ordine quil feissent crier
parmy la cite de Lundres qe tutes les gentz qe estoint iloques venuz,
par somonse ou par priere, feussent lendemayn a seint Poul devant
les ditz conestable e mareschal pur savoir e mettre en remembraunce
coment e de cum bien chescun de eux voleyt servir ou eydir le roi
en cest veyage de la outre, e lur dist le roi qe selonc la dite ordinaunce,
la quele lur fust baylle en escrit, il feissent faire la dite crie. E eux
receu le dit comaundement e la dite bille sen alerent. Puis mesme
le iour a la nuyter, les ditz contes enveyerent au roy par mons' Johan
Esturmi chivaler une bille escrit en ceste forme:

Pur ceo, chier sire, qe vus maundastes au mareschal par le conestable e par une bille quil feist crier parmy la vyle de Lundres qe tuz
iceux qe sunt venuz par vostre somounse ou par priere, fussent
demayn devant eux a seint Poul a houre de prime, e quil feissent
mettre en roule combien des chivaus des uns e des autres, e coe vous
faissent asavoir; vous prient vostre conestable e vostre mareschal, qe
ceste chose vousissez commaunder a autre de vostre hostel. E pur ceo
sire, qe vus bien savez qe eux sunt cy venuz par vostre priere e ne
mye par somonse, sil ceo faissent, il entroyent en lur office pur service
fere, par quay il vus prient qe vus les voillez comaunder a autre.

E le roi, resceu la dite bille e eu conseyl sur ceo, pur ceo quil lui
sembla quil avoyent meyns avisement maunde, e ne volayt mye quil
enfussent suspris, enveya a eux mons' Geffrey de Geneville, mons'
Thomas de Berkeleye, mons' Johan Tregoz, le conestable de la Tur,
le gardeyn de Lundres, mons' Roger Brabazon e mons' Willame de
Bereford', pur eux meuz aviser sur ceo e quil purvessent en teu manere
quil ne feissent chose qe peust turner en preiudice du roi ne de lur
estat demeyne, e si autrement ne vousissent aviser, qe lors lur fust
demaunde sil avoueynt la dite bille e les paroles iloqes contenues,
les queles il avouerent tut outre. E qaunt ceste avouement fust reporte

au roi, il, eu sur ceo conseyl, mist en lu du conte de Hereford' conestable mons' Thomas de Berkeley, e en lu du conte mareschal mons'
Geffrey de Genevill', pur ceo qe les ditz contes avoyent requis qe le
rey commaundast a autres sicom il est contenu en la dite bille, e sur
ceo sen aloyngerent les contes du roy e de sa curt. E cest apres ceo
le erceveske de Caunterbur' e plusurs eveskes Dengleterre vindrent
au roy e luy prierent quil peussent parler as ditz contes, e le roy lur
graunta, par quay le dit erceveske e les autres prierent as ditz contes
qil lur faissent a savoir ou il lur plerroit de venir pur parler a eux.
E les contes lur remaunderent par lur lettres quil serroient a Waltham
le vendredi lendemayn de la feste de seint Jak';[1] au queu iour les ditz
erceveske e eveskes vindrent a Waltham e les ditz contes ne vindrent
mye, mes enveyerent illoqes mons' Roberd le Fiz Roger, mons' Johan
de Segrave, chevaleres, qui distrent de par les contes quil ny purroyent
venir adunk par acunes resuns. E pus a la priere des ditz prelatz e
des ditz chevalers, qui vindrent au roy a Seynt Auban le dimayng
procheynement suant,[2] le rey graunta sauf conduyt as ditz contes, e
enbaylla ses lettres a ditz chevalers contenentz suffisent terme denz
le quel les ditz contes peussent sauvement e sur sun conduyt venir
au roy e demorer e returner. E ovesqes celes lettres se departirent les
ditz chivalers du roy a cele foiz, mes unqes puis les contes au roy
ne vindrent ne enveyerent, ne uncore ne venent ne enveyent, qe le
rey sache. Ore puit estre qe acunes gentz unt feit entendaunt au
pueple qe les contes mustrerent au roy certeyns articles pur le commun
profit du pueple e du reaume, e qe le roy les deveit aver refuse e
escundit tut outre, de quey le roy ne seit reiens, kar riens ne lui
mustrerent ne ne firent mustrer ne ne seit pur quey il se retrestrent,
eynz entendi de iour en iour quil venissent a lui. Entre les queus
articles contenu est, a coe qe hom dist de acunes grevaunces qe le
roy ad fait en son reaume, les queles il coneyt bien, com des eydes
quil ad demaunde sovente foez de ses gentz, la quele chose lui ad convenu fere par encheison des gueres qui lui unt este meues en Gascoyne,
en Gales, e en Escoce e ayllurs, des queles il ne poeyt lui ne son reaume
defendre saunz eyde de ses bones gentz, dunt il lui poyse mult quil
les ad taunt grevez e taunt travaillez, e leur prie quil lui en voyllent
avoir pur excuse, com celui qui ad les choses mises ne mye pur achater
terres ne tenementz ne chasteus ne viles, mes pur defendre lui e eux
meismes e tut le reaume. E si dieu lui doynt iames returner du veyage
quil fait ore, il voet bien qe tuz sachent quil ad volente e graunt desir
del amender bonement a la volente de dieu e au gre de son peuple
taunt avaunt cum il devera. E sil avenist qil ne returnast mye, il bye
ordener qe son heir le fra ausi com sil meismes returnast de ceo qe

[1] 26 July.
[2] 28 July.

fera amender, car il seit bien qe nul nest taunt tenuz au reaume ne
de amer les bones gentz de sa terre come il meismes. Dautre part puys
quil ont enpris de passer la outre pur eyder le conte de Flandres, qui
est son aliez, e nomement pur mettre en la busoygne de lui e de son
reaume tele fyn com dieu vodra, kar meuz vaut de mettre fyn en la
busoygne au plus tost qe hom purra, qe de languyr ensi longement,
les graunt seyngnurs, qui nadguers furent a Lundres ove lui, pur ceo
qe il virent bien qil ne poait ne ne[a] puyt si graunt chose pursuier ne
meyntenir du soin,[b] e qe le veyage est si hastif pur le graunt peril
en quey les amys le roy de dela sont, par les queus sil perdissent, le
reaume purrayt cheyir en graunt peryl apres, qui dieu defende. E
pur aver le confermement de la graunt chartre des fraunchises Dengleterre e de la chartre de la foreste, le queu confermement le roys leur
ad graunte bonement si li graunterent un commun doun tel come
lui est mult busoygnable en poynt de ore, dunt il prie a tutes les bones
gentz e a tut le pueple de son reaume, qui unqes ne lui faillent, qe
cest doun ne leur ennoye mye, e puys quil veient bien quil ne esparnye
son cors, ne ceo qe il ad, pur alegger eux e ly de grauntz suffreytes
quil unt suffert e suffrent uncore a graunt meschief de iour en autre,
e puys quil seyvent ausint qe la busoygne est plus graunde quele ne
estoit unqes mes a nul iour. E pur ceo qe par cest aler avendra, si
dieu plest, bone pees e pardurable, par unt chescun si deit meyns tenir
agrevez de ceste doun, e par quay il purrount estre le plus tost delivers
des angusses e des travaus quil unt e unt eu avaunt ceste houre. E
si nuls feissent entendauntz avaunt le pays qe le roy eust refuse articles,
ou autre chose contre le commun profit du reaume pur son pueple
honir e destruire ou quil eust autrement overe envers les contes qe
en la manere desusdite, il prie qe hom ne lui creyt mye, kar ceo est
le droit processe e tute la verite coment les choses sunt alez deskes[c]
a ore. E se avise chescun coment graunt descord ad este autre foiz
en ceste reaume par iceles paroles entre le seyngnur e ses gentz de
une part e dautre, e les damages qe en sunt avenuz. E si hom crust
ore cestes autrement qe eles ne sunt, purroit avenir qe ryote ensur-
droit, la quele serroit plus perillouse e plus greve qe nestoit unqes mes
nule en ceste terre. E sunt escumengez tuz iceux qui troblent la pees
de ceste reaume en quele manere qe ceo soit, e tuz iceus qui as turbeurs
en argent, ou en chivaus, ou en armes, ou autrement donnent ou funt
eyde, ou favour, privement ou apertement de quelque condicion ou
estat quil soyent, de la quele sentence descumenge nuls ne puyt estre
asouz, sauntz especial comandement del apostoyl, forsqe en article
de mort, sicome pert par une bulle qe le rey ad du temps la pape

---

[a] *Sic in MS., corrected by Bémont to* se.
[b] *Sic in MS., corrected by Bémont to* sien.
[c] *Sic in MS., corrected by Bémont to* jeskes.

Clement, la quele graunt partie des prelatz e des autres grauntz seyn-gnurs de ceste terre unt bien entenduz, par quey il est mestier qe chescun sen gard. E pri le roy tut ces bones gentz de son reaume qe pur ceo quil, al honur de dieu, e de lui, e de eux, e du reaume, e pur pardurable pees, e pur mettre en bon estat son reaume ad enpris ceste veyage a fere, e il ad graunt afiance qe les bones priers de ses bones gentz lui purrunt mult eider, e valer a mettre ceste busoygne a bone fyn, quil voillent prier e fere prier ententivement pur lui e pur ceux qui ovesk lui vunt. En tesmoigne etc., donez a Odymere[1] le xii iour de Augst. Auteles lettres sount envoies a touz les viscontes de Engle-terre.[2]

C 66/117, m. 7, printed in *Foedera*, I, i, 872–3, and by C. Bémont, *Chartes des libertés anglaises* (Paris, 1902), making use of the copy at Canterbury, for which see *Royal Commission on Historical Manuscripts*, viii (London, 1881), 347. A copy is also printed in *Cotton, Historia Anglicana*, pp. 330–34. A translation is in *E.H.D.*, iii, 477–80.

112. *Anonymous letter, 13 August 1297*

Saluz e touz honeurs. Je vous envoy une bille qui ceux del Escheker ont fait a sire Johan de Cobeham du mariage Roger le fiuz e heyr Adam de Bavent, le quel mariage meismes celi sire Johan ad achate du roy, e deust paier les deniers avant cest dimenge procheinement avenir, e nen voet rien paer avant quil eit la lettre le roy de conferme-ment de cele vente, e ceste chose vous tesmoigne ie par cestes lettres, issint qe vous lui peussez faire avoir sur ce lettres le roy qui lui soient covenables en ceste partie, e celes lettres soient hastees issint qe le roy peusse tost estre paiez de les deniers quil deit avoir pur le dit mariage. A dieu sire qi vous gard. Escrit a Winchelse, le xiii iour du mois daugst.[3]

SC 1/31/101. Original.

[1] Udimore, Sussex.
[2] Payment for messengers taking this document to various Midland counties is recorded for 14 August in the Jornalia Roll (E 405/1/11), and for 17 August to Surrey, Sussex and Kent in the wardrobe book (B.L., Add. MS. 7965, fo. 113).
[3] John de Cobham paid 200 marks for the marriage of Roger de Bavent, and the grant was formally made on 13 August 1297 (*C.P.R., 1292–1301*, p. 302). Cobham also received custody of some of Bavent's lands, in payment for a loan of 500 marks he made to the crown, on 3 November 1297 (*Ibid.*, p. 314).

113. *The deputy treasurer and barons of the exchequer to Edward I, 14 August 1297*

Excellentissimo principi suo domino reverendo domino Edwardo dei gratia regi Anglie illustri domino Hibernie et duci Aquitanie, devoti sui tenens locum thesaurarii et barones de scaccario suo, fidele semper obsequium cum omni reverencia et honore. Mandavit nobis vestra serenitas per breve de privato sigillo vestro, quod ad nos venit die Mercurii in vigilia Assumpcionis beate Marie,[1] quod diversas litteras vestras patentes *et clausas* quas una cum eodem breve vestro nobis destinatis diversis vicecomitibus iuxta tenorem earundem transmitteremus, circa cuius mandati vestri expedicionem noscat vestra serenissima dominacio quod eadem hora predicte diei qua ad nos dicte littere vestre venerunt eas transmitti fecimus ulterius iuxta mandatum vestrum. Valeat excellencia vestra per tempora diuturna.[2]

SC 1/17/42. Original. An enrolled version is in E 159/70, m. 36d.

114. *Edward I to the deputy treasurer and the barons of the exchequer, 14 August 1297*

1 Edward etc. au .. lieu tenaunt nostre tresorier e as .. barons del eschekier saluz. [Nous vous *2* man]doms fermement enoignantz qe hastivement veues cestes lettres entre vous e le Gard[ien de Loundres] *3* e le .. conestable de la Tour, a queux nous avoms semblablement maunde, faciez crier . . . *4* de Loundres qe toutz ceaux de nostre hostiel e toutz les autres qui la sount qui de . . . *5* ovesques nous a cest passage viegnent a nous a Winchelse ove leur chivaux, e ove leur . . . *6* [sanz] nule manere de delai. Car nous avoms ia feit lyverer une graunt partie de nostre nav[ie] . . . *7* qui sount es parties ou nous sumes, apparailliez de passer ovesques nous. E feront . . . *8* chevaux ycest Lundi procheinement avenir[3] a tot le plus tard e des adonqe . . . *9* nule du mounde, qe nous ne passoms sauntz delai si le temps le suefre. E faites . . . *10* nos gentz qe le facent hastier de iour en iour tant quil soient issiez de la . . . *11* vers nous. Dautre part nous vous chargeoms especiaument qe les leynes qe nous fe . . . *12* a noste oes pur mener la outre, faciez

---

a . . . a *Words interlined.*

[1] 14 August. The king's letter, written on 12 August, is in E 159/70, m. 36d.
[2] The exchequer Jornalia Roll (E 405/1/11) has payments to Richard de Clare, sent to various counties, and Roger de Southcote to Beds. & Bucks., and also to John de Droxford, keeper of the wardrobe, for payments to various messengers taking the king's letter of 12 August 1297 (no. 111), justifying his actions against the earls, to Hunts., Cambs., Northants, Rutland, Leics., Warw., Notts. & Derbs.
[3] 19 August.

hastier e eskiper e enveer entre . . . *13* vous unqes purrez, car en ce
tient une des plus grant choses de nostre busoigne . . . *14* lesse, sicome
vous volez qe nous ne soioms honys a toutz iours mes. E nous . . . fa
. . . *15* vos lettres ce qe vous averez fait sur cestes beusoignes, ensemblement ove le . . . *16* Londres e daillours qui vous verrez qe a mander
nous facent. Don' sous nostre [prive seal] *17* a Odymere le xiii iour
Daugst, lan de nostre regne vintisme quint.

E 159/70, m. 36d.

115. *The deputy treasurer and barons of the exchequer to Edward I, 14 August*
      1297

A treshonurable prince e lour treschier seigneur Edward par la grace
de dieu roy Dengleterre, seigneur Dirlaunde e duks Daquitaigne, [le
lieu tenaunt le] tresorier e ses barouns de son eschekier, touz iours
leau service ove tuttes reverences et honeurs. Nous manda vostre hautesce qe a [plus en haste] qe nous peussoms, vous feissoms saveir ceo
qe les marchauntz e les autres gentz qui ne ad gueres feurent enveez
en divers countiez pur achatier [leynes] a vostre oes ount feit de cele
busoigne e ceo qui est feit ausint de leide des lays qui se deit lever
a vostre oes a ceste foiz deinz vostre reaume, sour queu chose sache
vostre seigneurie qe endreit de la busoigne des leynes, ceaus qui a
cele sount assignez furent delivres e enveez en pais graunt piece ad
sicome avaunt vous avoms maunde, mes puis leur partir navioms
nule novele de eaus, mes tauntost apres vostre dit maundement rescue,
avoms maunde par briefs de vostre eschekier a les dites gentz quil
facent hastier e espleitier la dite busoigne des leynes, e celes leynes
carier as portz e chargier en niefs, ove tutte la diligence e haste quil
saveront e purront, issi qeles peussent estre prestes a passer a vostre
passage, si avaunt come il purront e saveront qe il nous certifient hastivement come avaunt la dite busoigne est espleitee e fete en touz
pointz. E si tost come il nous averont de ceo certifie, nous le vous
froums saveir hastivement. Endreit de la busoigne de leyde des lays
tuttes les choses qe touche cele busoigne furent fetes, espleitees, e
envees avaunt, avaunt la venue de vos lettres, a fere e espleitier, solom
la fourme de ceo ord[ine] devaunt vous meismes. Sire, endreit de ceo
qe vous nous chargiez qe nous mettoms tote la peyne e la diligence
qe nous purroms de lever deniers [a vostre oes] ove tutte la foison
e la haste qe nous unqes purroms e qe a ceo ferre enveoms gentz par
tot pur faire les venir a vostre eschekier hastivement, nous lavoms fet
e fesoms e froms en meisme la maniere solom vostre mandement, e
si avaunt come nostre sen e nostre poeir se estendent, sauntz aveir

regard a nuly persone. Sire, nostre seigneur vous doint bone vie e lunge e acresse vos honeurs. [Ceste lettre fut fete e envee au rei la veille del assumpcion nostre dame].

SC 1/17/36. Original or draft, slightly torn. The sections in brackets are supplied from the copy in E 159/70, m. 36.

116. *John le Breton, keeper of the City of London, to Edward I, 15–16 August 1297*

1 ... pryme e treshautyme seignur roy Dengleterre, pur le soen lyge Jehan le Bretun, gardeyn de sa citee de Lundres, quaun ke il seet e ... *2* ... pleysir vous est ore i ceo Joedi en la feste del assumpcion nostre dame a houre de Vespres me furent livereez vos lettres ke entre ... *3* ... Tour de Lundres e le leu tenaunt vostre tresorier e les baruns del escheker, tauntost veue vos lettres, feysoms crieer parmy ... *4* touz ceux de vostre houstiel e touz les autres ky la sunt ky deyvent passer oveks vous a ceo passage e veignent a vous a Wynchelse od ... *5* od leur armes saunz nule manere de delay e ke vous freyes eskyper vos chivaus le lundi procheynement avenir apres la dite feste de nos ... *6* ... unks vous ne atendryez nuly de munde ke vous ne passerez saunz delay, si le tens le suffrysist. Sire, tauntost veue vos lettres, feym ... *7* ... parmy la citee en la suzdite fourme, e assignames certeynz gentz ky les hastent de jour en jour taunt com il poent ke il seent en alaunt *8* ... endreit des noveles a Lundres e dailleurs ke vous facent a maunder, ne vous say ieo autres noveles maunder ore aparmenees, mes ke le *9* ... le cunte de Heref' e autres graunz seignurs serrent en la vile de Lundres iceo Samady procheynement avenir apres la dite feste de nostre Dame *10* ... dit. Celuy roy par ky touz roys regnent vous sauve e garde en lunge vie e bone.[1]

SC 1/15/107. Original, torn.

117. *Edward I to the deputy treasurer and barons of the exchequer, 17 August 1297*

Edward etc au lieu tenaunt nostre tresorier e as barouns del escheker, saluz. Nous vous mandoms fermement enioignantz qe entre vous e Roberd de Cotingham nostre clerk, portour de ces lettres, faciez sercher sanz nule maniere de delai en nostre tresorie a la Tour de Loundres e a Westmoster e ailleurs la ou vous verrez qe mieuz soit,

[1] This letter was evidently written in reply to one similar to that sent on 14 August to the deputy treasurer and barons of the exchequer (no. 114).

le testament qui nous feismes faire darreinement[1] ou autre testament
qui nous ou aucun de nos auncestres avoms fait avaunt ces houres,
sicome le dit Robert vous purra plus pleinement dire. E meismes le
testament nous enveez par lavauntdit Robert a plus en haste qe vous
unqes purrez. E ceste chose ne lessez en nule manere. Don, desouz
nostre prive seal a Odymere le xvii iour Daugst, lan de nostre regne
vintisme quint.

E 159/70, m. 35d.

118. *Edward I to the deputy treasurer and barons of the exchequer, 17 August
1297*

Edward etc au lieu tenaunt nostre tresorier e as barouns del escheker,
saluz. Nous vous mandoms qe trestot le ble, qui est meintenaunt a
Loundres e qui est purveu a nostre oes pur nostre passage la outre,[2]
faciez mettre en bons vesseaux e enveer iusqes en Flaundres au plus
en haste qe vous unqes porrez. Et tut le ble qui y vendra desoremes,
qui est purveu a nostre oes pur le dit passage, faciez enveer en
Flaundres en la maniere avantdite. Don' desouz nostre prive seal a
Odymere le xvii iour Daugst, lan de nostre regne vintisme quint.

Et in pretextu cuius brevis iniunctum est vicecomitibus London'
per barones de scaccario, xx die Augusti, quod premissa exequantur
omni celeritate qua fieri poterit iuxta tenorem brevis predicti. Et
nihilominus inde habeant breve sub sigillo scaccarii.

E 159/70, m. 35d.

119. *Edward I to the barons of the exchequer, 20 August 1297*

Rex baronibus suis de scaccario, salutem. Mittimus vobis sub sigillo
nostro formam cuiusdam ordinacionis per nos et consilium nostrum
facte de tercia vel quinta parte bonorum prelatorum, clericorum et
personarum ecclesiasticarum quarumcumque de regno nostro in subsidium instantis expedicionis nostre ad opus nostrum levanda, mandantes quatenus certas personas, de quarum[a] fidelitate et industria
considitis, per litteras sub sigillo scaccarii nostri sine dilacione assig-
netis ad dictam tertiam vel quintam partem taxandam et levandam

---

[a] quorum *in E 368/68 and E 159/70.*

[1] Edward had made his will at Acre on 18 June 1272 (*Testamenta Vetusta*, ed. N. H.
Nicolas (London, 1826), i, 7–10).
[2] In addition to grain purveyed in London and Midd., supplies from Beds., Bucks.,
Warw., Leics., Oxon. and Berks. were all assembled at London (E 159/70, m. 90d).

iuxta formam ordinacionis predicte, quam illis quos sic assignaveritis per vos liberari volumus per ipsos in comitatibus in quibus assignati fuerint publice ostendendam. Teste meipso apud Winchelse xx die Augusti, anno regni nostri vicesimo quinto.

Tenor forme predicte talis est.

Come le reis par lordinaunce de dieu eit resceu le governement du reaume par quei il est tenuz a defense de meisme le reaume e de toutz ses sozmis, clers e lais, e eit sentu e apercu les grauntz periels, maux e damages qe de iour en autre sur*a* lui e soun poeple en subversion du dit reaume e destruction de seinte eglise aperte sunt avenuz, par le grant poeir du rei de Fraunce e de ses aliez, quil ont*b* desherite, e seforcerent a tot leur poer, e uncore font, lui e son reaume destruire, ad fait aliaunce de counte de Flaundres e dautres grantz seignours, par leide de queux il entent al eide de dieu soun reaume defendre e ses enemis rebotier, e son dreit recoverir, dunt purceo quil ne perde ses aliez ne ses amis ne leide de eaux, nomement en cest busoigne quest si grande, les queux le dit rei de Fraunce seforce destruire a tot son poer, par la perte des queux, si ele avenist, qe ia deus ne voille, il ne porreit atteindre a soun dreit recoverir. E a coe son reaume e tote seinte eglise e le poeple de meisme le reaume serroient en peril de destruction e perdicion aperte, ad empris de passer la mer es partie de dela, non soulement pur sez aliez e ses amis eider, eynz pur son dreit recoverir e les ditz perils escheure, e ses enemis rebotier, e pur son reaume asseurer des damages quil*c* peussent avenir, si ses amis feussent en peril, les queux enemis porra al eide de dieu, e des ses aliez e amis mieuz e plus seurement rebotier*d* de loynz qe de pres. La quele emprise ne se peut faire a honour e a profit ne a la sauvacion de lui ne de son reaume, saunz commune eide des clers e de lais de son reaume, pur le comoun profit e defens devaunditz, ad ordeine qe pur ceo qe clers par fet darmes ne*e* se deivent defendre, la tierce partie des biens temporeus de lan qe ore est, des prelaz e des clers, e tuttes persones de seinte eglise, religieux e autres seit levee pur la dite necessarite*f* empris faire e meintenir, ensi qe rien ne seit levee par cele atcheson des dimes meismes, ne grantz oblacions, obventions, mortuaires, ne des biens assignez a la luminare, ou as ornementz de la eglise ou des autres biens purement espirituels, ne rien ne seit levee des clers qe benefices ne valent plus de v. mars, entotes choses solom la derreine taxation. E entent le rei qe les biens des clers en lour lai fez qe ne sunt pas aportenaunt as eglises ne seient pas en ceste taxation, mes courent en la taxation des lais. E auxi entent le rei qe ceaux qe voudrent doner la quinte partie de toutz lour biens tem-

---

a sur *omitted in* E 368/68.   *b* vout *in* E 368/68; lount *in Parl. Writs.*
c qui y *in Parl. Writs.*   *d* rebotier *omitted in Parl. Writs.*
e ne *omitted in* E 368/68.   *f* necessaire *in Parl. Writs.*

poreux et espirituels aportenaunz a lour benefices seient a quint. E
de ceste prise, qe le rei fera, entent il si tost come il purra en bone
manere faire la gree de ceux de qui il avera pris solom coe quil devera
faire en tiele manere quil sendeveront tenir paiez.

E 368/68, m. 58d; E 159/70, m. 125, badly damaged. Printed in *Parl.
Writs*, i, 396, from the Patent Roll. Translated in *E.H.D.*, iii, 480–1.

120. *Edward I to the barons of the exchequer, 20 August 1297*

Edward par la grace de deu etc. Pur ce qe nous avoms entendu qe
les gentz qe sont alez pur prendre leynes a nostre oes ount arestuz
aucunes leynes de marchaundz de Alemaigne, de Brabaunt e de
Flandres, les queles il achaterent a Seint Botolph' e aillors, la queu
chose nous ne volions unques, ne unquore ne voloms, car ce ne fust
unques nostre entencion ne uncore nest. Vous mandoms qe a la suit
de chescun de marchaundz avantditz, faciez deliverer lour leynes quil
averont achatees pur les mesner la outre a lour voluntez, feisantz pur
oek la custume qe y apent, cest asaver les leynes quil eurent achatees
avant qe les dites gentz comencerent a faire la prise avantdite. E ceste
chose voloms qe vous faciez prestement e santz delay pur le grant
avantage qe nous y veoms. E nous entendoms totes foiz e uncore entendoms qe la prise se face des autres leynes qe de celes qe marchandz
ont achatez. Don' souz nostre prive seal a Wynchels' le xx iour Daugst,
lan de nostre regne xxv.[1]

E 159/70, m. 35d.

121. *Indenture of agreement between Peter of Chichester and Alexander le
Convers, 20 August 1297*

Memorandum quod die Mercurii proximo post festum assumpcionis
beate Marie anno regni regis Edwardi vicesimo quinto apud Wyn-
cheles' concordatum est inter dominum Petrum de Cicestr' et Alexandrum le Convers, clericos regis, de denarios quos iidem Petrus et Alexander receperunt de garderobe eiusdem regis pro pontibus et cleiis
et diversis victualibus et aliis necessariis pro passagio eiusdem regis
versus partes transmarinas providendis et cariandis. Et inveniebatur
quod predicti Petrus et Alexander receperunt de predicta garderobe
per vices pro predictis faciendis centum et decem libras, de quibus
predictus Alexander liberavit predicto domino Petro pro victualibus
ad opus eiusdem regis providendis et cariandis viginti et tres libras.

---

[1] A similar letter on behalf of Gascon merchants, written on the same day, is in
E 159/70, m. 37.

Et sic remanebant penes predictum Alexandrum quater viginti et septem libre, de quibus predictus Alexander tenetur respondere pro se
et dicto domino Petro in garderobe domini regis predicto. In cuius
rei testimonium iidem Petrus et Alexander huic dividende sigilla sua
alternatim apposuerunt.

E 101/684/84/1. Original, indented.

122. *Edward I to the barons of the exchequer, 20 August 1297*

Edward par la grace de deu etc. Pur ce qe les gentz de Londres ont
taxez George Dacre, vallet la dame de Vescy, a faire contribucion
a nous si come les gentz de meismes la vile font orendreit, la ou
meismes celui George nest pas taillable a ce quil nous ad fait entendant; vous mandoms qe vous enquergez sour ce tote la certeinete e
si vous treifsez quil ne devera mie ceste taille ou quil seit taille en
autre manere qe en due, faciez sun estat redresser sicome vous verrez
quil soit a faire par reison. Don' souz nostre prive seal a Wynchelse
le xx iour Daust, lan de nostre regne xxv.

E 159/70, m. 37.

123. *Edward I to Henry de Guildford and the sheriff of Sussex, 20 August
1297*

Rex dilecto clerico suo Henrico de Gyldeford et vicecomiti Sussex',
salutem. Monstraverunt nobis prior et conventus de Lewes quod vos
averia caruce sue pro quibusdam debitis in quibus iidem prior et conventus nobis tenentur vendicioni facitis exponi, ubi intencionis nostre
non est quod averia caruce, per quod cultura terrarum impediatur,
pro debitis nostris vendantur. Et ideo vobis mandamus quod vendicioni averiorum caruce predictorum prioris et conventus, de quibus
pro cultura terrarum necessario indigetur, supersedeatis. Teste J. de
Cobeham etc. xx die Augusti, anno xxv. Quia predictus prior reddit
regi certum finem per annum pro omnibus exitibus domus sue.

E 159/70, m. 107d.

124. *Edward I to the deputy treasurer and barons of the exchequer, 22 August
1297*

Edward par la grace de dieu, rei Dengleterre, seignor Dirland e ducs
Daquitaine, a lieu tenant nostre tresorier e as barons del escheqer,

saluz. Nous vous mandoms qe vous suffrez nostre chier e ame cosin mons' Aymar de Valence, ou sez atornez, pur lui passer la outre iusqes a vint saks de sa layne qite de la custume e de tot ceo qui a nous en appent quil houre quil vodra ou qe ses gentz voudrent, issint totes voies qe ce seit feit le plus priveement qe vous porrez, si qe autres ne preignent ensample de nous charger de tieu chose. Done souz nostre prive seal a Winchilse le xxii iour Daust, lan de nostre regne xxv.

E 159/71, m. 5; E 368/69, m. 13d.

125. *Edward I to the barons of the exchequer, 22 August 1297*

Nous vous mandoms qe les leynes Talde Janyan,[1] lesqueles il ont leaument e santz fraude achatees avant qe nos gentz sont alez es countez pur prendre leynes a nostre oes urent comenceez a faire la prise avantdite, e les queles sont aresteez par meismes les gentz es countez de Nicole e Deverwyke ausint, a ce qe nous avons entendu, li faciez deliverer sanz delay, paiant la custume en du manere. Don' suz nostre prive seal a Wynchelse le xxii iour Daugst, lan de nostre regne xxv.

E 159/70, m. 37d.

126. *The deputy treasurer and barons of the exchequer to Edward I, 22 August 1297*[2]

Tenens locum thesaurarii et barones de scaccario miserunt domino regi quasdam litteras sub sigillo dicti scaccarii in hec verba:

Sir, ycest ioedy prochein devaunt la feste seint Bertelmeu a houre de tierce vindrent a vostre eschekier a la barre le . . counte mareschal e le . . counte de Hereford, monsire Robert le fiz Rogier, sire Alein la Zouche, sire Johan de Segrave, sire Henri le Tieys, sire Johan Luvel e plusours autres baneretz e bacheliers, e le counte de Hereford dit quil feust chargee a dire de par le counte mareschal e les autres qui illoeques furent, e pur tutte la comunaute du reaume, auxi bien clerks come lays, qe de deus choses se sentirent eaux e la dite communaute grevez; lune daukunes grevaunces dount il aveient fait moustrer les articles a vous, come a leur lige seignour, e lautre quil entendirent qe feust fet par nous del eschekier, sauntz vostre seu, come endreit del utime lever, e de leynes prendre, e dit qen les briefs qe sunt issuz pur lever le utime est contenu qe countes e barouns, chivaliers e la

---

[1] Taldo Janiani was one of the members of the Florentine firm of the Frescobaldi.

[2] The following letters of 22–25 August (nos. 127–131) are entered consecutively in the manuscript.

comunaute du reaume unt graunte le utime, sicom e eaux e leur auncestres unt fait cea en ariere, la ou le dit utime par eaux ne par la
dite comunaute unqes ne fu graunte, e dit outre qe nule chose ne
met plus tost homme en servage qe rechat de saunc, e estre taillie
a volente, e qe si le utime fust issi levee, ceo turnereit a desheriteson
de eaux e de leur heyrs. E dit apertement, e toutz les autres apres,
qe tiel taillage e prise de leynes ne furent mie suffrables, ne il ne le
suffreient en nule manere. E nous prierent qe cestes choses feissoms
redrescier, e a taunt senpartirent sauntz nule respounse attendre. E
pur ceo, sire, nous voilliez maunder, se vous plest, sur ceste chose
vostre volunte. Sir, nostre seigneur vous doint bone vie e longe, e
acresse vos honeurs. Escrit a Westmoustier le ioedy avantdit a houre
de noune.

Ista littera missa fuit domino regi per Robertum Dyvelyn hosti-
arium de scaccario ad predictam horam none.[1]

E 159/70, m. 125.

127. *Edward I to the deputy treasurer and barons of the exchequer, 23 August
1297*

Postea dominus rex rescripsit voluntatem suam eisdem per litteras suas
in hec verba:

Edward par la grace de dieu rei Dengleterre etc., au .. lieu tenaunt
nostre tresorier e as barons del eschekier, saluz. Nous avoms entendu
coment les deus countes vindrent al eschekier ove leur compaignie
e les choses ausint quil vous unt dites, les queles vous nous mandastes. E
quant a coe quil distrent, quil ne suffreient en nule manere de lever le
utime ne de faire la prise des leynes, nous voloms qe vous ne leissez mie
pur ceo qe vous naillez avaunt a taxer e a lever lutyme avantdit en
la fourme qui en est ordene, mais pur ceo quil disoient qe la levee tor-
nereit en preiudice e en desheritaunce de eaux e de leur heirs, nous
voloms bien qe vous facez saveir a toutz e criez parmy les countiez
ou la taxation del utime se deit faire, qe sil yad nul qui se doute de
tieu preiudice ne de tiele desheritance, qe le rei le quitera voluntiers
par ses lettres overtes en tieu maniere qe la taxation ne la levee de
cest utime ne puisse tourner en preiudice ne en servage de nuly, ne
estre tret ne usage en temps avenir, mes qe le rei sen puisse ore eider
pur soun graunt busoign, qe est si hastif, pur la sauvacion de lui e
de eux meismes, e de tut le reaume, e pur alegier lui e eaux des mes-
chiefs dont il unt este chargiez ia graunt piece. E sur coe voloms qe

---

[1] Payment of 5s. to Robert Dyvelin is recorded on 23 August, to cover his expenses
in going from London to Winchelsea. He then received a further 5s. on 26 August,
after his return (E 405/1/11).

nostre chauncelier Dengleterre leur face tieux lettres du seal quil gar-
dera tant come nous seroms la outre, e vous ausint du seal del eschekier
a ceaux qui purchacier les voudront come entre vous verrez qe bones
e suffisantes soient. E ceste chose avoms nous mande au chauncelier
avantdit par nos lettres. E quant a la prise des leynes, voloms qe lor-
denance qui en est faitre se tiegne, e qe dit soit par tut, auxibien par
vous come par ceaux qe senentremettent, qe le rei nen voet rien
prendre ne avier pur nient mais qe par achat, feisaunt gre pur vek
a chescun, e qe en autre volunte nous ne fumes unques ne en autre
manere la chose est mise en oevre. Quant vous averez a demander
autrefoiz avisement sur ceste beusoigne ou sur autre qui soit hastive,
vous le ferez savoir a nostre filz e a son counseil quil aura pres li, e
eaux y mettront tieu counseil par lavisement dentre vous come il verront qe bon seit. Don' souz nostre privee seal a Wynchelse le xxiii
iour Daugst, lan de nostre regne xxv.

128. *Edward I to the deputy treasurer and barons of the exchequer, 24 August
1297*

Edward par la grace de dieu etc., au .. lieu tenaunt nostre tresorier
e as barons del eschekier, saluz. Nous vous enveoms enclos denz ces
lettres le transcrit dunes lettres qui nous enveoms a Edward nostre
fiz e a son counseil pur faire une crie de par nous parmy les countiez
Dengleterre, sicome plus pleinement est contenu en transcrit
avauntdit. E vous mandoms, quant vous vendrez la ou nostre filz
serra, qe vous en amontenez e avisez lui e soun counseil, si qe par
lavisement dentre vous toutz, seit ent fait ceo quil vous semblera qe
seit a fere pur le meillour. Don' souz nostre privee seal en la mer au
devaunt Dovre le xxiii iour Daugst, lan de nostre regne vintime quint.
Tenor transcripti predicti talis est:

129. *Edward I to his son Edward and his council, 24 August 1297*

Edward par la grace de dieu etc., a .. Edward nostre cher filz, nostre
lieu tenant en Engleterre, e a son consail, saluz. Nous vous mandoms
ore, sicome nous vous mandasmes par nostre chancelier, pur ceo qe
les deus .. countes e leur eideurs par aventure bient a destourbier
la levee de cest utime e la prise de leynes, ausint qe vous facez crier
e dire solempnement parmy les countiez Dengleterre e nomement en
la presence des ditz countes e as countes meismes qe eaux e toutz ceaux
qui a nostre foi sount e voelent estre sueffrent qe la levee e la prise

avantdites se facent puis qe les choses sont ordinees pur la beusoigne qest si grande e si hastive e pur la sauvacion de nous e de tut nostre reaume. E faites ausint defendre qe[a] nul ny mette empeschement ne destourbe chose qe seit ordenee pur la sustenaunce de nous[b] qui suive leur seigneur lige e de ceaux qui ovesque nous vont. E leur faites saveir qe vous estes prestz quant a la levee du dit utime de faire lettres du seal de la chauncelrie dount home deit user taunt come nous serroms la outre, e del eschekier ausint, a toutz ceaux qui purchacier les voudront, qe ceste levee ne turnera en prejudice ne en desheritance de nuli ne autrefoiz tret ne demaunde ne serra par nous ne par nos heirs en nule manere de servage. E quant a la prise des leynes seit criez e defendu en meisme la manere, kar nous voloms faire gree pur cek a toutz ceaux de qui eles serront prises en tieu manere quil se deveront tenir appaiez par resoun. E il nous semble qe nous devoms estre auxi fraunk dachatier leynes en nostre pays come un autre. Ceste crie e ceste defense voloms qe seient faites hastivement e communement parmi toutz les countiez, citiez, burghs e viles marchaundes Dengleterre. E qe toutz seient chargiez sur lomage e la foi quil nous deivent e sur tut ce quil nous poent meffaire e sicome il ne voelent estre rettez de nostre desheriteson e de la perte de nous e de ceaux qui vont ovesque nous e du reaume ausint qe nul de fait ne de parole ne viegne par lui ne par autre contre la fourme de la criee e de la defense avantdites. Totes voies nous mettoms le fait de ceste criee en vos discrecions, si qele se face sil vous semble que bon seit. E pur ceo qe diverses noveles nous purront venir, de quei nous ne sauriens coment creire, vous mandoms qe vous nous facez savoir sovent tote la certeinte des dites beusoignes e de tuttes les autres qui vous verrez qui a maunder nous facent. Don' souz nostre privee seal en la mer a devant Dovre le xxiiii iour Daugust, lan de nostre regne xxv.

130. *Edward, son of Edward I, to the deputy treasurer and barons of the exchequer, 25 August 1297*

Edward filz au rei Dengleterre, tenaunt le lieu meisme le rei en Engleterre, au tenaunt le lieu le tresorier e as barons del eschekier, saluz. Nous vous enveioms par Willame de Blyburgh' nostre clerk le transcrit de une lettre, qe vint de nostre seignour nostre piere au chauncelier, enclos dedenz ceste lettre, e la quele il moustra devaunt nous e nostre counseil, sur la queu chose e auxi sour la serche du seal faire e dendreit des autres choses qe touchent la garde de la vile e de la

---

[a] defendre a trestouz qe, *in* E 368/68.
[b] eious, *in* E 368/68.

Tour e de criee faire en la cyte qe nul preigne vitaille santz paier.[1]
Le avantdit nostre clerk creez e faciez sour ceo quil vous dirra. Don'
a Pont Robert[2] lendemein de seinte Bertelmeu, lan du regne nostre
seignour le rei nostre piere xxv. Tenor transcripti predicti talis est:

131. *Edward I to the chancellor, 24 August 1297*

Edward etc. a nostre chauncelier, saluz. Nous vous mandoms qe par
lavisement de ceaux del eschekier faciez faire tieux lettres come entre
vous verriez qe suffisauntes seient coment lutyme qe nous fesoms taxer
parmi le reaume ne puisse turnier a preiudice ne en desheritaunce
de ceaux du reaume, ne de leur heirs ne iaumieis estre treit en usage
en temps avenir, les queux lettres nous voloms qe seient sealees du
seal de la chauncelrie dunt hom deit user taunt come nous serroms
la outre. Don' souz nostre prive seal a Wynchelse le xxiiii iour Daugst,
lan de nostre regne xxv.

E 159/70, m. 125; E 368/68, m. 59. The letter of the deputy treasurer
and barons to the king of 22 August is also in SC 1/17/31, and that
of the king to his son and his council of 24 August is also in SC 1/
45/76. This correspondence was printed from E 368/68, although the
version is slightly inferior to that of E 159/70, in 'Extracts from the
Memoranda Rolls (L.T.R.) of the Exchequer:—1. The negotiations
preceding the Confirmatio Cartarum (1297 A.D.). With Translation',
T.R.Hist.S., n.s., iii (1886), 281–91. A modern translation is in
E.H.D., iii, 482–5.

132. *Richard, earl of Arundel, to Edward I, after 9 July 1297, probably
August 1297*

1 A treshaut home e tresnobles e a soun treschier e tresame segneur
moun segneur sire Edward par la grace [de dieu roi Dengleterre, sei-
gneur] *2* Dyrlande e ducs Daquitaigne, le soen tut liges Richard counte
Darundel, quant qe il seet a poet de h ... *3* sire qe vous me mandastes
par vos lettres qe mes amys me aveyent garny trop tart de moun ...
4 de Escoce, par quei vous ne me poez riens fere, mes quant vous
verrez tans qe vous me eyderez so ... *5* plest. Altre foiz mavez promis

---

[1] For the text of a proclamation to this effect allegedly made in London on 26 August,
see *Monumenta Gildhallae Londoniensis; Liber Albus, Liber Custumarum, et Liber Horn*, ed.
H. T. Riley (Rolls Series, 1860), ii, pt. i, 71–2. The list of persons present on that
occasion, notably the chancellor, Reginald de Grey and Alan Plukenet, does not tally
with the fact that they were at Tonbridge on 27 August (*C.P.R., 1292–1301*, p. 306).
See also Rothwell, 'The Confirmation of the Charters, 1297', 177, n. 3.

[2] Robertsbridge, Sussex.

grace, e ie enteng, sire, qe la ley ne volez vyer a nully, ne ie ne ...
6 de diex puys qe ie ne puys altre grace trouver. De ce, sire, qe vous
me mandastes qe ie me hastace vers vo ... *7* passage e qe vous me
ferryez gages ou altre chose, sachez, sire, me eussez vous grante moun
droit ie ne eusse d ... *8* altre chose qar sur Fraunce de cele terre de
Escoce me eusse ie demys de mes terres par de ca de avoir done a
mes *9* genz pur vous servir e pur moi chevir, e fort, sire, me serroit
si cele dela me fausist e cele de ca ausint, qar sachez *10* certaignement,
sire, qe ie ne troef nuyl qi servir me voylle saunz ce qe ie ne ly doigne
grantmentes de mes terres e ie *11* en ay, sire, si poi qe me est tut asseez
busoign par quel, sire, ie nel puis pas fere, sanz grant abesement de
mon estat, *12* la queu chose, sire, ie enteng qe vous ne voderez mie.
Et sachez qe pur vos gerres e pur moun estat meyntenir, si me *13*
... re demys puis qe ie fu seigneur de terre al amountaunte de cink
cent liverees de terre, e ce grevereit, sire, a un grey[gnour] *14* ... segneur qe ie ne su. Et par la foi, sire, qe ie vous doi, ie ai perdu en
ceste deus gerres en vostre service pluys de quatre *15* ... archees de
chevaux de armes, que en Gales, qe en Escoce, qe en Gascoigne, de
quei, sire, ie ne avoi unqes dener *16* ... lle de vostre garderobe, e ce
teng ie bien emplye. Et del poer, sire, qe vous me donastes a demettre
moi de cent liverees *17* [de] terre;[1] sachez qe ie ne troef nuyl h[om]me
voylle nuyl deneres prester sur ce, si ie ne les voylle doner come qui
dit *18* ... yent, e ce ne purrere ie mye fere saunz grant abessement
de moun estat, la queu chose ie enteng qe vous ne vod ... *19* ... as,
e vostre patente, sire, ai ie preste en ma garde, quel hure qe vous
pleyse de la vous rendre. Chier sire, si vous *20* voyllez aver pur escuse
de ce qe ie ne suy de poer ore de passer ove vous pur les enchesouns
desus escrites *21* ... e poyse. Le seint Esperit, sire, vous ait en sa garde,
e me doint bones noveles de vous.

SC 1/17/64. Original, torn and holed for filing.

133. *Procuration directed against the archbishop of Canterbury, his suffragans,
all other prelates and others, 1 September 1297*

Et predictus Hugo de Jernemuth' procurator regis[2] fecit procuraciones et appellationes in ecclesia Cantuar' et inde per publicum instrumentum in hec verba. In nomine domini, amen. Per presens
publicum instrumentum omnibus appareat evidenter quod die

[1] On 9 July 1297 the earl of Arundel was given licence to let out land at farm for
ten years, to a value of £100 p.a. (*C.P.R., 1292–1301*, p. 289).
[2] This text is preceded by a royal notification dated 31 August to the archbishop
of Canterbury, his suffragans and others, of the appointment of Hugh of Yarmouth
as king's proctor, which is calendared in *C.P.R., 1292–1301*, pp. 307–8. That follows
in the manuscript immediately on the procurations of 24 March (no. 23).

dominica proxima post festum decollacionis sancti Johanni Baptiste,
scilicet Kalendis Septembris, [1] anno domini ab incarnacione millesimo
ducentesimo nonagensimo septimo, indictione decima, in presencia
mei notarii publici infrascripti et testium subscriptorum dominus
Hugo de Jernemuth' clericus procurator illustris regis Anglie, litteratorie destinatus prout infra patet, quoddam procuratorium dicti
domini regis sigillo signatum publice legit iuxta magnum altare
ecclesie Christi Cantuar', cuius tenor talis est:

Edwardus dei gracia etc., in predicto procuratorio. [2] Quo procuratorio lecto, dictus procurator quasdam procurationes et appellaciones
infrascriptas interposuit, legit et recitavit in hec verba:

In dei nomine, amen. Nuper in media quadragesima venerabili
patre domino R. dei gratia Cantuar' archiepiscopo ac suis suffraganeis
nec non et aliis prelatis Cantuar' provincie congregatis, magnificus
princeps dominus Edwardus eadem gratia illustris rex Anglie,
dominus Hibernie et dux Aquitanie, coram dictis archiepiscopo, suffraganeis et prelatis certis de causis et presumptionibus et coniecturis
verisimilibus per dominum Iterium de Engolisma clericum et procuratorem suum ad hoc litteratorie constitutum pro se, regno suo et
suis qui de sua fidelitate erant, justiciariis, consiliariis, clericis et
ministris aliis quibuscumque quasdam procuraciones et appellaciones
in scriptis fecit ad sacrosanctam Romanam ecclesiam interponi,
quarum tenor sequitur in hec verba:

In dei nomine, amen. Cum serenissimus princeps dominus
Edwardus etc. ut supra in alio instrumento, usque ibi 'et appellos
peto'.[3] Et tunc sic. Verum quia idem dominus rex et suum consilium
iam de novo tam per relatum plurimum fidedignorum quam per ges-
tum dicti archiepiscopi, dicta et facta ipsius manifestissime intellexit
quod ipse, spretis dictis appellacionibus de quibusdam sedis apostolice
constitutionibus et aliis que regno Anglie in necessitatis articulo in
quo positum est existente hiis diebus secundum sanctorum regulas et
una alia infinita locum sibi vendicare non possunt sumpto colore quedam preiudicialia et infamatoria dicto regi consiliariis, justiciariis,
clericis et ministris suis proponit promulgare vel facere promulgari,
declarare vel facere declarari. Ego Hugo de Jernemuta clericus et procurator eiusdem regis ad hoc litteratorie constitutus, volens sibi et suis
contra huiusmodi preiudicialia providere, vice et nomine dicti regis,
et pro ipso ac certis de ministris suis et fautoribus et eisdem adherentibus, predictas provocaciones et appellaciones innovo in hiis scriptis.
Et ne archiepiscopus predictus vel quivis predicti regni episcopus aut
prelatus vel aliter quispiam superiori sua vel cuiusvis vice, nomine,

---

[1] 1 September.
[2] The notification of 31 August, in *C.P.R.*, *1292–1301*, pp. 307–8.
[3] The procuration of 24 March (no. 23).

auctoritate vel mandato contra dictum regem aut eius consiliarios, justiciarios, clericos aut adherentes eidem cuiuscumque eminencie, status aut dignitatis existant, vel quoscumque sibi adherentes per ipsum vel per alium seu alios directe seu indirecte aliquid quomodo-libet attemptet vel faciet aliqualiter attemptari mandando, monendo, citando, statuendo, ordinando, diffiniendo, declarando, denun-ciando, publicando, suspendendo, excommunicando aut exequendo seu quicquam aliud in iudicio vel extra iudicium faciendo, ego dictus Hugo vice ipsius domini regis et pro ipso domino rege, consiliariis, justiciariis, clericis, ministris, fautoribus et suis adherentibus quibus-cumque et singulis eorundem ad dictam sedem apostolicam in hiis scriptis provoco et appello et appellaciones peto, quos si denegaverit ex hoc iterato appello.

Et postmodum dictus procurator omnia suprascripta palam et publice notificavit et informavit venerabili patri domino R. dei gratia Cantuar' archiepiscopo totius Anglie primati, tunc in dicta ecclesia predicanti, et coram ipso easdem innovacionem et provocacionem et appellacionem directe ad ipsum ordinans verba sua fecit et interposuit de verbo ad verbum loquendo sibi in secunda persona ubi superius de eodem in tercia loquentur. Presentibus tunc ibidem venerabili viro magistro Iterio de Engolisma, illustris regis Anglie clerico, domino Petro de Abindon', magistro Ricardo de Hauze, magistro Johannem de Luda, clericis, dominus Johanne de Norwode, Willelmo de Hauze militibus, Johanne de Midelton', Ricardo dicto Le Weable et aliis testibus in multitudine copiosa.[1]

E 159/70, m. 117d.

134. *Edward I to his son Edward and his council, 5 September 1297*

Edward par la grace de dieu roi Dengleterre, seigneur Dirland e ducs Daquitaine, a Edward son chier fiuz e a son consail, saluz. Nous vous fesoms a saver qe bientost apres ce qe nous esteiens arrivez en Flandres surdi tieux ... tens e tieu riote entre les gentz des Portz e ceux de Jernemue, qe homicide, robberie e arson des vesseaux, e autres damages en sont avenuz dun part e dautre, par qi par leur bon gre e par lour assent demeyne nous avoms pris ostages des uns e des autres,

---

[1] The manuscript continues at this point with the notarial certification by Walter le Norreys, in exactly the same form as after the procuration of 24 March (no. 23), with the addition at the end of the following: 'et abrasi superius de manu mei hoc verbum procurationem'. There then follows a much shorter public notification, in very similar terms, by Alan of Kent, appointed by the king to go to the bishoprics of Rochester, Chichester, Winchester, Exeter, Bath and Wells, Salisbury, Hereford, Llan-daff and St David's. He was accompanied by Walter le Norreys, and they were each paid £1 10s. on 16 September (E 405/1/11, m. 11).

pur eux e pur touz les autres qui sont orendroit es parties de decea, en
tieu manere qe le redrescement soit a nostre volunte, pard ... quant il
nous plerra, e que plus de damage navendra desoremes entres les parties
e ne nul sur autre ne meffera par mer ne par tere par acheison du
fait avantdit. E pur ce qe aucuns des uns e des autres sont ia retournez
en lour pays, a ce qe nous avoms entendu, par qui porreit avenir qe
plus de riote ensourdreit se les choses ne demorassent en certein estat
tant qe eles feussent redrescees, si avoms ordene par le consail des
ditz ostages qe hom preigne lettres overtes de chescune vile des Cync
Portz sealees de lour commun seal, par les queles chescune communaute se oblige sur forfaiture de corps e ... de terres e de tenements,
e de touz lour biens moebles e noun moebles queux quil unques soient,
quil esterrent haut e bas a nostre agard e a nostre volunte du dit fait,
quele houre qe nous en voudroms pa ... e quil ne meffront rien sur
eux de Jernemue par mer ne par tere par cele acheison en nule
manere. Dont nous v[ous man]doms qe hastivement, veues ces lettres,
enveez au ... gardeyn des Cync Portz, e a ceux de Portz meismes,
aucun ... ou deux de qui vous fiez, e lour mandez quil facent faire
e sealer sanz delay leur lettres overtes en la fourme [avant]dite, la
quele fourme vous leur enverrez, tele come vous ordenez qe soit suffisauntz, e outre ... e nous ... qe vous le facez crier e defendre de par
nous parmy les Portz le plus solempnement e le plus chargeaument
qe vous le saverez ... e faire. En ceste manere voloms qe vous mandez
a ceux de Jernemue, e qe vous y preignez autieux lettres de mise e
obligement a nous de service en tous poynts, come de ceux de Portz,
car tot ausint lour consaillez ceux de Jernemue qui sont ovesque nous
pur eux e pur les autres de leur vile. E quant vous averez les lettres
e les seurtez prises des uns e des autres, e les vues e les defenses faites
sicome est avantdit, si recevez les lettres sauvement devers vous, e nous
faciez saver le plus tost qe vous porrez, tot ce qui vous enaverez fait.[1]
Don' souz nostre prive seal a Erdenburgh[2] en Flandre le v. jour de
Septembre, lan de nostre regne vintisme quint.

SC 1/45/78. Original, holed for filing and slightly faded.

---

[1] The government had tried to put an end to the feud between the Cinque Ports
and Yarmouth as early as 14 April 1297, when instructions to that effect were sent
to Stephen de Pencester, warden of the Ports and constable of Dover. Steps were taken
by the government in England on 6 September to prevent further conflict, and arrangements for the communities to seal letters of submission were made on 11 September.
The actual form was sent to Yarmouth for sealing on 12 October (*C.C.R., 1296–1302*,
pp. 59, 62, 67). One estimate of damage was seventeen ships burnt, twelve more looted,
and 165 men killed (F. W. Brooks, 'The Cinque Ports Feud with Yarmouth', *Mariner's
Mirror*, xix (1953), 44), but the wardrobe book refers to twenty-one ships from Yarmouth being burnt (B.L., Add. MS. 7965, fo. 84v).
[2] Aardenburg, Netherlands, prov. Zeeland.

135. *Edward I to his son Edward and his council, 8 September 1297*

Edward par la grace de dieu roi Engleterre, seigneur Dirlande e ducs
Daquitaine, a Edward son chier fiuz e a son consail, saluz. Pur ce
qe nous avoms entendu qe Wautier de Burnham, qui ad terres en
lisle de Haxholm' en le conte de Nicole, receust nadgueres bien fait
de mons' Roger de Moubray pur aler ovesque li cea outre en nostre
servise, sicome plus pleynement est contenu es covenaunces sur ceo
faites, les queles les gentz le dit Roger vous porront moustrer,[1] e
meisme celi Wautier ne seit mye passe, a ce qe le dit Roger nous ad
fait entendant; vous mandoms qe a la suyte des gentz celi Roger faciez
venir le dit Wautier devant vous, e oyr sur ce les resons dune part
e dautre, e les covenances ausint bien entendues; si vous truefsez qe
le dit Wautier eyt le covenant enfreynt en la manere avantdite, faciez
tant qe le dit Roger en soit gardez de damage, e le devantdit Wautier
punyz selonc la demande du trespas quil en ad fait. Donees souz nostre
prive seal a Gaunt[2] en Flandres le viii iour de Septembre lan de nostre
regne xxv.

SC 1/45/79. Original.

136. *Edward I to the sheriff of Huntingdon, 9 September 1297*

Rex vicecomiti Hunt', salutem. Cum per nostras litteras patentes
assignaverimus Walterum de Mellesworth et Willelmum de Wals-
ingle ad octavam et quintam nobis in comitatu Bed' concessas taxandas et colligendas iuxta tenorem earundem litterarum et formam
inde provisam, ac idem Willelmus quamquam eum per diversa man-
data nostra fecerimus premunire, officium illud hucusque detulerit
admittere in nostrum contemptum manifestum et solucionis earundem
octave et quinte retardacionem, quod non solum nobis verum eciam
toti regno nostro periculum inevitabile, quod absit, maxime hiis
diebus poterit generare. Tibi precipimus quod terras, tenementa et
omnia bona et catalla eiusdem Willelmi in quorumcumque manibus
seu custodia existant in balliva tua in manum nostram capias, et ea
salvo custodias, ita quod nec ipse nec aliquis pro ipso ad ea manus
apponant quousque coram predicto Waltero venerit et ad premissa
una cum eodem Waltero fideliter in forma predicta facienda sacramentum prestiterit, et eciam invenerit tibi sufficientem securitatem
ad respondendum nobis ad voluntatem nostram de contemptu pre-

---

[1] Walter de Burnham was granted rents and lands in Lincolnshire to a value of £10
15s. for life by Roger de Mowbray, presumably as his fee of retainer (*C.P.R., 1292–
1301*, p. 297).
[2] Ghent, Belgium.

dicto. Teste P. de Wilughby, tenente etc. ix die Septembris, anno regni
nostri xxv^{to}.

E 159/70, m. 124d.

137. *Edward I to the chancellor, 13 September 1297*

Edwardus dei gracia rex Anglie, dominus Hibernie et dux Aquitanie,
dilecto clerico et fideli suo Johanni de Langton' cancellario suo, salutem. Continetur in quadam petitione quam vobis mittimus presentibus interclusam, quod Johannes Paternoster rettatus de morte
Willelmi de Gloucestr' interfecit ipsum Willelmum quod idem Willelmus quodamodo nos contempsit, prout potueritis intueri. Et quia
dictus Johannes in exercitu nostro nobis in cismarinis partibus agen-
tibus commoratur, perdonavimus ei sectam pacis nostre, que ad nos
pro morte pertinet, supradictam, si videlicet ea occasione fuerit et non
alia perpetrata. Et ideo vobis mandamus quod, inquisita super hiis
veritate, si inveneritis ita esse, tunc eidem Johanni litteras nostras de
huismodi perdonacione faciatis in forma debita fieri et habere. Dat'
sub privato sigillo nostro apud Gandavum[1] xiii die Septembris, anno
regni nostri vicesimo quinto.

C 81/12/1189. Calendared in *Calendar of Chancery Warrants, 1244–1326*,
p. 76.

138. *John Paternoster, goldsmith, to Edward I and his council (formerly
enclosed in the above)*

A nostre seigneur le roy de Engleterre e a sun counsail mustre Johan
Paternoster, orfever de Lundr', qe la ou meme cele Johan estoyt en
sa forge regardant la test Leulyn,[2] e seu a la hors a la tavern ove ses
compayngnuns, la vint Willame de Gloucestr' e despisoyt mon seigneur le roy, e dist qe il voleyt qe la test le rey estoit oveck lautre,
dount lavauntdit Johan e ses compayngnuns sey coroucerent e a mal
grauntment pristrent e luy baterent por le despit qe il avoyt dist,
issint qe il morut. Par quey lavauntdit Johan prie a nostre seigneur le roy pur deu e pur la line le rey Henry qe il puys avoyr la
pees.

C 81/12/1188. Calendared in *Calendar of Chancery Warrants, 1244–1326*,
p. 76.

[1] Ghent, Belgium.
[2] Llywelyn ap Gruffydd, prince of Gwynedd and Wales (d. 1282).

139. *Edward I to the sheriff of Kent, 14 September 1297*

Rex vicecomiti Kanc', salutem. Quia intelleximus quod quedam naves carcate de victualibus ad opus nostrum et nostrorum nobiscum in partibus transmarinis existencium apud diversos portus in balliva tua nuper applicuerunt, tibi precepimus quod statim, visis presentibus, omnibus aliis pretermissis, omnes naves de hiis victualibus carcatas per costeram maris et Thamisie in eadem balliva tua inventas usque portum Sandwici venire facias absque mora. Et scire facias magistris et nautis navium predictorum quod, cum ad portum venerint cum navibus suis predictis, Philipus de Everdon' clericus noster statim solvet eisdem frettum vel vadia racionabilia pro victualibus predictis ad nos in partibus predictis transducendis in comitiva flote navium in eodem portu existenti. Et hoc sub forisfactura omnium que nobis forisfacere poteris nullatenus omittas. Et quid inde feceris quam cicius poteris scire facere thesaurario et baronibus nostris de scaccario. Teste P. de Wilugby tenente etc., xiiii die Septembris, anno regni nostri xxv^{to}.

E 159/70, m. 118d.

140. *Adolf of Nassau, king of the Romans, to Edward I, 16 September 1297*

Magnifico principi domino Edewardo regi Anglie, domino Hibernie, duci Aquitanie, amico suo karissimo, Adolfus, dei gratia Romanorum rex semper augustus, salutem et sincere dilectionis continuum incrementum. Quia ea que nos adinvicem contingunt, negotia iuxta statum presentem planius et plenius vobis exprimi estimamus vive vocis oraculo quam annotatione tacita litterarum, Wigandum de Huftersheim, famulum nostrum dilectum, exhibitorem presentium, cui secure mentis nostre secreta deteximus tamquam a multis retroactis temporibus nobis noto, ad vos duximus transmittendum, excellentiam vestram attente rogantes, quatenus eidem super hiis, que vobis ex parte nostra retulerit, tamquam nobis fidem credulam apponatis. Datum in Oppenheim xvi kalendas Octobris, regni nostri anno sexto.

SC 1/20/38. Original. Printed in *Acta Imperii*, no. 122.

141. *Edward I to his son Edward and his council, 18 September 1297*

Edward par la grace de dieu, roi Dengleterre, seigneur Dirlande e ducs Daquitaine, a Edward nostre chier fiuz, tenant nostre lieu en

Engleterre, e a son consail, saluz. Nous vous mandoms e chargeoms, en la foi qui vous nous devez et sicome vous amez nostre honour, que le paement qui nous devoms faire au roi Dalemayne et au duk de Brebant, faciez haster vers nous ou en deniers ou en leynes ou en ambedeux, quant que vous porrez. Car nous avoms entendu qe le roi Dalemayne est en venant et sil ne trovast de nous ce qe il deust, nous nous tendriens a huniz et nostre busoigne en grant condicion de perdre pour touz iours. Par quoi il est mestiers qe vous en pensez en totes les bones manieres qui vous porrez, et coment nous eoms ausint quoi despendre es parties ou nous sumes. Donees desouz nostre prive seal a Gaunt le xviii iour de Septembre, lan de nostre regne vintisme quint.

SC 1/45/80. Original. Printed in *Acta Imperii*, no. 124.

142. —— *to Edward I, probably 18 September 1297*

Domine rex, dominus meus dominus rex Alemanie innotescit vestre magnificentie homines suos esse paratos ad expeditionem et dictos homines terram suam destruere. Unde quia dictus dominus meus, domine rex, expectabat vestros consiliarios, qui ipsum instruerent modum veniendi et per quam viam, rogat vestram dominationem ut vestros consiliarios expeditos super premissis ad ipsum transmittatis, ut ipse per ipsos instructus ita veniat sine mora, quod expediat hinc et inde.

SC 1/14/157. Original. Printed in *Acta Imperii*, no. 123.

143. —— *to* ——, *probably 19 September 1297*

Sire. Endroit de ce qe vous me mandastes qe ie vous feisse a savoir queu iour e quele houre ie me meisse en mer por passer, ie vous faz a savoir, sire, qe sire Willame de Leyburn' me delivera la nef qe est apelee la Rose de Sandwyz[1] e une autre nef en conduyt e la tierce nef petite[a] por mes petiz runcins. E quant ie quiday entrer en mer prestement por aler mon cheymin, ceux des Portz pristrent lor consail e disoient qil ne vodreient graunter en nule manere qe ie eusse les dites nefs, ne nule des grandes, mes a la fin me delivereient iii petites

[a] *Word interlined.*

[1] The *Rose* of Sandwich, commanded by John Furnivall, returned to Sandwich with a crew of one constable and thirty-two sailors on 8 September. She was then in port with a skeleton crew of six sailors until 16 September, and subsequently a full crew of one constable and thirty-four sailors were paid up to 18 October (B.L., Add. MS. 7965, fo. 103v).

nefs de lor mend, e ie les recevoie volenters, *e fu lieuz e avoie destrusse ma vitaille e mon herneys;* e puis vint sire Willame de Leyburn' e me fist avoir la Rose ... par lor iugement demeyn, *la quele ke ... pour autres choses qe nous avoms a fere de relevier*, voies ie fu destrourbe de un tyde, e la recouverai al mielz qe ie pus al aide de dieu, e nos mariners me ont dit qil sen irront a la eyde de ceste veynt de vendredi, si dieu tiegne le tens. Autres noveles ne savoi ie nules quant ces lettres furent fetes qe vous fiessent a maunder. Nostre seigneur vous donere bone vie e longe. Escrit en le port del Escluse[1] yce joedi contre le vespre.

SC 1/21/178. Original or draft, badly stained.

144. *Edward I to the barons of the exchequer, 1 October 1297*

Edward par la grace de deu etc. Nous vous enveoms unes lettres qe nous vindrent a Gaunt lendemeyn de la seint Michel du counte de Nicole,[2] e une aline qe vint en meismes les lettres, par les queles vous poez veer coment le counte e mons' Johan de Bretaine se sunt obligez en une certeine somme des deniers pur nostre grosses bosoignes faire en les parties de Gascoyne, par quei nous vous mandoms qe regardees e avisees les choses contenues es dites lettres, mettez peine de faire gre as gentz as quex le deniers sunt duz en la meillore manere qe vous porrez. Car nous ne vodrions mie qe ce qe nos gentz ont promis pur nous ne fust fait ausi avant come hom porra en bone manere. E pur ce qe nous avoms entendu par laline qe feust enclose denz celes lettres qe les gentz de Bayone qui sunt venuz a nostre escheker sunt surquis de vileines paroles e sunt treitez autrement qe nous navoms comande,[3] vous mandoms qe desoremes ne suffrez qe hom lour dit ne fait chose qui ne seit de reison, mais qe hom les honure come bones gentz e come ceux qe molt ont fait pur nous. Don' de souz nostre prive seal a Gaunt le primer iour Doctobre, lan de nostre regne xxv.

E 159/71, m. 6; E 368/69, m. 16.

145. *Edward I on the behalf of the bishop of Ely, 1 October 1297*

Rex omnibus ad quos presentes littere pervenerint, salutem. Noveritis nos recepisse die confectionis presencium a venerabili patre Willelmo Elyensis episcopo trescentas libras sterlingorum in pecunia numerata

---

a ... a Passage interlined.

[1] Sluys, Netherlands, prov. Zeeland.
[2] Henry de Lacy, earl of Lincoln.
[3] See no. 16.

de prestito nobis facto per manus thesaurarii nostri et camerariorum nostrorum de scaccario, recipiencium dictam pecuniam apud London' de episcopo supradicto. Quas quidem predictas trescentas libras volumus et promittimus dicto episcopo solvere in crastino Animarum proximo futuro.[1] In cuius rei testimonium has litteras nostras eidem fieri fecimus patentes. Teste W. Conventr' et Lich' episcopo, thesaurario nostro apud Westm' primo die Octobris, anno regni nostri vicesimo quinto.

Postea in termino sancti Michaelis anno xxvi⁰ incipiente, predictus Elyensis episcopus venit hic et reddidit litteras predictas qui in presencia Thesaurarii et baronum dampnantur, et instanter per eosdem concordatum est quod idem episcopus Eliensis habeat talliam scaccarii de denariis predictis in partem solucionis remanentis compoti sui de tempore quo fuit custos garderobe regis.[2]

E 368/68, m. 23d.

146. *Edward I to his son Edward and his council, 5 October 1297*

Edward par la grace de dieu roi Dengleterre, seigneur Dirland e ducs Daquitaine, a Edward nostre chier fiuz e a son consail, saluz. Pur ce qe le ... conte de Garenne e Hughe de Cressingham nous ont tesmoine par leur lettres qe mons' Johan de Vaus sest bien portez en nostre servise es parties Descoce ia une piece, e ad promis de venir cea outre pur nous servir, e il neit fait nule requeste pur reavoir ses terres qui sont en nostre mein ne ne soit uncore a nous venuz, vous mandoms qe, quele houre qe le dit Johan voudra venir a nous pur nous servir par decea, qe vous li faciez tele grace endreit de la deliverance de ses terres come vous verrez qe soit a faire, prenant totes voies de li tieu seurte com hom ad pris des autres qui sont de sa condicion. Don' desouz nostre prive seal a Gaunt le v iour de Octobre, lan de nostre regne vintisme quint.

SC 1/45/83. Original.

147. *Edward I to his son Edward and his council, 8 October 1297*

Edward par la grace de dieu roi Dengleterre, seigneur Dirlande e ducs Daquitaine, a Edward son chier fiuz e a son consail, saluz. Nous avoms entendu qe les executours du testament mestre William de Montfort qui mort est ont deseisez nostre foial e loial Henri de Leybourne du

[1] 3 November.
[2] In the roll this entry immediately follows the letters of 13 February 1297 (no. 2).

manoir de Bifleet en Surr', puys quil estoit passez pur nostre servise
vers les parties ou nous sumes. E pur ce quil affiert qe ceux qui especiaument nous servent ioyssent despeciale grace en les busoignes quil
ont a faire de nous, vous mandoms qe le dit Henri, ou sez gentz en
noun de li, faciez mettre sanz delay endroit du dit manoir en meisme
lestat quil avoit quant il sen parti pur nostre servise vers les parties
avantdites. Don' souz nostre prive seal a Gant le viii iour Doctobre,
lan de nostre regne vintisme quint.[1]

SC 1/45/84. Original.

148. *John, count of Holland, to Edward I, 9 October 1297*

A sage, noble, honorable et poysant prince, son tre cher segnour et
pere, mon segnour le roy Dengletere, segnour Dirlande et duc Daquitaine, Jehans coens de Hollande, de Zelande et sire de Frise, tout tans
apparellies de faire voustre volour si avant comme il porra, comme
drois est. Cher sire peres, autre fies nous vous havons requis ke il vous
pleust denvoyer noustre chere compaigne en sa tere; cher sires, encore
vous prions humelement pour le grant bien de li et de nous et de
noustre tere e de nous gens, ki mout durement desirent a veer loer
dame noustre chere compaigne, ke il vous plaise ke vous nous voillies
meitre un certein jour et un certein lieu la u nous porrons venir ausi
ke nous pusons, et ke il vous plaise del mener noustre compaigne en
sa propre tere ausi honorablement comme a luy affirt. Cher sires, nous
vous prions ke il vous plaise de remander a nous voustre volente sur
ces choses par le portoer de ces leitres. Noustre sires vous doint boene
vie et longe, et vous gart tout tant. Don' le jour sent Denise.

SC 1/18/125. Original.

149. —— *to Edward I, 10 October 1297*

Sire, le mardi qe nous partimes de vous,[2] alames a Erneburgh[3] e lendemeyn alames au Dam,[4] e tant com hom herbiga, sourt une mellee

---

[1] On 5 November the escheator was instructed to restore to Henry de Leburn the
lands which had been taken into the king's hands following Leyburn's marriage to
Elizabeth de Sharstede, whose marriage had been granted to William Latimer. Leyburn found sufficient security to satisfy Latimer. Similar orders were again issued on
7 March 1298 (*C.C.R.*, *1292–1302*, pp. 70, 152). It would appear, therefore, that on
8 October Leyburn's lands were in fact in the king's hands. Leyburn had only recently
acquired Byfleet, for on 30 July Geoffrey de Lucy received a licence to alienate it to
him (*C.P.R.*, *1292–1301*, p. 300).
[2] 8 October.
[3] Aardenburg, Netherlands, prov. Zeeland.
[4] Damme, Belgium, prov. W. Flanders.

par entre un vallet alemand e un Flemeng, taverner de memes la vile, e nos gentz de pie y aleyent e le cry se leva de eus, par qei nos gentz de pie y corurent et sasemblerent trop grant plente si qil y aveit des meesons ou Flemengs furent eenz brisees, e tue de eus bien a xxx ou xl, avant qe nous le peussoms saver, e des noz ne fust mort un soul, la merci dieu. E si tost come nous le savioms se y alames demeintenant et les apeisimes, si qe avant le vespre fust tout apeise, honore seit dieus. Sire, nous avioms oy dire qe gentz de France deveient aver este devant la vile de Dam, mes, sire, du iour qe la vile fust prise, ny vint onqes nul. Mes nous avoms entendu qe le roy de France y ad envee de ses gentz. E sachez, sire, qe *nous avoms* la vile de Dam *regarde e lavoms trovee si* avirone de braz de meer e de grant fosses pleins de eawe, qe apoy de eyde ele navera regard de gentz a cheval, e les entrees sont si longes e si estreites come ny peut aler mes qe a cinc chivaus de front, la ou la chaucee est plus large. E, sire, pur ceo qe mons sire Robert de Betoigne[1] enveit un chivalier au conte pur moustrer li lestat de cele vile e des gentz, si nous pria il qe nous enveisoms a vous pur vous certefier des choses, coment eles sont alees. Par qei, sire, nous priames mon sire Johan Randolf qil alast a vous e vous deist les choses teles come eles sont, a qi, si vous plest, veollez crere de ceo qil vous dirra, qe il seit e ad veu quantqil y ad. Sire, nostre seigneur vous gard. Escrites a Dam lendemeyn de seint Denis.

SC 1/21/116. Original. Printed in *Acta Imperii*, no. 129.

150. *Edward I to Aymer de Valence and Hugh le Despenser, 10 October 1297*

Edward par la grace de dieu roy Dengleterre, seigneur Dirlande e ducs Daquitaine, a ses foiaux e loiaux Aymar de Valence son chier cosyn e a Hugh' le Despenser, saluz. Pur ce qe nous voudriens molt ordener ce qui mieux serreit a faire de la flote qui est a Escluse, vous mandoms qe vous menyez ovesque vous cink ou sis les plus suffisantz de meisme la flote ensemblement ove le baillif de Sandwyz qui est illueques, si qe vous e eux soiez a nous a Gant icest Samadi[2] au veispre au plus tard. E qe nous peussoms aver avisement sur cele busoigne. Don' souz nostre prive seal a Gant le x iour Doctobre, lan de nostre regne vintisme quint.[3]

SC 1/47/76. Original.

a ... a Words interlined.

[1] Béthune, *dép.* Pas-de-Calais.   [2] 12 October.
[3] The great majority of the ships in Flanders were paid by the crown until 18 October, when they presumably returned to their home ports (B.L., Add. MS. 7965, fos, 103–5).

151. *De Tallagio Non Concedendo, probably before 10 October 1297*

I. Nullum tallagium vel auxilium per nos vel heredes nostros de cetero in regno nostro imponatur seu levetur sine voluntate et assensu communi archiepiscoporum, episcoporum et aliorum prelatorum, comitum, baronum, militum, burgencium et aliorum liberorum hominum in regno nostro.

II. Nullus minister noster vel heredum nostrorum capiat blada, lanas, coria, aut aliqua alia bona cuiuscumque, sine voluntate et assensu illius cujus fuerint huiusmodi bona.

III. Nihil capiatur de cetero, nomine vel occasione male tolte, de sacco lanae.

IV. Volumus eciam et concedimus pro nobis et heredibus nostris, quod omnes clerici et laici de regno nostro habeant omnes leges, libertates et liberas consuetudines suas ita libere et integre sicut eas aliquo tempore melius et plenius habere consueverunt. Et si contra illas vel quemcunque articulum in presenti carta contentum statuta fuerint edita per nos vel antecessores nostros, vel consuetudines introducte, volumus et concedimus quod huiusmodi consuetudines et statuta vacua et nulla sint in perpetuum.

V. Remisimus etiam Humfrido de Bown, comiti Hereford' et Essex', constabulario Anglie, Rogero Bigot, comiti Norfolk', marescallo Anglie, et aliis comitibus, baronibus, militibus, armigeris, Johanni de Ferariis ac omnibus aliis de eorum societate, confederacione et concordia existentibus, necnon omnibus viginti libratas terre tenentibus in regno nostro, sive de nobis in capite sive de alio quocunque, qui ad transfretandum nobiscum in Flandriam certo die notato vocati fuerunt et non venerunt, rancorem nostrum et malam voluntatem quam ex causis predictis erga eos habuimus; et eciam transgressiones si quas nobis vel nostris fecerint usque ad presentis carte confectionem.

VI. Et ad maiorem huius rei securitatem volumus et concedimus pro nobis et heredibus nostris, quod omnes archiepiscopi et episcopi Angliae, in perpetuum in suis cathedralibus ecclesiis habita presenti carta et lecta, excommunicent publice et in singulis parochialibus ecclesiis suarum diocesium excommunicare seu excommunicatos denunciare faciant, bis in anno, omnes qui contra tenorem presentis carte, vim et effectum in quocunque articulo scienter fecerint, aut fieri procuraverint, quoquo modo. In cuius rei testimonium presenti carte sigillum nostrum est appensum, una cum sigillis archiepiscoporum, episcoporum, comitum, baronum et aliorum qui sponte juraverunt quod tenorem presentis carte, quatenus in eis est, in omnibus et singulis articulis servabunt, et ad eius observationem consilium suum et auxilium fidele prestabunt in perpetuum.

This is the text as established by Rothwell, 'The Confirmation of the

Charters, 1297', 303–5, where full variant readings and editorial apparatus are given. The spelling has been altered in accordance with the version in *Guisborough*, pp. 311–12.

152. *Draft letter of pardon to the earls of Norfolk and Hereford, probably before 1 November 1297*

Concessimus etiam domino Rogero Bygod comiti Northfolk' et heredibus suis officium Marascall' Anglie et domino Umfredo comiti Hereford' et Estsexie et heredibus suis officium Constabular' Anglie tenenda et habenda predicta officia ita libere sicut ipsi vel eorum antecessores aliquo tempore melius habere consueverunt. Remisimus etiam eisdem comitibus Northfolk', Hereford' [et] Estsexie, et aliis comitibus de regno nostro, baronibus, militibus, Johanni de Ferariis et aliis armigeris et omnibus aliis de societate et confederatione eorum pro impetratione istius carte, necnon et omnibus xx libratas terre in regno nostro tenentibus sive de nobis in capite sive de alio quocunque ad transfretandum nobiscum in Flandriam certo die vocatis rancorem nostrum et malam voluntatem quam contra eos habuimus vel habere potuimus quacunque occasione, ac etiam omnes transgressiones ab eisdem omnibus et singulis nobis vel nostris factas a festo Pasche anno regni nostri xxv usque ad festum Omnium Sanctorum proximum sequens, ita quod nos vel heredes nostri ratione huiusmodi transgressionum quarumcunque contra predictos vel eorum aliquos aut suos heredes nullam actionem aut causam habere seu movere possimus in perpetuum.[1]

Bodleian Library, MS. Laud Misc. 529, fos. 88v–89. Printed in Denton, 'The Crisis of 1297 from the Evesham Chronicle', 579.

153. *Letters patent of Edward, son of Edward I, 10 October 1297*

A touz ceaux qui cestes presentes lettres verrount ou orrount, Edward filz au noble roi Dengleterre tenaunt soun liu en Engleterre taunt come il est es parties de dela, salutz. Come nos chiers a feaus H. de Boun, counte de Hereford e de Essex', conestable de Engleterre, e Rogier Bigod, counte de Norff' e mareschal Dengleterre, nous eyent fait entendre qil se doutoient qe nostre seigneur nostre piere avauntdite e nous eussoms conceu devers eaux rancour e indignacion pur

---

[1] For discussion of this text, which is closely related to *De Tallagio*, see Denton, 'The Crisis of 1297 from the Evesham Chronicle', 565–7. The actual pardon which the earls received followed closely on the form set out in the prince's letters patent of 10 October, and was issued at the same time as the Confirmation of the Charters, at Ghent on 5 November (*Reg. Winchelsey*, pp. 207–8).

aucunes desobeisaunces qil avoient fait nadgueres a ceo qom disoit,
en ceo qil ne vyndrent pas a dist nostre piere par soun mandement,
e en ceo qom disoit qil avoient aucuns de ses comaundementz destur-
biez e targie, e aukunes aliaunces e assemblez des gentz darmes fait
countre la volentie e le defens lavaundit roi nostre piere, nous, regar-
dauntz qe des choses avauntdites nul maufait par eaux ne est sui uncore, coment qe paroles eyent este dites, e bien veiauntz qe, si ceste
chose ne feust appese en bone manere, e la rancour e la indignacion
du dist nostre piere e de nous, si nule y feust, ne feust relaisse, moutz
grauntz damages e grauntz perilz purroyent legierement venir au
roiaume, nomement taunt come le dit nostre piere est es parties de
dela; a la requeste des ditz countes e pur escheure tieus maneres de
damages e de perils, grauntoms e permettoms par lordinaunce e
lassent des honurables pieres Willame evesqe de Ely, Richard evesqe
de Lundr', Wautier evesq de Coventr' e Lichefeud, e Henri elyt de
Everwyk, e des nobles homes mounsire Edmon counte de Corne-
waille, mounsire Johan de Garenne coun e de Surr' e de Sussex',
mounsire Willame de Beauchamp counte de Warrewik, mounsire
Johan Giffard, mounsire Reynaud de Grey, munsire Aleyn Plukenet
e de touz les autres conseilliers qui le dit nostre piere nous ad baille,
qe nous porchaceroms par tutes les voies qe nous purroms qe le dit
nostre piere relerra e pardurra pleinement as ditz countes e Johan
de Feriers e a touz leurs meinengs e toutz leur aliez tute manere de
rancour e dindignacioun, si nul eit conceu devers eaux pur les encheisouns avauntdites, ou nules de eles, issi qe nul des ditz countes ne
Johan de Feriers ne nul de leur meinengs ne de leur aliez avauntditz
ne serrount chalangiez, enchesoinez ne greivez par le dit nostre piere
ne par nous ne par nos heirs en nule tens par nules des choses susdites.
E promettoms e grauntoms qe sour le reles e le pardoun de la rancour
e de lindignacioun avauntdites, nous feroms avoir as ditz countes,
Johan de Feriers e a leur meinengs e a leur aliez les lettres du dit
nostre piere patentes, sealez de soun graunt seal. E nous par cestes
presentes lettres avoms a eaux relaisse e pardone tute maniere de
rancour e de indignacioun qe nous avioms conceu devers eaux pur
nule des encheisouns susdites. E promettoms e grauntoms qe nous
les garderoms de damage devers nostre piere avauntdit de tutes les
choses avauntdites. En tesmoigne de quieu chose nous avoms fait faire
nos lettres overtes sealees de nostre seal. Doneez a Loundr' le disme
iour de Octobr', lan du regne nostre piere avauntdite vintisme quint.

DL 34/1/6. Original, with portion of seal attached. A copy is in *Reg. Winchelsey*, i, 203–4.

154. *List of the household of Roger Bigod, probably autumn 1297*

Rogerus le Bygod, comes Norff' et marescallus Anglie [first column]

Banerretti	Dominus Robertus filius Rogeri Dominus Johannes de Segrave Dominus Alanus la Souche Dominus Gilebertus de Umfravile Dominus Johannes Lovel
Maiores clerici	Magister Thomas de Sudington' Dominus Johannes le Bygod Dominus Willelmus de Spanneby
Milites	Dominus Reginaldus de Cobeham Dominus Richardus de Skolaund Dominus Thomas de Akeny Dominus Nicholas de Wokindon' Dominus Ranulphus de Monte Canis' Dominus Ricardus de Daunteseye Dominus Petrus de Tatington Dominus Johannes de Holebrok Dominus Hamo le Parker
Minores clerici	Dominus Johannes de Boseham, capellanus ....
Armigeri	Willelmus de Belinges [second column] Thomas de Valle Hugo le Breton Jolanus Cocus Willelmus Vys de Len Willelmus de Winkfeld Radulphus de Waltham Walterus de Metingham Johannes de Ticheburne Edmundus Gascelyn Robertus de Mildenhale Nicholas de [Staunton]ᵃ Willelmus de Haukeswel .... Rogerus de Beauchamp

ᵃ *MS. unclear at this point:* Staunton *is conjectural.*

Johannes Costyn
Rogerus de Hereford

[Note sewn to the above]
Les servauns de armes qe la protection demandent:
Henr' de Greneford
Thomas de Flete
Robertus de Heketon'
Johannes de Kelvedon[1]

C 81/1698/130, 131. Originals.

155. *The Confirmation of the Charters, 10 October 1297*

I. Edward par la grace de deu, rey de Engleterre, seygnur de Yrlond[a]
e duks Aquit', a tuz ceus qe cestes presentes lettres verrunt ou orrunt,
saluz. Sachez nous al honur de deu e de seint eglise e al profit de
tut nostre reaume avum graunte pur nous e pur nos heyrs qe la graunt
chartre de fraunchises e la chartre de forestes,[b] les queus furrunt fetes
par cummune assent de tut la reaume en le tens le rey Henri nostre
pere, seient meintenu en tuz lur poinz saunz nule blemisement. E
voloms qe memes celes chartres desuz nostre seal seient enveyez a nos
justices ausi bien de la foreste cum as autres, e a tuz les viscountes
de countez e a tuz nos autres ministres e a tutes nos cites parmi la
terre ensemblement ove nos brefs en les quels serra contenu qe il facent
les avaundites chartres pupplier e qe il facent dire au pople qe nous
avum graunte a tenir les en tuz lur poinz; [c]e a nos justices, viscountes,
meyres e autres ministres qe les leys de la terre de suz nous e par nous
unt a guier memes les chartres en tuz lur poinz enpleydez[d] devaunt
eus e en jugement le facent alower, cest asaver la chartre de fraunchises cum ley commune e la chartre de la foreste solum la assize de
la foreste au mendement[e] de nostre pople.
II. E voluns qe si nul jugemenz seient donez desormes encountre les

---

[a] *Both the original issued on 5 November 1297 (Bémont, 'Chartes des libertés anglaises', p.96), and the copies on the statute roll ('Statutes of the Realm', i, 123), Winchelsey's register ('Reg. Winchelsey', pp. 201, 207) and Guisborough's chronicle ('Guisborough', p. 309), have the more conventional Dengleterre and Dirland or Dyrlaund. This suggests that possibly this manuscript is not the work of a royal scribe.*
[b] *Other versions have the normal* de la foreste.
[c] *The following section to* en tuz leur poinz *was accidentally omitted in the Guisborough version ('Guisborough', p. 309).*
[d] *The other versions have* en pledz, *save for Guisborough, which has* en pledaunt.
[e] *The other versions have* al amendement.

---

[1] Another list, dating from 1294-5, of the earl of Norfolk's retinue and household survives; the only names common with this one are Thomas de Akeny, Peter de Tatington, Magister Thomas de Sudington, John de Boseham and Walter de Metingham (C 47/2/10, no. 8).

poinz des avauntdites chartres par justice ou[a] par autre de nos ministres qui countre les poinz des chartres tenent plez devaunt eus, seient defetes e pur nent tenuz.

III. E volums qe celes[b] chartres desuz nostre sel seient enveyez as eglises cathedrales parmi nostre reaume e la demurgent, e seient deu fez par an luwes devant le pople.

IV. E qe ercheveskes e eveskes doynent sentences de graunte escomenge countre tuz iceus qui countre les avauntdit chartres vendrunt, ou en fet, ou en eyde, ou en counseyl, ou en nul point enfreindrent ou countre vendrunt. E qe celes sentences seient denunciez e puppliez deu fez par an par les avauntdiz prelaz. E si memes les prelaz, eveskes, ou nul de eus seient negligent en la denunciacion suz dit fere[c] par les ercheveskes de Cant' e de Everwyke pur[d] tens serrunt, sicum covent, seient requis[e] e destreint a meme cele denunciacion fere en la furme avauntdite.

V. E pur ceo qe acuns gent de nostre reaume se doutent qe les eides e les mises, les quels il nous unt fet avaunt ces oures pur nos guerres e autres bosoignes, de lur graunt e de lur bone volente, e quele manere qe fet seient,[f] pussent turner en servage a eux ou lur heyris,[g] par ceo qe il serreint autrefez trovez en roules, e ausi prises qe unt este fetes parmi le reaume par nos ministres en nostre noun, si avom graunte pur nous e pur nos heirs qe memes celes[h] eydes 'mises' ne prises ne trerrums a custumes pur nule chose qe seit fet ou qe par roule ou par autre manere pot estre trove.

VI. E ausi avums graunte pur nous e pur nos heirs as ercheveskes, eveskes, abbes, priurs e autre gentz de seint eglise, e a countes e a baruns e a tut la communaute de la terre qe mes, pur nule bosoigne de tele manere de eyde,[i] mises ne prises de nostre reaume ne prendrums fors qe par commune assent de tute la reaume e a commune profit de meme le reaume,[j] sauve les auncien eydes e prises dues e coustumez.

VII. E pur ceo qe tut le plus de la communaute del raume se sentent grevez durement de la maltout de leynes, cest asaver de chescun sake de leyn xl. sous, eus unt prie[k] qe nous lur vousisums relesser; nous

[a] *Only Guisborough has* ou (*'Guisborough', p. 310*) ; *other versions have* e.
[b] *Other versions have* memes celes, *save Guisborough, which has* memes les.
[c] *Guisborough adds at this point the phrase* en la forme avauntdite.
[d] *Other versions read* qui pur.
[e] *Other versions read* soient repris.
[f] *The original (Bémont, 'Chartes des libertés anglaises', p. 98) has* qe fez soient.
[g] *Other versions all have* e a lur heirs.
[h] *Guisborough agrees with* memes celes (*'Guisborough', p. 310*), *other versions read* mes teles.
[i] *The original (Bémont, 'Chartes des libertés anglaises', p. 98) has* busoignie tieu manere des aydes, *and is followed by the other versions, although Guisborough ('Guisborough', p. 310) has* teus maners, *not* tieu manere.
[j] *MS.* raume.
[k] *Other versions all have* e nous unt prie.

a lur prier les avums pleinement relessez e avum graunte qe celes ne autres mes ne prendrums saunz le*a* commun assent e lur bone volunte, sauve a nous e a nos heirs la custume des leynes, peaus e quirs avaunt grauntez par la communaute del reaume avauntdite. En temoyne des quels choses nous avums fet ceste nos lettres overtes. Temoyne Edward nostre fiz a Lundres le dyme jour de Octobre, le an de nostre regne xxv.*b*

E 175, file 1/11, contemporary copy. For other versions, see Bémont, *Chartes des libertés anglaises*, p. 96; *Statutes of the Realm*, i, 123. A translation is provided in *E.H.D.*, iii, 485–6.

156. *John, count of Holland, to Edward I, probably after 9 October 1297*

A noble homme, sage et excellent prince, son tre cher segnour e pere, mon segnour le roy Dengletere, segnour Dirlande e duc Daquitaine, Jehans conte de Hollande, de Zelande e sire de Frise, tout diis apparellies en tous vous services si avant comme il porra. Cher sires, nous havons bien entendu les lettres ke vous envoyastes par voustre messagier. Sire, pour se nous vous faisons a saver ke nous ne vous puons nulle certeine response ne*c* escrire avant ke nous serrons certifie des choses ke nous vous mandames par nostre messagier. Cher sire, commandes nous. Nostre sire vous gart.

SC 1/18/127. Original.

157. *John, count of Holland, to Edward I, probably between 9 and 18 October 1297*

A tre sage, noble, poisand et excellent prince, son tre cher seignor et pere, mon segnour le roy Dengletere, segnour Dirlande et duc Daquitaine, Jehans conte de Hollande, de Zelande et sire de Frise, ses services apparellies si avant comme il poet. Cher sires, nous havons bien entenduez les leitres ke vous envoyastes par noustre messagier, par les quieles nous sumes mout lies et durement conforte ke il vous

---

a Other versions all have saunz leur.

b The Statute Roll version ('Statutes of the Realm', i, 123) continues at this point: E fet a remembrer qe meismĕ ceste charte, suth meismes les paroles, de mot en mot, fust sele en Flaundres de suth le grant seal le rey, cest asaver a Gaunt, le quint jour de Novembre, lan del regne lavauntdit seignur le rey vintisme quint, e envee en Engleterre. *The final clause of the version issued in Ghent accordingly reads:* En tesmoinaunce des quieux choses nous avuns fait faire cestes nos lettres overtes. Donees a Gaunt le quint jour de Novembre lan de nostre regne vintisme quint. (*Bémont, 'Chartes des libertés anglaises', p. 98.*)

c essc struck out at this point and ne *interlined.*

plaet ke noustre chere compaigne venge en sa propre tere e ke vous metter y volontirs boen consail. Cher sires, pour ce ke nous ne savons mie voustre estaet et quant serres haysies daconplir noustre requeste endreit de noustre compaigne, vous requirons comme a noustre segnour et pere ke vous nous voillies mettre un certeyn jour au queil nous nous porrons si[a] apprester comme il affirt a voustre autesse et al honour de noustre compaigne. Sire, dou lieu vous faisons a savoer ke il nous sanle [b]boen et[b] covenable pour vous et pour nous a Bieru-liet e li mieus aysies. Cher sire, se li lieu vous plaet, se nous remandes un jour convenable par le poertoer de ces leitres, nous i vendroms, ce dieu plaet, si convenablement come il nous affirt. Cher sires, endroit de nous marchans ke vous gens nous ont novelement ociis, e de roberies faites de vous gens en noustre tere, si sacies, sire, ke tout ce fu fait entour le sen Remi ki ore fu.[1] Sire, commandes moy comme le voustre. Noustre sires vous gart.

SC 1/18/126. Original.

158. *John, lord of Cuyk, to Edward I, 15 October 1297*

Illustrissimo domino suo domino Edwardo dei gratia regi Anglie, domino Hybernie et duci Aquitannie, Johannes de Kuyc miles, quantum obsequii poterit et honoris. Vestre excellentie, domine carissime, significo dominum Reynaldum et magistrum Rychardum vestros nuncios et me die Lune post diem beati Dyonisii[3] mane invenisse dominum romanorum regem ad octo miliaria supra Coloniam iuxta Renum quodque non vidimus ipsum tantam habere multitudinem armatorum [b]penes se,[b] quod ad profectum et honorem vestrum et suum versus vos venire potuisset, secundum quod de[a] vobis fuimus separati. Est tamen in bona voluntate veniendi versus vos, et exspectat quosdam hominum suorum secum venturorum. Preterea dominus exspectat adventum archiepiscopi Trevirensis et langravii Hassie et aliorum quorundam dominorum, qui sunt in eodem confinio in quo ipse iacet, et illis consultis, nobis die Mercurii post diem beati Victoris[3] super nuntiationibus seu legationibus nostris finaliter respondebit, et quam cito responsum suum habuerimus, ad vos omni festinantia qua potuerimus revertemur. Valeat vestra excellentia temporibus in-

---

[a] *Word interlined.*
[b . . . b] *Words interlined.*

---

[1] 1 October.
[2] 14 October.
[3] 16 October.

finitis. Datum apud Zynsike,[1] videlicet in eo loco in quo memoratus rex iacet, de civitate Coloniensi octo miliaribus distante, die Martis sero post diem beati Victoris.

SC 1/18/179. Original. Printed in *Acta Imperii*, no. 130.

159. *Edward I to the treasurer and barons of the exchequer, 16 October 1297*

Edward par la grace de dieu etc., al honourable peere en dieu W. par la meisme grace evesque de Cestre, nostre tresorier, e as barouns del escheker, saluz. Nous vous feisoms a savoir qe nous de la guerre meue entre nous e nos aliez dune part, e le roi de Fraunce e les suens, dautre, avoms grante e fait suffrance a durer quant a la duchee Daquitaine iusques a la Typhene,[2] e quant as autres terres iusques as oytanes de la feste seint Andreu procheine.[3] Cest a savoir de roiaume a roiaume, de terre en terre, de gent a gent, par mer e par terre en tieu maniere qe touz marchandz e tote maniere de gentz peussent aler, venir, demorer e marchaunder sauvement e seurement de un roiaume a autre la suffrance duraunt. E tendroms nous e nos aliez, e le dit rei e li seon, duraunt la suffrance tot ceo qe nous e il tenioms au iour de la confectioun des lettres seur ce faites, cest a savoir le iour de seint Denys procheinement passez.[4] E qe le roi Dalemayne peusse cele suffrance rompre, si li plest, en tieu maniere totes voies qe ele dura quinze iours apres ce quil lavera fait savoir a .. lesvesque de Tournay ou a son official a Tournay. E avoms promis damender les damages qui serrount faitz durant la suffrance avauntdite. E par ce vous maundoms e fermement enioignoms qe vous lavauntdite suffrance gardez e facez garder en touz pointz par tot nostre roiaume e nostre poer par terre e par mer, e fermement commaunder qe rien ne soit fait a lencontre, pur ce nomement qe, si rien estoit fait encountre, nous sumes tenuz, sicome dit est, de lamender e ovesque ce de garder le dit suffrance. E vous mandoms sicome nous chargeames vous, evesque, quant vous departistes de nous, qe vous mettez hastif cunsail qe nous eoms tost les deniers e les autres chose qui nous deussoms avoir pur nous e pur les paementz du roi Dalemaygne e du duk de Brabant, e pur les autres busoignes qui nous avoms a faire par decea, come des gages qui sount a paer as gentilshommes e as autres gentz de nostre ost, e pur le counte de Sauvoie e pur ses gentz, e pur les autres quil nous covendra retenir a nos gages. E sachiez qe, si nous eoms bone e sufisaunte aide de deniers e des autres choses e qe nous peussoms faire les paementz, sicome dit est, nous entendoms

---

[1] Sinzig, Germany.   [2] 6 January 1298.
[3] 7 December 1297.   [4] 9 October 1297.

qe par laide de dieu nous averoms bone pees, ou poer de faire tel
espleit seur nos enemys qe ce serra al honeur de dieu e de nous e de
nostre roiaume e de touz nos amys. Mais nous voloms totes voies qe
vous eez tieu regard as busoignes de Gascoigne qe nos gentz qui la
sount seient sauvez e aidez en ce qe homme peut en bone maniere.
E qe les gent de Bayone seient en tieu maniere paez e treitez quil
se peussent tenir apaez. Car nous nentendoms qe nous navoms eu ne
avoms rescet ne entre en la terre de Gascoigne fors qe parmy Bayone,
e serroient nos gent qui sount illeoques en grant peril, si ceaux de
Bayone se tenissent a mal paez. E dautre part nous ne veoms ne entendoms qe le roi de Fraunce peusse nule part avoir ne purchacer navie,
si ce ne feust parmi ceaux de Bayone sil tournassent countre nous.
E pur ce voloms qe home met peigne de retenir leur bon gre en tote
les bones manieres qe homme peut. E pensez e mettez au queur qe
totes ces choses seient hastees si avaunt come vous purrez. E vous devez
entendre e savoir le ennoy e les angoisses qui nous suffroms e en queul
meschief nous demorroms taunt qe nous eoms aide e recoverir des
choses avantdites. Car en ceste busoigne gist nostre honeur ou nostre
deshoneur e de touz ceaux qui nous aiment e nomement de ceaux
qui de nos busoignes se entremettent en les parties ou vous estes. E
sachiez qe ce serreit trop desavenaunt chose e deshonorable a nous
e a noz si le dit rey Dalemaygne ne venist mye par defaute des
covenaunces, ou quant il fust venuz, qe homme ne li tenist les pro-
messes.[1] E vous evesque, faciez tenir les covenaunces qui nous avoms
au duk de Brabant endreit des laynes qui sount a ceaux de Brebant
dount il avera la custume si qe nul de nos gentz ne mette enpesche-
ment countre la fourme des dites covenaunces.[2] Endreit de ceaux Dirlaunde, cest asaver le counte de Ulvestere e mons' Johan le filz
Thomas e des autres, nous ne pleisent mie les convenaunces qe len
leur ad faites.[3] E si hom ne les peusse attemprier e amesurer, nous
voloms qe hom sen departe a plus beal qe hom porra. E ce dites a
nostre filz e a son cunsail, as queux nous avoms ces meismes maunde
par nos lettres. E endroit des choses desus dites, e daucunes autres
qui nous tuchent, creez nostre cher clerk Johan de Drokenesford, gardein de nostre garderobe, de ce quil vous dirra de par nous. Don'

---

[1] The agreement was for £20,000 to be paid to Adolf: see no. 97.
[2] On 2 February 1297 the duke of Brabant had been granted £25,000 out of the
custom to be paid by Brabantine merchants (C.P.R., 1292–1301, p. 232). A liberate writ
for £4,000 to be paid out of such duties had been issued on 3 February (C 62/73).
£779 15s. 5d. was paid to the duke out of the Yarmouth customs (E 372/145).
[3] By agreement made with the justiciar of Ireland, they were to receive higher rates
of pay than was normal: 2s. 9d. for a knight, and 1s. 4d. for a squire. Instructions were
issued on 23 October that the earl of Ulster, Richard FitzThomas, and the other Irish
should remain at home, but FitzThomas was already in Flanders in receipt of royal
pay at the high rate (Lewis, 'The English Forces in Flanders', p. 313, n. 1; C.C.R.,
1296–1302, p. 69; B.L., Add. MS. 7965, fo. 68v).

suz nostre prive seal a Gaunt le xvi iour Doctobre, lan de nostre regne vintisme quint.

E 159/71, m. 7d; E 368/69, m. 19d.

160. *John, count of Holland, to Edward I, 18 October 1297*

A tres noble et tres excelent prince, son tres cher segnour et pere, mon segnour le roy Dengletere, segnour Dirlande et duc Daquitaine, Jehans [conte] de Hollande, de Zelande e sire de Frise, apparelliet de faire pour vous ce ke nous porrons. Sire, nous havons bien veues et oyes les resp[ounses] ke vous nous mandastes sur la lettre que nous*a* vous envoyames par Ernaut de Ranst, que vous ne havies mie en propoes ne en volente . . . sire Jehan de Renesse,[1] e nous autres ennemiis en noustre tere encountre noustre profiit, et encountre noustre honoer. Et encore, sire, vous nous . . . ke apertement au dont nous dires voustre volente et voustre entencion quant vous haries parle a nous en aucun certein lieu. Sire, il nous semble . . . a nous gens que james nen poroit estre noustre honoer ne noustre profiit ke chil ki sont banis de noustre tere par loy et par droit jugement de nous hommes, et chil ausi ke si pitoesement mordirent noustre tres cher segnour et pere, a qui dieus face vray merci, ducent revenir en noustre tere encountre noustre volente, che ke james ne havendra, ce dieu plaet. Et pur se, sire, ke vous ne nous mandastes mie clerement et appertement en voustre lettre ke vous les devant diis ne remerries mie sicomme nous vous haviemes priet avan ces hoeres par nous lettres ke clerement voustre entencion nous feicies a savoer si entre . . . et nous gens ausi, ke vous haves en propos et en volente de remener les devant diis en noustre tere encountre noustre volente, si ce nest ensi ke . . . et clerement nous remandes ke vous ne le voles mie faire. Sire, apres nous vous faisons a savoer ke nous ne volons mie venir pour oyeir voustre volente ne voustre entencion en lieu u chil habitent et demoerent ki si vilenement mordrirent noustre tres cher segnour et pere ni en la pres . . . ki apertement pourvoyent au diis mordroers de quant ke mestir loer est si longement comme il le font. Apres, sire, avan ches heures haves escrit . . . en vo lettres overtes ke les choses ke nous faisons ke nous ne le faisons mie de noustre propre quer, mes par le consail dautres gens, sire, bien sachiez . . . ausi ke nous soyons encore jovene, nous ne sumes mi si enfant ne si fol ke nous ne conisons bien ke nous par droite nature devons*b* . . . ki si pitoesement nous hont mordri noustre tres cher

a Word interlined.   *b* hayr struck out.

[1] Edward I's favour to John de Renesse, one of the murderers of Florence, count of Holland, is demonstrated by his gift to him of a horse worth £40 (B.L., Add. MS. 7965, fo. 57v). Earlier in the year Count John had not taken any exception to John de Renesse, who was present with him at Ipswich (*Treaty Rolls*, i, 176).

segnour et pere, et ke nous nous devons bien pleindre de cheaus ke
a diis mordroers troevent tout quant ke mestir loer est. Sire, et ce
nous faisons par consail, de che ne sumes mie a blamer, kar plus grant
segnour de nous ... et plus ancien hoevrent a la fie par consail. Sire,
noustre segnour vous gart. Doneies en lile de Walcre[1] en noustre tere,
le ioer seint Luc ... evangeliste.[2]

SC 1/18/124. Original.

161. *Edward I to his son Edward and his council, 20 October 1297*

Edward par la grace de dieu roi Dengleterre, seigneur Dirland e ducs
Daquitaine, a Edward nostre chier fiuz, tenant nostre lieu en Engleterre e a son consail, saluz. Pur ce qe nous avoms suffert e grante
qe les gentz de Sandwyz e les autres qui mesnerent cea outre les gentz
la contesse de Gloucestr' e les autres qui vindrent en ceste darrein
flote retourgent en leur pays[3] qe pur la suffrance qui est orendroit
prise parentre nous e le roi de France qe pur eux mieuz purveer e
estorer de venir autrefoiz en nostre servise pardecea quele houre qe
nous en eoms a faire; vous mandoms qe Reg' Cousin baillif de Sandwyz e les autres qui y ont este eez especiaument recommandez come
ceux de qui nous nous looms molt e qui nous ont fait pardecea servise
qui molt nous agree. E faites garnir les avantditz mariners e trestouz
les autres des Ports qui eux soient totes foiz prestz de venir a nous
quele houre qe nous enverroms querre touz ou partie de eux selonc
lestat des busoignes qui nous avoms a faire es parties ou nous sumes.
Doneez sous nostre prive seal a Gaunt le xx iour Doctobre, lan de
nostre regne xxv.

SC 1/45/88. Original.

162. *Edward I to his son Edward and his council, 20 October 1297*

Edward par la grace de dieu roi Dengleterre, seigneur Dirland e ducs
Daquitaine, a Edward nostre chier fiuz, tenant nostre lieu en Engleterre e a son consail, saluz. Nous vous mandoms qe, si mons' Johan
de Forton', qui est en nostre prison a Berewyk,[4] vous troefse suffisaunte
seurte de venir par decea pur demoerer en nostre servise es parties

---

[1] Walcheren.
[2] On the same day the count wrote to the inhabitants of s'Hertogenbosch, warning them against his father's murderers. The letter was intercepted by the duke of Brabant, and sent to Edward I (*Acta Imperii*, nos. 131, 132).
[3] The fleet was paid wages up to 18 October (B.L., Add. MS. 7965, fos. 103v–105).
[4] Berwick-on-Tweed.

ou nous sumes, sicome les autres qui sont de sa condicion on fait e fount encore, adonques le faciez delivrer sanz delay par la seurte avantdite. Donees desouz nostre prive seal a Gaunt le xx iour Doctobre, lan de nostre regne vintisme quint.

SC 1/45/87. Original.

163. *Edward I to his son Edward, 21 October 1297*

Edward par la grace de dieu roi Dengleterre, seigneur Dirland e ducs Daquitaine, a Edward nostre chier fiuz tenant nostre lieu en Engleterre, saluz ove sa benezon. Nous vous mandoms qu vous faciez garnir e aprester quarante ou cynquante bones nefs des Ports e deux barges contre le finissement de la suffrance qui est prise entre nous e le roi de France; issint qe nous pussoms avoir meismes les nefs e les barges bien eskipees e suffisaument aparaillees prestement quele houre qe nous les enverroms quere pur garder le port del Swyne[1] ou pur autre chose faire selonc ce qe nous verroms qe mieux seit. Don' souz nostre prive seal a Gaunt le xxi iour Doctobre, lan de nostre regne vintisme quint.

SC 1/45/89. Original.

164. *John, lord of Cuyk, to Edward I, 21 October 1297*

Illustrissimo domino suo domino Edwardo dei gratia regi Anglie, domino Hybernie et duci Aquitannie, Johannes de Kuyc ad eius magnificentie beneplacita debitum in omnibus obsequium et paratum. Cum intellexerim, domine carissime, vos domino meo duci Brabantie filio vestro nuntiasse, quod ipsum in hoc instanti festo Omnium Sanctorum[2] una cum consanguineis vestris filiis quondam domini mei Edmundi vestri fratris memorie recolende et cum filiis domini comitis Flandrie militem facere vos velitis, et nuper taliter a vobis recesserim, quod propter quasdam rationes, quas vobis explicaveram, militiam suam induciari velletis usque ad Natale Domini proximo nunc futurum, vestre dominationis excellentiam instantissime deprecor et requiro, quatinus militiam ipsius domini mei ducis usque ad memoratum festum natalis domini nostri causa vestri ac ipsius honoris dignemini prorogare, cum tunc tam propter adiutorium de hominibus suis sibi faciendum quam propter alia finamenta procuranda medio tempore multo decentius et melius ad vestrum honorem suumque et honorem et profectum quam plurimum ad statum militie valeat

[1] Zwin.   [2] 1 November 1297.

devenire. Alioquin vere, domine, preparationes suas necessarias ad *militiam suam ante* dictum festum Omnium Sanctorum habere non poterit ita quod ad honorem vestrum et suum in militem valeat ordinari. Si autem vobis placuerit militiam ipsius induciari usque ad Natale Domini, extunc, carissime domini, prorogare velitis militiam consanguineorum vestrorum predictorum[1] et filiorum comitis Flandrie quousque ipse dux miles efficiatur; alioquin ipse dux male contentus esset. Et si volueritis, domine, eius militiam usqe ad Natale Domini prorogari, hoc ei nuncietis taliter, quod non se male teneat pro pagato, et quidquid super hoc vestre voluntatis fu [erit] ... quanto citius potueritis, dignemini remandare. Scientes quod ego una cum nuntiis vestris domino Reynaldo et ma[gistro Rychardo a] domino meo Romanorum rege reversus sum in Brabantiam et ad vestre magnificentie presentiam venire diligenter ... ius regis Alemanie plenius relaturus. Valeat et vigeat vestra magnificentia honorum multi ... oppido sancti Trudonis,[2] die Lune post diem beati Luce evangeliste.

SC 1/18/178. Original, bottom left-hand corner torn. Printed in *Acta Imperii*, no. 133.

165. *Letters patent to all royal officials and others, 30 October 1297*

Rex omnibus ballivis, vicecomitibus, ministris et ceteris fidelibus suis salutem. Quia intelleximus quod cum quedam naves que nuper infra quosdam portus regni nostri bladis et aliis victualibus cartate et in partibus Vasconie per preceptum nostrum ad sustentacionem hominum nostrorum ibidem transducende extra predictos portus versus partes predictas velificassent, magistri et marinelli earundem navium spreto mandato nostro, contra fidelitatem suam debitam, non absque suspicionem sedicionis et in periculum tocius regni nostri cum predictis navibus predictis bladis et victualibus sic cartatis gressus suos divertentes ad partes Anglie per diversas costeras maris sunt reversi, de quo non modicum movemur. Assignavimus dilectos et fideles nostros Galfridum atte Schire et Radulphum de Bray ad inquirendum tam infra libertates quam extra in quibus locis predicte naves applicaverunt et ad eadem naves arrestanda, et bona in eisdem inventa, et magistros et marinellos earundem attachiandos nisi sufficientem manucapcionem invenire poterunt, ad standum inde recto quandocumque super hoc loqui voluerimus, et ad alia super hoc facienda

---

a ... a Words interlined.

[1] Thomas of Lancaster was in fact knighted by the king at Ghent on 1 November 1297 (B.L., Add. MS. 7965, fo. 57v).
[2] St Truiden.

quatenus eisdem Galfrido et Radulpho plenius iniunximus. Et ideo vobis mandamus quod eisdem Galfrido et Radulpho cum per partes vestras venerint, sitis eis intendentes, respondentes et facientes secundum quod ex parte nostra vobis plenius exponent. In cuius rei testimonium has litteras nostras eisdem Galfrido et Radulpho fieri fecimus patentes. T. P. de Wylugby, tenente locum W. de Langeton thesaurario nostro apud Westm', xxx die Octobris.

Et mandatum est vicecomiti Surr' et Sussex quod in propria persona sua sit respondens et intendens, et eciam faciens prout dicti Galfridus et Radulphus ei ex parte regis iniungent. T. ut supra.

E 159/70, m. 100.

166. *Edward I to his son Edward and his council, 8 November 1297*

Edward par la grace de dieu, roy Dengleterre, seigneur Dirlande e ducs Daquitaine, a Edward nostre trescher fiz, e nostre lieu tenant en Engleterre, e a son conseil, saluz. Moustre nous ad nostre ame e feal Thomas de la Roche, qi est en nostre service de ca la mer en la compaignie Hug' le Despensier, qil est disseisi de aucunes fraunchises, apartenans a sa baronie de la Roche, puis son departir Dengleterre, en grief, preiudice de lui, e aperte desheriteson. E por ce qe nous ne voloms mie, si come reson nest, qil por son bon e leal service encourge damage, nous vous mandoms qe vous le facez mettre endreit de ses dites franchises en autre tiel estat come il esteit qant il sen departi de son pais a venir par de ca en nostre service, e ce ne lessez. Donees desoutz nostre prive seal a Gant le viii iour de Novembre, lan de nostre regne vint e cinkime.[1]

SC 1/45/95. Original.

167. *Edward I to his son Edward and his council, 12 November 1297*

Edward par la grace de dieu, roi Dengleterre, seigneur Dirlande e ducs Daquitaine, a Edward nostre chier fiuz, tenant nostre lieu en Engleterre, e a son consail, saluz. Pur ce qe nous avoms entendu qe Robert le Poer e Alice sa femme ont arraine une assize de novele disseisine vers nostre foial e loial Hughe de Seint Philibert, qui demoert en nostre servise es parties ou nous sumes, daucunes choses dont meismes celui Hughe feut en peisible possession al houre quil se meust

[1] *C.C.R., 1296–1302*, p. 147, has an acquittance, dated 20 February 1298, for £259 demanded from Thomas de la Roche of the arrears of his account when he was sheriff of Cork, in view of his good service.

Dengleterre pur venir oveque nous en nostre servise; nous mandoms qe vous faciez mander as justices qui sont assignez a prendre assises en le counte ou les dites choses sont qe meismes lassise si ele soit arraines sicome est desusdite, preigne delay e soit mise en respit tant qe au retourner le dit Hughe en Engleterre ou tant qe nous en eoms autre chose commande. Don' souz nostre prive seal a Gaunt le xii iour de Novembre, lan de nostre regne vintisme quint.[1]

SC 1/45/95. Original.

168. *Exchequer memorandum, 15 November 1297*

Memorandum quod cum dominus rex nuper assignasset diversos homines in diversis comitatibus simul cum vicecomitibus eorundem comitatuum ad lanas emendas ad opus regis, videlicet certum numerum saccorum in quolibet comitatu, et ad lanas illas preparandas, paccandas et ad diversos portus cariandas collectoribus custume regis in portubus illis liberandas, exinde ad partes transmarinas transducendas, prout in rotulo memorandorum de termino sancte Trinitatis proximo preterito plenius continetur;[2] dilectus et fidelis regis Johannes de Drokenesford custos garderobe ipsius regis modo tenens hic locum thesaurarii, ipso in partibus predictis agente, recordatus est hic coram baronibus, videlicet xv die Novembris etc., quod videtur consilio regis quod expedit pro rege quod lane ille que occasione assignationis predicte empte sunt ad opus regis et ad portus nondum cariate, set in manibus eorum a quibus empte fuerunt adhuc remanent, ad portus non carientur nec ad opus regis detineantur, sed quod illi quorum lane ille fuerunt eas retineant, et comodum suum inde facere valeant prout melius viderint expedire. Quia consilium predictum pro certo accepit quod computatis solucionibus quas rex fieri pro lanis illis necnon sumptubus quos circa cariagium et preparationem earundem apponi facere teneretur, soluciones et sumptus huiusmodi valorem lanarum illarum excederent, quod ad dampnum regis foret manifestum et non modicum, per quod per predictum consilium est[a] concordatum quod huiusmodi lane sic empte et nondum

---

[a] *E 159/71 has* per consilium predictum est.

[1] A further letter on behalf of Hugh de St Philibert, ordering an action of novel disseisin brought against him by Roger de la Hide to be held over until Hugh's return to England, also issued on 12 November, is in SC 1/45/96. It seems likely that these letters are those referred to in the prince's letter to the chancellor of 10 January 1298 (no. 187). St Philibert's wife acquired some land while her husband was in Flanders without proper licence, but they were later pardoned as result of his service in Scotland, Flanders and elsewhere (*C.P.R., 1292–1301*, pp. 390–1).

[2] These appointments had been made on 30 July 1297 (no. 97, n. 3).

ad portus cariate set penes[a] eos a quibus empte fuerunt existant in manibus eorundem remaneant absque diminucione et ipsi inde como-dum suum faciant prout melius etc., et quod singulis vicecomitibus quibus preceptum fuit ad lanas ad opus regis emendas in forma pre-dicta fiant brevia quod de lanis emptis et nondum cariatis, ut est dic-tum se non intromittant, sed in manibus eorum a quibus empte fuerunt sine diminucione remanere et ipsos inde suum commodum facere permittant. Et preceptum est vicecomitibus in forma illa sicut continetur in rotulo brevium retornabilium pro rege[b] de hoc termino, hoc signo anteposito.[c1]

E 368/69, m. 21; E 159/71, m. 14d.

169. *Edward I to his son Edward and his council, 16 November 1297*

Edward par la grace de dieu roy Dengleterre, seigneur Dirland, e ducs Daquitaine, a Edward nostre cher fiz e nostre lieu tenant en Engleterre, e a son conseil, saluz. Come le roy de Portugal nostre chier amy nous eit enve ses lettres overtes par les queles il ad asseure touz marchantz, e totes autres gentz de nostre reaume Dengleterre, de Gascoigne e des autres terres de nostre pouer de venir par tout en sa terre e en sa seignurie, e illoqes demorer e marchander a lour volunte. E nous ausi lui eioms envoie noz lettres overtes semblables por marchantz e totes autres gentz de son reaume e de sa seigneurie de la quele nous vous envoioms le transcrit enclos dedeinz ceste lettre. Nous vous mandoms qe vous faciez crier par totes les citez e viles e autres lieus de nostre reaume e de nostre pouer par la ou vous verrez qe bon seit, qe nuls ne face mal, damage, destourbance ne grevance par terre ne par mer as marchantz ne as gentz le dit roy de Portugal, contre la forme de noz lettre avantdites. E ce ne lessez. Donees desoutz nostre prive seal a Gant le xvi iour de Novembr', lan de nostre regne vint e cinkime.[2]

SC 1/45/98. Original.

---

[a] *E 159/71 has* quibus *for* penes.
[b] pro rege *is only in E 368/69.*
[c] *No sign is given in E 159/71, but in E 368/69 a drawing of a hand holding a small bell is placed at this point.*

---

[1] The writs to the sheriffs are enrolled in E 368/69, m. 107, and were issued on 15 November.
[2] For a similar letter to the Cinque Ports, see SC 1/45/99. Letters close ordering the proclamation to be made were issued on 28 November 1297 (*C.C.R., 1296–1302,* p. 139).

170. *Edward, son of Edward I, to the chancellor, 17 November 1297*

Edward fiuz a noble roy Dengleterre a son chier e bien ame sire Johan
de Langeton', chaunceler nostre seigneur le roy, saluz e bon amour.
Pur ceo qe nous avoms entendu par le message mons' Johan le fiuz
Thomas qil nad mye congie du consail de remuer nule part tant qe
a nostre venue a Londres, par qe il nous ad prie qil peut aler auqune
part dedure dentre ci e nostre venue, nous vous mandoms qe vous
lui facez aver une lettre au bailif de Banested, qil le resceive corteisement e soeffre aver son deduit en park a prendre leviz iekes a deauz
bestes ou a trois ou tant qil semble a vous, sir chaunceler, qil face
a faire. E qil le soeffre ausint aver les esementz du manoir pur sa
demeure e du busche a sa volente e a raison. Don' a Eltham le xvii
iour de Novembr' desouz le seal mons' Guy Ferre nostre chivaler,
pur ceo qe nous naviem mye le nostre prest.[1]

SC 1/26/169. Original.

171. *Edward I to his son Edward and his council, 18 November 1297*

Edward par la grace de dieu roi Dengleterre, seigneur Dirland e ducs
Daquitaine, a Edward nostre chier fiuz tenant nostre lieu en Engleterre e a son consail, saluz. Come les executours du testament mestre
Willame de Montfort, iadis dean de leglise seint Pool de Londres eent
aucunes grevances faites a mons' Guilliam de Leibourn' puis qil vynt
ceo outre en nostre service, sicome ses gentz vous porront plus pleinement moustrer, vous mandoms qe sa moustrance e ses resons bien
entendues, mettez y tieu consail e tieu redrescement come vous porrez
sanz mesprendre. E tant en faciez qe son estat seit sauvez en tieu manere
quil se pusse tenir appaiez par reson, e quil aparceive qe sa demoere
devers nous li tiegne profit e nient de damage. Don' souz nostre prive
seal a Gant le xviii iour de Novembre, lan de nostre regne xxv.

SC 1/45/101. Original.

172. *Letters patent of Edward I to the knights, freemen and others of Kent,*
23 November 1297

Rex militibus, liberis hominibus, ballivis, ministris et omnibus aliis
et singulis de comitatu Kanc' ad quod presentes littere pervenerint,

---

[1] Letters close were issued on 21 November, ordering the keeper of the royal park
at Banstead, Surrey, to allow John FitzThomas to have four does and two leafless tree
stumps, by information of the bishops of London and Ely (*C.C.R., 1296–1302*, p. 138).

salutem. Quia blado, victualibus et aliis necessariis ad opus nostrum et nostrorum nobiscum in partibus transmarinis existentium quamplurimum indigemus, assignavimus vicecomitem nostrum comitatus predicti et dilectos clericos nostros Ricardum de Brummesgrave et Alexandrum le Convers ad MD quarteria frumenti et D quarteria avene infra comitatum illum ad opus nostrum iuxta forum patrie emenda et capienda, prout iidem vicecomes, Ricardus et Alexander melius viderint faciendum. Ita quod predicti vicecomes, Ricardus et Alexander blada illa sic empta et capta in comitatu predicto usque Sandwicum sine dilacione aliqua cariari et ibidem in navibus poni usque ad nos in partibus predictis transduci faciant, et quod pro bladis predictis illis a quibus ea ceperint statim in captione eorundem satisfaciant prout eis ex parte nostre plenius est iniunctum. Et ideo vobis mandamus quod eisdem vicecomiti, Ricardo et Alexandro ad premissa facienda intendentes sitis et respondentes, consulentes et auxiliantes, quotiens ab ipsis vel uno eorum super hoc fueritis requisiti. Et hoc sicut comodum nostrum et vestrum et salvacionem regni nostri diligitis nullatenus omittatis. In cuius rei testimonium has litteras nostras fieri fecimus patentes. Teste W. Coventr' et Lich' episcopo, thesaurario nostro, apud Westm' xxiii die Novembris, anno regni nostri vicesimo quinto.[1]

E 368/69, m. 7; E 159/71, m. 64.

173. *Edward I to the sheriff of Staffordshire, 23 November 1297*

Rex vicecomiti Staff', salutem. Cum nos ad instanciam communitatis regni nostri remisimus custumam quadraginta solidorum nobis nuper in subsidium guerre nostre contra regem Francie concessam, de quolibet sacco lane exeunte regnum nostrum percipiendam per biennium vel triennium, si tantum durasset guerra illa, concedentes custumam illam vel aliam sine voluntate et communi assensu eiusdem communitatis minime capiemus, salvo tamen nobis et heredibus nostris custuma lanarum, pellium et coriorum per communitatem dicti regni nobis prius concessa; tibi precipimus quod in pleno comitatu tuo civitatibus, burgis et villis mercatoriis et alibi per totam ballivam tuam ubi melius videris expedire publice proclamari facere quod omnes

---

[1] Similar writs were issued as follows:

Hampshire. The sheriff and Peter de Aulton, 1,500 qu. oats, to be taken to Southampton.

Essex & Herts. The sheriff and Thurstan de Hamslape, 1,000 qu. wheat, 1,000 qu. oats, to be taken to London and Colchester.

Norfolk & Suffolk. The sheriff and John de St Ivone, 1,500 qu. wheat, 1,000 qu. oats, to be taken to Yarmouth and Ipswich.

Sussex. The sheriff and Thomas de Warberge, 1,000 qu. oats, to be taken to Shoreham.

mercatores et alii qui lanas, pelles et coria ducere seu cariare volentes ad partes transmarinas salvo et secure duci et cariari faciant ad portus ubi cokettum nostrum existit, solvendo ad opus nostrum custodibus custume ibidem dimidiam marcam pro quolibet sacco lane et pellium lanutarum et similiter unam marcam per quolibet lasto coriorum exeuntium dictum regnum, prout prius fieri consuevit. Mandavimus enim custodibus custume nostre in portubus predictis quod custumam huiusmodi de sacco lane et pellium lanutarum et lasto coriorum exeuntium dictum regnum capiant ad opus nostrum et quod capcioni dictorum quadraginta solidorum de sacco lane et pellium lanutarum et quinque marcarum de lasto coriorum omnino supersedeant. Teste Edwardo filio nostro apud Westm' xxiii die Novembris, anno regni nostri vicesimo sexto.[1]

Consimile modo mandatum est singulis vicecomitibus Anglie. Teste ut supra.

E 159/71, mm. 108, 108d; E 368/69, mm. 27, 27d.

174. *Edward I to the collectors of the customs at Newcastle-upon-Tyne, 23 November 1297*

Rex custodibus nove custume sue apud Novum Castrum super Tynam, salutem. Cum nos ad instanciam communitatis regni nostri remiserimus custumam quadraginta solidorum nobis nuper in subsidium guerre nostre contra regem Francie concessam de quolibet sacco lane exeunte regnum nostrum percipiendam per biennium vel triennium, si tantum durasset guerra illa, concedentes quod custumam illam vel aliam sine voluntate et communi assensu eiusdem communitatis minime capiemus, salva tamen nobis et heredibus nostris custuma lanarum, pellium et coriorum per communitatem regni nobis prius concessa; vobis mandamus quod, receptis custuma dimidie marce de quolibet sacco lane et pellium lanutarum et similiter custuma unius marce de quolibet lasto coriorum exeuntium dictum regnum, prout prius fieri consuevit, capcioni dictorum quadraginta solidorum de sacco lane et pellium et quinque marcarum de lasto coriorum supersedeatis omnino. Teste W. Coventr' et Lich' episcopo, thesaurario nostro apud Westm' xxiii die Novembris, anno regni nostri vicesimo sexto. Per consilium.[2]

E 159/71, m. 108; E 368/69, m. 27. Translated in *E.H.D.*, iii, 488–9.

---

[1] Calendared in *C.C.R.*, *1296–1302*, p. 187, version addressed to the sheriff of York, and dated 24 November.

[2] Similar writs were issued on the same date to the customs collectors at Hull, Boston, Yarmouth, Ipswich, London, Sandwich, Southampton and Bristol.

175. *Edward I to his son Edward and his council, 23 November 1297*

Edward par la grace de dieu roi Dengleterre, seigneur Dirlande e ducs Daquitaine, a Edward nostre chier fiuz, tenant nostre lieu en Engleterre e a son consail, saluz. Come aucunes gentz soient tenuz en diverses dettes a nostre foial e loial Johan Engayne, qui demoert en nostre servise es parties ou nous sumes, par lettres obligatoires, sicome aucun de par lui vous porra plus pleinement moustrer; vous mandoms qe, les dites lettres obligatoires regardees e diligeaument entendues, facez lever les dites dettes e paer au dit Johan, ou a son attorne en noun de lui, le plus en haste qe vous porrez, selonc les leys e les usages de nostre roiaume. Don' souz nostre prive seal a Gaunt le xxiii iour de November, lan de nostre regne vint e quint.

SC 1/45/102. Original.

176. *Edward I to his son Edward and his council, 27 November 1297*

Edward par la grace de dieu roi Dengleterre, seigneur Dirland e ducs Daquitaine, a Edward nostre chier fiuz, tenant nostre lieu en Engleterre, e a son conseil, saluz. Sachiez qe entre la terme de la souffrance qui estoit prise entre le roi de France e nous, la[a] qele nous vous feissoms a savoir par nos lettres, est pur certeynes achesons e par consail e commun assent dambes partz le dit terme de cele souffrance esloignez e continuez de les utaves la feste seint Andreu[1] iusques a quaresme prenant prochein[2] avenir, en maniere qe le dit roi de France e nous nous deyvoms entreveer meen temps a iour certeyn nomez. Cest a savoir lendemeyn del an renoef, e deyt le dit roi de France venir e estre au dit terme a Tournay, e nous a Audenarde.[3] E avoms bone esperaunce qe par la grace de dieu la busoigne se prendra ensi par cele voie qe bone pees ensuira a profit e greynure quiete e tranquillite de la Crestiente. E pur ce qe tant come nos adversaires plus fortz e plus efforciez de bones gentz nous verroient plus tost descenderoient a meilleure fourme de pees e plus honourable pur nous e pur nos alliez, vous mandoms qe sicome vous amez loneur e le profit e le bon estat de nous e de vous e de quantqe nous touche, mettez peine e tote la diligence qui vous porrez de nous purchacier e enveer tot le pouer qui vous porrez de gentz darmes, ensi quil peussent estre a nous au dit terme qe la dite veue se doyt faire, si estre puet, ou dedeinz la vintisme iour apres le Noel. Car sicome dit est qe, de tant come il

---

[a] *Word interlined.*

[1] 7 December 1297.   [2] 19 February 1298.   [3] Oudenarde, Belgium.

nous verroient venir bone aide de nostre roiaume Dengleterre e nostre force crescez, a meilleure e plus honurable pees pur nous e nos alliez descendreient e la freint. E entendoms totes veies e voloms qe forspris soient celes gentz darmes endroit de faire venir a nous qui deyvent entendre as les busoignes e deffens Descoce, cest a savoir de ceux qui sont plus pres de celes marches qe de les parties vers ou nous sumes. E vous mandoms uncore qe vous mandez a touz ceux de nos portz e a ce les mettez qe eux contre lissue du terme de la dite souffrance assemblent, e facez assembler tot leur navie a un porte ensi quil soient prestz.e apparaillez ove tote cele navie ove bon e suffisaunt apparaillement totes les houres qe nous leur feroms a savoir. Don' souz nostre prive seal a Gaunt le xxvii iour de Novembre, lan de nostre regne xxvi.

SC 1/45/105. Original.

177. *Edward I to his son Edward and his council, 27 November 1297*

Edward par la grace de dieu roi Dengleterre, seigneur Dirlande e ducs Daquitayne, a Edward nostre chier fiuz, tenant nostre lieu en Engleterre, e a son consail, saluz. Queux mandementz qe nous eoms faitz a entre vous ore e autrefoiz, vous chargeoms especiaument, sicome vous volez sauver nostre honeur, qe vous mettez aucun bon consail en la busoigne de Gascoigne, coment nos gentz qui la sount se peussent meyntenir celes parties, tant qe nos busoignes par decea soient mises en plus certeyn estat qe eles ne sont uncore. E par vos lettres les confortez ausint quantque vous porrez, si les requerrez molt quil se voillent tenir come bones gentz, sicome il ont fait touz iours cea en arrieres, e quil facent semblant de bon covyne, nomeement ceste souffrance durant. Car si nos adversaires veent qe ceux de Gascoigne se portent bien a ce qe nos amys par ailleurs se porteront ausint, nous esperoms certeynement qe nous trouveroms bone issue de nostre busoigne. E pur ce vous soviegne bien de ceux de Gascoigne, coment il soient par temps confortez en aucune bone manere, car de nient ne puent il estre de bon covyne. Don' souz nostre prive seal a Gaunt le xxvii iour de Novembre, lan de nostre regne vint e sysme.

SC 1/45/103. Original.

178. *Edward I to his son Edward and his council, 29 November 1297*

Edward par la grace de dieu roy Dengleterre, seigneur Dirland e ducs Daquitaine, a Edward nostre chier fiz, e nostre lieu tenant en Engle-

terre e a son conseil, saluz. Come puis la soffrance prise entre le roy
de France e nous, venist une nief de les parties de Espaigne oveques
marchandie en la port del Swyn, e illoqes par genz de noz portz qe
lors y esteint feust cele nief arestee. E nous suz ce a la mostrance e
la suite Johan de Cortray, burges de Bruges, pur lui e por autres de
la dite vile, claimantz cele nief e les biens qe leins furent por lour
biens e por lour chateaus, mandissoms sor greve forfeiture as gentz
de nos portz qe illoqes esteient qe la dite nef ove les ditz biens que
en cele esteient feissent santz delai deliverer as devantditz burgeys.
E *eaus por nostre maundement* rien de ce ne feissent, mes mesme
cele nief menerent en Engleterre, si come il nous ont fait puis entendre.
Nous vous mandoms qe vous facez diligeaument enquerre a la suite
des avantditz burgeis ou cele nief ove les biens leins contenuz feut
devenue. E ce ne lessez de fere por ce qe nous sumes tenuz a la restitution par reson qe ce fu fait puis la dite suffrance prise. Donees desoutz
nostre prive seal a Gant le xxix iour de Novembr' lan de nostre regne
vint e sisime.

SC 1/45/106. Original.

179. *Edward I to the sheriff of Wiltshire, 30 November 1297*

Rex vicecomiti Wiltes', salutem. Meminimus nos tibi nuper prece-
pisse quod omnes lanas per dilectos et fideles nostros Walterum de
Bello Alneto, Laurentium de Aune de Wynton', Johannem de Tyting'
et Philippum Aubyn una tecum assignatos ad certum numerum saccorum lane emendum ad opus nostrum in comitatu predicto emptas
occasione assignationis predicte que apud Suth' nondum cariate
fuerunt, set in manibus eorum a quibus empte fuerant, remanentes
in manibus eorundem*b* absque diminucione remanere et ipsos inde
comodum suum facere permisses;[1] et per predictos Laurencium et
Johannem datum est nobis intelligi quod pretextu [precepti] nostri
predicti diversas lanas ad opus nostrum emptas occasione assignationis predicte et ad sumptus nostros preparatas, paccas et usque Sar'
cariatas feceris et facis deliberari, quod pretextu illius precepti nostri
fieri nostre non erat intencionis nec esse dinoscimus quod huiusmodi
lane sic empte, preparate et paccate ad portum predictum cariate
fuissent ad partes transmarinas transducende. Et ideo tibi precepimus
quod de lanis per predictos Laurencium, Johannem, Walterum et
Philippum et te aut unum vestrum ad opus nostrum emptas et ad

a...a Passage interlined.
b in manibus eorem repeated in MS.

[1] See no. 168.

sumptus nostros preparatas et paccatas ubicumque in comitatu predicto existant hiis a quibus empte fuerunt nichil deliberari, set eas sic preparatas et paccatas usque portum predictum facias cariari sine mora custodibus custume nostre liberandas, ibidem ad partes predictas transmittendas, proviso siquidem quod [si] ante receptionem presentium de huiusmodi lanis aliquid deliberaveris occasione precepti nostri supradicti, tunc id sine dilacione recapere et ad portum predictum facere cariari in forma predicta. Et quid inde feceris scire facias thesaurario et baronibus de scaccario nostro apud Westm' in crastino sancte Lucie[1] sub sigillo tuo distincte et aperte, remittens ibi hoc breve. Teste W. Coventr' et Lich' episcopo, thesaurario nostro etc. xxx die Novembris, anno vicesimo sexto.

E 368/69, m. 107d.

180. *Petition of Cecily de la More of London, November 1297*

A nostre seigneur le rey e a son conseil monstre Cecille de la More de Loundres qe la ou ele aveit lessee en la meyn des custumiers de Loundres iusqes a x saks de leyne en gage por xxx livres por la custume des leynes qele aveit fete passer graunt piece devant Pasche, si sont mesmes celes leynes prises e arestues e mandez par dela a vendre, e les pernours de leynes a Loundres si unt fet priser les dites leynes a liii livres xviii sous iiii deniers. Dunt ele prie por dieu qe les xxx livres qe ele deit por la custume ly seient allowez en la dite leyne, e qe nostre seignor le rey ly face sa grace du remenaunt qar ele ad mout perdue en la mer por ceste guerre.[2]

E 368/69, m. 20; E 159/71, m. 13.

181. *Composition by the master and knights of the Temple for taxation, Michaelmas 1297*

Magister et fratres milicie Templi in Anglia dant domino regi pro defensione regni et pro confirmacione magne carte de libertatibus Anglie et de foresta una cum ceteris articulis nunc additis eidem carte et concessis, et pro nona omnium bonorum temporalium predictorum magistri et fratrum et villanorum suorum in Anglia DCC marcas.

[1] 14 December 1297.
[2] On 15 November 1297 settlement was made at the exchequer, with Cecily being allowed £29 3s. 9½d. against the customs duties she owed (E 368/69, m. 20). A writ in pursuance was issued to the collectors of customs at London on 17 November 1297 (E 159/71, m. 108).

Ita tamen quod istud donum nunc factum alias non vertatur in servitutem vel consuetudinem contra libertates suas. Postea solvunt DCC marcas per i talliam et quieti sunt.[1]

E 159/71, m. 79.

182. *Edward I to the barons of the exchequer, 4 December 1297*

Edward par la grace de deu etc. Nous vous mandoms fermement enioignantz qe de la forest de Dene nous faciez venir le plus en haste qe vous porrez cinquante bons mineurs, issint quil seient a nous ove lour ustiz e tot lour attyl a la chandelour procheinement avenir[2] a plus tard; e seie avises e prenez bone garde qe meismes les minou[r]s seient bien eluz, e quil eient avant lour partir Dengeleterre touz lour ustiz qui a eus apendent, mais qe les choses nous deivent custer, si lour faciez trover passage e gages tant quil seient venuz a nous e quil seient a nous au dit terme en totes maneres. Don' souz nostre prive seal a Rode le iiii iour de Decembre, lan de nostre regne xxvi.[3]

E 159/71, m. 10.

183. *Edward I to his son Edward and his council, 6 December 1297*

Edward par la grace de dieu roy Dengleterre, seigneur Dirland e ducs Daquitaine, a Edward nostre cher fiz, nostre lieu tenant en Engleterre, e a son consail, saluz. Moustre nous ad Thomas de Verdon nostre chier e ame vallet, qui est ovesque nous la ou nous sumes en propre persone, qe Gerard de Bathesham le destreint par ses biens en le conte de Suff' por un relief qil lui demande, por quei nous vous mandoms qe vous faitz mettre en respit le dite demande de ci qil puisse venir en Engleterre e qil seit en pes de totes maneres destresces e grevances tant come il est ove nous en nostre guerre. Donees desoutz nostre prive seal a Gant le vi iour de Decembre, lan de nostre regne vint e sisime.

SC 1/45/107. Original.

---

[1] A similar memorandum records an identical arrangement made by the Prior and brothers of the Hospital. It is printed in Rothwell, 'The Confirmation of the Charters, 1297', 190–1.
[2] 2 February 1298.
[3] Letters patent appointing the constables of the castles of Bristol and St Briavels, with the sheriff of Gloucestershire, to select fifty miners to go to London were issued on 14 December 1297 (E 368/69, m. 6d; E 159/71, m. 64d).

184. *Edward, son of Edward I, to the chancellor, 12 December 1297*

Edward fiuz a noble roy Dengleterre, tenaunt son lieu en Engleterre,
a son chier clerc sire Johan de Langeton' chanceler le dit nostre piere,
saluz e bon amur. Nous vous envoiom close dedenz ceste *a demorer
ver vous* une lettre nostre seignur le roy nostre piere,[1] la quele il
manda a nous e a nostre consail pur feire resun a mon sire Roger
de Mounbrai sur les choses en la dite lettre contenues, e vous mandom
ke solom la tenur de meisme la*b* lettre facez a ceux qui suyent pur
le dit monsire Roger ceo qe vous verrez a fere par dreite e resun. Don'
a Langele[2] le xii iour de Decembre.

SC 1/26/170. Original.

185. *Edward I to the exchequer or to his son and his council, 2 January 1298*

Edward par la grace de deu etc. Come nous seioms tenuz par nos
lettres overtes a les bones gentz de la vile Dypre en une summe des
deniers, sicome plus pleynement est contenuz en les dites lettres, e
le iour qui leur feut assignez a receivre le paement des avauntditz
deniers a nostre dit Escheker soit passez, e le paement ne leur seit
uncore fait seur ceo a graunt grevaunce de eaux, a ce qe nous avoms
entendu, vous maundoms qe le paement des avaundiz deniers leur
faciez faire le plus tost e en la meillure manere qui vous purrez. Don'
a Gaunt le secund iour de Janevoir, lan de nostre regne vint e sisime.

E 159/71, m. 24; E 368/69, m. 55.

186. *Edward I to his son Edward and his council, 2 January 1298*

Edward par la grace de dieu roi Dengleterre, seigneur Dirland e ducs
Daquitaine, a Edward nostre chier fiuz, tenant nostre lieu en Engleterre, e a son consail, saluz. Come nostre ame clerk mestre Pieres
Emerik demoerge pres de nous e bon lieu e profitable nous tiegne
e nous uncore nel eoms regarde selonc ses travaux, e les merites de

---

a ... a Passage interlined.
b Word interlined.

---

[1] This may relate to the letter of 8 September (no. 135) or, more probably, to the
grant Mowbray made of lands and rent to John de Creppinges, which received royal
confirmation on 22 December, by which time Mowbray had died (*C.P.R.*, *1292–1301*,
p. 325).
[2] King's Langley, Herts.

sa personne; e tot soit qe nous a nostre passage de Wynchelse vous
eussiens mande par nostre chancelier qe de benefice deglise a nostre
doneison aportenant, qui pur lui suffissant e covenable feust du primer
qui escherreit, li feissez purveer. Nous vuellantz qe cele chose se face
ausi tost come temps se dorra, vous mandoms et chargeoms qe du
primer benefice deglise a nostre doneison aportenant qe escherra, e
qe por le dit mestre Pieres soit covenable e suffisant, li faciez porveer
e doner. E ce ne lessez. Don' souz nostre prive seal a Gant le second
iour de Janevoir, lan de nostre regne vint e sisime.[1]

SC 1/45/109. Original.

187. *Edward, son of Edward I, to John Langton, the chancellor, 10 January
1298*

Edward fiuz au noble roy Dengleterre, tenant son leu en Engleterre
a son treschier e bien ame sire Johan de Langeton', chanceler nostre
seigneur le roy avantdit, saluz e bon amour. Nous vous mandoms par
le porteur de ses lettres ii lettres les queles nous viendrent a Langel'
y ceo vendresdi prochain devant la feste saynt Hillary de par nostre
seigneur le roy mon piere pur les bosoignes mons' Hughe de Saynt
Philibert qui demoere outremer ovesques lui e en son service;[2] e vous
mandoms qe solom le mandement que est contenuz en les avantdites
lettres, voillez lavantdite bosoigne fere e ordener solom dreiture en teu
manere que nous ne puissoms autrefoiz estre repris. Nostre seigneur
vous eit en sa garde. Donez a Langel' le iour avantdit desouz le seal
nostre cher chivaler mons' Reignaud de Gray pur ceo qe le nostre
nestoit mye prest.

SC 1/26/171. Original.

188. *Exchequer memorandum, 15 January 1298*

Memorandum quod quintodecimo die Januarii concessum fuit per W.
Coventr' et Lich' episcopum, thesaurarium, quod venerabilis pater
R. archiepiscopus Cantuariensis habeat respectum de suis debitis que
regi debet donec rex aliud inde preceperit.

E 368/69, m. 65; E 159/71, m. 73.

[1] Pierre Emerik had been granted the church of Peckham on 27 January 1295. In
1296 he was described as being 'attendant constantly on the king's service', and on
24 August 1299 he was granted a canonry at Beverley (*C.P.R., 1292–1301*, pp. 129,
208, 436). See also no. 4.
[2] For the king's letters on behalf of Hugh, see no. 167.

189. *Edward I to the collectors of customs at Hull, 28 January 1298*

Rex collectoribus custume sue apud Hull', salutem. Monstraverunt nobis Coppus Josep et Taldus Janian mercatores de societate Friscobaldorum Alborum de Florencia quod licet nuper vobis mandaremus quod omnes denarios, quos vos habueretis de custodia predicta vel extunc essetis recepturi, ipsis mercatoribus vel eorum certo attornato liberaretis in partem solucionis debitorum in quibus eis tenemur quousque aliud inde vobis mandassemus; vos tamen, spreto mandato illo, denarios provenientes de custuma illa solvi facitis hiis qui ad expensas faciendas in instanti exercitu nostro versus partes Scocie deputantur contra formam mandati nostri predicti, et ad dampnum mercatorum predictorum non modicum et gravamen. Cumque nostre intentionis non existat quin mercatores predicti pecuniam provenientem de custuma predicta per manus vestras habeant et percipiant iuxta formam prioris mandati nostri vobis inde directi aliquo alio mandato nostro vobis postea directo de memorata pecunia ad expensas predictas solvendas non obstante; exceptis dumtaxat denariis illis provenientibus de custuma lanarum mercatorum Brabantie a portu predicto exeuntium quos karissimo filio nostro Johanni duci Brabantie assignavimus prout alias vobis meminimus mandasse. Vobis mandamus firmiter iniungentes quod mercatoribus de Florencia antedictis, vel eorum certo attornato, omnes denarios provenientes de custuma predicta, exceptis denariis dicto duci Brabantie assignatis ut predicitur, habere et liberari faciatis in partem solucionem debitorum predictorum quousque aliud inde vobis mandaverimus, recipientes a Coppo et Taldo predictis vel eorum attornato litteras suas patentes receptionem denariorum eis per vos liberandorum testificantes hoc pro aliquo alio mandato nostro vobis directo nullo modo omittentes. Et nos vobis super compotum vestrum debitam inde allocationem fieri fecimus. Teste W. Coventr' etc. xxviii die Januarii, anno regni nostri xxvi^to.[1]

E 368/69, m. 59; E 159/71, m. 111.

190. *Edward I to the chancellor, 30 January 1298*

Edward par la grace de dieu roi Dengleterre, seigneur Dirland e ducs Daquitaine, a son chier clerk e feal Johan de Langeton' son chancelier,

---

[1] Writs had been issued on 4 October 1297 assigning the customs revenue from Boston and Hull to the merchants of the Frescobaldi, saving the revenue already assigned to the duke of Brabant (E 159/71, m. 107; E 368/69, m. 24d). For full details of the repayments to the Frescobaldi of the forced loans of 1294-5, see Kaeuper, 'The Frescobaldi of Florence and the English Crown', 48-52.

saluz. Pur ce qe nous avoms mande a levesque de Cestr' nostre tresorier quil face tant vers quatre compagnies ou cynk de marchandz
qe eux e leur compaignons de decea meinpreignent mons' Johan de
Seint Johan pur vint mil livres de tournays, e li avoms mande qe il
les face si seures qe il porra qe nous les garderoms de damage; pur
quei nous vous mandoms qe tieux lettres come le dit tresorer vous
devisera sur ceste busoigne qe vous les facez ausi come nous meismes
les vous devissioms de bouche. E ce en nule manere ne leissiez. Don'
souz nostre prive seal a Gaunt le xxx iour de Janevoir, lan de nostre
regne vint e sisime.

C 81/16/1483. Original.

191. *Edward I to the chancellor, 30 January 1298*

Edward par la grace de dieu roi Dengleterre, seigneur Dirland e ducs
Daquitaine, a son chier clerk e feal Johan de Langeton son chaunceler,
saluz. Come la suffrance soit esloignee entre nous e le roi de France,
e la fourme ne soit mie uncore venue a nous de la ou nos gentz sont,
e nous voloms bien qe la terme est pris a issir, qui avant fait entre
nous, pur quei nous vous mandoms qe veues ces lettres, facez mander
par tot la ou vous estes acustumez de mander qe tot soit il issi qe la
fourme de lesloignance ne leur soit mie venue souz nostre seal au terme
qui lautre feut, qe eux a plus tard gardent e continuent la dite suffrance ausi bien ou mieux come unques furent avant, iusques tant
qe la fourme leur soit venue souz nostre seal, sicome est avantdite,
la queu fourme nous vous enverroms qu plus tost qe nous lauroms
de nos gentz. Don' sous nostre prive seal a Gant le xxx iour de Janevoir, lan de nostre regne vint e sisime.[1]

C 81/16/1485. Original.

192. *Edward I to John de Lisle, 30 January 1298*

Rex dilecto et fideli suo Johanni de Insula salutem. Quia propter
expensas multiplices que nobis continue diebus istis incumbunt tam
ad expugnacionem inimicorum nostrorum regni Francie potencius
resistendam, quam proterviam Scotorum rebellionem severicius
reprimendam, pecunie promptitudine necessarius indigemus, vobis
mandamus in fide et dileccione quibis nobis tenemini quod ad presen-

---

[1] The continuation of the truce was agreed at Tournai on 28 January 1298 (*Treaty
Rolls*, i, 143–4).

ciam dilecti in Cristo H. Ebor' electi accedatis et omni diligencia qua poteritis eidem in auxilium assistatis ad denarios nostros qui nobis a retro sunt, tam de quinta bonorum cleri sue diocesis quam de aliis debitis quibus idem clerus nobis debet de diversis subsidiis nobis per eundem clerum alias gratanter concessis, ad opus nostrum levandos. Exasperantes siquidem et inducentes taxatores et collectores none et aliorum subsidiorum de quibus nobis arreragia debentur et eciam vicecomes Ebor' ut omni dilacione postposita huiusmodi debita nostra celeriter levari faciant, considerando quantum periculum, quod absit, defectus pecunie possit inducere, et quanta examinatio inimicorum nostrorum erit si super pecunie potenciam nos sciant excellere. Mandavimus enim vicecomiti nostro Ebor' quod ipse una cum ballivis suis omnibus modis quibus poterit quandocumque et quotienscumque a vobis seu uno vestrum fuerit requisitus vobis intendant ad dicta debita levanda, secundum quod ex parte nostra ei plenius iniungetis. Et hoc nullo modo omittatis, sicut honorem vestrum diligitis, et regni nostri periculum vitari volueritis. Teste W. Coventr' et Lich' episcopo, thesaurario regis, xxx die Januarii anno xxvi[to].[1]

E 368/69, m. 59d.

193. *Edward I to the treasurer and barons of the exchequer, 5 February 1298, with an indenture of credence for William of Gainsborough and John Lovel*

Edward par la grace de dieu etc., al honourable piere en dieu W. par la meisme grace evesque de Cestre, nostre tresorier, e as barons del escheker, salutz. Nous enveoms a vous nos feaux e loiaux frere Guilliame de Geynesburgh, e mestre Johan Lovel nostre clerk, pur la suffraunce qui est pris entre le roy de France e nous e noz aliez dune part e dautre, e pur aucunes grantz busoignes qui nous touchent, les queles sont les plus hastives qe nous eoms a faire es parties ou nous sumes, e sanz les queles nous ne pooms partir diloeqes. E vous mandoms e chargeoms en la foi qe vous nous devez qe vous les encreez e faciez ceo quil vous dirront depar nous. E ceo en nule manere ne soit lesse, sicome vous amez loneur de nous. Don' souz nostre prive seal a Gaunt, le v iour de Feverier, lan de nostre regne xxvi.

Les ditz frere Guillame, e mestre Johan, porterent une endenture de leur creaunce en ceste paroles:

---

[1] Immediately preceding this writ, on m. 59, is a writ giving similar instructions to Henry Newark, archbishop-elect of York; and following it is a writ to the sheriff of Yorks., ordering him to assist Henry Newark and John de Lisle.

Frere Guillame de Geynesburgh e mestre Johan Lovel deivent haster tant come il porrunt, qe deniers viegnent pur le paement des Burgignons,[1] e pur deliverer le rei e ses gentz de cest pais. Car il sen partira taunt quil les eit. Item, il dirrount au filz le rei e a son conseil quil facent la suffraunce crier e garder solonc la fourme quil portent ovesques eux. Item, quil facent venir al Escluse iusqes a cent nefs covenables au meins, pur le passage le rei e de ses gentz, au plus tost quil unqes porront.[2] E se hom demande purquei li rois ne maunde nul certein iour, respondi soit quil ne puet, ne ne voet partyr de cest pays, tant quil eit le paement des Burgoignouns, e tant outre, quil peusse deliverer li e ses gentz sicome il devra faire, e qe les nefs soient venues, car il demorra sour le port de son passage, attendant ces choses tant qe eles viegnent. E dient ausint quil affiert a eux de faire savoir au roi le iour qe les deniers e les nefs soient prestz de venir ver ly, e quel iour il entendent quil porrount estre par decea. Car le roi natent autre chose. E veut le roi qe les nefs passageres de Dovre viegnent entre les autres pur porter chevaux, e ke celes e la plus grant partie des autres soient apparailles de cleies e de pontz, e de ceo qe mester serra pur les chevaux. E qe eles ne eent fors qe simple eskipeson de gentz, car il ne covient mie, quil en eent tant come sil deussent aler de guerre. E les ditz frere Guillame e mestre Johan porterent desouz le prive seal le roi le fourme de la trwe la quele est contenu en la roulle precheyn suivaunt, ou en la margine sont ces paroles escrites: Forma sufferencia guerre inter regem Anglie et regem Francie.[3]

E 368/69, m. 53d; E 159/71, m. 21.

194. *Edward, son of Edward I, to his council, 13 February 1298*

Eadward fiuz a noble roy de Engleterre a son consail, saluz. Nus receumes ceo Joedi une lettres que vont a nous e a vous de par nostre seigneur le roy, la quele Robert de Chishull' nostre clerk nous porta, par la quele nous entendom quil y soit bosoignes a faire que demandent tut haste. E receumes ausint par meisme cely une lettre que mestre Jehan Lovel nous envea par la quele nous avom entendu

---

[1] For the payment of the Burgundians, see J. de Sturler, 'Le paiement à Bruxelles des alliés Franc-comtois d'Edouard Ier, roi d'Angleterre (Mai 1297)', *Cahiers Bruxellois*, v (1960), 18–37.

[2] Commissions had already been issued for ships to be collected in Norfolk and Suffolk, to be ready at Sluys by 23 February for the king's passage to England (*C.P.R., 1292–1301*, p. 328). On 15 February the men of Portsmouth were instructed to send ships to Sluys by the first favourable wind, by view of Richard de Kerstan sent to those parts to collect ships. (E 159/71, m. 114).

[3] Details follow of the agreement reached at Tournai on 28 and 31 January: see *Treaty Rolls*, i, 143–5; *Foedera*, I, ii, 885–6.

kil est mester ke nous viegnom a vous pur meisme celes bosoignes.
E si nous dist il de buche qe vous aviez charge Guill' de Bliburgh,
nostre cher clerk, kil nous deist kil fu bien mester qe nous venisom
a vous pur celes bosoignes, par quei nous vous fesom asavoer ke nous
veom estre a Fuleham, si deu plest, ceo Lundi prochein avenir;[1] issint
ke hom ne puisse dire ke les bosoignes nostre seignur le roy preignent
delay par·nostre absence. Nostre seignur vous gard. Don' a Langele
le xiii iur de Fevrer, seuz le seel mon sire Renaud de Grey, par ceo
ke nous navioms mie prestement le nostre.

SC 1/32/61. Original.

195. *Edward I to his son Edward and his council, 20 February 1298*

Edward par la grace de dieu, roy Dengleterre, seigneur Dirlaunde
e ducs Daquitaigne, a Edward nostre chier fiuz, tenant nostre lieu
en Engleterre, e a son consail, saluz. Nous vous[a] enveioms la moustraunce daucuns burgeis de La Rochele enclose denz ces lettres, les
queux puis la suffrance prise entre le roy de France e nous ont perduz
par aucuns des gentz de Portemue une nef qui est appelee la nef Seinte
Marie de Castre en Ordiales[b2] chargee de leur vins a ce qe nous avoms
entendu, sicome plus pleynement est contenuz en la meisme moustraunce. E vous mandoms, sicome avant ces houres vous avoms
mande, e chargeoms especiaument qe enquise la verite de la dite
moustraunce, si trove seit sicome en est contenuz, adonques faciez les
choses redrescier en due maniere au plus en haste qe vous porrez.
Car vous savez bien qe nous sumes tenuz a la restitution, si ce estoit
fait puis la dite souffrance prise. E cestes choses faciez faire si bien
e si reddement qe nostre serment y soit sauvez, e qe ceux qui ont le
damage receu se peussent tenir appaez par reson. Don' souz nostre
prive seal a Gaunt, le xx iour de Feverer, lan de nostre regne vint
e sysime.

SC 1/45/112. Original.

196. *Edward I to his son Edward and his council, or to the chancellor, John
Langton, 24 February 1298*

Edward par la grace de dieu roi Dengleterre, seigneur Dirland
e ducs Daquitain, a Edward nostre chier fiuz, tenant nostre lieu en

---

[a] *Word interlined.*
[b] *MS.* Castre enordiales.

---

[1] 17 February.   [2] Castro Urdiales, Spain, prov. Santander.

Engleterre e a son consail, ou a Johan de Langeton' nostre chancelier, saluz. Nous vous mandoms qe as Galois de Morganno[1] qui ont este ovesque nous en nostre servise, e qui sont ia retornez vers Engleterre par nostre conge, faciez avoir nos lettres overtes de conduit que soient bones e suffisantz parmi les contez ou il passeront, a durer iusques tant quil pussent venir en leur pays. Don' sous nostre prive seal a Gant le xxiiii iour de Feverer, lan de nostre regne xxvi.[2]

SC 1/45/113. Original.

197. *Thomas Paynel to Edward I, February 1298*

A nostre seignour le roy Dengleterre, suen bacheler Thomas Paynel, reverence e honour. Sire, la besoigne de la deliverance mon seignour[3] est delaye plus qe hom ne quidoit, car les marchandz ne se paient point de aver seurte de vous, mes ont refusez tot outre, e demandent seurte del Ercevesqe de Canterbir', e de Everwyk, del abbe de seint Austyn, del prior de Canterbir', del abbe de Westmoster, del abbe de seint Eymon e de lour eglises. Sire, il a aucuns qe grant despit vous ont fait les marchandz qui par seurte de vous en vostre terre demeine ne voilent la chose enprendre. E si les marchandz qui demorent en France se fussent en teu manere portez vers le rey de France, il en preit grandz amendes. Sire, si vous mandissez a sire Johan de Cobe-ham, Johan le Breton e Rauf de Sandwyz trenchant bref quil meissent les merchands a reson du despit quil vous ont fait, e quil les menassent ausi come il ont deservi, ie entenk qe par tant se avancereit la bosoigne, car par beel ne ferront il rien. Sire, vostre volunte, si vous plest, me mandez, car ie entenk cy tant qe aye de vous autre mande-ment. A deu, sire, qui vous doint bone vie e longe.

E 159/71, m. 20d; E 368/69, m. 57d.

198. *Edward I to the barons of the exchequer, 23 February 1298*

Edward par la grace deu etc. Nous avoms entendu par unes lettres qe mons' Thomas Paynel dount le transescrit est enclos dedenz cestes, coment aucuns marchanz demoranz a Londres ount refuse tot outre de faire nostre requeste qe nous leur feismes faire nad gueres, endreit

---

[1] Morgannwg, Glam.

[2] Similar letters were sent on behalf of the men of North Wales and West Wales (SC 1/45/114, 115). The strength of this particular contingent was nine constables and 900 foot (B.L., Add. MS. 7965, fo. 83).

[3] John de St John appointed Thomas Paynel his attorney on 5 October 1296 (E 159/70, m. 75d).

de meinprendre la somme qe est acordee sour la deliverance mons'
Johan de seint Johan e en ont grossement respondu, la quele response
nous tenoms estre faite en despit e en grant vuente de nous, si el seit
faite sicome est contenu en transescrit avantdit. Dont nous vous mandoms fermement enioinanz qe si ensi est, adonqes entre vous e mons'
Johan le Breton, gardein de la Cite, e mons' Rauf de Sandwyz, nostre
conestable de la Tour de Londres, a queux nous avoms semblablement mande par nos lettres, faciez venir devant vous a aucun certeine
iour touz iceux marchandz qe ont respondu a nostre dite requeste
en la manere avantdite, e qui en seent cupables, si les faciez chastier
e punir si reddement e en teu manere qe le despit e le utrage quel
nous ont faitz en cele partie seit bien e hautement amendez, par quei
eux e autres marchanz peussent estre chastiez e avoir doute de faire
tieux responses a les requestes qe nous leur ferroms par aventure apres
ces houres en cas semblable ou en autre. Don' souz nostre prive seal
a Gaunt le xxiii iour de Feverer, lan de nostre regne xxvi.

E 159/71, m. 20d; E 368/69, m. 57d.

199. *Exchequer memorandum on a case of smuggling, Hilary 1298*

Memorandum quod Henricus Darderne attachiatus in partibus
Flandrie pro transgressione facta regi de lanis per ipsum ductis ab
Anglia sine custuma venit coram W. Coventr' et Lich' episcopo,
domini regis thesaurario, in partibus predictis, et recognovit transgressiones subscriptas; videlicet quod idem Henricus transducere fecit
a portu London' usque partes Flandrie in navi Finche de Colecestr'
in comitiva flote regis versus dictas partes x saccos lane Johannis
Bokerell' de Dowaco sine coketto et absque custuma inde regi solvenda, et recepit de dicto Johanne xl solidos de quolibet sacco ad opus
suum proprium pro custuma, ac si talem custumam regi solvisset. Et
quod transducta fuerunt in eadem navi dicto tempore duo dolea ad
vinum reneis' plena lokettis que fuerunt Johannis Golde, socii dicti
Henrici, sine custuma regi inde solvenda. Et quod pro xx solidos quos
idem Henricus recepit de Roberto de Wendlesworth ut lanam suam
transducere faceret sine custuma, idem Henricus transducere fecit in
eadem navi eodem tempore ii saccos et i poketto lane predicti Roberti
sine custuma inde regi solvenda. Item recognovit quod Thomas de
Bolonia in sua propria navi eodem tempore transducere fecit a dicto
portu vi pokettos de propria lana dicti Thome sine custuma inde regi
solvenda. Et quod idem Thomas plura talia facta fecit. Et quod
Johannes Golde socius dicti Henrici transducere fecit in eadem navi
dicto tempore i saccum de propria lana ipsius Johannis sine custuma
inde regi solvenda. Item idem Henricus recognovit quod ipse ad

Pentecosten anno xxv^{to} transducere fecit a dicto portu London'
versus dictas partes in navi Johannis de Bolonia iiii saccos lane Claii de
la Porte absque custuma et coketto, et recepit de dicto Claio xl solidos
pro quolibet sacco ad opus suum proprium. Et quod ipse transducere
fecit in eadem navi et eodem tempore i saccum lane et i saccum de
lokettis de propria lana ipsius Henrici et nichil solvit regi pro custuma.
Postea, in redditu dicti thesaurarii ad partes Anglie, idem Henricus
super hoc allocutus in scaccario recognovit omnes transgressiones predictas prout superius annotatur. Et ideo consideratum est quod libere-
tur prisone de Flete. Postea predictus Henricus fecit finem cum regi
pro xx marcis pro transgressione predicta, de quibus solvet regi ad
Pascha proximo futuro x marcas, et ad festum sancti Michaelis proximo sequentem v marcas, et ad Natale Domini proximo futurum v
marcas. Et ad dictas xx marcas terminis predictis solvendas idem Henricus invenit manucaptores predictos, videlicet Willelmum Darnerne
qui manucepit pro x marcis. Postea solvit iiii^{or} *li*. x *s*. per i talliam
de scaccario.[1]

E 159/71, m. 82d. Printed with some omissions in H. Hall, *A History
of the Customs-Revenue in England* (London, 1885), ii, 40–1.

200. *Edward I to his son Edward and his council, 1 March 1298*

Edward par la grace de dieu etc. a Edward nostre chier fiuz, tenaunt
nostre lieu en Engleterre e a soen^a conseil, saluz. Nous vous enveoms
une escrowete e un roulle encloz denz ces lettres, en les queux est contenu qe les burgeis de Bruges e aucuns autres du poer le roi de France
ont perduz aucunes niefs par aucuns de nos gentz Dengleterre e de
Baion, chargees de lur biens, sicome pleus pleinement est contenuez
en le meisme escrowete e roule. E vous mandoms e chargeons especiaument qe enqise saunt delai sur ceo la verite si trove soit sicome
en est contenuz, adonqes facez les choses redrescer en due manere
au plus tost en haste qe vous purrez. Car vous savez bien qe nous
sumes tenuz a la restitucion, si ce estoit fait puis la suffrance prise.
E ceste choses faciez faire si bien e si reddement qe nostre serment
y seit sauvez, e qe ceux qi unt la damage receu se puissent tenir apaez
par reseon. Don' souz nostre prive seal a Erdenbourgh le primer iour
de Marz, lan de nostre regne vint e sisime.[2]

E 159/71, m. 24.

^a *MS*. seon.

---

[1] For an earlier report of alleged non-payment of customs, after Easter 1297, see
E 159/70, m. 28.
[2] The detailed complaints of the merchants follow in the memoranda roll.

201. *Proceedings regarding wool seized at Haverford, 4 March 1298*

Walterus de Hakelute' custos regis ville et castri suorum de Haverford' cum pertinenciis modo videlicet iiii die Martii veniens hic sua petitione que invenietur inter inquisitiones hic retornatas anno presenti, thesaurario et baronibus monstravit quod, cum rex assignasset dilectos et fideles suos Robertum le Veel et Walterum de Pederton' ad lanas et salita coria capienda ad opus regis in Westwellia ad pascha proximo preteritum predicti Robertus et Walterus pretextu assignationis illius ceperunt in partibus predictis xxxii saccas, xix petras et dimidiam petram lane appreciatas ad iiii^{xx} *li.* xlviii *s.* viii *d.*, et iii lestas xvi dacras coriorum et xi coria appreciatas ad xli *li.* viii *d.*, et lanam et coria illa liberarunt Stephano de Castro Martini et Roberto Cas custodibus custume regis in portu de Milford' pertinente ad Haverford', in quorum custodia adhunc existunt, et petiit pro rege certiorari quid thesaurarius et barones vellent inde fieri ; quo petito, ipsi thesaurarius et barones vehementer admirati de eo quod lana et coria illa per tantum tempus fuerunt detenta, maxime cum ordinatum fuerat in captione predicta quod lane et coria in partibus predictis et alibi ad terminum predictum capta a tempore captionis eorundem sine mora ad partes transmarinas fuissent transmissa, et in eisdem partibus custodibus lanarum regis liberata, et etiam de eo quod dictus Walterus ipsos thesaurarium et barones prius inde certiorare non curavit, maxime cum predicta diutina detentio in dampnum regis cedere videtur ; ipsum Walterum inde posuerunt ad rationem, qui dixit quod tempore captionis lanarum et coriorum predictorum non extitit ballivus de Haverford', nec magno tempore post, set H. de Cressingham qui nuper obiit, unde dicit pro memorata diutina detentione merito culpari non debet, tamen dicit se modo venire fecisse hic Johannem Cokay et Ricardum le Parmenter de balliva sua de Haverford', paratos ad lanas et coria illa emenda. Et super hoc thesaurarius et barones adinvicem consulentes concordarunt quod lane et coria illa vendantur. Et incontinenti, inspecta indentura per dictos Robertum le Veel et Walterum de Pederton' nuper hic liberata de captione predicta, comperta est in eadem summa lanarum et coriorum qualiter supradicitur in peticione supradicta et eodem modo appreciata ut supra. Et eo comperto thesaurarius et barones concesserunt dictis Johanni Cokay et Ricardo le Parmenter quod habeant lanam et coria predicta per precium supradictum, cuius summa est cxxiii *li.* ix *s.*, ita quod ultra idem precium reddant regi xl marcas. Et sic est summa totalis cl *li.* ii *s.* iiii *d.* Et iidem Johannes et Ricardus instanter concesserunt se teneri domino regi in illis cl *li.* ii *s.* iiii *d.* pro lanis et coriis predictis habendis. Et concessum est eis quod solvant inde unam medietatem ad festum nativitatis sancti Johannis Baptiste proximo

futurum,[1] et aliam medietatem ad festum sancti Egidii proximo sequentem.[2] Et mandatum est custodibus custume supradicte quod lanas et coria predicta prefatis Johanni et Ricardo liberent indilate habenda ut predictum est.

E 368/69, m. 50; E 159/71, m. 29.

202. *Memorandum on the ransom of John de St John, 7 March 1298*

Cum dilectus et fidelis regis Johannes de Sancto Johanne, senescallus ipsius regis in ducatu suo Aquitanie, in conflictu nuper in partibus illis habito inter fideles dicti regis in eisdem partibus existentes, et alios de potestate regis Francie, nomine ipsius ibidem venientes ad dictum regem Anglie de ducatu predicto vi exheredandum, captus esset, et ad prisonam dicti regis Francie ductus, in qua detinetur, ac inter dictum regem Anglie in partibus transmarinis agentem, pro guerra inter ipsum et prefatum regem Francie ob predictum ducatum suborta, sustinenda et exequenda, [et regem Francie] concordetur sufferencia vel guerre predicte abstinencia, videlicet a festo Epiphanie domini proximo preterito per biennium proximo sequens et completum. Et quod interim dictus Johannes a prisona memorata deliberetur in hac forma que subsequitur, videlicet quod mercatores societatum transmarinarum in cismarinis partibus conversantes manucapiant dicto regi Francie teneri in viginti milibus libris tornesiorum nigrorum, valentibus v. milia librarum sterlingorum, solvendis post lapsum sufferencie predicte, nisi eadem prorogetur vel super guerra predicta interim contingat pax finaliter formari, vel, quod absit, prefatum Johannem viam universe carnis ingredi, vel quod corpus dicti Johannis prisone predicte restituatur in fine sufferencie predicte, nisi illa ut premittitur prorogari contingat, ac etiam dominus rex Anglie maxime ut tenetur affectans pro fideli obsequio dicti Johannis ipsius deliberationem ut est dictum minime differri, set fieri festinanter, mandavit thesaurario et baronibus quod huiusmodi mercatores coram eis vocarent et ex parte sua sibi premissa exponerent; quibus vocatis ut predicitur, venerunt nolentes summam pecunie predictam manucapere nullo modo, nisi a viris religiosis sufficientibus ad dicte summe pecunie solucionem obligationem sufficientem optinerent. Thesaurariusque et barones, considerantes viam celeriorem non esse, qua expeditio negotii istius celerius fieret, quomodo providere securitatem fieri prefatis mercatoribus in forma prepetita, per eosdem concordarunt quod abbates Westm', Waltham', Sancti Albani et Evesham mandentur veniendi hic die Lune proxima ante festum sancti

[1] 24 June 1298.   [2] 1 September 1298.

Gregorii pape, et abbas sancti Edmundi et abbas de Burgo sancti Petri die sabbati proxima post festum predictum, audituri et facturi ea qua iidem thesaurarius et barones eis exponerent ex parte regis super premissis. Quo concordato, mandatum est dictis abbatibus quod veniant hic in forma supradicta. Teste thesaurario, vii die Marcii. Postea predictus abbas Westm' venit hic et gratanter concessit.

E 368/69, m. 55; E 159/71, m. 21d.

203. *Ordinance for redress of grievances, 4 April 1298*

Come le rey avant son passage vers Flandres eust volente e desir de fere redrescier e amender les grevances faites a son pueple en nun de lui, e suz ce envoiast ses lettres par tous les contees Dengleterre por ceste chose mettre en effect; ordene est par lui e son conseil qe en chescun contee soient assignes qatre, ce est asavoir deus chevalers, des queus le un serra mis par lui e lautre *serra pris* du conte, un clerk e un homme de religion qui seient bone e leaus e bien avises por enquerire de tous maneres des grevances, come des choses prises hors de seinte eglise, des prises de leynes, peaus, quirs, blez, bestes, charz, peyssons e de totes autres maneres des choses *parmi le reaume des clers e des lais* puis la gerre comencie entre le rey de France e lui, fust ce por garde de la mer ou en autre manere. E enqueriront meismes ceaus par queus e as queus e de quant e de combien e de la value e coment e en queu manere ices prises e grevances furent faites au pueple. E ceus assignes eient plein pouer de enquerire, oir e terminer ausi bien par office come a suite de partie. E qant la matere de ces choses serra ateinte, le quel qe ce seit, par garant ou sans garant, ce qe serra pris sans garant seit retorne a ceaus qe la damage ont receu, si le tortz fesantz eient de quei, e outre ce puni por le trespas. E si il neient de quei, ceaus as queus les garants e les commissions sont venus come vyscontes, clerks assignes, baillifs e autres tiels maneres de ministres respoignent por lor souzmis qui averont fait telz prises. E qe de ce qe serra trove*b* par garant le rey soit certifie a ce en fera tant qe il sentendront apaie par reson.

[Dorse]
[First column]

Fiant commissiones ad exequendum istud negotium infrascriptis personis.
Domino Johanni de Insula in comitatibus
Lincoln'   Adiungatur sibi dominus Thomas de Snetterton'

---

a ... a Passage interlined.   *b Word interlined.*

Rotland'
Northampton'
Nottingham'ᵃ
Derb'ᵃ
Norff'   episcopo Norwyc' sibi
Suff'

Domino Willelmo de Den in comitatibus
Essex'   adiungatur dicto domino W. dominus Rogerus Brian
Hertford'   Middelsex, Lond' episcopo
Cantebreg'   Elyensi
Huntindon'   Lincoln' episcopo, similiter de Hertf'

Domino Willelmo de Ormesbyᵃ ᵇdominus. J. de Baukewell' loco militisᵇ
    in comitatibus
Kanc'   adiungatur dicto J. de Baukwell', dominus J. Sauvage
Sussex'   Cicestr' episcopo
Surr'   episcopo Wynton'
Suthampton' et Wilton'   episcopo Sarum

Domino Johanni Randulf' in comitatibus
Wilt'ᵃ Berk'   episcopo Sarum
Somerset'   Bathon'
Dors'   adiungatur dominus Ricardus de Coleshill', dominus
                    J. Randulf
Devon   episcopo Exon'
Cornub'

[Second column]

Dominus Willelmo Trussel'ᵃ   Domino Ade de Crokedey
Dominus Nicholas Fermbaudᵃ in comitatibus
Glouc'   episcopo Wigorn'
Wigorn'   adiungatur sibi dominus Robertus de Knyttele
Hereford'   Hereford' episcopo
Salop'   Cestr' episcopo
Stafford'

Domino Willelmo de Sancto Quintino in comitatibus
Ebor'   electo Ebor'
Lancastr'   adiungatur sibi dominus Petrus Bocard
Nottingham'   episcopo Coventr'
Derby   episcopo Coventr'

Domino Johanni de Burn' in comitatibus
Bokyngham

ᵃ *Words printed in italics are cancelled in the manuscript.*
ᵇ...ᵇ *Passage interlined.*

Bedeford   adiungatur sibi dominus Johannes de Wyleby
Oxon'
Berk'   episcopo Linc'
Leyc'
Warwyk   episcopo Coventr'   *Cantebr'*[a]

Predicti milites assignantur ad premissa facienda, una cum clericis et religiosis quos episcopi singulos dicti duxerint deputandos, et super hoc ex parte regis scribantur eisdem episcopis.[1]

C 49/2/26. Draft. The first paragraph was printed by J. F. Baldwin, *The King's Council during the Middle Ages* (Oxford, 1913), p. 465.

204. *Edward I to the barons of the exchequer, 26 April 1298*

Cum rex nuper ob aliquas certas causas temporalia archiepiscopatus Cantuariensis capi fecerit in manum suam et exitus de temporalibus eisdem per ministros regis tunc ad ipsorum temporalium custodiam deputatus ad opus regis sunt levati, ut rex accepit; rex venerabili patri R. Cantuariensis archiepiscopo volens in hac parte gratiam facere specialem, mandat baronibus quod vocatis coram eis ministris predictis, et audito compoto eorundem de tempore quo dicta temporalia sit in manibus regis erant prefato archiepiscopo tantam pecunie summam, quantam eis evidenter constiterit ad opus regis levatam[b] fuisse de dictis temporalibus tempore supradicto, in debitis que nobis debet ad scaccarium predictum allocent. Teste rege apud Sanctum Albanum xxvi die Aprilis, anno regni nostri xxvi.[2]

E 368/69, mm. 74d, 76.

---

[a] *Words printed in italics are cancelled in the manuscript.*
[b] *Followed by* esse, *struck out.*

---

[1] Commissions in accordance with this memorandum were issued on 4 April 1298 (*C.P.R., 1292–1301*, p. 338). In these William Inge and John de Cokefield replaced John de Lisle and Thomas de Snetterton, although in the letters sent to the bishops the latter were specified (*C.C.R., 1296–1302*, pp. 204–5). See also *C.P.R. 1292–1301*, p. 354, where on 17 June Cokefield was replaced by Richard de Walsingham. For further details of these proceedings, and an edition of the record of the inquest for Lincolnshire, see *A Lincolnshire Assize Roll for 1298*. Appendix 1, p. 136, contains a transcript of the ordinance from the Patent Roll. The clause defining those who are to make the enquiry is omitted, and there are in addition several minor changes.

[2] Details follow (E 368/69, m. 76) of the account of William Trussel, sheriff of Kent, who was charged with £400 profits from the archbishop's manors, and with prises of grain and timber totalling £547 5s. 2d. Some of the grain had been taken before the lands had been taken into the king's hands, however, and payment of £80 in alms was allowed in the account, leaving £447 10s. 2d. to be credited against Winchelsey's debts.

205. *Edward I to the treasurer, 11 May 1298*

Edward par la grace de dieu etc., a honurable peere en dieu W.
par la meisme grace evesqe de Cestre[1] e de Lichefeld, nostre tresorier,
salutz. Nous vous enveoms par mons' Thomas Paynel les nouns des
abbez Dengleterre qui nous resqueismes nadgueres sur la bosoigne
mons' Johan de seint Johan, sicome bien savez. E vous maundoms
qe a ceux qui ont responduz soiez auxsi gracious, favorable e deboniers
en tutes les busoignes quil averont a faire devers vous come vous porrez
par reson. E as autres, voloms qe vous faciez droit saunz nule grace
du munde. Done souz nostre prive seal a Culeford,[2] le xi iour de May,
lan de nostre regne vint e sisme.

Les nouns des abbez qui ont bien respondu a la volunte le roy, e
as queux veut le rei faire tote manere de grace, cest asavoir labbe
de Glastingbur', le abbe de Weymonster, labbe de Burg' seint Peere,
labbe de Evesham e labbe de seint Eymon.

Les nons des abbez qui ne voillent en nule manere faire la volunte
le roy endreit de la deliverance de sire Johan de seint Johan, as queux
le rei ne veut faire qe commune ley, cest asavoir labbe de Rammeshey,
labbe de Abindon', labbe de Wautham, labbe de seint Auban e labbe
de la Hide.[3]

E 159/71, m. 43; E 368/69, m. 78.

206. *Memorandum on the delivery of jewels pledged for a loan in Brabant,
16 May 1298*

Memorandum quod septimo die Aprilis anno regni regis Edwardi
xxvi[to] apud Westm' iniunctum fuit ex parte domini regis Roberto de
Segre clerico et Elye Russel de London' per venerabilem patrem W.
dei gratia Coventr' et Lich' episcopum, thesaurarium, et Johannem
de Drokenesford', custodem garderobe regis, ad proficiscendum[a] ad

---

[a] proficissendum *in* E 368/69.

[1] Although his proper title was bishop of Coventry and Lichfield, Walter Langton
was frequently also styled bishop of Chester. See no. 97.
[2] Culford, Suffolk.
[3] For a letter of obligation by the abbot of St Peter's, Gloucester, see C 47/13/94.
Orders to the houses to pay the money to six Italian companies were issued in 1306.
The full list of monasteries was: Evesham, 500 marks; Glastonbury, 1,000 marks; Gloucester, 300 marks; Peterborough, 500 marks; Westminster, £500; Reading, 500 marks;
St Mary's, York, 500 marks; Selby, 300 marks; Whitby, 400 marks; Bridlington, £100;
Guisborough, £100; Kirkham, 200 marks; Newburgh, £100; Nostell, 100 marks (E
159/79, mm. 35, 35d). For financial assistance for the release of hostages provided by
alien houses, see E 159/71, mm. 34, 34d, where in return for guarantees of 3,000 and
1,000 *livres tournois* respectively, Meremoutier and Holy Trinity, Caen, were restored
their confiscated English lands.

partes Brabantie pro quibusdam negociis regis specialibus. Et dictus Johannes liberavit eisdem Roberto et Elie quedam scripta confecta super jocalibus regis per dictum Johannem invadiatis per preceptum regis Henrico de Mercato mercatori ducis Brabancie, Opetino Guaretto et aliis Lumbardis mercatoribus ad deferendum cum ipsis ad partes transmarinas pro deliberacione eorundem jocalium ibidem habenda, videlicet quoddam scriptum indentatum inter dictum Johannem et dictos mercatores de dictis jocalibus sic invadiatis, et forma super hoc facta, una cum alia indentura procuratoria et patentibus litteris, prout patet in quadam indentura eisdem inde liberata per predictum Johannem. Qui quidem Robertus et Elias accedentes usque Brusseles predicta jocalia de predictis mercatoribus per satisfactionem eisdem confectam receperunt et liberaverunt eisdem mercatoribus quoddam scriptum procuratorium factum eisdem Roberto et Elye sub pupplico instrumento sigillis dictorum Dunelmensis et Coventr' et Lich' episcoporum ac dicti Johanni sigillatum, et duas litteras patentes sigillo ducis Brabantie signatas receperunt, quas iidem mercatores cancelarunt ab eisdem mercatoribus quamdam indenturam sub hiis verba: Memorandum quod die Jovis tertio die mensis Octobris anno domini millesimo ducentesimo nonagesimo septimo apud Andwerp' in Brabantia conventum fuit inter dominum Johannem de Drokenesford' custodem garderobe illustris regis Anglie in presencia dominorum Johannis de Benestede et Johannis de Hustwayt clericorum eiusdem domini regis ex parte una, presente Henrico de Mercato, Lumbardo, mercatore ducis Brabancie necnon, et Oppetinum Guarettum, Waletum de le Cheyn, Bartholomeum de Jasse et Gandulphum de Al', mercatores de Ast, Lumbardos, ex altera parte, videlicet quod idem Johannes de Drokenesford' et socii sui supradicti tradiderunt dicto Henrico et mercatoribus antedictis nomine pignoris jocalia infrascripta super quadem summa pecunie quatuor milium sexcentarum librarum turonensium nigrorum parvorum appreciata ad dictorum mercatorum estimationem voluntariam, quamquam precium huiusmodi ad medietatem seu ad terciam partem veri valoris ipsorum jocalium nullatenus se extendat. Et sunt jocalia ... *[a lengthy inventory follows, concluding with]* Item i. capellum largum quod fuit quondam unius regine operatum et coopertum grossis perlis et auro et lapidibus preciosis apreciatum ad M. libras turonensium nigrorum, quod quidem capellum morari debet apud Brussell' in custodia dicti Henrici de Mercato, mercatoris ducis Brabancie, et est in quodam vase ligneo cooperto de corio, nec debet mitti usque Lieges nec alibi cum jocalibus supradictis secundum preceptum et ordinacionem eiusdem ducis, unde summa totalis predictorum jocalium sic per predictos Henricum et Oppetinum appreciatorum ad septem milia et quindecim libras turonensium nigrorum

parvorum extendit. Et mercatores predicti dicta jocalia absque alicuius illius diminucione seu detrimento sane custodient atque salve,
satisfactoque mercatoribus de Ast predictis vel attornatis ipsorum de
quatuor milibus et trescentis libris turonensium nigrorum parvorum
vel alterius monete valoris eiusdem abhuc usque ad primum diem
mensis Januarii, iidem mercatores jocalia suprascripta integraliter
sane ac salve sine diminucione quacumque restituent dicto Johanni
de Drokenesford' vel dicto Roberto[a] predicte garderobe custodi qui
pro tempore fuerit, aut ipsius custodis in hac parte specialiter assig-
nato, nec ultro exigent pecuniam aliqualem. Et si dicto primo die
mensis Januarii de summa predicta quatuor milium et trescentarum
librarum turonensium nigrorum parvorum mercatoribus prenom-
inatis minime fuerit satisfactum et in ipsorum mercatorum manibus
ipsa priuscripta jocalia, capello excepto predicto, remanere contin-
gant usque ad primum diem mensis Aprilis instantis proximo, extunc
habeat custos predictus dictis mercatoribus satisfacere de quatuor
milibus et sexcentis libris turonensium nigrorum parvorum, aut
alterius monete valoris eiusdem. Et si postmodum post primum diem
mensis Aprilis ultra remaneant ipsa jocalia per tres menses in manibus
dictorum mercatorum, liceat eisdem mercatoribus inpignorare
jocalia pro tantundem pecunia librarum, videlicet in septimana qualibet predictorum trium mensium pro duobus turonensis parvis. Et
si ipsa jocalia post dictos tres menses ulterius remaneant, liceat extunc
mercatoribus antedictis ipsa jocalia velud propria vendere ac etiam
alienare pro sue libito voluntatis. Factisque solucionibus suprascriptis
in forma premissa et moneta prescripta vel in alia equivalenti monete
tradite in hac parte iidem mercatores teneantur ipsa jocalia omnia
et singula restituere ut premittitur cum quadam littera obligatoria
dictis mercatoribus in hac parte confecta sigillis dictorum ducis
Brabancie et domini Johannis de Drokenesford' suprascripti cance-
landa in eventum satisfaccionis suprascripte. Super hiis autem fiunt
due littere cirograffate, quarum una residet penes dominum Johannem de Drokenesford' prenotatum, et altera penes predictos mercatores ipsiusque transcriptum cirographatum penes Henricum pre-
scriptum que etiam restituentur cum premissis jocalibus cancelate que
jocalia suprascripta tenetur mercatores de Ast, capello excepto predicto restituere quod penes dictum Henricum nomine pignoris
remaneat cum jocalibus antedictis in eventum satisfaccionis faciende
dictis mercatoribus in hac parte. Et predicta indentura sic cancelata
remanet in custodia dictorum camerariorum, et alia pars dicte indenture similiter cancelate remanet penes dictos Robertum et Eliam,
et tertia pars eiusdem remanet penes dictum Henricum de Mercato,
ut iidem Robertus et Elias dicunt. Premissis itaque peractis, predicti

[a] *MS.* Rogero.

Robertus et Elias cum predictis jocalibus redientes in Angliam venerunt ad scaccarium die Veneris in crastino ascensionis domini xvi die Maii, anno regni regis Edwardi xxvi^{to}, predicto domino W. Coventr' et Lich' episcopo et camerariis de eodem scaccario iocalia predicta contenta in uno scrineo rubeo, uno circulo lingneo et quodam vase ligneo coperto de coreo sub sigillis Ade le Convers aurifabri regis et Coppe Cotenni mercatoris Friscobaldorum et Henrici de Mercato mercatoris ducis Brabantie, ut dicti Robertus et Elias asserebant. Et eadem jocalia in scriniis et vasiis sic sigillata liberata fuerunt dictis camerariis custodienda in thesauro regis in Turrim London', predicto xvi die Maii quousque alias super hoc fuerit ordinatum.[1]

E 159/71, m. 36; E 368/69, m. 76d.

207. *Petition from the burgesses of Cardigan, May 1298*

A nostre seignor le rei si luy plest ses burgeys de Cardigan prient sa grace de ce qe vos ministres ount arestuz nos leynes e nos quirs par vostre comandement, sicum nous entendoms, au quel resteiement, trescher seignor, vous prioms remedie e vostre grace. E tant plus tost, cher seignor, qe nostre estat est enfebliz e enpoverez par diverses guerres come vous le savez, e pur ce, cher seignor, qe les uns de nous autres marchandises navoms fors solement en les leynes e les quirs qui sunt arestuz, qui ne amonte utre entre nous touz forsqe xxxiii livers. E si vous plest, trescher seignor, de ceste chose voillez faire vostre grace pur nous poures burgeis qui tant sumes destruz. E si autre grace ne puissoms aver de vous qe vous, trescher seignor, si vous plest nous voillez regranter qe nous seioms plus pres a nostre petit chatel qe autres estraunges a mesme le jour qe vos ministres les ount taxez.[2]

E 368/69, m. 70; E 159/71, m. 37d. Printed by Hall, *History of the Customs-Revenue*, ii, 181.

[1] The initial negotiations for this loan were carried out by Hugh Bush, and the sum actually borrowed was 4,000 *livres tournois*, which was brought by the merchants from Liège to Brussels (B.L., Add. MS. 7965, fos. 22v, 31). Repayment by the Frescobaldi on Edward I's behalf was 5,140 *livres tournois*, or approximately £1,290 (E 101/126/13, 15; C 47/13/1/28). The rate of interest works out at 28·5 per cent, or approximately 42 per cent p.a. Letters patent of the duke of Brabant are in Exchequer Warrants for Issue, E 404/481/2, no. 12. See Fryde, 'Financial Resources of Edward I in the Netherlands', 1178.

[2] This petition was sent to the king at Fulham, and was forwarded by him to the treasurer on 5 May 1298. It was discovered that at Easter 1297 wool had been seized at Cardigan to a total value of £9 19s. 10d., and hides to a value of £15 2s. od. Orders were issued to the keepers of the customs at Haverford to allow the men of Cardigan to have their wool and hides returned to them in full (E 159/71, m. 37d).

208. *Petition from the community of the realm to Edward I, 1297 or 1307*

A nostre seignur le roi e a son conseil, prient les bones gentz de sa terre qe come nostre seignur le roi aveit fait crier lan xxv qe chescun home, qui leynes eust, les feist carier as certeins lieus a lendemayn de Paskes, lan xxv avauntdit, sur forfeture des leynes, e quil trovereient marchauntz qui les achatereient. A quel iour le roi fist prendre a son oeps totes les dites leynes cariees, e en fist tailles saunz rien paier. E les leynes qe ne furent nient cariees fist il auxi prendre auxi come forfaites, e nules tailles nen feurent faites. Par quei il prient qe cele forfeture seit pardonee, e qe le roi face gree de celes leynes auxi come des autres, solonc ceo qe serra trove par roulles des prenurs qe sont a lescheqer.

Dorse

Rex perdonat forisfacturam, et vult quod satisfiat de lanis sic captis sicut apparere poterit per rotulos captorum, qui sunt ad scaccarium, non obstante quod non fuerunt cariate, et quod illi, quorum lane ille fuerunt, tallias inde non habent.[1]

Ancient Petitions, SC 8, no. 3808. Original. Printed by G. L. Haskins, 'Three Early Petitions of the Commonalty', *Speculum*, xii (1937), 316–17.

[1] This petition was dated by Haskins ('Three Early Petitions of the Commonalty', 318) as 1297, for he assumed that it formed the basis for the pardons from the forfeiture of wool which were issued in May and June 1297 (*C.C.R.*, *1296–1302*, pp. 33, 35). These, however, were issued on an individual basis, and it seems unlikely that they were inspired by this document. T. H. Lloyd has argued more plausibly that the petition was presented in 1307, and that the pardon and promise of payment issued on 20 June 1307 resulted from it (Lloyd, *English Wool Trade*, pp. 95, 325; *C.C.R.*, *1302–07*, pp. 504–5).

APPENDIX

The events of 1297 according to the Hagnaby Chronicle

Anno regis Eduuardi xxv°, [exstitit] papa Bonifacius vii[i], archiepiscopus Cant' Robertus de Winchelse, episcopus Lincoln' Oliverus.
Hoc anno comes de Hoyland' desponsavit filiam regis Anglie, nomine
Elizabeth, dominica infra Epiphaniam domini.[1] Nova sunt quod die
mercurii proxima ante festum Purificacionis Virginis gloriose[2] fuit
bellum in Wasconia inter nostros et Francos, in quo nostri succu-
buerunt ac quibusdam militibus captis et quibusdam interfectis seu
submersis, magna permultitudine aliorum torruente fugam ceteri in-
ierunt et se Baiona receperunt. Nomina militum captorum sunt hec:
dominus Johannes de Sancto Johanne seniore, Willelmus de Mortuo
Mari, Johannes de Rois, Willelmus de Burnigham, Adam de Hudles-
ton, Thomas de Morse, Reginaldus de Noers, Reynerus de la Warde,
Willelmus de Suleie, Willelmus de Ponteine, Gerardus de la Spineie
ac Henricus de Schadwrd.[3] Submersi sunt dominus Jacobus de Bello
Campo, germanus domini comitis Warwik', qui in diocesi Lincoln'
clericus beneficiatus existens, arma militaria sumpserat, clericali
milicia derelicta, et Phillippus de Matilden.[4] Dicitur atque eodem
die dominus rex, audito cleri responso, illum de sua protectione sus-
pendit. Dicitur atque in illo bello iiii^or mille hominum corruerunt
de nostris. Post Purificacionis tenuit rex apud London' concilium ubi
sicut prius petiit a clero auxilium, sed respondit archiepiscopus pro
clero se nichil daturus sine speciali licencia domini pape. Rex mandavit vicecomitibus Anglie ut nullus in baliva sua sineret aliquam personam religiosorem seu personam ecclesiasticam terram operare sive
seminare nisi concederent domino regi quintam partem omnium
bonorum et ut quilibet haberet protectionem domini regis citra Pasca
sequens. In hoc concilio iussit rex omnes equos archiepiscopi detineri.
Congregatio prelatorum et cleri erat in medio quadragesime, ad
quam Lincoln' episcopus personaliter est citatus, et per eum omnes
abbates [et] priores sue diocesis quod ipsi personaliter suarumque
ecclesiarum capitula seu conventes per procuratores idoneos, et clerus
per unum procuratorem dictis die et loco convenerint de statu ecclesie
anglicane et regni una cum domino archiepiscopo tractaturi.

---

[1] 6 January 1297. The marriage in fact took place on 7 January (*Foedera*, I, ii, 850).
[2] 30 January 1297.
[3] This list is very similar to that provided by *Cotton, Historia Anglicana*, p. 319, though
he does not include Reyner de la Warde.
[4] *Cotton, Historia Anglicana*, p. 319, makes no mention of James de Beauchamp, and
states that Philip de Matesdon was killed, and that Alan de Tuycham and his son
were drowned.

Item post Pasca mandavit rex vicecomitibus Anglie ut uni-
usquisque in baliva sua caperet ad opus suum frumentum et avena
ubicumque inventa fuerant, boves et porcos et caseum, necnon et
carnes bovinas et porcias, et congregarent ad mare apud Portism' in
expedicionem domini regis in Wasconia.

Eodem tempore dominus Walterus de Langeton mandavit domino
regi nomina principum et numerum equorum armatorum de diversis
terris quos ad opus suum conduxerat. In primis, comes Flandrie cum
tribus milibus pungnatoribus, comes de Hoyland cum tribus milibus
pungnatoribus, dux de Braban cum iii. milibus pungnatoribus, comes
de Gerls cum ii. milibus pungnatoribus. Iidem iam destruxerunt mag-
nam partem Campanie, et ibidem lucratus est xl. milia marcarum
argenti. Rex Alemanie cum x. milibus pungnatoribus, episcopus
Colonie et episcopus de Legis cum iiii. milibus pungnatoribus, comes
de Bar cum ii. milibus pungnatoribus, comes de Sauvey cum v.
milibus pungnatoribus, comes de Hermaunde[a] cum iiii[or] c. pungnatoribus, xii. comites et barones de Burgundia qui morantur cum rege
habent m. et vc. pungnatores, dominus Elyas de Campania cum l.
pungnatoribus. Summa xxviii[m]. iiii[c]. l. pungnatores.[1] Hii omnes in
adventu regis in Flandriam defecerunt.

Item post festum sancti Johanni Baptiste tenuit rex concilium apud
London' ubi petiit a populo auxilium, scilicet ix partem omnium
bonorum, qui sub obtentu carte libertatum Anglie et foreste eidem
concesserit. Precepit igitur rex comitibus, baronibus et omnibus de
se tenentibus ut essent parati cum armis in assumpcione beate Virginis
ad transfretandum cum eo in Wasconia.[2] Qui responderunt se nullatenus cum eo transfretare propriis sumptibus, quorum primus erat
comes Marschall' et comes Herefordie, ob quam causam privavit
comitem Marschall' de baliva qua de se habuit, et discordes discus-
serunt, cartam vero tunc non confirmavit.

Rex vero constituit dominum Reginaldum de Gray custodem
Anglie et filiim suim Edwardi, et circa festum sancti Bartholomei[3]
cum paucis transfretavit in Flandriam, quo honorifice susceptus est
a comite et devenit in civitatem quam vocatur Gaunt cum suis.
Interim comites et barones consilium habuerunt cum filio regis et
domino Reginaldo custode Anglie de pace et cartis libertatibus
Anglie. Qui pro se concesserunt et scripto confirmaverunt. Audientes

---

[a] sic in MS. Perhaps Hainault is intended.

[1] This list may derive from some lost newsletter sent by Walter de Langton. It is
highly optimistic: although a treaty with the bishop of Liège was envisaged, none seems
to have been concluded. The count of Guelders in fact agreed to serve with 1,000 men,
the duke of Brabant with 2,000, the count of Bar with 1,000 (*Treaty Rolls*, i, 106, 168;
C 62/71, 20 April).
[2] 15 August. Flanders, not Gascony, must be intended.
[3] 24 August.

igitur Scoti transitum regis Anglie in Flandriam surexerunt inter illos quidam malignus nomine Willelmus Waleys et congregata magna multitudine expungnavit Northumberland, occidendo et comburendo et vastando fere tres comitatus. Comites et barones audientes dampnum tunc factum in Anglia congregati sunt in magna multitudine et profecti sunt versus Scociam. Quam audierunt, Scoti se subtraxerunt et sic morati ibidem nostri usque ad Purificacionem. Interim dominus Reginaldus destinavit nuncium regi ex parte filii sui et comunitatis Anglie pro carta libertatum et foreste, ac quomodo Scotti iterum Angliam expungnaverunt. Rex vero cartam concessit et sigillo suo coroboravit et in Angliam misit per quemdam fratrem predicatorem citra festum sancti Andree[1] Carta hec est eadem quam pater suus concessit postquam magna multitudo hominum occisa est apud Lewes et Evesham.[2]

B.L., Cotton MS. Vesp. B.xi, fos. 41v–42v.

[1] 30 November.
[2] The manuscript continues with a version of Magna Carta, the Charter of the Forest, and the sentence of thirteen bishops issued in 1253 against all transgressors of the Charters. The *Confirmatio Cartarum* is not included.

INDEX

Aardenburg (Erdenbourgh, Erdenburgh, Erneburgh), Netherlands, prov. Zeeland, 145, 152, 188

Abergavenny (Bergeveny), Mon., franchise of, 124

Abingdon (Abindon'), Berks., abbot of, 194

—, Peter de, 144

Acre, Israel, 133n

—, Joan of, *see* Joan

Adam, *see* Beel

Adolf of Nassau, king of Germany (1291–8), 3–4, 24, 33–4, 80, 113, 148–9, 161–3, 167, 200

Akeny, Thomas de, 157, 158n

Al', Gandulph de, 195

Albrecht of Habsburg, king of Germany (1298–1308), 34

alien priories, 23, 98–9, 194n; *see also* Lewes

Amadeus, count of Savoy, 162, 200

Amarici, *see* Emerik

Andwerp, Andwerpe, *see* Antwerp

Angouleme (Engolisma), Itier de, 55–7, 143–4

Antwerp (Andwerp, Andwerpe), Belgium, 81, 83, 195

Aquinas, Thomas, 30

Aquitaine, France, duchy of, 162, 190; *see also* Gascony

Ardern (Darderne, Darnerne), Henry de, 187–8

—, William de, 188

Arundel, Sussex, 4

—, earl of, *see* FitzAlan

Assaldon', Nicholas de, 95

Asti (Ast), Italy, prov. Piemonte, merchants of, 35, 195–6

Aubyn, Philip, 176

Audenarde, *see* Oudenarde

Aulton, Peter de, 172n

—, William de, 97n, 98n

Aune, Laurence de, 176

Aveneu, John de, prior of Lewes, 98, 136

Axholm (Haxholm'), Lincs., isle of, 146

Aylesbury, Bucks, 88

Aylseton, Richard de, 94

Baa, *see* Bath and Wells

Bacon, Adam, 10–11

Baion, *see* Bayonne

Banested, *see* Banstead

bannerets, appointed to receive clerical fines, 16, 20, 25, 47n, 51, 52n, 53, 54n, 59, 66, 68, 71n, 74; *see also* Engayne; FitzRoger; Knoville; Lovel; Segrave; Tieys

Banstead (Banested), Surrey, 171

Bar, France, count of, *see* Henry

—, county of, 69

Bartholomew, Simon, 45

Basings, Robert of, 98

Bath (Baa) and Wells, bishop of, *see* March

—, bishopric of, 144n

Bathesham, Gerard de, 178

Batlesford, John de, 97n, 98n

battles, *see* Bellegarde; Evesham; Lewes; Stirling Bridge; Veurne

Baukwelle, John de, 91, 192

Bavent, Adam, 129

—, Roger, 129

Bayonne (Baion, Bayon, Bayone), France, dép. Basses-Pyrénées, 24, 58, 64, 78, 150, 163, 188, 199

Beauchamp (Bello Campo), James de, 199

—, Roger de, 157

—, Walter de, steward of the royal household, 22, 92, 96, 103

—, William de, earl of Warwick (1268–98), 6, 14, 107, 156, 199

Beaufey, Robert, 77n, 93n, 97n

Bedfordshire (Bed', Bedeford), 8, 50n, 77n, 97n, 103n, 115n, 121, 130n, 133n, 146, 193

—, and Buckinghamshire, sheriff of, 92

Beel, Adam known as, 45

Bek, Anthony, bishop of Durham (1283–1311), 22, 39, 107, 195

Bel, Robert le, 78n

Belinges, William de, 157

Bellafago, Roger de, 103n

Bellegarde, France, dép. Landes, battle of, 3, 35, 199

Bello Alneto, Walter de, 176

Bello Campo, *see* Beauchamp

Benstead (Benestede), John de, 195

Benton, Robert de, 103n

Berchey, Henry le, 88

Bristol (Bristeud, Bristoll'), 103, 178n
—, customs collectors at, 81n, 173n
—, St Augustine's abbey, 94–5
Brittany (Bretaine), John of, 150
Brochere, Richard le, 87
Bromfield (Bromfeld'), Salop, prior of, 66
Brommore, see Breamore
Bromsgrove (Brummesgrave), Richard de, 172
Bruges, Belgium, prov. West Flanders, 32, 176, 188
Brumbelschete, William de, 94
Brummesgrave, see Bromsgrove
Brummore, see Breamore
Brussels (Brusseles, Brussell'), Belgium, 195, 197n
Buckinghamshire (Bokyngham, Buk'), 50n, 68, 77n, 97n, 103n, 115n, 121, 130n, 133n, 192
—, sheriff of, see Bedfordshire and Buckinghamshire
bulls, papal: Clericis Laicos, 15, 19, 25, 28; Coram illo fatemur, 19; forgery, 25, 44, 77–8
Burg' seint Peere, see Peterborough
Burgh, Richard de, earl of Ulster (1280–1326), 163
Burgh', see Bourg-sur-Gironde
Burghersh, Robert de, 65
Burgo sancti Petri, see Peterborough
Burgundians, 35, 184, 200
Burn', John de, 192
Burnham, Walter de, 146
Burnigham, William de, 199
Burwelle (Burewelle), John de, 100, 104
Bury St Edmunds (Seint Eymon, Seynt Eymun), Suff., 15, 50; see also parliament
—, abbot of, 186, 191, 194
Bush, Hugh, 197n
Byfleet (Bifleet), Surr., 152
Bygod, see Bigod

Caen, France, dép. Calvados, 194n
Cambridgeshire (Cant', Cantebreg'), 11, 50n, 93n, 103n, 115n, 121, 130n, 192
Campania, see Champagne
canon law, 19, 28–9, 143
Cant', Cantebreg', see Cambridgeshire
Canterbury (Canterbir', Cantuar', Cantwarbere), 4, 17, 42, 91–3
—, archbishop of, see Winchelsey
—, cathedral, 19, 93n, 142–4
—, cathedral priory, 17, 42–3, 45–6
Canterbury, convocation of, 18, 124
—, diocese of, 100, 193
—, prior of, see Eastry
—, province of, 43–4, 55, 57, 124
—, St Augustine's (Seint Austyn), abbot of, 186
—, St Gregory's, prior of, 100
—, John de, 83, 92
Cardiff (Kaerdif), Glam., 66
Cardigan, 197
Cardoil, Cardoyl, see Carlisle
Carleton, William de, 52, 83n, 84n
Carlisle (Cardoil, Cardoyl, Karl'), 51
—, bishop of, see Halton
—, bishopric of, 17, 20, 60–1, 66n
Cas, Robert, 189
Castle Martin (Castrum Martini), Stephen de, 189
Castro Urdiales (Castre en Ordiales), Spain, prov. Santander, 185
Castrum Martini, see Castle Martin
Celeby, Richard de, 43
Cestre, bishop of, see Langton, Walter
Champagne (Campania), France, 200
—, Elyas de, 200
chancellor, see Langton, John
chancery, 18, 20, 114, 140–1; see also great seal
Chanu, John le, 117n
charters, confirmation of, 8, 18, 110, 112, 124, 128, 155n, 158–60, 200–1; see also Confirmatio Cartarum; Forest, charter of; Magna Carta
Chartham, Kent, 17
Chastel Gaweyn, see Walwynscastle
Chatham (Chetham), Kent, 98
Cheddeley, see Chudleigh
Chepstow (Estrugoil), Mon., 14, 66
Chester (Cestre), 22
—, bishop of, see Langton, Walter
Chetham, see Chatham
Cheyn, Waletus de le, 195
Chichester (Cicestr'), bishop of, 192
—, bishopric of, 144n
—, Peter de, 86, 87n, 135–6
Chiltham, Glos, 95
Chishull', Robert de, 184
Chudleigh (Cheddeleye), Devon, 4n, 83
Cicestr', see Chichester
Cinque Ports (Cync Ports, Ports, Portz), 4, 32, 58, 74–5, 144–5, 149, 165–6, 170n
—, warden of, see Pencester

Gascony (Gascoigne, Gascoygne, Vasconia), France, 3–6, 12, 14, 20, 23, 26, 35–6, 50, 53–4, 58–60, 63–4, 70, 88, 95, 127, 142, 150, 163, 167, 170, 175, 199–200
—, merchants of, 135n
Gatecoumbe, Reginald de, 77n, 92, 97n
Gaunt, see Ghent
Geneville (Geynville), Geoffrey de, 107, 126–8
Gerls, see Guelders
Germany, 3
—, king of, 34; see also Adolf
—, merchants of, 135
Gersingham, Alice de, 55
—, Geoffrey de, 55
Geynesburgh, see Gainsborough
Geyneville, see Geneville
Ghent (Gandavum, Gant, Gaunt), Belgium, prov. East Flanders, 31, 33, 146–53, 155n, 160n, 164–6, 168–71, 174–6, 178–80, 182–3, 185–7, 200
—, Simon of, bishop of Salisbury (1297–1315), 192
Giffard, Godfrey, bishop of Worcester (1268–1302), 2, 192
—, John, 156
Gildeford, see Guildford
Gildon', John de, 98n
Gillingham, Dorset, 59
—, John de, 54
Gipwicum, see Ipswich
Glamorgan, see Morgannwg
—, sheriff of, 106
Glastonbury (Glastingbur'), Som., abbey, 194n
—, abbot of, 194
Gloucester (Glouc', Gloucestr'), abbey, 94, 194n
—, abbot of, 194n
—, countess of, see Joan
—, earl of, see Clare; Monthermer
—, William de, 147
Gloucestershire (Glouc'), 21, 50n, 97n, 103n, 115n, 121, 192
—, sheriff of, 55n, 94–5, 178n
Godele, John de, 103n
Golde, John, 187
Goldsmith, see Paternoster
grain, 12, 21, 52, 58, 60, 75–7, 85, 93n, 193n; growing, 67; putrefying, 45; see also prise

Gravesend, Richard, bishop of London (1280–1303), 56–7, 78n, 107, 124, 156, 171n, 192
Graunt, David le, 50n
Gray, see Grey
great seal, letters under, 44, 56, 63, 72, 106, 110, 125–9, 133–4, 172–3, 193
Greneford, Henry de, 158
Grey (Gray), Reginald de, 30, 36, 141n, 156, 180, 185, 200–1
Grinegone, Henry, 88
Guaretto, Opetinus, 195
Guelders (Gerls), count of, 200
Guildford (Gildeford, Gyldeford), Adam de, 88
—, Henry de, 47, 103n, 136
Guisborough, Yorks, priory, 194n
—, Walter of, 2–3, 21, 31, 37
Guy, count of Flanders, 3, 5, 128, 134, 166–7, 200
Gyldeford, see Guildford

Habsburg, see Albrecht
Haclutel', see Hakelute
Hagnaby, Lincs., chronicle of, 2, 26, 199–201
Hainault (Hermaunde), count of, 200
Halton, John, bishop of Carlisle (1292–1324), 65, 84, 91n
Hakelute (Haclutel'), Walter, 106, 189
Hampshire (Suth', Suthampton'), 21, 46, 50n, 84n, 97n, 103n, 115n, 121, 172n, 192
—, sheriff of, 47, 55n, 172n
Hamslape, Thurstan de, 97n, 121, 172n
Hardy, John, 100
Harriss, G. L., 28, 30
Hassie, see Hesse
Hastings (Hastingg', Hastinges), John de, 7, 14, 106–7, 123–4
Haukeswel, William de, 157
Hauward (Haward), William, 81–2
Hauze, Richard de, 144
—, William de, 144
Haverford, Pembs., 67, 189, 197n
—, keepers of customs at, 197n
Havering, Richard de, 25, 83–4
hawks, 52, 55
Haxholm', see Axholm
Hegham, Roger de, 50n, 103n
Heketon, Robert de, 158
Helton, John de, 73
Henry III, king of England (1216–72), 110, 147, 158, 201

Norfolk, earl of, *see* Bigod
—, and Suffolk, sheriff of, 55n, 67, 101n, 172n
Norreys, Walter le, public notary, 57, 58n, 144n
Northamptonshire, 4, 50n, 64, 69, 77n, 85, 93n, 97n, 98n, 103n, 115n, 121, 130n, 192
—, sheriff of, 74
Northleach (Northlegh'), Glos., 95
Northumberland (Norhumbr', Northumbr'), 64, 77n, 85, 93n, 97n, 103n, 110, 121, 201
Norton, Roger de, 97n, 103n, 121
Nostell Priory, 194n
Norwich (Norwyc'), bishop of, *see* Walpole, Ralph
Norwode, John de, 144
notarial instruments, 1, 42–3, 45–6, 55–8, 142–4
notaries, *see* Norreys; Titchfield
notarial sign, 58
Nottinghamshire (Notingham), 50n, 64, 77n, 85, 93n, 97n, 103n, 115n, 121, 130n, 192
— and Derbyshire, sheriff of, 55n
novel disseisin, 36, 168–9
Novum Castrum, *see* Newcastle upon Tyne
Nympsfield (Nimdesfeld), Glos., 95

Oakham (Ocham), Rutland, 69
Odymere, *see* Udimore
Odiham (Odyham), Hants., 72
—, Ralph de, 103n
Oppenheim, Germany, 148
ordinances, 48–50, 75–7, 87–90, 96–7, 102, 133–5, 191–3
Ormesby, William, 192
Orpington (Orpigton'), Kent, 120
Oudenarde (Audenarde), Belgium, 174
Oxford (Oxenford), 68
Oxfordshire (Oxon'), 50n, 55n, 97n, 98n, 103n, 115n, 121, 133n, 193
— and Berkshire, sheriff of, 53, 55n

Palacio, Walter de, 42
pardons, 36, 154–6, 165–6
Parker, Hamo le, 157
parliament, 4, 8, 14, 28, 67
—, at Bury St Edmunds (1296), 15, 50, 65
—, at Salisbury (1297), 3, 6
—, at Westminster (1297), 99, 108

Parmenter, Richard le, 189–90
Paternoster, John, 147
Paynel, Ralph, 97n
—, Thomas, 35, 186, 194
Peckham (Pecham), Kent, 41, 180n
Pederton', Walter de, 189
Pembroke (Pembrok), 67
—, countess of, *see* Valence, Joan de
Pembrokeshire, 67
Pencester, Stephen de, warden of the Cinque Ports and constable of Dover, 65, 74–5, 145
Percy, Henry de, 109
Pershore, William de, 50n
Peterborough (Burg' seint Peere, Burgo sancti Petri), Cambs., abbey of, 194n
—, abbot of, 191, 194
Philip IV, king of France (1285–1314), 3, 19, 28, 30, 32–3, 36, 86, 92, 97–8, 125, 134, 153, 162–3, 165–6, 172–4, 176, 182–6, 188, 190–1
Pichard (Pychard), Miles, 109
Plimmuth, *see* Plymouth
Plukenet, Alan, 46n, 141n, 156
Plymouth (Plimmuth, Plummue, Plymue), 51, 54, 64, 80n
Plympton, Devon, 63, 69–72, 80
—, prior of, 63n
Plymue, *see* Plymouth
Poer, Alice le, 168
—, Robert le, 168
Ponteine, William de, 199
Pontoise, John of, bishop of Winchester (1282–1304), 192
Pont Robert, *see* Robertsbridge
Pope, *see* Boniface; Clement; Honorius
Porte, Claius de la, 188
Portemue, Portism', *see* Portsmouth
Portland, Isle of, Dorset, 103n
ports, guardians of, 89n
Ports, Portz, *see* Cinque Ports
Portsmouth (Portemue, Portism'), 4, 184n, 185, 200
Portugal, king of, *see* Dinis
prises, 12–13, 20–1, 26–8, 31, 37, 116, 154, 159, 191, 193n; from clergy, 19, 39, 41, 63–4, 76, 82, 92, 118, 191; of victuals, 1, 12–13, 20–1, 26, 39, 41, 54–5, 63–4, 75–7, 85–7, 92–5, 133, 171–2, 191, 193n, 198, 200; of wool, 1, 9–12, 20, 22, 24, 26, 88, 92, 114–15, 117–19, 125, 131, 135, 137–40, 169–70, 176–7, 189, 191, 197–8